Taming the Wind of Desire

COMPARATIVE STUDIES OF
HEALTH SYSTEMS AND MEDICAL CARE

For a complete list of titles in this series, please contact the
Sales Department
University of California Press
2120 Berkeley Way
Berkeley, CA 94720

Taming the Wind of Desire

Psychology, Medicine, and Aesthetics in Malay Shamanistic Performance

CAROL LADERMAN

University of California Press
Berkeley Los Angeles London

University of California Press
Berkeley and Los Angeles, California
University of California Press
London, England

Printed in the United States of America
1 2 3 4 5 6 7 8 9

First Paperback Printing 1993

Library of Congress Cataloging-in-Publication Data

Laderman, Carol.
Taming the wind of desire : psychology, medicine, and aesthetics in Malay shamanistic performance / Carol Laderman.
p. cm. — (Comparative studies of health systems and medical care)
Includes bibliographical references and index.
ISBN 0-520-08258-3
1. Malays (Asian people)—Medicine. 2. Malays (Asian people)—Religion. 3. Shamanism—Trengganu—Kampong Merchang. 4. Folk medicine—Trengganu—Kampong Merchang. 5. Kampong Merchang (Trengganu)—Social life and customs. I. Title. II. Series.

DS595.L33 1991
615.8′82′095951—dc20 90-38031

The paper used in this publication
meets the minimum requirements of American
National Standard for Information Sciences—Permanence
of Paper for Printed Library Materials,
ANSI Z39.48–1984 ♾

For my parents, Sylvia and Philip Ciavati,
and Pak Long Awang Bin Ali

and for my children,
Raphael and Michael Laderman

CONTENTS

PREFACE

A Note on Fieldwork

My research on Malay rituals of healing began as a result of the kind of serendipity that seems to enhance the work of many anthropologists. When I arrived in Trengganu State, in 1975, prepared to study Malay childbirth and nutrition, I was unaware of the persistence of shamanism in the area. I expected to learn as much as I could about the cultural and ecological context in which Malay ideas and practices regarding food and reproduction are embedded. Understanding the Malay medical system as a totality, I believed, would be vital to the wider implications of my study. As I discovered, without the knowledge I gained from my association with Malay shamans, I might never have known even the basic "facts of life." Almost a year after I had begun to work as an apprentice to a traditional midwife and had assisted at numerous births, I attended a seance at which I was startled to hear one of the ritual specialists sing of the father's pregnancy. When I asked my midwife-teacher what that meant, she was equally startled. Imagine a grown, highly educated woman not knowing that a baby develops within its father's brain for forty days before its mother takes over! She pointed to her husband as an example, reminiscing about the time he carried their youngest child, and how he had craved sour foods during his pregnancy.

Had I not been privileged to attend shamanistic seances, I might never have understood the concept of the Inner Winds, a key to the traditional medical system. My understanding of the Winds came slowly, nurtured by my shaman-teachers and reinforced by conversations with Malay patients, friends, and neighbors. It was not until many years later, when I had read extensively in Western psychoanalytic and art historical literature, that I realized the important implications this concept had for my own society.

My principal informants, Pak Long Awang bin Ali (a shaman) and Tok Daud bin Mat (his partner, or *minduk*), lived in my parish; I spoke to them frequently and taped their seances whenever and wherever they occurred, as part of their entourage. I also attended the seances of eight other practitioners of Main Peteri (pronounced approximately like the English "mine pet tree"), all of whom were born in Kelantan, although many had long been resident in Trengganu, and interviewed them extensively over a period of two years (1975–1977). I transcribed the tapes in the field and attempted a preliminary translation. I returned to Malaysia during 1982, on a grant from the Translations Program of the National Endowment for the Humanities, to check the accuracy of my previous transcriptions and translations of Main Peteri with the original performers and to study their meaning and symbolism further. All research and interviews were conducted in Malay local dialects, primarily Kelantanese, often intermingled with Trengganu expressions.

During the fifteen-odd years I have worked with these ritual dramas of healing, they have revealed the wit of their comedy and the beauty of their poetry, their validity as medicine as well as philosophy, and their profound understanding of the human condition. The unfolding process by which these texts have spoken to me has seemed at times like the unfolding that takes place during the shaman's divination, "Open the message, one fold within the gloomy darkness. Two folds shows a grayish haze. With three folds we can now see clearly." I hope that I have been able to reveal some of the clarity of the Malay shaman's vision of the universe.

A Note on Translation

Discussions of the Malay shaman's seance in the past were seriously hampered by the lack of texts transcribed from actual performances. Cuisinier, and earlier writers, had to rely on the dictation of informants after the fact. Skeat, who was present at part of a seance held for a sick man, remarked on the difficulty of following the language (1972[1900]:436–444). He was able to collect only part of an incantation that was dictated to him later. Cuisinier's generally excellent translation is excerpted from longer formal songs and incantations and omits the extensive colloquial dialogues between the spirits (speaking through the voice of the *tok 'teri*) and the master of the spirits (the minduk). Of the performances that Cuisinier describes, one was a special ceremony ordered by the Sultan of Kelantan for reasons of state (1936:97), and the other was staged for Cuisinier's benefit with no real patient or practical purpose (1936:39). Since Cuisinier based her analysis on these, rather than upon personally experienced rituals performed for health reasons, her comments about the Main Peteri, particularly in its function as a healing ceremony, are often wide of the mark.

Gimlette, who provided eight pages in English and a corresponding number in Malay of selections from Main Peteri songs, attests to the difficulty for non-native speakers of a language that he said was "made up of many elements: besides illiterate Malay it includes corrupt Arabic, broken Siamese, mutilated Javanese, debased Sanskrit, words from the spirit language" (1971[1915]:73). Cuisinier (1936) also notes the inclusion of "Sakai" [Orang Asli] words. Gimlette laments his shortcomings in understanding the language, but leaves one with no doubt as to the possibility of further scholarship's ability to unravel these problems. A more recent scholar, however, rather than improving on Gimlette's understanding, came to the conclusion that "there is little point in translating all of the incantations completely, as most are repetitious and full of mumbo-jumbo that means little in another language" (Shaw 1973:78).

Native speakers of Kelantanese Malay have little trouble understanding the language of the seance. Rather than finding it incomprehensible and repetitious, they find it endlessly diverting and meaningful.

Although seeking the "original form" of Malay texts appears to be a serious occupation of some Malay scholars, for example, Ismail Hussein (1974), it is fruitless to attempt to reconstruct "the original form" of the Main Peteri because of the emergent quality of each performance. Every seance is its own "original" whose plot and staging develop, to a large extent, out of particular circumstances, as well as owing a debt to specific performers and their audiences. I have attempted to show the great variety this form can attain by transcribing and translating three complete seances, presided over by six different ritual specialists. These were chosen from among the dozens of performances I witnessed—performances including one done for a boy suffering from a spirit attack that had been aimed at his father but struck the more vulnerable child; one for a new mother who refused to attend to her infant; one for a fat woman who annually took to her bed as a result of unrealized theatrical ambitions; one for a forestry official whose divorced wife periodically sent spirits to confuse his mind; one done in an attempt to evict a Chinese family from a Malay-owned house using the help of spirit familiars; and many rituals designed to encourage love or hate, or to return an errant spouse to his wife. Of the three performances I chose, the first ("A Stifled Talent") was held primarily to ease the virulent frustration that resulted from the thwarting of the patient's Inner Winds (a concept discussed in chapter 4); the second ("Seance for a Sick Shaman") combined exorcism with the strengthening of the sick shaman's professional Wind; the third ("Breaking Contracts with the Spirit World") was purely exorcistic, designed to rid the neighborhood of unsatisfied marauding spirits.

Readers of these texts should be aware that the Malay audiences at these performances are, for the most part, not intent on hearing every word, and for many reasons may miss some of the dialogue. Silence is not enjoined upon audiences. People come and go, there may be conversations carried on in low tones by members of the audience, and children are often present, sometimes making noise and often drifting off to sleep on floor mats in the area in which the ritual is taking place.

Transcriptions, based on tapes made by the author during performances, were done with the help of my field assistant, Yusof bin Hassan (a Trengganu Malay who had spent a good deal of time in Kelantan with his Kelantanese father), and the ritual specialists who presided over the seances. The greater part of the words, whether spoken or sung, could be heard clearly on the tapes, but problems arose when two performers spoke or sang simultaneously. Moreover, most elderly Malays (including many of the ritual specialists) have lost all or most of their teeth, which makes for diminished clarity of speech. The only section dictated to me after the fact was the tok 'teri's invocation while going into trance, which, at a performance, is recited during the singing of the minduk's Bestirring Song. On my tape, the minduk's song was a good deal louder than the shaman's invocation, making it impossible to hear the invocation clearly. In these instances, my readers have been presented with material that was not completely audible to the Malay audience.

Words that were unclear on the tapes were listened to time after time by the author, her field assistant, and the ritual specialists. Prof. P. L. Amin Sweeney also listened to and commented on the material, using copies of the original tapes. Where it was impossible to hear words or phrases even after extensive re-listening, I have so indicated. Although there may be questions about the accuracy of some isolated words, an alternate reading would not significantly change the meaning.

Inquiring about particular words during interviews with ritual specialists many years after the event proved unfruitful, since much of the dialogue is ad lib improvisation on underlying themes. Aside from the formulaic phrases that ornament the Main Peteri, bomoh can no more be expected to remember exactly what they said in the past (even when prompted by tape recordings) than can anyone who does not perform according to an unvarying script.

Like the Zuni storytellers described by Tedlock (1983), Main Peteri bomoh differ in the stresses, pitches, and intonations of their performance from ritual pair to ritual pair, as well as in the music they sing and the words they repeat. While these differences add to the impact of the performance, I believe that an attempt to reproduce them in the lengthy texts of the Main Peteri would detract from, rather than add to, the reader's understanding.

Although it is unreasonable to expect that a translation of ritual material could evoke a response in members of another culture similar to the one evoked by the original performance in its own setting (*pace* Nida), an adequate translation should make sense to the reader, convey the manner of the original, and be "natural and easy to read" (Nida 1964:162); it must not become "literary" where the original was not, introducing elegant variation where there was none in the text (Hymes 1981). The translator must surrender herself to the performance, to experience it as a participant, as well as an observer. It is only by learning to live another kind of life, and to speak another language, in the fullest sense, that a translator can hope to bring her readers any of the rich flavor of a performance she has experienced with all of her senses (cf. Asad 1986) as a participating member of the shaman's entourage and a member of the audience.

Scholars can read the original Malay transcriptions of these Main Peteri in my monograph, *Main Peteri: Malay Shamanism* (forthcoming). The original tapes are in the archives of Columbia University's Center for Ethnomusicology, Department of Music.

The Structure of the Book

The book is divided into two major parts, followed by an afterword, two appendixes, and a glossary. Part I, *Malay Medicine, Malay Person*, discusses the concepts and practices of traditional Malay healing. The initial chapter introduces the reader to Malay shamanism, first as I myself was introduced to it, and later through a review of changing Western attitudes toward the phenomenon. The second chapter relates the Malay humoral system, the cornerstone of both medical and cosmological theory, to medieval Islamic humoralism and to the beliefs of aborigines who live in the Malayan rain forest. The third chapter discusses "unusual illnesses," their etiology, and their relations to Malay concepts of the Self. Chapter 4 expands on the Inner Winds, a key component of the Malay Person, and compares Malay theories of personality development, creativity, and frustration with those of contemporary Western psychoanalysis. Chapter 5 considers the performance aspects of the shaman's seance, discussing its dramatic form, music, movement, and props. While Part I prepares the reader to understand the cultural context of the ritual dramas that follow, the epic sweep and poetic qualities of the Malay shaman's healing seances give them intrinsic value as oral literature and dramatic performance, beyond their anthropological interest. In Part II, *Ritual Dramas of Healing*, the anthropologist's voice fades further into the background and the ritual practitioners' voices come to the fore. The three chapters that make up Part II include translations of three complete performances of shamanic seances, extensively annotated. In these ritual dramas, the noble philosophy of the minduk's long introductory song and the lyric beauty of the Bestirring Song that helps the shaman achieve trance alternate with passages of striking metaphor and coarse humor. The brief Afterword, "Words and Meaning," an appreciation of the language of healing, concludes the book. Of particular interest are the appendices, including a transcription of some of the music of the Main Peteri (courtesy of Marina Roseman), and a lengthy interview with a shaman. The anthropologist confines herself here to short questions for the shaman, and interpolated comments to the reader. The shaman himself is the central figure—his intelligence, understanding, and verve for his profession flow from his mouth with the force of a waterfall.

ACKNOWLEDGMENTS

I would like to acknowledge the graciousness of the government of Malaysia in allowing me to conduct research under the auspices of the Institute for Medical Research of the Malaysian Ministry of Health. My research during 1975–1977 was supported by the Social Science Research Council and the National Institute for Mental Health, with logistic assistance from the Hooper Foundation of the University of California, San Francisco. My research during 1982–1985 was supported by the National Endowment for the Humanities Translation Program, and by grants from Fordham University. Support from the John Simon Guggenheim Memorial Foundation allowed me to take a leave of absence from teaching during the academic year 1987–1988 and concentrate on writing. The National Endowment for the Humanities Program for Interpretive Research supported my work during 1987–1990 and Fordham University awarded me a Faculty Fellowship for 1989–1990. Final revisions were done at the Rockefeller Foundation's Study Center in Bellagio. I thank them all for their generous support. I also wish to express my gratitude to Profs. P. L. Amin Sweeney and Marina Roseman for their invaluable help as my consultants. Many people kindly read and commented on earlier versions of portions of this manuscript, or helped by listening to my tapes, including Barbara Ribakove Gordon, Barbara Kirshenblatt-Gimblett, Nancy Scheper-Hughes, Charles Leslie, Patricia Matusky Yamaguchi, Vivian Garrison, Mario Rendon, Clifford Waldman, Rena Gropper, Laurel Kendall, Barbara Ismail, John Hollander, Thomas Bolt, Jed Perl, and Gabriel, Raphael, and Michael Laderman. Most of all, I want to express my love and appreciation for Pak Long Awang bin Ali and Tok Daud bin Mat, of blessed memory, who were unstinting with their time and patient in their teaching. They, and all the traditional healers mentioned in this book, have ceased their practice, due to death, infirmity, or religious considerations.

PART I

Malay Medicine, Malay Person

1

An Introduction to Malay Shamanism

We had recently moved into a house in Merchang, a Malay village on the South China Sea, in the state of Trengganu, Malaysia: myself, a graduate student hoping to write a dissertation on childbirth and nutrition,[1] my husband, and our ten-year-old son. We were the only foreigners who had ever lived in Kampung (Kg.) Merchang, except for Japanese soldiers during World War Two. The village was chosen after consultation with the director and staff of the General Hospital in Kuala Trengganu, the state capital. Located on the main highway, twenty-five miles away from cosmopolitan medicine in either direction, Merchang seemed perfect as a research site. The director of nursing told me that although a government-trained midwife had been in attendance for seventeen years, traditional midwives (*bidan*) and indigenous medical practitioners (*bomoh*) were still very much in demand. She said that the most common medical problems were intestinal worms, infected cuts, and scabies and asked me if I would be willing to do some first aid. The hospital pharmacy provided me with a supply of medicines.

When word got around that I had medicine that could take away the maddening itch of scabies and was giving it away free, people came to my house in ever greater numbers. Not only my close neighbors ap-

1. I did write the dissertation I had intended to, "Conceptions and Preconceptions: Childbirth and Nutrition in Rural Malaysia" (Department of Anthropology, Columbia University, 1979). A revised version, *Wives and Midwives: Childbirth and Nutrition in Rural Malaysia*, was published by the University of California Press in 1983. Interested readers will find an overview of the village's society and cultural ecology in this work.

peared, but others as well, who told me they lived in nearby hamlets. It seemed unreasonable to me that they should have to walk to my kampung when there was medical help available close at hand—the bomoh they had always called in times of need. I decided to pour some of the benzyl benzoate that was so effective in treating scabies into several bottles which I brought with me on visits to the local bomoh, many of whom I had not yet met.

Two of the bomoh lived in Kg. Padang Pauh, a hamlet located up a steep hill leading past the cemetery, toward the jungle. The first one I visited, Tok Kemat, claimed to have come from a long line of wonder-working (*keramat*) bomoh. Although he accepted the benzyl benzoate graciously, he declined to speak to me about his own methods, saying that, although other bomoh might be willing to speak to me, his knowledge could be passed down only to his children. The other bomoh, Pak Long Awang, lived far off the dirt road in a small house reached by climbing over a stile. He was a sturdy old man with short white hair whose tiny, skinny wife I recognized as one of the people who had come to me for aspirins. He told me that he specialized in curing crazy (*gila*) people, people with soul sickness (*sakit jiwa*), and invited me to come back in about two weeks when he expected to treat some interesting cases.

Pak Long's wife stopped at my house one afternoon to inform me that her husband was expecting me later. Night falls suddenly near the equator. The sun takes only minutes to set, and when the moon is full it seems much larger and feels much closer to earth than it does in the temperate zone. That night, however, was dark of the moon. My assistant, Yusof, and I started up the hill to Padang Pauh, our way lit by flashlight. I should have checked the batteries before we started out, because as we neared the graveyard, the light grew dimmer and disappeared. I couldn't see ahead of me in the blackness. The air seemed denser in the absence of light, and the scent of jasmine more intense. Yusof took my hand and told me not to worry—he could find his way around the kampung with his eyes shut. We climbed slowly up the hill until we reached the path that ended in a stile. As we approached Pak Long's house, the sounds of drum and gong, fiddle and song grew louder.

The house was lit by flickering oil lamps. A crowd of people sat on floor mats woven of strips of pandanus leaves dyed in pinks and purples, the men sitting cross-legged and the women with their legs bent to the side, invisible under their sarongs. Some of the children were still awake while others slept soundly on the mats, despite the loud percussive sounds of the little band. One man beat a hand drum decorated with three stars and a crescent moon. A woman hit an overturned pot with sticks. Another man sang as he drew a bow in the shape of a feathered arrow across the strings of an intricately carved spike fiddle painted red, green, and silver. Smoke rose from a dish of incense; in another dish jasmine blossoms floated in water. Pak Long danced slowly to the music, taking small steps, gesturing gracefully with his arms, and shaking his head from side to side.

I was still a recent enough arrival in the village to cause a sensation when I walked in the door. The women exclaimed at the whiteness of my skin and the fact that I was dressed in a sarong, as they were; they asked to try on my ring and my earrings. Some of the children tentatively smiled; others hid their faces in their mother's laps. Everyone's attention seemed to turn toward me, except for Pak Long, the musicians, and a middle-aged man who sat before them, his face immobile. After a while the music stopped. It was only then that the man's stony expression left his face. He turned toward his neighbor and asked, "Who's she?"

I found out later that he had been one of the patients that Pak Long spoke of, a person suffering from soul sickness. In order to cure the patient, Pak Long said, it was necessary to put him into a state of "not remembering" (*tak ingat*); his immobility and apparent lack of interest in his surroundings was due to his being in trance.

The treatment, I was told, was called Main 'teri—the ceremony I had read about in English accounts of Malay ritual life at the turn of the century. It was the oldest kind of medicine there was, said Pak Long, in fact it dated back to the time of Adam and Eve:

> *In the time of the Prophet Adam [he said], Eve was sick. Adam looked for medicine, he looked and he looked but he couldn't find any. Then he looked for a bomoh, and he found one. Then he asked the bomoh, "Do you have medicine to treat Eve?" This is what Tok Kumar Hakim [the bomoh] said: "I have medicine for everything!" He brought over a*

gebana [hand drum]; he had a rebab *[spike fiddle]. Adam asked what those things were. "This is a bowl for medicine," he said, pointing to the gebana. "This is a medicinal herb," he said, pointing to the rebab. Then he treated his patient—he played [*main*]. He played and he played Main 'teri. After Main 'teri, Eve was cured of her sickness. When she was cured, then God said, "I can't afford to keep this Datuk Kumar Hakim around. It would be better if I sent him to a cave. I'll tell him to go into that cave. If I don't tell him to go into the cave," he said, "no one will ever die," he said, "none of the followers of Muhammad." So he entered the cave, and he is still living there.*

*Its name is even older than that [said Pak Long]. When God made Adam he was just a lifeless image. God called Gabriel and breathed into his hands. He told Gabriel to fly over to Adam's image and put the breath up his nostrils. Adam sneezed, and the breath traveled all over his body. His body was too weak for the breath, and it broke into little pieces. God told Gabriel to weld (*pateri*) it back together, to make it whole. That's why it's called Main 'teri. When we do it, we weld people together, we make sick people well.*

I had heard from one of my professors at Columbia, Clive Kessler, that the healing ceremony was still being performed in Kelantan, the state to the north, but was assured by my colleagues in Kuala Lumpur that it had died out long ago in Trengganu, so I had not expected to see it in Merchang. I was fascinated by Main 'teri. I attended the seances whenever and wherever I could, and, although I became acquainted with many other bomoh, I soon joined Pak Long's entourage and became his student, and, later, his "daughter." Tok Daud, the man who had played the rebab on the first night I witnessed Main 'teri, took my education in hand as well. In the second year of my research, I also attended an impromptu school for shamans that flourished briefly in Merchang. Like so many foreigners before me, I had become entranced by the work of the Malay shaman.

A History of Western Accounts of Malay Shamanism

Malay shamanism has attracted the attention of foreign writers and researchers for more than a hundred years. The spirit-raising seance (variations on a theme known in different states of the Malay peninsula as *berhantu*, *berjin*, *main bagih*, *main gebiah*, *main mok pek*, *main belian*, *main peteri*, *puteri*, or *'teri*)[2] first appeared in Western literature as "demon worship [whose] very existence is scarcely known [since] there are not probably many Englishmen who have witnessed the frantic dances of the *Pawang*, or listened to the chant and drum of the *Bidu* [bomoh] beside the bed of some sick or dying person" (W. E. Maxwell 1881:12). Maxwell, who referred to all Malay indigenous treatments, other than bone-setting and simple herbal remedies, as "the black art," described a seance held for a sick young woman in Perak, in which the spirits were exorcised but the patient died (W. E. Maxwell 1883). Blagden was more charitable when he said that the shaman's familiar spirits were "by no means necessarily evil" (1896:4), but his characterization of Malay beliefs as "quaint notions" (1896:11) was perhaps even more condescending than Maxwell's "downright heathenism" (1883:222).

Skeat (1898, 1972 [1900]), and Annandale (1903*a*, 1903*b*, 1904*a*, 1904*b*), following the inspiration of Tylor and Frazer, discussed such rituals as "superstitions found among the lower races." Skeat declared himself devoted to collecting "every jot or tittle of information" on the folklore and "popular religion" of the Malays; Annandale was equally meticulous as a collector of data. The temper of the times, however, was not conducive to the analysis of the material they had collected. English students of Malay culture believed that "it is evident . . . that these ideas do not form a system, being rather a jumble of confused and sometimes incongruous superstition" (Annandale and Robinson 1904:33). Wilkinson (1908:64) compared Malay culture to "a sort of museum of ancient customs—an ill-kept and ill-designed museum in which no exhibit is dated, labelled or explained." Under the circumstances, it seemed a

2. Although the seance was almost invariably referred to as Main Teri by the ritual practitioners and their patients, its usual reference in the literature has been Main Peteri or Main Puteri. I prefer Main Peteri (Main 'teri for short) because of its multiple resonances: *peteri* as princess (*tuan 'teri*), as shaman (tok 'teri), and in closeness of sound, to *pateri* (to weld). The Malay shaman does not send his soul on a journey, but I do not believe that this must be the primary criterion for employing the term "shaman". In fact, the original Tungus word, *saman*, from which this term derives does not specify a spiritual journey, but, rather, means "one who is excited, moved, raised." This definition brings it close in content to the Malay role of the tok 'teri (one whose Inner Winds are excited, moved, raised—see chapter 4).

thankless job to try to make systematic sense out of these irrational beliefs. More recent scholars must, however, appreciate the wealth of information amassed by these earlier investigators and respect their modest goals: to confine themselves "almost entirely to describing things as they are, without attempting either conjecture or comparison" (Skeat 1898:1).

Early accounts of Malay seances show that they occurred in many parts of the Peninsula, although even at the turn of the century we are cautioned that they were "very seldom undertaken" (Annandale 1903*a*:102). Annandale described a shamanistic ceremony performed for a little girl in Perak and discussed many beliefs connected with Malay theory and practice of curing spirit-inflicted problems in Perak and Patani. Zainal-Abidin described a similar ritual in Negri Sembilan (1922), Kloss (1908) spoke of the pawang's activities in Johore, and Gimlette (1913) wrote of shamanism in Pahang and Kelantan. Skeat recorded an eyewitness account of a seance held in Selangor in which the Tiger Spirit was invoked for the benefit of a sick man, and described a berhantu, conducted by a female pawang, which cured the Sultan of Perak of a grievous illness (1972 [1900]:436–449).

A description of this Perak seance had appeared previously in one of Sir Frank Swettenham's *Malay Sketches* (1895). Sir Frank's stories, particularly "Ber-hantu" and "Malay Superstitions," and those of Sir George Maxwell (1907), particularly "The Pinjih Rhino" and "A Deer Drive," brought the rituals of the Malay shaman to the English reading public, who eagerly devoured these colorful tales of colonial exotica.

Winstedt, writing later in this century (1951 [1925]), attempted to tease Hindu and Sufi elements out of the shaman's seance, as well as those that he ascribed to an indigenous religion practiced by Malays before their conversion, first to Hinduism and later to Islam. Although he mentioned in passing the microcosm/macrocosm relation of man and the universe found in the symbolism of the Kelantan shaman's exorcism (1951 [1925]:85–86), he found no system or unity in Malay beliefs, which he compared to a cultural "lumber-room," full of "gracious and beautiful" items perhaps, but nevertheless carrying the distinct connotation of useless objects piled helter-skelter in no particular order. Winstedt warned his English readers not to expect anything better of Malays since their "primitive minds" could not grasp theories and systems that required abstract thinking: "Although, for example, the Malay, like many other races, arrived at what has been termed animatism or the idea of a vital force in stone and plant and beast and man, it would be absurd to suggest that he proceeded to postulate uniformity in nature, an idea too abstract for the Malay language even today" (1951 [1925]:14).

Although Winstedt's dictionary, even in its fourth edition (1966), contains no Malay gloss for "uniformity," perhaps because he had convinced himself there could be none, earlier English-Malay dictionaries (e.g., Shellabear 1916) found no problem in locating an equivalent.

Later scholars were less interested in separating the strands of historical influences in the shaman's seance than they were in analyzing its form and content. Cuisinier (1936), who has provided the most extensive treatment to date, concentrated on its dramatic and symbolic aspects, finding order in the parallelisms the Malay shaman makes between the universal macrocosm and the human microcosm. Her later book (1951) discussed the abstract idea of uniformity in nature that Winstedt believed was beyond the capabilities of Malay minds: the essence that binds the universe together in totality is *semangat*, the vital force that permeates all creation—fire and rock as well as plant and animal. Endicott (1970), using both the descriptive essays of earlier writers and the more analytical writings of Cuisinier, claimed that the basic content of Malay magic was the manipulation and maintenance of boundaries between spirit and matter.

Social and cultural anthropologists of the 1960s and 1970s were more concerned with relations between human and human than between human and spirit. They described the ways in which the shaman's ritual reveals the structure of the social interactions and the thoughts, beliefs, and values salient to Malay society. Mohd. Taib Osman (1972) placed the institution of the bomoh within its social context and the beliefs surrounding his practice within the traditional Malay world view. Raybeck (1974) and Kessler (1977) discussed the Main Peteri as a response to social stresses and gender hostility in Kelantanese village life; and Kessler (1977) brilliantly analyzed the political content of the ceremony.

Anthropologists working in other Malaysian states have provided insights into related phenomena in traditional Malay healing, for example, Banks's illuminating discussion of shamanism in Kedah (1976), Provencher's provocative comments on the prevalence of orality in the symbolism of Malay healers (1979), and Benjamin's comparisons of Malay and aboriginal animism (1979).

Firth discussed Main Peteri as sheer entertainment as well as social drama (1967), continuing Cuisinier's perceptive linkage of the seance with *Mak Yong* (a dramatic performance with music, song, and dance) and *wayang kulit* (the shadow play). Sheppard (1972) extended this linkage by his inclusion of Main Peteri as one of the many Malay traditional arts and pastimes. Ghulam-Sarwar Yousof (1976) described the fusion of Mak Yong and Main Peteri in a healing genre of Kelantan that promotes an identification of patients suffering from depression and other mental disturbances with the characters of Mak Yong stories. This genre appears to be the type of healing ceremony used in the case studies analyzed by Kessler (1977).

Firth's treatment of Main Peteri as entertainment takes on the flavor of dramatic criticism rather than social anthropology when he complains that "the language is stereotyped and follows conventional formulae" and suggests that what is "needed to convert this ritual performance into dramatic art [is] a sense of general statement about human experience and the human condition; and more deliberate focus on the development and unity of the form of statement" (1967:203). These criticisms fall very wide of the mark, since the heart of the Main Peteri is precisely its statement about human experience and the human condition.

The Main Peteri, although it takes the form of a dramatic performance and can be used for a variety of purposes (including inducing a straying spouse to return home, breaking contracts between spirit and mortal, and giving a supernatural nudge to recalcitrant tenants who refuse to be evicted), is essentially a healing ceremony that has interested physicians as well as ethnographers, from Gimlette, writing in 1913, to Chen in 1979. Gimlette's *Malay Poisons and Charm Cures*, which first appeared in 1915, includes several short excerpts and a description of a performance. His discussion of shamanic cures (which he attributes to "suggestion") assumes a purely demoniac theory of causation as the basis for the seance and exorcism as its only means of treatment, an assumption that Gimlette held in common with Malayanists of all persuasions.

More recent research has focused on the seance's psychotherapeutic implications. In the mid-1960s, the Hooper Foundation of the University of California, San Francisco, in cooperation with the Malaysian Ministry of Health, supported the investigations of two psychiatrists, Gerald Resner and Joseph Hartog, and a graduate student specializing in medical anthropology, Brett Hart Kramer, into aspects of traditional Malay treatments of mental disorders. Hartog and Resner, who had undertaken a two-year study to compare Malay folk treatment concepts and practices with Western counterparts (Hartog and Resner 1972), spent only a few paragraphs in a general article on Malay folk treatments discussing Main Peteri, which they characterized as psychodrama. They enthusiastically supported Kramer's investigation of Main Peteri[3] with a view to considering its psychotherapeutic effectiveness within its cultural context, since they believed that such a study would enhance understanding of the relationships between culture and traditional psychiatric practice. The short-term, highly focused nature of Kramer's investigations, however, and his lack of fluency in the language limit the usefulness of his observations. These investigations were cut short by the deaths of Resner in 1969 and Kramer in 1971.

Paul Chen, a physician trained in hospital-based medicine who formerly taught at the University of Malaya, observed Main Peteri in Kelantan. He commented that it was highly successful in treating psychoneuroses and depression, since the ritual "draws the sick individual out of his state of morbid self-absorption and heightens his feelings of self-worth" (1979). A vital element in this treatment, he felt, was the involvement of the patient's family and friends in the ritual, which enhances group solidarity and reintegrates the patient into his social group.

This evolution of opinion about the Main Peteri, from "devil worship" and "the black art," through a view of it as a ritual that cures by

3. Kramer spent a total of ten weeks in Kelantan. His observations exist only as a few pages contained within an unpublished paper written for a course; a short, unpublished mimeographed report; and a summary of the latter in the *Transcultural Psychiatric Research Review* (7(1970):149–150).

faith alone, to a consideration of the psychotherapeutic elements to be found in an essentially magical enterprise, reflects the changing attitudes of representatives of Western culture in general, over the course of this century, toward traditional forms of healing.

"Primitive" Psychotherapy

From the early days of this century, psychiatrists and psychoanalysts have recognized that some types of "primitive" healing methods must be classed as examples of psychotherapy, since, as Freud (1924:250) put it, in order to effect a cure, a "condition of 'expectant' faith was induced in sick persons, the same condition which answers a similar purpose for us today." Scholars from the fields of medicine and psychology writing later in the century, such as Kiev (1964, 1972), Kim and Rhi (cited in Kendall 1985), Devereux (1956), and Frank (1974), while conceding that shamanistic rituals can be effective, believed that their psychotherapeutic elements were primarily by-products of magical activity, reinforced by the moral support that patients receive from the community. The greater efficacy of Western methods was proclaimed, primarily on the ground that shamans provide merely symptomatic relief rather than the true cure provided by Western psychotherapists. The shaman's patients experience "remission without insight," whereas patients in psychotherapy are expected to undergo a basic learning experience. The insights that patients achieve in the course of this learning experience are assumed to help them form a more workable self-image, and, as a result, improve the way they function in daily life (Frank 1974).

Kiev exemplifies the mid-century medical viewpoint: "Although primitive therapies are fundamentally magical, that is non-rational attempts to deal with non-rational forces, they often contain elements of rational therapy" (1964:10). According to Kiev, the assistance that healers might provide to their patients occurs in spite of, rather than because of, the healer's theories regarding the cause and treatment of disease.

Many anthropologists (and some sociologists, e.g., Rogler and Hollingshead 1961), rather than considering the shaman's role a pale shadow of its Western counterpart, have viewed it as more important within its cultural context, since its practice includes a wider range of illnesses and misfortunes than that of the psychiatrist, and it obliges the shaman to be a master of the unseen world as well as a healer. Psychiatrists and psychologists of considerable anthropological sophistication (for example, Torrey 1972; Katz 1982; and Kleinman 1980, who combines psychiatric and anthropological expertise) have joined contemporary anthropologists in searching for the logic inherent in the shaman's ministrations and in finding similarities in, as well as differences between, biomedical and nonbiomedical healing methods. Lévi-Strauss points out that the purpose of the treatment, in both cases, is to bring repressed material to a conscious level, resulting in an abreaction. The difference between psychoanalysis and shamanism, he believes, concerns the origin of the myth employed in the healing process. Patients under psychoanalysis present their individual myths to the healer, while the myth of the shaman is received from collective tradition (Lévi-Strauss 1963:198–204).

The work of the shaman involves the manipulation of symbols that serve as appropriate metaphors for the articulation of the patients' experiences (see, e.g., Crapanzano 1977 for numerous examples). Shamans provide their patients with material from outside their normal experience; in the words of Lévi-Strauss (1963:199), the patient "receives from the outside a social myth which does not correspond to his former personal state." The locus of this symbolic expression of the patient's conflicts may be found in ancestral ghosts, elemental spirits, or other entities. These serve as projective symbols of stressful social relationships, couched in terms common to the healer, the patient, and their social milieu, and conceived of as external to the patient's personality. The trancing shaman becomes a conduit for these embodied symbols, and the patient who achieves trance is considered to have escaped from harsh reality into the world of symbols (e.g., Lewis 1971) (although I believe an equally strong case could be made for considering confrontation with the spirit world an often frightening and demanding means of facing familial and social problems). Analysis of the shamanistic ritual has elucidated the logic and rules of what, in essence, have been viewed as projective systems.

Garrison (1977) has pointed out that many concepts in Puerto Rican *Espiritismo* may be close parallels of psychoanalytic concepts: the superego being equivalent to the protective spirits, the ego to the individual spirits, and the id to base or ignorant spirits. But, although parallels may be drawn between many cosmologies and psychoanalytic formulations of the self, Prince believes that the gulf between Western psychotherapies and non-Western therapeutic systems is "of the order of the difference between alchemy and chemistry, or between astrology and astronomy" (Prince 1980:335) due to the superiority of Western theoretical formulations.

Although the Main Peteri contains all the elements of a projective system, the theory of Malay ritual practitioners goes far beyond that of simple possession and exorcism, and, as I shall demonstrate, is comparable to some of the most respected contemporary Western theories regarding personality types, creativity, and frustration, especially as they refer to psychosomatic medicine. Like Western psychotherapies, the Main Peteri can provide patients with insight by locating problems within the patients' own personality components. This aspect of the Malay ceremony is nonprojective: its metaphors are archetypes of the Self, and its agents are the Inner Winds, an integral part of the patient's being, rather than disembodied spirits or other external entities.

The concept of the Inner Winds (*angin*) is central to the Malay theory of personality, its expressions, and vissicitudes. The treatment of those ravaged by its inhibitions and frustrations, as exemplified by the Main Peteri, must be understood within the contexts of Malay medical theory and the restraints in rural Malay society that can lead to problems that respond to this indigenous form of conscious psychotherapy.

2

Islamic Humoralism on the Malay Peninsula

Rather than dividing the causes of illness into "natural" and "supernatural" categories, a dichotomy that often appears in Western comments on non-Western medical theories (e.g., Foster and Anderson 1979), rural east coast Malays speak of "usual" (*biasa*) and "unusual" (*luar biasa*) sicknesses.[1] The distinction is based more on incidence than on etiology. There is no emphasis on the "un-naturalness" of the spirit world and its manifestations.

"Usual" health problems may be attributed to a number of causes, either singly or in conjunction: accidents, poor personal or communal hygiene, a bad diet (whether due to poverty, bad habits, or other causes), too many intestinal worms (a small number is considered normal), changes in the weather that upset the body's internal balance, overwork, and worry, among others. A specialist known as a *mudin* treats broken bones and sprains. Obstetric and perinatal problems are the province of the bidan (midwife). Masseurs and masseuses are in demand for muscular aches. Other "usual" problems are treated by patients and their families, often with the aid of a bomoh whose services are sought after by villagers for both "usual" and "unusual" problems in spite of the increasing availability of the cosmopolitan medicine and in the face of objections from the Islamic hierarchy.

1. My remarks derive from fieldwork in the states of Trengganu and Kelantan. Variations in belief and behavior undoubtedly exist in other Malaysian states.

Islam and Traditional Malay Healers

Islam is the state religion of Malaysia. It is impossible to be Malay without being Muslim as well. The criteria for classification as Malay, as defined in the Constitution of the Malaysian Federation, include habitual use of the Malay language, conformity to Malay customs, and the profession of Islam (Hamid 1964:180). Malays have been Muslims for more than five hundred years, following centuries of Hindu-Buddhist influence.

For much of this time, there appears to have been a large measure of tolerance for the practices of traditional healers, in whose incantations appeals to Allah, Muhammad, and the archangels mingle with references to the Hindu triumvirate and to nature spirits who can afflict the unwary. The Ninety-Nine Laws of Perak, compiled in the eighteenth century by a family that claimed descent from Muhammad, state that "Muslims must feed the district judge, the officials of the mosque, the bomoh and the bidan. The muezzin is king in the mosque, and the bomoh is king in the house of the sick . . ." (Winstedt 1951:72). In Malay feudal society, nonaristocratic bomoh ranked higher than all other commoners, except for the wealthiest farmers and merchants (Syed Hussein Alatas 1968). Aristocrats, and even royalty, also assumed the office of medical-magical practitioner. As late as the middle of the twentieth century, the title of State Bomoh still existed in Perak. The holder of this title, usually a younger brother of the reigning sultan, was expected to conduct an annual seance, to keep the spirits of the sacred weapons and royal drums in place, and to make offerings to the state genii (Winstedt 1951: 10–11).

Even in recent times the king and his representatives have not abjured the bomoh's practices. In 1977, for example, a bomoh was hired by a district officer in Penang to ensure that the visit of the Yang di-Pertuan Agung and his queen would not be spoiled by rain.

Although rulers of the Malay states have, on the whole, not interfered with magico-medical practitioners (and have even, on occasion, officiated as shamans at a seance; see Winstedt 1951:11), relations between the bomoh and Islamic orthodoxy have long been equivocal. While some bomoh claim to have first received the call to practice their art during a pilgrimage to Mecca, turn-of-the-century ethnographers recount stories of bomoh magically barred from entering the holy city (Annandale and Robinson 1903). Letters from Islamic teachers have been preserved, protesting English Residents' interest in shamanism, a "practice which is a deadly sin to the Muhammadan faith" (Swettenham 1895:208–210).

In recent years, Malay religious leaders have objected to the practices of the bomoh in increasingly strenuous terms. The bomoh's duties as a healer extend from clinical (private treatment of sickness) to preventive medicine (public rites for warding off impending disaster). They are all perceived as anathema by the Islamic establishment. In a publication of the Trengganu Office of Religious Affairs (Haji Mahmud Salim 1976), many of the bomoh's practices are cited as dangerous deviations from Islam. They are said to "treat sick people by means of worshipping spirits and devils, and to throw away trays of propitiatory food offerings." Their public performances, such as *tolak bala*, done to ward off evil at the erection of a new house, or at the time of an epidemic or other calamity; *buka hutan*, the ritual connected with opening the jungle for agriculture; and *puja pantai* (invocations at the seashore), a yearly celebration featuring offerings to the sea spirits, are listed as examples of the kinds of superstition that must be rooted out.

When I asked officials at the Trengganu Office of Religious Affairs in 1976 about their efforts to curb bomoh, I was told that, although speakers were often sent to village mosques to enveigh against them, there was little hope that serious inroads could be made at that time in their rural patronage. The situation appears to have changed radically during the succeeding decade. Colleagues who have worked in Malaysia during the late 1980s have informed me that all types of traditional theatrical performances, including the Main Peteri, have become well-nigh defunct on Malaysia's east coast, due to religious objections.

Private treatments do not carry the risk of prosecution by ecclesiastical courts. Public performances, however, such as puja pantai, which traditionally included large-scale propitiatory offerings of water buffalo and goats, have been outlawed for well over two decades and anyone undertaking their performance could be subject to criminal prosecution entailing a fine or jail sentence.

Bomoh have long been required to obtain permission from the police to hold seances. They have often ignored this rule, however, holding their seances far from the local police compound, where the sounds of singing and drumming will not reach the ears of the civil authorities.

Although disdained by the Islamic hierarchy, many native healers are, in fact, devout Muslims. To a greater or lesser degree, they are concerned about the negative attitude of Muslim orthodoxy toward their activities and attempt a number of accommodations to Islam. For example, one bomoh who had received her first call to practice while on a pilgrimage to Mecca replaced the usual Malay incantations with Koranic sentences, although she otherwise employed the same techniques as her colleagues. Another, who frequently participated in Main Peteri, taught a large children's Koranic class nightly. He worried about his neighbors' opinions and even about the possibility of divine censure and punishment on Judgment Day, but he never hesitated to leave his pupils to attend a patient. Another bomoh, the muezzin of the local mosque, apparently did not perceive any dissonance between his two roles, although he, like all bomoh, maintained that magical healing was ineffective on Thursday nights, the eve of the Islamic sabbath. One shaman always prayed in the mosque before commencing a seance. The seance itself, although primarily about nature spirits, genii, and demigods, employs Islamic prayer. Some shamans' theories regarding the nature of spirits are essays in reconciliation with Islam. One explained to me that only ignorant people believe in a multitude of spirits. In truth, he said, there is only one, the Father of Lies, who pretended to give birth to other spirits but merely "gave birth" to many names.[2]

Bomoh who discussed the problem with me felt that the religious

2. Malay shamans differ in their beliefs regarding the origin and nature of hantu. One school of thought says that only one hantu was created. This spirit "gave birth to names" rather than proliferating. It is addressed by one name when it appears in the village, by another when out at sea, by a third in the jungle, and so on. Another school of thought says that the Breath of Life sent out many sparks, creating untold numbers of spirits. The disagreement was graphically illustrated one day when Pak Long Awang came with me while I interviewed another shaman, Pak Mat Daud bin Panjak. Pak Long listened silently while Mat Daud explained to me that there was only one hantu called by many names. On the way home, however, Pak Long remarked that if such were actually the case, it would be simple to catch that one hantu and confine it in a jar, fasten the lid on tight, dig a pit, and put the jar in, upside down, so that, should the spirit escape, it would go farther into the earth and never come back to the surface and harm humanity. Although Pak Long had done this several times, people continued to get sick due to spirit attacks, thus proving that there must be many hantu.

authorities judged them unfairly on the basis of misconceptions. They maintained that their traffic with spirits in no way constituted worship; that food used in offerings did not go to waste but was eaten by people, or at least by animals; and, most important, that their work was meant to heal, not to hurt. "I realize that what I am doing may be a sin," said one, "but it is only a small sin. Why don't the religious authorities stop bothering us and worry about all the people who commit really serious sins, like adultery?"

In spite of religious disapproval and secular attempts to control the work of the bomoh, indigenous medical-magical practitioners still carried on a thriving practice, in the cities as well as in the countryside in the 1970s. Bomoh have joined the jet set, flying in to Kuala Lumpur from Kelantan and advertising their services in the capital's newspapers. A local chief of police who had spent many years abroad and was fluent in several languages was a steady client of Tok Hitam, a famous female bomoh living in Trengganu. A retired general who specializes in love magic received his customers at the Kuala Lumpur Hilton Hotel; and an official of the *Dewan Bahasa dan Pustaka* (Malaysian Council on Language and Literature), after advising me that my material on Malay shamanism was likely to be judged offensive to Islam by the government censor, spent the next hour attempting to persuade me to use my magical knowledge to secure his wife's affections and cure her sterility.

Bomoh and bidan are roles integral to village life. Although no longer supported by public funds, they are referred to by the honorific, '*tok*, and accorded the respect due valued members of the community.

No one is a full-time healer in village Malaysia. Pak Long Awang, for example, grows vegetables and tobacco, as well as attending to his patients. Sapiah, the most popular village midwife, plants tobacco and also taps rubber for sale. The practice of healing, however, can add significantly to one's income. Pak Long told me that before he became a bomoh life was very hard, but now he can count on enough extra money to provide for himself and his wife and even have some left over for gifts to young relatives. When he taught me his incantations, he was particularly enthusiastic about love magic. With that kind of knowledge, he said, I would never want for clients. Mat Daud bin Panjak said that curing illness not only brought him great satisfaction but allowed him to support his wife and children in style. Occasionally, the trust and respect engendered by successful healing can generalize to other economic arenas. Pak Su Umar, one of the most respected bomoh in Merchang, was able to build upon his reputation as a powerful healer in order to advance his trade in dried fish. His expanding business has made him one of the wealthiest men in Merchang.

The work of the bomoh is not confined to curative medicine. Besides the protective measures they employ for the health and safety of the community, mentioned previously, bomoh advise individuals who intend to build new houses, attempt to bring back errant husbands by magical means, send their spirits to urge undesirable tenants to vacate their houses, try to increase a fisherman's chances of getting a good catch or a prospective driver's chances of getting a license, and help clients abrogate their contracts with the spirit world. But, although their range of expertise is vast (I have mentioned merely a few examples), the bomoh's practice is primarily that of healer.

Bomoh are called upon to treat a wide range of illnesses. The means they employ include prescriptions for rest, dietary adjustments, and medicines (which may have plant, animal, and mineral components), as well as incantations and trance cures. In Malaysia, the etiology of the great majority of illnesses and their treatment fit into a humoral model. In many respects contemporary Malay humoralism is remarkably similar to the humoralism of the medieval Islamic world, but it incorporates significant differences in both theory and practice.

Humoralism on the Malay Peninsula

The bases of medical thought in three of the world's great civilizations, ancient Greece, India, and China, are remarkably similar. All define health as the balance of universal and opposing elements, though each plays its own variation on the broad theme of humoral pathology. The similarities can be explained in part by early, continuing, and deliberate cross-fertilization. In the ancient world, Greek and Indian humoral traditions traveled from east to west and back again through Persia (Filliozat 1964). In the centuries following Chinese conversion to Buddhism, Chinese pilgrim-monks traveled to India and returned bearing Indian medical texts in Chinese translation (Huard and Wong 1968).

Malaya, located on the periphery of both the Indian and the Chinese spheres of influence and trade, has exchanged medical and philosophical ideas as well as goods with representatives of both cultures for close to two thousand years. Although we cannot date the first Indian voyages to Malaya with any precision, there is evidence dating from the third century A.D. of a growing ocean-borne trade. Success of this trade depended on the establishment of restapling ports in the Malay archipelago, where Indian merchants could remain during the monsoon season before returning home. Third-century Chinese sources mention a terminus port for Indian shipping, apparently located near the Melaka Straits (Andaya and Andaya 1982).

Indian traders were drawn to Malaya in search of gold and silver, aromatic woods, and spices. Their religious concepts, notions of kingship, and the vocabulary of Sanskrit pervaded Malay life and thought, although nothing in legend or history points to a dramatic conversion such as occurred with the adoption of Islam. There appears to have been little in the way of actual colonization, although there is evidence of small coastal and riverine settlements, and remains of Buddhist temples dating from 300–550 A.D. have been found in Kedah (Ryan 1965). Hindu as well as Buddhist inscriptions, attributed to the fourth century, have been found in Prai (Province Wellesley) as well as in Kedah (Andaya and Andaya 1982).

Few Chinese sources prior to the fifth century mention Southeast Asia, but there is suggestive evidence of earlier contact, such as the fragments of Han dynasty (206 B.C.–221 A.D.) pottery found in Malaya (Ryan 1965). From the fifth century on, Chinese trade in luxury items from western Asia, which had previously been conducted overland, made increasing use of the sea. Harbors in the Melaka Straits provided shelters for the sailing ships that had to wait for the winds to change before continuing on their voyages or returning home. Although the influence of Chinese thought and culture in Malaya was not as pervasive as that of India, the association of China and Malaya has been long and continuous.

By the fourteenth century, when Greek-Arabic medical theories reached Malaya along with Islam, its inhabitants had had more than a thousand years of exposure to similar traditional Hindu Ayurvedic theories, tempered by contact with Chinese medicine. Over the following centuries, Islamic humoral theory has been shaped by and integrated into Malay thought. Elaborated humoral ideas of contemporary Malays extend from such mundane matters as food and illness to the workings of the universe and the nature of its inhabitants, both seen and unseen.

Historians have theorized that the establishment of peaceful relationships between traders and natives was often aided by an exchange of medical treatments, amulets, herbs, and other curative and preventive ingredients (e.g., Ferrand 1919; Coèdes 1968; Winstedt 1935; see also Golomb 1985). The sharing of materia medica and materia magica, and their practical application, is a common feature of culture contact. The transfer of the underlying theories behind treatments is considerably rarer.

It has become increasingly evident that in societies throughout the world people will often accept the treatments a foreign medical system provides while rejecting their theoretical basis. The prestige of a donor culture whose technology is not only more sophisticated than the recipients' own, but whose religion has been accepted as the true faith, is a powerful stimulus to the acceptance of other aspects of the exogenous culture. It is doubtful, however, that foreign ideas will take root and flourish as thoroughly as humoral theories have done among Malays in the absence of a preexisting world view that could incorporate them without dissonance.

Just as the humoral system brought to the New World by Spaniards found acceptance among Native Americans who believed the universe to be ordered by a balance of opposites, so may such theories have found points of resemblance in pre-Hindu Malayan beliefs about sickness and health, humanity and the cosmos. Since we lack written records of Malay life and thought in ancient times, we must turn for clues to ethnographic accounts of the Negritos, Senoi, and Proto-Malays, the aboriginal peoples (Orang Asli) of the interior of Malaya who were converted neither to Hinduism nor to Islam.

Concepts of Heat and Cold Among Orang Asli

Although they do not employ a humoral classificatory system, a hot-cold opposition is dominant in the cosmological, medical, and social theories of all Orang Asli groups. The distinction refers to actual temperatures, both on the physical and spiritual planes, and is not related to either the Chinese or Malay concepts of humoral "heating" or "cooling" properties (Endicott 1979). The heat of the sun and all its earthly reflections are associated with excrement, blood, misfortune, disease, and death (Endicott 1979; Howell 1981; Wazir-Jahan Karim 1981; Roseman 1984). Heat, in fact, is the primary cause of human mortality. The Chewong believe that our world has become hot and unhealthy, due to its burning sun, the heat emanating from the slaughter of animals, and the accumulation of urine and feces. The Original People, who live on another world with a cool sun, have cool white blood and cool eyes. Unlike us, they never sicken or die (Howell 1981). The Batek Negritos place their benevolent supernaturals on the moon, but they, too, attribute their immortality to their cool breath, colorless blood, and cool bodies (Endicott 1979).

The hot blood of humanity makes us mortal, and the need to eat hot bloody animal flesh accelerates the process toward death (Endicott 1979; Howell 1981). Those who take animal life may expose themselves, as well, to *badi*, a hot spiritual force found in all living things but concentrated especially in human corpses and jungle animals and released upon death (Mohd. Hood Salleh 1978).

Although humans must eat meat and other foods that have been rendered less wholesome through their exposure to heat by cooking, it is possible to avoid the harmful effects of the sun's heat by depending upon the jungle for one's sustenance rather than venturing out into the open for the long hours necessary to cultivate a garden. This is the argument most often advanced by Batek Negritos for resisting agriculture, an activity that removes one from the coolness and comfort of the forest and exposes one to the harmful rays of the sun (Endicott 1979).

Coolness is considered to be so vital to health that, when a Negrito or Senoi takes ill in a jungle clearing, the entire group prefers to withdraw to the forest (Endicott 1979; Roseman 1985). The jungle is not only cool in itself, it is the source of cooling herbs and leaves used internally and externally to counteract the heat of disease (Laird 1985; Nagata 1985). It is also the only environment in which spells become truly effective (Howell 1981).

Disease is most often associated with heat, whether carried by malevolent spirits or resulting from contact with badi. Aboriginal healers' treatments are designed to remove the heat and substitute coolness. Skeat and Blagden (1906) cite spells used by Senoi and Aboriginal Malay healers to plead with supernatural forces to "Cool the heat, be cool, be cold," "Let the hot grow cold and frigid," "Give coolness within the body." Like the immortal gods they resemble, healers' bodies are superhumanly cool, and the healers take steps to retain their coolness by bathing in cold water and sleeping far from the fire (Endicott 1979; Howell 1981). Their eyes are especially cool, enabling them to see the true nature of things, hidden to ordinary people (Howell 1981). After removing their patients from the hot clearing to the cool jungle, they blow their cooling breath upon their patients' backs, treat them with cooling medications, and call upon beneficent spirits to assist them in magically infusing the sick body with cool, refreshing, spiritual liquid, which they draw from a bowl placed under hanging leaf ornaments, or from their own breasts (Roseman 1984, 1985). The spirits are enjoined to carry the patient's ailing soul to the sky, where supernaturals bathe it in cooling dew (Endicott 1979).

Heat and dryness are associated with psychic as well as physical discomfort. Temiars describe longing for the absent beloved, longing of the living for the dead, and longing of the male healer for his female spirit-guide, as a hot, dry wind: "One hears it in one's ear like wind: 'Yaaw-waaw-waaw.' If we sit, dream, we hear this in our ear; it's uncomfortable. We must have a singing ceremony, it orders us to have a trance-dancing ceremony. Only then are we relieved. Otherwise, after a while, we would go mad. [It] is like a hot, dry wind rustling the leaves when there is no rain; we must hold a ceremony" (Roseman 1986:210).

Coolness and moisture are associated with everything positive in aboriginal society: self-control, harmony, fertility, health, and life. Heat epitomizes disease, death, destruction, and disorder, not only within the individual person but also, metaphorically, within aboriginal society. The spirits of disease are not the only hot entities; so is a spirit who causes monthly bleeding in women and punishes incest by hurling a hot lightning bolt at the perpetrators (Howell 1981). Forbidden sexual relations themselves are referred to as "hot," as are other threats to society, such as incompatibility between mother and child attributed to the mother's "hot body," which may destroy the child unless it is removed to another household (Wazir-Jahan Karim 1981). Violent emotions, aggressive behavior, and drunkenness, all potentially disruptive to the harmony of aboriginal society, are manifestations of heat and call for cooling remedies (Laird 1985).

Although coolness is much preferred to heat, extreme cold can also harm the body. The problem is rare in normal life, except for a woman who has recently given birth. During pregnancy, a Senoi mother-to-be and her midwife should be ceremonially bathed "to make them supernaturally 'cool,' that is, healthy" (Dentan 1965). While in labor, women are asperged with cold water to keep them cool and healthy and protect them from destructive heat (Roseman 1984; Dentan 1965). After a woman has delivered, however, her body is no longer normally cool, but has become very cold and vulnerable. She must avoid decreasing her heat further by refraining from drinking or bathing in cold water (Dentan 1965; Endicott 1979; Skeat and Blagden 1906). She augments her body heat by tying sashes containing warmed leaves or ashes around her waist, bathing herself and her newborn child in warm water, and lying near a fire source (a practice known as "mother roasting," widespread throughout Southeast Asia, as is the theory of the healer's cooling breath; e.g., Hart, Rajadhon, and Coughlin 1965; Errington 1983; Laderman 1981, 1983).

These beliefs, which make general statements about heat and cold, set the stage for the acceptance of an exogenous humoral theory that systematically categorizes particular diseases, treatments, and foods according to the hot, cold, wet, and dry properties of their components. Indianized Malays had undoubtedly been influenced by Ayurvedic theory before the arrival of the Greek-Arabic medical system based upon Galen's humoral concepts, which reached the Malay peninsula in the fourteenth century along with Islam and was incorporated into the medicine and cosmology of Islamicized Malays. Islamic humoralism differed from indigenous theories in two important respects: (1) it attempted to deal with illness by employing a rational, scientific approach, which located the problem in the natural world and measured degrees of humoral qualities precisely; and (2) the aboriginal emphasis on the danger of heat and value of coolness was reversed.

Medieval Islamic Humoral Theory

In medieval humoral theory, foods, diseases, medicines, and many other aspects of nature could be scientifically classified according to their inherent qualities of heat, cold, dryness, and moisture. Heat and cold did not refer, necessarily, to thermal qualities, that is, squash hot off the stove was still considered to be extremely cold. The precise classifications used by Islamic theoreticians were far from the generalized hot and cold notions of the aboriginal peoples of Malaya. Foods and other things were meticulously positioned in terms of humoral degrees, often being placed, for example, at "the beginning of the third degree" or "the end of the second." Health handbooks, such as the *Regimen Sanitatis Salernitanum* (Harington 1920) and the *Tacuinum Sanitatis* (Cogliati 1976) (translated into Latin from the work of Ibn Botlan), advised readers about the effects and usefulness of various foods and the means of neutralizing their dangers. For example, cucumbers, which are cold and humid in the third degree, are useful in cooling fevers, but may cause pain in the loins and stomach. They can be neutralized by the addition of honey and oil (both "hot"). Spinach, cold and humid in the second degree, should be fried with "hot" salt and spices to balance its humoral qualities.

Although medieval Islamic humoral theory emphasized the importance of balance for the maintenance of health, the ideal human body was not located on the humoral scale midway between the cold and hot, wet and dry polarities, but was hot and moist in the second degree (McVaugh 1975). Heat that is not natural to the body was believed to imperil it by causing putrefaction, but natural internal heat was thought to increase the virility and courage of its possessor, and was considered "the great instrument with which the system . . . destroys hot things which are inimical to life . . . and protects also against injurious cold." Cold "produces only weakness and damage. It is for this reason that heat is called the innate heat while cold is not termed the innate cold" (Shah 1966:116).

Medieval physicians, such as Avicenna (Shah 1966; Krueger 1963), Averroes (Blumberg 1961), Ibn Ridwan (Dols 1984), Ibn Botlan (Cogliati 1976), and Maimonides (Gorlin 1961; Maimonides 1981), advised their patients to live prudent lives, since moderation in all things was productive of innate heat. Moderate amounts of sleep, a moderate degree of wakefulness, moderate exercise, moderate mental exertion, moderate quantities of food, moderate use of hot baths, moderate indulgence in pleasurable activities, moderation in the expression of emotions—all of these are beneficial to human well-being. Excess of any kind is destructive to health, since it disturbs the innate heat. Thus, extremes of atmospheric temperature or topical applications, whether hot or cold, are destructive to innate heat; excessive activity disperses it, excessive repose surpresses it, excessive food and drink smother it, insufficient food depletes it, strong emotions and too much pleasure destroy it—all are productive of cold, the absence of health. (Anger, in fact, was considered to deplete the innate heat by causing it to boil within the heart [Cogliati 1976].) The predominance of heat and moisture ensures long life, since death is nothing more than cold and dryness (Blumberg 1961).

When one considers the negative connotations of cold in medieval Islamic medical theory, it is not surprising to learn that women, the imperfect half of humanity, are naturally colder than men, and moister, since "their greater cold leads to the excessive formation of excrements" (Krueger 1963:93). Females are deficient in heat from the time of their conception. They are produced from the imperfect semen of their fathers' left testicles and deposited in the left side of their mothers' wombs, both of which are naturally colder than those on the right (Maclean 1980; Maimonides 1970). Women's slower metabolism burns food less efficiently. The residue changes to fat, which is stored to nourish unborn babies and, later, used in milk production. The female form, broader in the hips and narrower in the shoulders than the male, is due to deficiency of heat, the driving force that sends matter up toward the head (Maclean 1980:34). Women's brains, therefore, lack the mental characteristics of heat: courage, liberality, moral strength, and honesty (Maclean 1980:32). Their lesser amounts of innate heat make women weaker and more vulnerable to sickness, particularly in their womanly parts and functions. They were advised to avoid drinking cold water, sitting on cold stones, or staying too long in a cold bath, since these actions would further deplete their innate heat and cause the uterus to ache, or even to slip its moorings (Rowland 1981). A cold, wet womb is a sterile womb, since "just as a wet soil and too much rain [it] will destroy seed" (Elgood 1970:69).

The production of male seed was encouraged by the external application of heat (Elgood 1970) and by a diet emphasizing foods that increased heat, and excluding foods that increased cold. Although medieval and Renaissance theoreticians were careful to measure humoral qualities in precise degrees, a layman could arrive at a rough estimate by using this rule of thumb: foods that taste sweet, salty, bitter, or sharp are heating, as are oils, fats, alcohol, and the flesh of animals, whereas foods which are sour, astringent, or tasteless are cooling (Gorlin 1961; Maimonides 1981).

Once the seed was planted, it could still be imperiled by the mother's coldness. Miscarriage and premature labor were usually attributed to a disproportionate measure of cold and damp within the womb (Rowland 1981). Childbirth further depleted a woman's innate heat, putting her in a colder than normal condition for the duration of the postpartum period.

The intensely pleasurable sex act was considered to be fraught with danger for the male. Intercourse depleted his body of hot, moist semen, decreasing his body's strength, and rendering his brain dry (Gorlin 1961). Averroes counseled moderation in sexual activity, explaining that those whose lust is excessive often die young (Blumberg 1961), and Maimonides warned that only "one in a thousand dies of other diseases, the rest of the thousand of sexual overindulgence" (1981:38). Men were advised to avoid cold water and fruits after intercourse and to shun old women and women who had recently delivered, since both were extremely cold and would rob the man of his innate heat. The young mother would regain her heat in time, but the old of both sexes were permanently cold, a cold that increased with age, ending with death, the total absence of heat (Gorlin 1961). A man who aspired to a long and healthy life, therefore, should locate himself in a warm climate, conduct himself with moderation in all things, avoid cold foods except in hot weather (unless the cold foods were balanced by heating ingredients), and marry a young wife.

Many of the precepts of medieval Islamic theory were incorporated into the Malay medical system, but acceptance was selective. Some beliefs that were accepted remain essentially unchanged, others have been modified. Precepts that reversed the hot and cold polarities of pre-Islamic, aboriginal cosmology were never accepted.

Contemporary Malay Humoralism

Malaya was introduced to Islam and its elaborate post-Galenic humoral traditions during the fourteenth and fifteenth centuries by Indian merchants (and an occasional Persian or Arab trader), who combined proselytization with commerce (Andaya and Andaya 1982). Sparsely settled and provincial to all major centers of humoral theory, Malaya received a less than perfect transfer of knowledge through the agency of nonprofessionals and low-level practitioners. This may help to explain why humoral classifications became less precise, why moisture and dryness virtually disappeared as independent qualities (in common with contemporary humoral systems found in similarly provincial areas), and why a neutral category, neither hot nor cold, took on importance.

The universe of contemporary Malays is composed of the four elements of Greek-Arabic doctrine: earth, air, fire, and water (rather than the universal building-blocks of China or India). Their humoral concerns are very salient: Within days after arriving at my east coast village, I was warned that eating *durian* fruit in conjunction with hospital-type medicines was dangerous since their combined heat might prove fatal, and that papaya should be limited to the noon meal when the body is at its hottest and can withstand the coldness of the fruit.

Although Malays do not attempt to categorize foods according to precise humoral degrees, their general rationales concerning their heating or cooling qualities are essentially those of medieval Islamic theory. Both agree that "hot" foods include alcohol, fats, oils, the flesh of animals, and foods that are salty, bitter, or spicy, whereas "cold" foods are sour or astringent. Malays add other criteria to these basic humoral distinctions: juicy fruits and vegetables, plants that exude viscous matters reminiscent of phlegm (the cold humor), or those that need a great deal of moisture to grow, are "cold," as are vines and creepers (which cling or are dependent upon larger plants and thus partake of feminine, and therefore cooler, qualities). Islamic humoral theory differentiated

between the active qualities of heat and coolness, and the passive qualities of moisture and dryness, and assigned both active and passive qualities in independent assortment. Thus, sugar was hot and moist, spinach cold and moist, and garlic hot and dry. Contemporary Malays speak only of "hot" and "cold" foods, but it is clear from their discussions of humoral characteristics that "passive humors," rather than acting independently, are tied to the "active humors." Moisture is associated with coolness and dryness with heat, whether in terms of the innate qualities of foods and medicines, in connection with physiological processes, such as the cooling properties of sweat, or in relation to the seasons. In Malaysia, the dry season is the hottest time of the year, whereas the monsoon season is justifiably known as the cold season. According to the Malay view of nature, rain should be associated with cold, and dryness with heat. That is why sunshowers (called *hujan panas*; literally, "hot rain"), because of their anomalous position in nature's scheme, are believed to carry risks to the health of vulnerable people.

Although the daily diet of contemporary Malays differs from that of medieval Arabs or Europeans in the species of foods available, where foods overlap there is a surprising amount of agreement as to their humoral qualities. For example, all would agree that cucumbers, squash, and spinach are very cold, that meats and egg yolks are quite hot, and that, while sugar and honey both are heating, honey is "hotter." Like the medieval theoreticians, Malays believe that humoral qualities of foods can be neutralized by eating them in conjunction with ingredients of opposite qualities, but that intensely "cold" foods, such as squash, should be eaten only during the hottest months.

Humoral concerns become most pressing during illnesses and other times of physical vulnerability. Most diseases are attributed to natural causes, and their treatments, in the main, follow rationally along an Islamic humoral model. These include dietary changes, ingestion and topical application of medicines (most of which are classified humorally), massage (believed to break up the lumps of cold "phlegm" that cause muscular pain and allow the hot blood to flow properly), and thermal treatments, such as steam inhalation and cold compresses.

Illnesses are classified as hot or cold, using the following criteria that interpret symptoms by means of empirical evidence in the light of humoral reasoning:

1. External heat: those illnesses, such as fever or boils, that are hot to the touch.

2. Internal heat: illnesses that make the patient experience hot or burning sensations, such as sore throat or heartburn.

3. Visible signs: hemorrhages are evidence that the hot element has boiled over; clotted phlegm indicates that the cold element has become still colder.

4. Deficiency or excess of a humor deduced from internal evidence: *Kurang darah* (literally, "not enough blood," roughly equivalent to anemia, a concept they have become acquainted with through clinic and hospital visits) is cold since its sufferers have insufficient amounts of the hot humor; *darah tinggi* (literally, "high blood," which produces headaches and dizziness in its sufferers) is hot since an excess of blood is presumed to have gone to the head (considered by Malays to be normally hotter than the rest of the body), thereby overheating it. Malays diagnosed in the hospital as hypertensive equate their condition with darah tinggi.

5. Pulse reading: A fast pulse denotes heat, since its speed is owing to the rate at which blood travels through the veins; a slow pulse is a sign that inner cold has thickened the blood and made it sluggish.

6. Behavioral considerations: Some forms of madness are thought to occur as a result of the brain overheating, causing violent and angry behavior. Such behavior is called *panas* (literally, "hot"). Madness can result from too much thought (such as excessive amounts of studying), or violent emotions. Prescribing hot medicines for hot conditions can also lead to madness when their combined heat reaches the brain.

7. Response to treatments: If illnesses respond to treatments already classified as hot or cold, this indicates that these illnesses have the opposite humoral quality, that is, asthma is cold since it responds to steam inhalation; heatstroke is hot since it responds to cold water.

8. In reference to age: Malays follow medieval Islamic medical theory in attributing a greater degree of cold to the aged. Since rheumatism is most often found in old people, it is classified as cold.

Malays are so convinced of the empirical reality of humoral qualities that when I sent off food samples to the Institute for Medical Research for nutrient testing, my neighbors were sure that the institute would also test for inherent heat and cold.

The great majority of illnesses are attributed by Malays to natural causes, and treatments follow along a humoral model. Illnesses that do not respond to these treatments, or which otherwise deviate from the normal course, are often blamed on incursions from the unseen world and must be treated by means other than dietary changes and pharmaceuticals. Etiology and treatment, although they do not locate the problem in the natural world and would not qualify as either scientific or rational by Galenic standards, are congruent with a humoral model employing the Greek-Arabic concept of a four-fold universe. The spirits, lacking the earthy and watery components of fleshly bodies, consist only of superheated air. They were created, Pak Daud said, owing to the curiosity of the archangel Gabriel. God blew the Breath of Life into Gabriel's hands and ordered him to place it near Adam's nostrils so that his lifeless body, made of earth and water, might be animated. Gabriel, wanting to see what it looked like, opened his hands as he flew toward Adam, and the Breath escaped. Having no body to receive it, the Breath became *hantu*, the disembodied older siblings of humankind, born before Adam. Like all siblings, hantu are sometimes beset with feelings of envy toward their younger brothers, the children of Adam, since humans are beings of the light whereas spirits must live forever in darkness. And like human siblings, they occasionally find ways to even the score.

For example, by blowing their hot breath on a victim's back, they upset his humoral balance. Treatment involves increasing the cool and moist elements and ridding the body of excess heat and air. Healers employ "neutralizing rice paste," recite spells, blowing their magically cooled breath on their patients, and bathe them in cooling water.

Divinations employed to discover the cause of these illnesses often follow a humoral model. One method uses rice popped by dry heat. The shaman places handfuls of this rice on a pillow and counts out the grains in pairs, two each for earth, air, fire, and water. If the count ends on earth, it might point to a cold illness, or one caused by the earth spirits. If it falls on fire, it might signify that the patient has incurred someone's hot wrath, whether human or spirit, or it might simply mean that the condition was hot. Another method consists of reading the flame of a beeswax candle. No other type of candle can be substituted. The bee partakes of the spirits' unholy heat. Found in the jungle, beyond human control (at least on the east coast of Malaysia), and commanding a remarkably hot sting, bees are called friends of the spirits.

Malay incantations invariably include Koranic sentences and other appeals to Allah, his Prophet, and his saints. Although Malays have reinterpreted their beliefs about the spirits in the light of stories about the angel Gabriel, Muhammad, and other Islamic references, their treatments for extra-normal problems are fundamentally the same as those of non-Islamic Orang Asli.

The Malay belief in the dangers of badi, that hot, impersonal, destructive spiritual force emanating from the corpses of jungle animals and human beings, which also parallels beliefs of the Orang Asli, makes no appeal to Islam for the authentication of its power. Badi holds particular danger for the unborn, working indirectly through their parents. To avoid its risk, prospective fathers are advised to forgo hunting for the duration of their wives' pregnancies, and mothers-to-be are warned against visits of condolence to homes of yet-unburied dead.

Although Malay ideas concerning appropriate and inappropriate degrees of heat according to individual temperaments and the changing seasons are common as well to the Galenic, Ayurvedic, and Chinese humoral traditions, Malays locate the normal, healthy male body in the very center of the hot-cold continuum, rather than toward the hot polarity preferred by Islamic humoral doctrine. Some believe that women are slightly colder than men, owing to their monthly loss of blood, the hot body humor; however, this is not considered an important distinction, nor is it elaborated upon as it was in medieval Islamic theory. It is important to stay near the humoral center, and nature assists one by encouraging the outpouring of cooling sweat during the hot, dry season. Freely flowing sweat in the presence of heat is considered essential to the maintenance of health. This concept disagrees with medieval Islamic and Jewish theory: Maimonides maintained that "sweat is an abnormal occurrence because the body is such that if a man conducts himself properly and eats natural foods and digests them properly, [a healthy man] will not sweat excessively" (1970:81).

In common with all adherents to humoral theory, and in common as well with Orang Asli, Malays believe that childbirth precipitates a woman into an abnormally cold state. They attempt to redress this problem by means of dietary changes that follow a humoral pattern, and by treatments, such as "mother-roasting," bathing with warm water, and tying protective sashes about the waists of new mothers, that can be interpreted humorally but are also the counterparts of Orang Asli post-partum procedures.

Although Islam was successfully implanted in Malaya, and Islamic concepts are used by Malays to interpret and reinterpret empirical realities, received theories of Islamic humoralism have been radically altered by the pre-Islamic aboriginal view of the workings of the cosmos and the positive valence of coolness in the universe and its human microcosm.

Moderation in all aspects of life is seen as a positive good by contemporary Malays and Orang Asli, as it was by medieval theoreticians. Overeating to the point of obesity is derided by Malays, and drunkenness or drug use puts one beyond the pale. Malays rarely exhibit strong emotions in public—neither great joy at a wedding or birth, nor grief at a funeral. Such lack of public emotional expression appears to be rare: using material from the Human Relations Area Files (seventy-three societies), Rosenblatt et al. (1976) found that crying during bereavement was nearly universal.[3] They suggest that the impulse to cry is present, but in rare cases people have learned to suppress it as socially inappropriate. Malays go beyond the convention that public display of strong emotions is unseemly. Most of my neighbors in Merchang, in fact, denied that they had ever experienced such feelings and believed that violent emotions could do harm to their possessors.[4]

3. Bali was the notable exception of the seventy-three societies considered in this study. I suspect that there would have been several more if other Southeast Asian cultures had been included.

4. My remarks are based both on long, intimate conversations with Malay friends and neighbors and on a survey I did of four kampung in Merchang. One question in my survey inquired into the effects of parental emotions upon the developing fetus. Gerber (1985), discussing a similar situation in Samoa, comments that where feelings are disapproved, it may be difficult for people to acknowledge their strength or their existence, even to themselves.

An admiration for "coolness" in regard to personality can also be found in Ayurvedic doctrine, which values the *kapha* phlegmatic disposition in which coolness and moisture predominate. This is the ideal personality type of the Brahmin: peaceful, tolerant, calm, forgiving, and loving (Lad 1984). Heat is valued in Ayurveda for digestion and the trans-

Although contemporary Malays would agree with Avicenna et al. about the benefits to one's health accrued by following the middle road, their humoral beliefs associated with such behavior are polar opposites of those of medieval Islam.

While Greek-Arabic medical theory stressed the importance of "innate heat," Malays associate coolness with self-control and health, and heat with vulnerability to illness. Violent emotions, like anger and passionate love, are hot and dangerous and can lead to an overheated brain and madness. A person quick to anger is known as *panas hati* (literally "hot-livered"); the heat rises from the liver, the center of emotions, which is ordinarily cool, to the head, which is ordinarily warm. Malays believe that the head is normally hotter than the rest of the body and try to avoid heating it further. That is why the heads of newborn babies are subjected to cold water, although the rest of their bodies, which are in other respects "cold" compared to adults, are washed in warm water. This is in direct contradiction to the advice of medieval Islamic and Jewish physicians who recommended that "the whole body should be washed, but water used on the head may be very hot" and never cold or lukewarm, since the head was considered to be the source of phlegm, the cold humor (Maimonides 1981:37).

All other humoral systems associate sterility with cold wombs, conception with coital heat, and pregnancy with either an intensely heated maternal condition, or a mother who starts out "hot" and is gradually polarized toward cold due to loss of her own hot blood, used in her baby's development (e.g., Fabrega 1974; Thakkur 1965; Pillsbury 1982). Malays, on the contrary, believe conception cannot take place unless both parents' bodies are in a cool state, an event that occurs once a month on "the day the seeds fall." The mother's body must continue to be cool throughout her pregnancy to safeguard the developing child, at first a lump of blood that may be liquified by heat, and later, a creature in danger of being driven from the womb prematurely by heat. Prospective mothers must guard their unborn children against fevers and "hot" medicines, whereas women who find themselves pregnant incon-

formation of body substances (seven *dhatus*), but in terms of temperament heat is associated with violence and promiscuity. (My thanks to Charles Leslie for pointing this out.)

veniently try to destroy the fetus by making their wombs uncomfortably hot, through their use of "hot" medicines and heating massage.

The Malay identification of heat with destruction and coolness with life and health is reflected in their daily language. *Sejuk* (literally, "coolness") can be used as a synonym for "healthful, energetic, and pleasant." *Menyejukkan* ("to make cool") can mean "to calm, to revive, to repair, to amuse." A person whose liver is cool (*hati sejuk*) is tranquil and carefree. In contrast, *panas* ("heat") can be used as a synonym for unlucky, ominous, disastrous. Those with *panas rezeki* ("hot livelihood," or difficulty in earning one's living) are poor unfortunates. A generally ill-tempered person is described as a "glowing ember" (*panas bara*); a person quick to anger has a "hot liver" or "hot blood" (*panas hati*, *panas darah*). *Memanaskan hati* ("to cause the liver to become hot") means to instill hatred in one's breast. Black magic is called *ilmu panas* ("the hot science") because it carries out a mission of hatred (Awang Sudjai Hairul and Yusoff Khan 1977; Iskandar 1970; Wilkinson 1959).

Malay preference for coolness and anxiety about heat extend beyond individual health concerns to concern for the health of the body politic. A successful sultan embodies the coolness that balances the destructive heat of nature, men's emotions, and the spirit world. The highest praise a ruler can receive is that his reign was cool (*perentah-nya sejuk*). An ordinary Malay, though limited in his powers, can still help to keep universal balance situated toward the cold polarity by reciting "the blessed cooling prayers" of Islamic obligation (Zainal-Abidin 1947).

Aboriginal peoples of Malaya have many ideas concerning the effects of foods in health and illness. Some of these are related to heat, although not in its humoral sense. There was nothing to prevent the acceptance of a system that accorded humoral qualities to foods and much to encourage it in specific aboriginal food beliefs as well as in the basic hot/cold opposition dominant in aboriginal cosmology. Many of the criteria for assigning foods to the "hot" category employed by adherents of humoral systems may have already existed as characteristics of "hot" foods in Negrito and Senoi (nonhumoral) belief systems before contact. Both Negritos and Senoi agree that animal flesh is hot, owing to its blood (Endicott 1979; Howell 1981), and some Senoi also add salt, chilis, and sugar to their "hot" category (Howell 1981), all of which are also humorally "hot" according to medieval Islamic and contemporary Malay theory. The Semelai, a group of aboriginal Malays, believe as well that foods in which the hot destructive force of badi inheres may themselves become hot (Mohd. Hood Salleh 1978).

Malaya proved a remarkably receptive soil for Islamic religion and medical theories. Islamic humoral provided Islamicized Malays with a new grammar with which to organize ideas about humanity and the universe. Medieval Greek-Arabic humoral theories concerning foods, medicines, and diseases whose etiology stems from the natural world appear in simplified but otherwise virtually unchanged form in contemporary rural Malaysia. Malay attributions of heat or cold to particular foods, and the reasons behind these attributions, would be very familiar and acceptable to their medieval Arab and European counterparts. Their conceptions of the values and dangers of heat and cold in the universe and within the human body, however, would not.

The aboriginal peoples of Malaya found nothing discordant in Islamic humoral dietary beliefs. Their ideas concerning the workings of the human body and the relations between the unseen world and the earthly life of mortals, however, were in direct opposition to the tenets of Greek-Arabic medical theory, both in their reversal of the hot and cold polarities and in their inclusion of "nonrational" etiologies.

Although contemporary Malays are wary of the jungle, fearing its wild inhabitants, both visible and invisible, the positive value that Orang Asli have always given to coolness and moisture, strongly associated with the rain forest, has remained an integral part of Malay cosmology. This insistence on the ascendancy of the cool over the hot polarity, although contrary to Islamic humoral doctrine, has its counterpart in aspects of Islamic religious doctrine, which, curiously, reinforced aboriginal Malay ideas about heat and cold in the universal macrocosm and within the human body's microcosm.

The Islamic conception of the afterlife stresses the pleasure of coolness and moisture and the destructiveness of heat. Paradise is a garden watered by running streams in a cool shade where the righteous drink from a refreshing spring: "In paradise there are a great river of water, a great river of honey, a great river of milk, and a great river of wine" (Mishkat Al-Masibih:1204; Koran I:221). There the righteous will dwell in cool pavillions (Koran II:253), in eternal shade (Koran I:272), and feel "the north wind blow and scatter fragrance on their faces and their clothing" (Mishkat Al-Masabih:1206). The home of the unrighteous will be a scorching fire, a destroying flame, a place where garments of fire are prepared for unbelievers (Koran, *passim*). Further reinforcement of the dangers of spiritual heat comes from the Islamic belief that the jin were created from fire (Koran II:251).

Orang Asli who have considered the possibility of an afterlife conceive of it as a cool place of fruit trees, where the dead remain (Schebesta 1957), or where only the worthiest stay, the rest being reborn (Wazir-Jahan Karim 1981). Most, however, are extremely skeptical about the likelihood of any life after death (Dentan 1964, 1965). Their beliefs are strongly centered on life and on the daily interactions between mortals and spirits. Neither they nor contemporary rural Malays recognize a clear division between the "natural" world and the "supernatural." Operating alongside the Malay model of disease causation based on the Greek-Arabic system, which locates medical problems in the sensory world, is a theory that certain illnesses are caused by disembodied hot spirits. Treatments for these illnesses and beliefs concerning their etiology closely parallel those of Orang Asli, although Malays have reinterpreted these ideas and practices using an Islamic and/or humoral idiom. Their ideals of coolness as attributes of beneficent spiritual powers and important components of treatments for illnesses caused by maleficent spiritual powers are echoed in their belief that coolness is necessary for the creation and development of the spirit made flesh in conception and pregnancy. In accepting the doctrine of humors, Malays have kept its "rational" superstructure, as well as individual categories, but have retained a vision of the universe (mankind writ large), and of humanity (the cosmos in miniature), that is its mirror image. Because they were able to identify the aboriginal belief in the coolness of the Immortals and their world with the coolness of the Islamic Paradise, and because they continued to believe in a participatory relationship between the human microcosm and the celestial ideal, the Malays succeeded in detaching the grammar of the Islamic humoral system from its emphasis on the ideal of innate heat.

Islamic Humoralism

The seeds of Islamic thought, transplanted on the peninsula, have proliferated to every corner of Malay life. Seeds sown in a foreign soil, however nourishing, often throw up sports, hybrids, and new combinations of familiar characteristics, and such was the case with humoralism among the Malays.

3

"Unusual" Illnesses

The great majority of illnesses are those Malays call "usual." Ordinary fevers, respiratory ailments, or digestive upsets are believed to result from a humoral imbalance, either to the hot or the cold polarity. They are treated with herbal remedies, dietary adjustments, and thermal treatments such as steam inhalation and cold compresses calculated to restore the patient's body to its normal state. Muscular aches are believed to be caused by lumps of phlegm (the cold humor) blocking the flow of blood (the hot humor). They are treated by massage, which breaks up the clots of phlegm and allows the hot blood to flow unobstructed through the muscle. None of these remedies can be considered a nonrational therapy, nor can the theory of humors, the cornerstone of Western medicine from before the time of Hippocrates until the modern era, be considered magical, although it no longer enters into the etiologies or therapies of contemporary cosmopolitan medicine.

Should ordinary health problems not respond to these treatments, or should an illness appear to be unusual in kind or in its course, a suspicion may arise that the sufferer's problems are due, at least in part, to the attacks of spirits, sent by an illwisher or acting on their own initiative. A whole, healthy person normally has little to fear from hantu, but, should an imbalance of his component parts occur, whether due to depletion of semangat or accumulation of angin, the integrity of the person is breached, his "gates" no longer protect the "fortress within," but have opened to allow the incursions of disembodied spirits. The bomoh aims to return his patient to a state of balanced wholeness. That is what Pak Long meant when he said that in the Main Peteri, "We weld people together, we make sick people well."

The Malay Person

The person, in the Malay view, is composed of more than a body that decays after death and a soul (*roh*) that lives on in Heaven or in Hell.

Inner Winds (angin) that will determine the child's individual personality, drives, and talents are already present at birth.[1] Their presence, type, and quality can be deduced from the behavior of their possessor, but they are palpable neither to observers nor to their owner, except during trance, when they are felt as actual presences: high winds blowing within their possessor's breast.

Human beings, like all God's creatures, must inhale the Breath of Life (*nyawa*)[2] at birth, if they are to live. The nyawa, containing the elements of air and fire, animates the watery, earthy body; without it the body must die. It drives the blood in its course; its effects are felt within the body and its presence is obvious to observers when it emerges as breath, just as the presence of a breeze, though itself invisible, is signaled by the rustling of leaves and the feeling it produces as it blows on the skin.

Semangat (Spirit of Life) is not limited to animals. It permeates the universe, dwelling in man, beast, plant, and rock (cf. Endicott 1970). The universe teems with life: the life of a fire is swift and soon burns out; a rock's life is slow, long, and dreamlike. Semangat strengthens its dwelling place, whether the human body or a stalk of rice, and maintains its health and integrity. However, it is extremely sensitive and can

1. The Malay emphasis on angin as a determinant of individual personality structure casts doubt upon Hsu's contention (1985:24–55) that "the concept of personality is an expression of the western ideal of individualism" which does not correspond to concepts in other cultures. Perhaps the concept is most salient in cultures without strong lineage or cohort ties.

For recent discussions of "the self" in various cultures, see Marsella, DeVos, and Hsu 1985; Shweder and LeVine 1984; White and Kirkpatrick 1985; Marsella and White 1984.

2. *Nyawa*, the Breath of Life, is related to the Greek *pneuma*, both conceptually and etymologically.

be depleted; it can even flee, startled or frightened, from its receptacle. The vulnerability of the semangat governs the conduct of the traditional Malay rice harvest, whose performance has become increasingly rare as modern technology supplants the handiwork of traditional methods of rice production. Modern methods may be more efficient, but they are not calculated to spare the feelings of the Rice Spirit (*semangat padi*). To a traditional Malay, the field of rice is like a pregnant woman, and the harvest is equivalent to the birth of a child. It is inaugurated by the taking of the Rice Baby, a stalk of rice swaddled like a human child after being cut from its plant with a small, curved blade concealed in the hand, so as not to frighten the Rice Spirit by its brutal appearance. The harvested rice crop is stored in a special bin with a coconut, coconut oil, limes, *beluru* root (used for shampoo), bananas, sugar cane, water, and a comb, all for the use of the Rice Spirit, personified as a timid young woman (see also Firth 1974:192–195). Since she is easily frightened, the rice must be brought back to the storeroom and left there in silence for three days.

Semangat in humans is similarly timid and must be cherished and protected. It can be summoned by spells such as thwarted lovers may use to regain their beloved. It can be called by a bomoh, using the same sound Malays use to call their chickens[3] (kurrr), to assist a woman in childbirth. Where the semangat goes, the body must follow, and so the loved one is drawn to her lover, and the baby is encouraged to make its way into the world.

The timidity of semangat makes it prone to leap and fly at the approach of a frightening object or the sound of an unexpected noise. The effect of the startle reaction is most serious in people who are already in a vulnerable condition, such as pregnant women whose fear may be communicated to their unborn children, resulting in infantile abnormalities.

Although most people live secure within the "gates" of their indi-

3. Cuisinier (1951:204) writes that the conception of the soul or spirit in the form of a bird is a common belief throughout the Malay Archipelago. The semangat or roh is often personified as a bird in the Main Peteri. Malay identification of semangat with the chicken (the bird most in evidence in their lives) is shown by the use of the chicken in circumcision feasts, rituals to release a new mother from the postpartum period (Laderman 1983:205–209), and in the paper models of chickens often seen at wedding parties. Skeat (1972:587) notes that bomoh of his day called the soul by the sound used to call fowl.

viduality, some people's boundaries are riddled with tiny openings, more like a permeable membrane than a wall. At times, such people find their thoughts becoming confused, their actions less than voluntary. The heightened permeability of some individuals was offered to me by many Malays, both professional healers and laypeople, as the explanation of *latah*, a condition in which being startled at a loud noise or an unexpected event triggers a spate of obscene language or imitative behavior.[4] This startle reaction in turn increases the permeability of the membrane, allowing the thoughts of others to mix with those of the latah victim's own and govern his or her actions (cf. Lutz 1985 on similar beliefs among the Ifaluk). It can also open the way to spirit attacks.

A short prayer (*doa*) or spell (*jampi*), recited by the patient, a family member, or a bomoh frequently accompanies treatments even of "usual" illnesses, both to add to their effectiveness and to strengthen the patient's "gate" against incursions from the spirit world. Shamans, by the very nature of their profession, must have the means of strengthening their bodily defenses, particularly when going into trance. They mobilize their inner resources, personified as the Four Sultans, the Four Heroes, the Four Guardians, and the Four Nobles, to "guard from above and become a shelter; guard from below and become a foundation; guard from before and become a crown; guard from behind and become a palisade." They call upon their familiar spirits (*penggawa*) to "guard the inner fortress closely; guard and strengthen the outer gates." Shamans who omit these basic precautions may put their lives in jeopardy. Pak Long warned his apprentices never to forget the fate of Pak Dollah, a bomoh who had lived in a nearby kampung. He neglected to summon his penggawa at the proper time during a seance. A powerful jin, sensing that his "gates" were ajar, entered his body and squeezed his heart until he died.

The natural barrier between spirit and mortal usually ensures an adult protection from spirit attacks. Children are more vulnerable, since their semangat has not yet "hardened" (cf. Massard 1988). Illness, overwork, and fright cause breaks in the barrier, allowing the spirits to come

4. Freud believed that hysteria began with a violent emotional shock (fright, anxiety, shame, or physical pain): "In traumatic neuroses the operative cause of the illness is not the trifling physical injury but the affect of fright—the psychical trauma" (Freud and Breuer 1895:40).

into contact with the unprotected body. Spirit attacks are particularly dangerous to those already weakened by "usual" problems. A divination will often reveal that the patient was startled and fell just prior to attack from the spirits (see Kapferer 1983:50 for similar beliefs in Sri Lanka).[5] Hantu, sent by an enemy, may fail to penetrate a strong man's "gates" and, in their anger and frustration, attack his more vulnerable wife or children instead.

These disembodied spirits are composed of only air and fire and lack the earth and water of which our own bodies are made. Their attacks can range in force from merely greeting the victim to striking him, but most often consist of blowing on the victim's back, which increases the elements of fire and air in the body, thereby upsetting its humoral balance.

The Bomoh's Treatments

Herbal treatments and dietary changes cannot alleviate the symptoms of spirit attack, since the cause is spiritual, though its effects may be physical. Excess fire and air must be removed and earth and water increased. Bomoh counteract the spirits' hot breath with their own, made "cool" by an incantation. After blowing on patients' backs, the shaman often advises that they bathe in cold water made still cooler by the addition of lime juice and the chanting of a cooling spell. Earth and water are further increased by applying *tepung tawar*, neutralizing rice paste, to the patient's forehead. Destructive spiritual influences may be swept away from the patient's body with leafy branches. If the semangat has been lost, measures must be taken to entice it back to the body, using sweet-smelling incense and the sweet words of the bomoh's incantation.

Bomoh are usually well acquainted with the life circumstances of their patients, and ask telling questions. They take the pulse and assess the patient's physical and emotional state. If the cause of an illness is still not apparent to the bomoh, a divination may provide the answer.

5. Similar metaphors can be found in other cultures, such as *babana* in the Solomon Islands, a term that describes building a barrier, conceptualized as making one "hard" and hence less vulnerable to penetration by dangerous forces such as spirits or malevolent human stares (White 1985:334).

The divination used by Pak Su Weng, when he was called by my assistant, Yusof, to treat me for a mysterious ailment, reminded me of tea-leaf readings offered in Gypsy tea rooms in New York City. I had been ill with a raging fever for three weeks, two of which I spent in the General Hospital in Kuala Trengganu, and was extremely weak when I returned to Merchang. After testing me for eleven other diseases, the doctors discovered I had mononucleosis. They had not suspected it sooner because mononucleosis appears to be rare in Malaysia. No wonder it seemed like an "unusual" illness to Yusof and Pak Su Weng!

Before the divination, Pak Su felt the pulse at my fingers, wrist, inside my elbow, at my shoulders, ears, and finally my toes. Had I been a man, he would also have felt the pulse in my chest, but he was afraid that if he did so it would make my husband angry. Bomoh feel the pulse in many places, he said, because the pulse can travel. If the ears and fingers are cold, the fever has lodged in the body but not in the head. If the toes are warm and the fingers are cold, the fever is going down. If the fingers are warm and the toes cold, the fever is traveling up. In my case, the coldness of my fingers, toes, and ears showed that the heat was buried within, making me weak and taking away my appetite. The doctors at the hospital were not able to find this internal fever, he said, since it can't be measured with a thermometer.

Pak Su asked Yusof to chew a betel quid and spit into a cup. His saliva, bright red and frothy from the betel quid, formed patterns in the cup. Pak Su pointed to a winding bubbly line in the saliva. This, he said, was the path I traveled when I visited Kg. Durian Pahit, the farthest inland of Merchang's hamlets, recently claimed from the jungle. The hantu there, living at the jungle's edge, are more hostile toward people than those who dwell in the village. Not only had I been working long hours and was tired and thus more vulnerable, I had also neglected to take elementary precautions when I went to Durian Pahit, he said. In the future, I must be sure to keep my fists together when traveling to such places, to make a protective "fence" for my body, and I must ask permission of the hantu before intruding on their land.

The hantu responsible for my sickness was the Hantu Bisu (Mute Spirit), who was beside himself with envy at meeting up with a person who spoke so much and in so many languages. The hot breath that he blew on my back caused heat to travel through my body, causing fever, and later settling in my throat, causing swellings. It was lucky that the hantu in question was a comparatively weak spirit, said Pak Su. A really powerful one could have caused my whole body to swell up, killing me instantaneously.

After he divined the cause of my illness, Pak Su cut the red saliva with a sharp knife, destroying the picture he had seen in the cup and breaking the hantu's power over me. He dipped a sirih leaf (one of the components of the betel quid) into the liquid. Using the leaf as a brush, he painted two crossed lines on my forehead, representing the four cardinal directions. He made red circles around my ears, on my shoulders, elbows, wrists, knees, and lastly on my ankles. This would cause the hantu's heat to leave my body, exiting by way of my toes. Then he sat behind me and recited a jampi, periodically blowing his supernaturally cooled breath on my back, to counteract the hantu's hot breath.

The bomoh still had to deal with the problems remaining after the hantu's influence had left. I was very weak and needed medicine to strengthen me. He prescribed two kinds of *akar kayu* to be taken internally (the literal meaning of akar kayu is "woody roots," but it is used as the generic name for all herbal medicines). Both were made of humorally cold ingredients, which would help to rid me of any vestiges of noxious heat. They would act like vitamin pills, said Pak Su, and give me back my strength and my appetite.

One, consisting of the following roots, was to be boiled in water, and the resulting potion to be drunk:

isi periok kera (*Nepenthes*)
akar sirih (*Piper betle*)
akar julong (*Ancistrocladus*)
akar terung asam hutan (*Solanum aculeatlissimum*)

The second potion, a much more complex medicine, was prepared by rubbing the following botanical ingredients on the rough inside of a stone bowl:

janggi padang (*Breynia reclinata*)
kederang (*Caesalpinia spp.*)
sepang (*Caesalpinia sappan*)

akar mayong (*Myristica cinnamomea*)
sirih (*Piper betle*)
akar mahang (*Macaranga*)
tekak biawak pianggu (*Clerodendron umbratile*)
akar julong (*Ancistrocladus*)
pasang hantu (unidentified botanically; Pak Su said the markings on this leaf were messages written by hantu, illegible to humans)
terung asam (*Solanum ferox*; a kind of sour eggplant)
akar rambutan (*Nephelium lappaceum*)
akar beras putih (*Chasalia chartacea*)
getang guri (*Spilanthes acemella*)
akar gelimbing keris (not identified)
gelimbing bolos (not identified)
akar cermai (*Cicca acida*)
nalu (*Henslowia umbellata*)

to which was added beleran gebang (red sulphate of arsenic) and water.

Before being discharged from the hospital, I had complained of a fiery spot on my shoulder. The doctor shrugged his own shoulders—there was nothing visibly wrong and nothing he could do about it. Pak Su Weng made a cooling lotion to apply to the fiery place, by rubbing the following on the inside of his medicine bowl:

akar tera keluak (*Pangium edule*)
isi teras kait hijau (*Zizyphus elegans*)
kayu tiga lapis (unidentified plant root)
pasang hantu (mentioned earlier)
butir kuini (*Mangerifera odorata*, the seed of a type of mango)
duri landak laut (the spine of an unidentified sea fish)
tempurong lutut unta (camel's knee bone; the camel being nearly a holy animal in Malay eyes, since it is closely associated with Muhammad's birthplace)
timah kaci (tin ore)
mucong batu pacat (unidentified sharp stone)
akar bahar laut (coral)
batu Bukit Bintang (a stone [the variety doesn't matter] collected on Bukit Bintang, a hill near Besut, Trengganu, famed for being

the dwelling place of invisible people [*orang ghaib*])
ketam batu laut (a stone brought up in a fisherman's net, from far out in the ocean, where it is very cold).

In all, the ingredients comprised elements of the animal, vegetable, and mineral kingdoms, some (like the stone from Bukit Bintang and the camel's kneebone) undoubtedly receiving efficacy from their associations with holy or magical persons; others (such as isi teras kait hijau) having been noted by researchers (e.g., Burkill 1966:2347) for their use in treating fevers. Pak Su combined the scrapings with water and poured the lotion into a bottle. I patted some on my shoulder. After the first application, the fiery feeling was noticeably diminished; after the next, it disappeared.

Before he left, Pak Su asked my husband to fill a large pail with the water from the well in our backyard and to pick three limes (*limau nipis*) from the tree that grew in front of our house. He recited a jampi, made two cuts in each lime, tracing the four cardinal directions, and squeezed their juice into the water, throwing the fruit in as well. He advised me to bathe in the cold water, made still cooler by the addition of the lime juice and the chanting of a cooling spell, to cool down my inner fever. The treatment was complete; both the symptoms and their underlying cause had been dealt with.

I gradually recovered from my illness, and my treatment was considered a success due both to Pak Su's skill and the harmony that existed between us. A bomoh's treatments, no matter how skillful, may not help if his relationship to his patient is not harmonious (*sesuai*). Internal and external harmony are the keys to good health and a peaceful life, in the view of rural Malays. Traditional healers and midwives attempt to bring their patients into greater harmony with their own inner being and with the outer world. A mother-to-be who is not in harmony with her unborn child risks spontaneous abortion. Should the child survive, this lack of harmony may cause him to be sickly and develop badly, unless he is adopted (usually informally) and raised in a household more compatible with the child's nature. Even the lack of harmony between a child's individual nature and his name may seriously affect his well-being. Because of this, many children have two names: a school name, given to them at birth, which appears on their birth certificate, and a home name, given as a prophylaxis during childhood ailments.

Adults and adolescents can also suffer from the effects of disharmony, particularly during illnesses, following the birth of a child, and after circumcision. During these times of vulnerability, they will avoid eating foods considered *bisa* (ordinarily glossed as "poison," but having a deeper meaning of "intensifier of internal disharmony" [see Laderman 1983:62–72]).

If one bomoh's ministrations do not work, patients may seek another, more harmonious practitioner, or they may look to biomedicine for a cure. Should the patient still not improve, it may be necessary to hold a Main Peteri.

Main Peteri

Bomoh can be found today in every part of Malaysia (including the capital, Kuala Lumpur), but the spirit-raising seance seems to have long disappeared from, or become rare in, most Malaysian states. In Kelantan, however, and in its neighboring state, Trengganu, to which Kelantanese have migrated in large numbers, the seance was still thriving until very recent times.

During twenty-one months of research in Kelantan, in the late 1960s, Kessler attended ninety-eight performances (1977:302). I attended a similar number in Trengganu, during 1975–1977. They occurred irregularly: occasionally weeks went by with no performance, but often performances were held almost every night.

The Main Peteri is often a measure of last resort, not undertaken lightly. It involves a substantial expenditure, since the patient's family must hold a feast for the shaman's entourage before the seance begins, pay a fee to each performer, and distribute refreshments, when the night's proceedings have come to an end, to the audience of friends, neighbors, and relatives who have come to offer moral support and to be entertained. At a minimum the performers include the *Tok 'teri*, or shaman (often referred to in the literature as bomoh or pawang), the *Tok Minduk* who plays the spike fiddle and acts as interlocutor (he is also a bomoh, and was sometimes referred to, in the literature, as *bidu* or *biduan* [seance-singer] when acting in this capacity), a drummer, and a player of the floor gongs (often merely overturned pots). Larger scale Main Peteri can include several tok 'teri and minduk, players of gongs, large drums, and other percussion instruments, and a *serunai* (a variety of oboe) player. They usually attract a large audience, luring them away from "Kojak" and "The Six Million Dollar Man" on television, since the Main Peteri is a drama whose elements of comedy, tragedy, melodrama, surprise, music, song, and dance are played out before the onlookers' eyes with a force of reality and truth that rivals the spell of other entertainments.

Both students of culture and practitioners of medicine have been attracted by the Malay seance. Physicians' views of the ritual center around questions of the processes and psychodynamics involved in its treatment of the ill, whereas ethnographers have been concerned with its social, political, and symbolic implications, but accounts of the ceremony written by medical scientists and social scientists are remarkably similar. The following description is excerpted from Firth (1967) and Chen (1979), the former representing anthropology and the latter medicine (for an extended account of the ritual, see Cuisinier 1936):

The performance is held at the home of the patient or the shaman, or in a structure built especially for the occasion. A tray of offerings is hung up for the spirits; the musicians cense and dedicate their instruments; the minduk sings an invocation to the spirits; the bomoh goes into trance and is possessed by ancestral spirits; he proceeds to a divination; and thereafter is possessed by one spirit after another until a "suitable" spirit (hantu) has been identified. The spirit is questioned by the minduk regarding the nature of and reason for the illness, the name of the guilty spirit, and so forth. The minduk then instructs the bomoh [officiating shaman] to exorcise the spirit. The patient, now entranced, is encouraged to dance as a sign that benign influences had come to him and he would be better (Firth 1967), or as entertainment for the spirits, or even as a medium possessed by a series of spirits (Chen 1979). The positive involvement of the patient with the healers and spectators provides a cathartic mechanism for his personality (Firth 1967) and a heightened feeling of self-worth (Chen 1979).

From the foregoing, typical of descriptions of the Main Peteri,[6] one would be justified in concluding that, aside from some minor local idiosyncracies, the ceremony was essentially the same as many varieties of trance-healing exorcisms described in cultures around the world—a ritual that undoubtedly contains psychotherapeutic elements within its essentially magical framework but lacks a rational theoretical basis. Characterizing the Malay ritual in this way is misleading since it is based on an impoverished view of a singularly rich phenomenon. For imbedded within the matrix of this Malay spirit-raising seance is a mode of trance-healing based upon an indigenous theory of personality development and frustration which, rather than merely providing patients with external symbols, allows them to face their own personalities with the help of concepts that clarify their problems.

Unlike patients in the Zar cults of Ethiopia (Lewis 1971) or the Hamadsha of Morocco (Crapanzano 1973), the Malay shaman's patients do not incarnate possessing spirits (*pace* Chen). Malay shamans help their patients move into an altered state through the force of their own personalities. This force, conceptualized as a powerful Wind, is intrinsic to the patient, not an outside entity.

Inside and Outside

Before discussing the Inner Winds and their relation to the Main Peteri, let us consider the elements of possession and exorcism from the viewpoint of the ritual practitioners.

Before becoming associated with Main 'teri bomoh, I had been instructed in the use of jampi (spells) by a nontrancing bomoh, Pakcik Su, the local muezzin. He had insisted on my learning each spell by rote, testing me as to my accuracy, and disdaining to answer most questions. Although he was willing to recite his spells slowly and clearly so that I could learn them, his recitation for the purpose of curing was delivered in a fast low murmur, impossible to understand. He emphasized the exclusiveness of the knowledge he was passing on to me and made me

6. Kessler's sensitive and intelligent account of Main Peteri in Kelantan (1977) is a notable exception.

swear that I would not reveal it to others. His methods of treating patients and instructing students were very similar to those reported for other areas of Southeast Asia. Ethnographers of many Southeast Asian cultures have stressed the importance of secrecy in the workings of magic. Cuisinier (1936) averred that Malays consider secrecy a condition for success, necessitating the use of mumbling and whispering when reciting spells. More recently, Errington (1975) remarked that in Luwu (Indonesia) whispers have a higher status as a ritual medium than clearly audible words. Atkinson's (1989) Sulawesi ritual instructors stressed accurate memorization and secrecy.

My training under the tutelage of Pak Long Awang and Tok Daud contrasted with that of Pakcik Su in every stylistic respect: the content of each song and spell, which they delivered in loud, ringing tones, was more important than word-for-word accuracy (and in fact their own delivery varied at each performance); they entered into long discussions regarding the meanings of their words and the philosophy upon which their performances were based; and they were eager for me to learn and to record what I had learned, to preserve their knowledge for future generations of Malays, and pass it on to my own countrymen, since they feared their profession was in decline.

Main Peteri bomoh, although they also practice other types of village medicine, differ from other bomoh both in their breadth of knowledge and in their style of treatment. Pakcik Su and Pak Long Awang epitomize two distinct traditions that exist side by side in the northeast states of peninsular Malaysia: those who value secrecy and accuracy, and those who are open and generous with their knowledge and are not dismayed by variation in their students' or their own delivery. Far from according greater status to bomoh who whisper their incantations, Pak Long and others in his tradition mocked their mumbling and secretive attitude as owing to their desire to hide a lack of knowledge. Pak Long felt that the essential difference between him and Pakcik Su was that Pakcik Su was stingy and secretive because he was "poor in knowledge," while he, himself, "had truckloads full" and could afford to be generous.

What defines the two traditions, however, is more than individual knowledge or generosity. The most salient difference is that bomoh who belong to the tradition that does not insist on secrecy have usually been performers in the Main Peteri, the Mak Yong (a traditional dance-drama), and the shadow play—and often in more than one. In their view, the words themselves are not permanently fixed and in danger of losing their efficacy if they are not learned and employed verbatim. The power of words lies in their contextual meaning rather than in their inflexible recitation. What is essential to practitioners of Main Peteri is that the tok 'teri and minduk be in harmony and that the ritual pair be in harmony with the patient.

Pak Long Awang's story of his career and search for a partner are almost mythic in their elements: born in Bachok, Kelantan, he developed into a young man who "liked to play around, to go here and there and never settle down." Life was hard around the turn of the century. He studied with a famous *dalang* (puppet master), but didn't have the angin (talent) to succeed in the shadow play. He did, however, acquire several familiar spirits that were to be useful during his young adulthood and essential later on. Many of his relatives were dalang, players in the Mak Yong, midwives, and bomoh, and they encouraged him to learn the healing as well as the theatrical arts, but, although he was open to learning short charms for his own use (as are many rural Malays), he avoided the responsibility of becoming a healer and caring for others. He tried growing rice, but land was scarce in Kelantan and he was able to earn barely enough to live on. He moved to Pasir Puteh briefly, where he cut firewood, and then, seeking better opportunities in Trengganu, to Kg. Buloh (Besut), where he laid train tracks. When that job came to an end, he traveled to Bukit Besi (Dungun). There he broke stones for the roads he helped to build. "Those days were torment," he said. "It was enough to make men cry. You were lucky if you got any work at all." Life improved when he learned to tap sugar palms. His training combined instruction in tapping methods with the "inner knowledge" vital to success as a tapper: the proper offerings to give to the spirit guardian of the palm tree, and the magic called *pejujuh* (from *jujuh*—to flow continuously) which makes the sap flow abundantly. He became so successful at tapping that he aroused someone's envy, and his pejujuh spells started to make him flow as well as the tree. His constant urination caused him to retire from tapping and seek help from a bomoh. His roving life came to an end when he married in his thirties and settled down in Merchang (Marang), where he fished and felled trees. His wife gave birth to a little girl who died before she could walk. "She suddenly ran a high fever early in the morning, and died in a couple of hours [he said]. I didn't know what caused it, and I was sorry I hadn't learned to be a bomoh. I couldn't help her. After she died, I started to study seriously."

About this time, Pak Long decided to try his hand at performing in the Mak Yong as well as learning techniques of healing, but, although he worked as an actor for three years, he never became a star. His training as a healer culminated in his training as a tok 'teri, a shaman who combined the healing arts with the performance skills he had achieved in the Mak Yong. His entrance into shamanism was precipitated neither by a personal health crisis or psychotic episode, nor by a prophetic dream, all of which seem to be common in many accounts of shamanism in other cultures. The precipitating factor for Pak Long—the feeling of impotence in the face of a loved one's sickness or death—is one that shaman after shaman recounted to me as a turning point in their lives, one that appears to be pertinent in the lives of Western doctors and medical students as well.

After Pak Long learned to perform in the Main Peteri his life took a turn for the better, both financially and in terms of prestige. He had finally found his metier. He worked with many partners, but never felt the closeness that comes with the perfect pairing of tok 'teri and minduk until one day he went to treat a patient in nearby Kg. Serating. An unfamiliar face appeared at the door, and Pak Long asked him to enter, but he would not. Pak Long was drawn to this man. Something told him that here at last was his partner. He recited the first two lines of a *pantun* (a traditional Malay four-line poem, the first two lines of which suggest the second):

> *"Ta'dak selut, cari selut*
> *Taruh atas situ."*
> (If there's no fertile soil, seek fertile soil,
> Put it over there.)

meaning that their association would be fruitful. Tok Daud, the stranger at the door, felt challenged. He entered the house and said,

"Ta'dak minduk, cari minduk
Minduk mulut bisu."
(If there's no minduk, seek a minduk,
The minduk's lips are sealed.)

Tok Daud had been a star of the Mak Yong during his youth in Kelantan, playing the romantic lead, but never using his personal attractions to seduce young girls as other men did. Always sober and serious, he became more pious as he grew older and was celebrated for his wisdom and kindness. He spent his days farming, caring for the sick as a bomoh, and teaching a nightly class in Koran to the local children. He was a skilled singer and played a rebab that he carved and constructed himself. After he teamed up with Pak Long Awang, they never lacked for patients. As Tok Daud grew older, he worried about the consequences of performing in a ceremony of which he knew religious purists disapproved, but he never hesitated to leave his Koranic students when a patient needed him. God, he felt, would weigh his actions and understand the necessity of his performances, and would forgive him.

Pak Long and Tok Daud's partnership extended to their teaching as well as to their performance. During the second year of my research, they presided over an impromptu school for aspiring shamans and minduk into which they accepted me as a student. Malay students of magic and ethnomedicine are rarely taught en masse; the usual method is the master-apprentice relationship. But, as Pak Long remarked, whichever way it is done, every bomoh must study. Some people like to claim they got their *ilmu* (magical knowledge) from a dream, he said, but that's a lie!

My fellow students were villagers from the surrounding hamlets—farmers, fishermen, and employees of the local sawmill. The majority of the students wanted to learn the role of the tok 'teri. The tok minduk's role, which includes the study of rebab playing, seemed to them more arduous and less rewarding. Each student paid a fee of M$100, a substantial amount for people whose monthly wages came to about M$150.[7]

7. I was not asked to pay a fee, since the teachers felt that I had contributed enough by volunteering to pick up and deliver the teachers, students, players, and their instru-

Three bomoh formed the teaching faculty: Tok Daud, the minduk, Pak Long, the tok 'teri, and Awang Jalal, who was adept at both roles. The students built a small wooden structure roofed with palm fronds (called a *bangsal*) and placed woven mats on the ground inside. Before the lessons could begin, offerings to the bomoh's familiar spirits were hung from the rafters and a *kenduri* was held, to which all the spirits in the sound of Tok Daud's voice, and in the smell of the offerings, were invited. Tok Daud censed the yellow rice, pancakes with custard, betel quid, cigarettes, popped rice, and water that form the usual spirit offering, and Pak Long put bits of each ingredient on a large banana leaf and placed it in the underbrush. Then Awang Jalal censed the drum and fiddle, a plate of raw rice mixed with pieces of turmeric, and a dish of popped rice. After he sang the prelude, reiterating Tok Daud's invocation of the spirits, he invited Cik Mas (the wife of the drum player, who had often kept rhythm by beating on an overturned pot during seances) to sit in the center of the bangsal and begin her instruction. The first lessons concentrated on the abilities of the students to achieve trance, in the beginning with the help of the teacher and finally by themselves, with only the cues of the minduk's song and the music of the players to assist them. Cik Mas was unable to trance during the first lesson. Perhaps she tried too hard and was too tense to allow herself to slip into an altered state. Her keyed-up frustration caused her to fling herself to the ground in despair and cry (a very rare occurrence in rural Malay society, where public display of emotions is scorned). Azizah, whose husband was attending classes as an advanced student, took Cik Mas's place, but she was also unable to achieve trance. Pak Long ended the lesson, saying they would try again the following night. "If you can't trance, you can't dance," he said, "and if you can't dance, you can't play (*main*)."

On the second night, Azizah still could not trance. She said she was having trouble because she was too shy (*malu*). Pak Long whispered in my ear, "If she's so shy, who asked her to come here? It was her own idea." Cik Mas was also unsuccessful in achieving trance, and her place on the mat was soon taken by Wahab, Azizah's husband. He easily went

---

ments to Pak Long's kampung and back again. Pak Long worried that the school wouldn't survive after I (and especially my car) left Merchang, and this, I learned later, was the case.

into trance and began to sing and dance, but his teachers, judging that his style was too reminiscent of the Mak Yong, stopped his performance and motioned to Sani, a neighbor of Pak Long, to take his turn. When Sani had achieved trance, Pak Long tried to get him to answer questions in the persona of Sulung Kecil Penganjur Raja (The Little First-born Advance Guard of the King), a personification of the eyes, the first human attribute that appears in an unborn baby. Sani could not reply, so Tok Daud answered for him. They encouraged Sani to sing, providing him with musical and verbal cues. His glorious voice was filled with emotion, and when he began to cry, still in trance, Pak Long said it was time the lesson was over because too much trancing would make their pupil dizzy. Tok Daud put an end to the lesson by reciting a jampi while Pak Long threw protective rice to the four corners, up in the air, and down to the ground.

Classes did not meet again until the following week, but Cik Mas came privately to Pak Long for instruction and arranged to have the next meeting at her house, which, she felt, would be more conducive to her trance. I asked Pak Long why he had accepted her as a student, since it was common gossip that she stole from her neighbors and harbored a *pelesit* (a familiar spirit harbored by some women, which makes its owner attractive to the opposite sex but is capable of harming others, particularly young children), and thus didn't fit his specifications for a bomoh—a person of good character. He said, "Don't worry, she won't make it, but there's no harm in accepting her money while she tries."

When the class met again, Cik Mas's ceiling was decorated with a yellow cloth hung with flowers, a sign of her noble ancestry.[8] Her best floor mats had been laid out, and one had been covered with a new white cloth. A pillow with a batik slip was placed atop the white cloth, for possible use in divination. Toki Latip, a retired dalang (see chapter 6), had been hired to play the hanging gongs. He joined Pak Long, Awang Jalal, Tok Daud, who played the rebab, and the students, who took turns playing the floor gongs and the drums. Cik Mas tranced

8. A surprising number of Malays, including some of the poorest, identify themselves as descendants of nobility. This does not entitle them to any privileges, but, to avoid internal disharmony due to neglecting their noble heritage, such people are obliged to use the royal color, yellow, in situations such as the one in which Cik Mas was participating, or during childbirth.

quickly this time, but the transition was violent. She rose to dance, only to fall to the ground. Azizah washed Cik Mas's face with perfumed water, and the men helped her to a seated position. The teachers urged her to sing, but when she tried, she merely repeated her words over and over and was not able to respond to the minduk's questions. Pak Long gave me a telling look: Hadn't he told me what would happen to her?

The other students achieved a smooth transition. They learned their lessons, in trance and out, like children in a Koran class, repeating the words of their teachers a moment after their utterance. Finally they had an easy command of the duets that they would sing with their ritual partners, and the stock phrases and mnemonic patterns, with their use of the parallelisms, assonance, alliteration, and so forth that ensure the distinctive rhythm of the Main Peteri (see Sweeney 1987). But, unlike Koranic students, they would not be required to repeat their teacher's every word. Pak Long's teaching aimed at enabling students to become adept at generating formulaic expressions on the models they were given, attaining fluency without a fixity that would deaden the performance (see Lord 1976). The performance emerges as a combination of formulae in a style of speech that is meant both to mimic the speech of nobility and to allow for free variation in colloquial style.

Besides learning how to control their own trances, students had to be taught to call upon their penggawa (spirit familiars). Since they had not found penggawa of their own, they used their personified bodily attributes: Awang Kasim Gila (the eyes of a trancing bomoh), and Awang Jiding (the pulse). Students learned the order of the Main Peteri, including the expected procession of spirit visitors. Generally speaking, the earth spirits come first, followed by spirits of the village, familiars created to serve their masters, sea spirits, *dewa* (the gods of Kayangan), and finally, spirits of the jungle. But, since one cannot be sure that the invisible guests will follow the usual procedure, it is important to be aware of their presence, signaled by the raising of the shaman's body hair and his feeling that his head is swelling;[9] and to know which type of spirit has arrived. For instance, the arrival of a sea spirit causes the shaman to feel a rolling motion within his stomach.

The students had to learn the names of the most important spirits of

9. Similar reactions to "the uncanny" have been described in other cultures, for example, Tahiti (Levy 1984:222).

each domain. There is really only one spirit for each natural division, they were taught, but they are capable of dividing themselves up infinitely. Each division has its own headman and army. Usually the headman appears during a seance, but if one of his soldiers appears, he can go back and inform the chief. It's like God, the students were told, who is One, but who divides Himself up so that little pieces of Himself can live as individual souls within people. Sickness is not a punishment from God, they were taught. Good people get sick as often as bad, and we humans aren't capable of understanding why God allows hantu to afflict us any more than we can understand why He found it necessary to make mosquitoes.

Students proceed at their own pace and are not allowed to receive the shaman's blessings (*menerima*) until the teacher considers them capable of starting their healing careers. Formal recognition by a teacher takes place at a ceremony in which the student presents the master with money, cloth, a betel quid, and a large mold of *nasi semangat* (glutinous rice colored yellow with turmeric) into which hardboiled eggs, dyed red and pierced with slivers of bamboo, are placed like candles on a birthday cake. Without this ceremony, the master's teachings will not adhere to the student, but will slip away like water. After the student has menerima, the master will take him along on professional calls and gradually allow him to take over responsibilities until they are both confident that the student can work on his own.

Pak Long said there was no danger to the teacher in sharing his knowledge with his students. Knowledge is not like money, he said. If you give someone all your money, you won't have any left, but if you give someone your knowledge, you still have everything you had before. It's only people who have very little knowledge who are stingy about teaching others. Tok Daud compared his shamanic students to people learning how to drive a car: some people get their license quickly while others may never have anything but a learner's permit. Therefore, there can be no set time range for an apprenticeship.

Students are not usually provided with penggawa by their teachers, but must seek them on their own, finding them in their families, through dreams, or in the performance of Mak Yong or wayang kulit. As Pak Long's daughter, however, I was presented with four penggawa at my "graduation ceremony." The first was Pak Long's favorite, Mek Bunga

(Miss Flower), his great grandaunt who had been stolen from her cradle by *orang bunian* (invisible creatures, something like fairies), who took her to Bukit Bintang (a hill in Besut renowned for spirit activity), where she herself became invisible. Pak Long delivered her completely into my hands, forever depriving himself of her aid. He bade farewell to her and told her to follow me back to New York City when I returned to my country. The other three, which we would share (since they were capable of traversing the world in minutes), were a legacy of Pak Long's career as a puppet master:[10] Raja Hanuman the White Monkey and two of his children, Hanuman Ikan (Fish Hanuman) and Hanuman Bongsu (Youngest Hanuman), characters from the shadow play.

My teachers taught me that much of what appears to an outsider to be possession by and exorcism of external spiritual forces is not nearly as straightforward as it may seem. While exorcism is an integral part of the ritual, all parts of the Main Peteri, to a greater or lesser degree, including the exorcism, take place within the self. As Pak Long taught me, "*Semua dalam diri kita* (It is all inside ourselves)."

The minduk's invocation not only invites the spirits to the seance but recounts the story of Creation—a double Creation: first, of the universe, second, of humanity, the universal microcosm. All of the minduk's allusions contain multiple meanings since the ritual operates simultaneously in the external world and within the human body and soul (see Kessler 1977 for elaboration of this point). The sea of which the minduk sings is at once the Sea of Creation, the South China Sea, and the human stomach. The vast fields stretching as far as the eye can see (*padang luas saujana padang*) are not only the homes of invisible hantu, they are inside the human bosom as well. The mountaintop is not merely the haunt of powerful jin; the patient, the healers, and the audience all know that it is also the human head.

symbolism-everyone uses these metaphors

10. These particular *penggawa* are not the tiny spirits of dead persons mentioned by Firth (1967). Most Main Peteri bomoh are, or have been, performers in the Mak Yong or shadow play. Their penggawa may be spirits derived from these other forms of entertainment—which include rituals and, on occasion, are used for exorcistic or healing purposes (see Sweeney 1972; Ghulam-Sarwar 1976). They are also inherited from teachers or family members. Pak Long's penggawa included many characters from the shadow play and one (Miss Jasmine) inherited as a gift from his midwife sister, who had acquired her in a dream.

Following the minduk's invocation, the shaman achieves trance. He is aided by another song sung by the minduk, intended to move the shaman's Inner Wind (angin). Firth (1974) recognizes angin as a hereditary disposition that allows the bomoh to trance, but, as will become clear from the following discussion, it is a wider and more profound concept. While in trance, the shaman evokes the Four Sultans, the Four Heroes, the Four Guardians, the Four Nobles. Firth understands these to be ancestral spirits that possess the shaman, but they are ancestral only in the sense that everything, physical or spiritual, inherited by humanity is ancestral. They are forces within the human body, the patient's and the bomoh's own, that the shaman mobilizes to help maintain and regain health—a kind of spiritual immune system. These forces are not individualized: questions about their specific powers or locations are considered unanswerable; they do not inhere to specific parts of the body (unlike those discussed by Banks [1976] in connection with a similar ritual in Kedah).

After the divination that follows, a series of hantu and jin appear, speaking through the shaman in a dialogue with the minduk (and occasionally with the patient and members of the audience). When speaking in the persona of hantu, the shaman is not "possessed" in the usual meaning of the term. He briefly experiences trance, which sensitizes him and allows him to express the personality and wishes of the hantu. The spirit, itself, does not invade the shaman's body but is thought to be present just outside the house where the seance is taking place. The shaman knows which category of spirit has manifested itself, since he has learned the pattern of their visitation, and how to interpret the sensory feelings each evokes within him. He knows the names of the chief spirits of each realm and the names of their lieutenants and followers; and he is aware of their characters, the demands they are likely to make, and the sounds and movements that personify them. Jin, unlike hantu, do "possess" the shaman. They come right into the room, causing the shaman to temporarily lose all awareness of his own personality, but they do not usually invade the shaman's body, which is protected by the familiar spirits who perch upon his shoulders. Bodily invasion by jin is considered almost invariably fatal.

While all of these spirits are believed to be external to the patient,[11] their attacks are ineffectual unless the victim's own vital forces (semangat), have been depleted by physical illness, overwork, shock, or fright. Furthermore, the external spirits depend upon the cooperation of their internal counterparts, as recounted in the following story told to me by Pak Long:[12]

> *Once there was a poor couple who didn't have any good things to add to the* sura *[a pudding containing fruit, vegetables, and meat, made and eaten communally during the month of Muharram] that the village people were planning to make. The poor man's wife asked her husband, "What can we do? I'm so embarrassed." Her husband replied, "You'll see later, when the devil's child comes again to our house to play with our child." That night the devil's child slept at the house of the poor people. While the human child and the devil's child slept, the poor man sharpened his knife. His wife asked, "What are you doing with that knife?" He answered, "I'm going to slaughter the devil's child." He cut up the flesh and took it the next morning to the place where the people were making sura. They cooked it in the sura, and everyone ate it up. Later, the devil's wife came to look for her child. She said, "I can't find my child. Where did the little devil go?" No one replied. The devil's wife said, "I'll go fetch my husband." Father Devil appeared. He asked, "Is my child here?" The poor man replied, "No, he isn't." Then Father Devil became angry. He said, "Don't think you can fool me. I know that you slaughtered my child and ate up his flesh. But you won't get any pleasure from what you did. Now my children are both inside and outside you forever." And that's how it is. Now we all have devils[13] inside our bellies.*

11. Malays believe that spirits can affect people from a distance, just as fire makes one hot even though it may be located several feet away, and the effects of its heat may continue for some time after exposure, even if one leaves the site of the flames. It was rare, I was told, that external spirits *entered* a human body, whether patient or healer. In those cases, death quickly ensued.

12. This story, and the others recounted in this book, were told to me by practitioners of Main Peteri to explain points of theory. Translations were done by the author from the original Kelantanese Malay (in some cases the speakers' dialect derived as well from Trengganu Malay, since, although all of the bomoh mentioned in this book originally came from Kelantan, several had lived many years in Trengganu).

13. The "devils" (*syaitan*) referred to here are hantu, not Satan, the ruler of Hell. East coast Malays usually refer to the Archfiend as Iblis.

During the Main Peteri, the patient (and occasionally a member of the audience) may achieve trance. This is not intended to entertain the hantu, nor is it merely a sign that benign influences have come and the patient will be better (Firth 1967). The patient is not possessed by external spirits; the trance proceeds from the very depths of the patient's being. It is an outward expression of the inner workings of the personality, a sign that the Inner Winds have begun to blow freely within the bosom.

4

Angin: the Inner Winds

Before the Main Peteri can proceed, the patient's problem must be diagnosed by means of divination. A divination that points to any combination of earth, fire, or water usually points to hantu or jin as causal factors. These spirits may have been bribed by an enemy of the patient, or they may be acting on their own volition, angered, perhaps, by the trampling of their invisible abodes or a shower of urine on their invisible heads.

The spirits, created before Adam, are humanity's disembodied older siblings. The children of Adam are beings of the light, while their spirit-brothers must dwell forever in darkness. Like all siblings, they are sometimes beset with feelings of envy toward their younger brothers, the favored of God. And, like human siblings, they occasionally find ways to even the score. On the whole, however, a healthy, complete person has little to fear from the hantu. Hantu, I was told, are much like dogs. Left to their own devices, they will rarely attack. Unlike dogs, however, they are invisible. One therefore runs the risk of inadvertently disturbing and offending them, thus arousing their wrath, but they are never truly vicious unless they are harbored by people who use them to harm others. Occasionally, too, they may turn feral if their human "master" has abrogated an agreement without their consent, or if he has neglected them, or died, leaving them unfed and uncared for (see, e.g., chapter 8).

Although they are our older brothers, God did not grant them the power of reason (*akal*) that makes us truly human. Lacking reason, they behave like simpletons or children, easily flattered, cowed by threats, satisfied with the symbol in place of reality, and easily caught out in their lies by clever bomoh, whose insulting remarks make the audience roar with laughter but elude the spirits' understanding. When, for example, a jin appears during a seance, announcing that his name is the Jin with the Lookalike Face (Anak Jin Serupa Muka), and the minduk answers, "Oh, you are the Jin with the Asshole Face" (Anak Jin Sejubor Muka), the spirit completely ignores the insult, rushing ahead with his speech.[1]

But, although they seem like ignorant children, Malay spirits in the second half of the twentieth century (like contemporary Malay children) are literate and can be reached by letter as well as through speech. Written communications, such as those given to the spirits who were being induced to break their contracts with Mat Din (see chapter 8), are powerful supplements to spoken requests. A letter addressed to the Hantu Raya, the most feared of all spirits on the east coast, was believed to have protected my neighbors from his mighty wrath.

The hamlet in which I lived was nicknamed Feverville (Kampung Demam) because of the high incidence of fevers, particularly afflicting newcomers. A bomoh divined that they were caused by one of the Mighty Spirits (Hantu Raya) who lived in a large tree in the middle of the hamlet. The only way to stop these fevers was to cut down the tree, depriving the Hantu Raya of his home. This, however, was extremely dangerous, since the spirit was bound to resent their actions and take his revenge. The solution was to counterfeit a letter from the sultan of Trengganu, ordering the villagers to cut down the tree and, in effect, giving the spirit his eviction notice. This letter, along with another signed by the village headman, was placed in a crotch of the tree. The second letter explained that none of this was the fault of the people: they were only following orders.

As Amin Sweeney recently remarked (1987:109), "It is not surprising that writing should be associated with magic power in a society newly introduced to writing or one which remains radically oral. . . . Writing is highly mysterious to oral man: the power to capture speech in signs is awesome indeed, for the written message appears to be in-

1. In this respect, the Malay seance has much in common with that of Sri Lanka, as described by Kapferer (1983, see especially p. 224).

vested with secret meaning, even though the text may have no magic intent."

Although the spirits may be easily duped by human intelligence, they insist upon receiving their proper due—the offerings that were promised to them in good faith. In the case of Pak Long Awang's sudden illness (see chapter 7), spirits, disappointed at not receiving the gifts they were offered at a seance, attacked the shaman rather than his delinquent clients.

If an illness shows signs of spirit-connected etiology, the suspected spirits must be brought to the seance by the officiating shaman's own familiar spirits (penggawa). The minduk flatters the hantu, coaxes, promises them offerings, and occasionally insults and threatens them, to induce them to restore the patient to health. Their victim's humoral balance has been put awry by the spirits' airy heat. To complete their healing task, they must remove their unbalancing presence: "clear every stifling vapor from the body and soul" of the patient. The minduk exhorts them to return to their origins and restore, as well, the balance of the universe, whose integrity is threatened by their encroaching upon humanity.

Complications can arise when the patient's birth-sibling joins the disembodied hantu's attack. The birth-sibling, the afterbirth that accompanies the birth of every human child, is the mirror image of the hantu. Both are incomplete: the spirits lack the earthy and watery elements of which the body is made, while the birth-sibling never receives the airy and fiery Breath of Life that animates its human sibling when the baby takes its first breath. Semihuman, the birth-sibling deserves a decent burial. The midwife washes the placenta in water into which limes have been squeezed as carefully as if she were laying out a corpse. Then she wraps it in a white winding sheet and lays it in a half coconut shell coffin. The father buries it beneath a coconut palm, "the sky for its cover, the earth for its pillow." The birth-sibling is not a malevolent force, but, like all siblings, it may experience the pangs of sibling rivalry. Although they "traveled down the same path" (the mother's birth canal), they are unequal heirs. The human child receives all the love and property of the parents, the birth-sibling only a half coconut shell and a scrap of cloth. The afterbirth, although it resents its unequal treatment at the hands of its parents, is not an implacable enemy of its human sibling. In fact, it and the blood of parturition are referred to as "black caretaker of the soul, yellow[2] caretaker of the spirit" (*hitam gembala roh, kuning gembala semangat*) in the Main Peteri.

In order to effect a cure, the good will of the older siblings, both spirit and afterbirth, must be obtained by offering them fair words and property. Spirits are satisfied with the essence of things, which they can extract from food without damaging it for future consumption by creatures with bodies (animals, if not humans), and will accept statuettes of animals and models of kitchen utensils (as were offered by Mat Din in chapter 8) in lieu of real objects.

When the shaman counts out the grains of popped rice arranged in three piles during the divination, if the count in any pile ends on air (angin), it points to the diagnosis that the patient's problem was not caused solely by external entities, either disembodied hantu or his own birth-brother. It lies as well within the patient's own personality.

Angin is a word with multiple meanings, many of which are connected with notions of sickness and treatment. It can refer to the wind that blows through the trees, a wind that may carry dirt and disease. As my field assistant (a Trengganu Malay man) put it:

> *People are careless about where they burn garbage. They let their children and animals defecate everywhere, and some adults aren't so particular about where they do it, either. Animals die and their smell gets in the air. The air is full of dirt and* kuman *[usually glossed as "germs," but characterized by my assistant as tiny white insects which people in the past, whose eyesight and other faculties were superior to our own, could see]. They enter through the nose, mouth, pores, and feet.*

A strong cold wind can make you sick if it chills your body, upsetting your humoral balance and causing upper respiratory symptoms and pains in the joints. Angin (in the sense of gas, or stomach wind) is produced spontaneously when a person overeats, making his belly swell and producing heartburn and nausea. Diseases that are not suspected of occurring as a result of spirit attacks, but are not readily diagnosed, are often called *sakit angin* (wind sickness), meaning essentially, "I don't

2. Yellow often substitutes for red as symbolic of blood in Malay magic. Belief in birth-siblings is widespread in Southeast Asia (see, e.g., Hart et al. 1965; Connor 1984).

know what it is." Oils and plasters containing menthol, used for headaches and fever (both humorally "hot"), are called *minyak angin* (wind oil) because of their cooling properties. All of these meanings of angin are everyday usages, with little relation to the concept of angin within the context of the Main Peteri.

Another common meaning of angin, however, is much closer to its core meaning as used in the shaman's seance. Capricious desires are also called angin by east coast Malays. If these whims are not indulged, the whimsical one may feel a kind of sadness known as *angin dalam hati* (literally, wind within the liver, an organ that substitutes for the Western "heart" in Malay expressions of emotion). The concept of angin, however, goes far beyond the whimsical, and the thwarting of the Inner Winds can result in consequences more serious than sadness (see also Kessler 1977:309).

The Inner Winds, as understood by east coast Malays,[3] are close to Western concepts of temperament, both in the medieval sense of the four temperaments and as artistic temperament. Everyone is born with angin, the traits, talents, and desires representing our ancestors' heritage, but some have more, or stronger, angin than the common run. If they are able to express their angin, they can lead untroubled and productive lives and, in fact, will usually be respected for their strong and gifted characters. If they cannot, their angin is trapped inside them, where it accumulates and produces *sakit berangin*, or sickness due to blockage of the Inner Winds.[4] We recognize this problem in artists and writers whose creativity is blocked, or whose art is insufficiently appreciated, and would not find it difficult to understand why Malays say that musicians, actors, and puppeteers are attracted to their professions because of angin and could not succeed without it. Malays do not recognize a split between the arts, the sciences, and sports, and therefore what we call artistic temperament refers to a wider range of behavior among east coast Malays than it does in Western culture. Most of the

3. See also De Danaan 1984 on sakit angin in Kelantan. For an enlightening discourse on the meaning of angin in Kedah, see Banks 1976.

4. "Blockage" (frustration, lack of emotional expression) as a metaphor for conceptualizing the premises of a theory explaining failure, misfortune, and illness in terms of socioemotional conflict is salient in other non-Western cultures (e.g., the A'ara of the Solomon Islands discussed in White 1985; the Ifaluk of the Carolines discussed in Lutz 1985), as well as in contemporary Western usage.

healers are also performers in the Malay opera or shadow play or masters of the art of self-defense. Healers of all types must possess the angin specific to their calling and suffer when their talents are ignored. A bomoh whose patients have forsaken him, a midwife with limited mobility, even a masseur without a steady call on his services can develop sakit berangin. Malays take the concept yet further. Everyone who hopes to be successful in any of the specialized roles that Malay village society provides (most of which are, or were, connected with rituals) must not only study diligently. He or she must also have the angin specific to that role. No amount of study can substitute for angin. Those whose angin is not appropriate to their role may be particularly at risk for sakit berangin, such as a man who has inherited the angin of a midwife but has no opportunity to assist a woman in childbirth.[5]

The meaning of angin, and the problems it may entail, extend beyond professional temperament to the basic personality. The majority of conditions treated by Main Peteri are sakit berangin, and the most prevalent is due to the thwarting of the personality type known as *Angin Dewa Muda* (The Wind of the Young Demigod), a personality whose archetype is the hero of a story from the Mak Yong. The following is the story of Dewa Muda as told to me by Pak Long to explain the meaning of Angin Dewa Muda:[6]

> *Little Dewa Muda was the Prince of Java, the son of the King and Queen of Java, or so he believed. One night he dreamed about a beautiful princess who lived in Kayangan [an abode in the sky where supernatural beings live]. He fell madly in love with her and wanted to find her, no matter what the danger, no matter what the cost. He saw an old man in his dream, an old man with three humps on his back, who told*

5. Male midwives are extremely rare in Malaysia. Of all the registered traditional midwives, only three are male (Siti Hasmah 1975). One of the bomoh in my subdistrict actually had practiced as a midwife in his jungle-outpost hamlet until a female midwife moved in and took over the bulk of his clientele. Both he and another man, who had inherited midwife's angin from his mother and grandmother, but who had never delivered a baby, needed occasional treatments for blocked Winds.

6. The significance of this story (and the tales of Abdul Jinah and Dewa Penchil which follow) as an archetypal source for a particular kind of angin is commonly understood by rural east coast Malays. The stories were told to me by ritual practitioners to clarify my understanding of the concept of angin. This version of the story of Dewa Muda varies somewhat from the version found in Sheppard (1974).

*him that if he ever wanted to meet the beautiful princess he would have to wake up immediately and go to the forest, to the clearing in the forest where the white sand lay, and there he must hunt the golden barking deer (*kijang mas*). "If you don't go hunt the golden barking deer," said the old man, "your people will riot, your kingdom will be in ruins, there will be great fires and the country will sink beneath a flood." Dewa Muda quickly awoke and called his trusted servant, Awang. He told Awang to fetch a bomoh skilled in divination. The bomoh did a divination and told Dewa Muda that he had dreamed a true dream. He said, "You had better go hunt the golden barking deer. If you don't, your kingdom will be torn apart." Up in Kayangan, Princess Ulana Mas had dreamed of Dewa Muda. She said to herself, "I want to go see Dewa Muda who loves me so much. I'll fly down to earth and find him." So she soared down to earth, and she took the form of a golden barking deer. She ran in front of Dewa Muda. He called to Awang, "Quick, let's go catch that golden barking deer." They went chasing after her, but they got thoroughly lost. Dewa Muda began to cry. "I must go hunt that golden barking deer," he said. "It isn't an ordinary barking deer, it's really Princess Ulana Mas, the daughter of Saksa Bota [an ogre]." Awang found the way out of the forest, but the golden barking deer had vanished. Dewa Muda said, "The only way I can find Princess Ulana Mas is to fly to Kayangan. I have to borrow my mother's golden kite. We'll hold on to the kite strings and fly up to Kayangan." So they climbed on to the golden kite. As they approached Kayangan, Saksa Bota yelled down to Dewa Muda, "Hey, Dewa Muda, there's no use your coming here. You can never marry Ulana Mas, because you are my child as much as she is. Your mother is the Queen of Java, but I am your real father." When he heard those words, Dewa Muda became so unhappy that he went crazy. He couldn't sleep, he couldn't eat, he couldn't bathe. He was so sick that the King and Queen of Java called a tok 'teri, a tok minduk, and the players to have a Main 'teri, so he could be cured.*

To Malays, Dewa Muda is the archetype of a personality whose needs are the needs and privileges of royalty: fine clothing, delicate food, aromatic perfumes, comfortable living, and the love and respect of kin, friends, and neighbors. Many people have inherited Angin Dewa Muda but few can satisfy its demands. Such people need to be pampered and admired, provided with life's luxuries, and reassured often of their charm and worth. Malay village society, where neither material goods nor overt expressions of affection and admiration are in plentiful supply, is a difficult setting for the Dewa Muda personality. It is not enough to say that the expression of strong emotions is frowned upon in rural Malaysia. Most people deny that they ever have any. Malays rarely cry or complain. Women suffer through difficult and prolonged labors without raising their voices, and mourners at funerals remain dry-eyed. Married couples normally exhibit no signs of either connubial affection or outright aggression in public.

I would never have known that my next door neighbor had been almost strangled to death one night by her mistakenly jealous husband had she not confided to me, as stranger and friend, and shown me his finger marks on her throat. No telltale sound had broken the peace of the night. Her husband is a classic example of *Angin Hala*,[7] the Wind of the Weretiger, which makes its carrier quick to anger and heedless of its consequences.

The archetype of this personality comes from a folk legend, the following version of which was told to me by Tok Daud, Pak Long's minduk, as part of his teachings about angin:

> *Once there was a young virgin named Siti Zarah who plucked some* buah kemunting *[a kind of berry] and ate them. After awhile her belly began to get big. She was pregnant and she had no husband. The berries she had eaten had had drops of Weretiger's semen on them.*[8] *She gave birth to a son who she named Abdul Jinah.*[9] *As the boy grew older, he acted more and more like a tiger. He started to demand raw meat for his dinner, and he couldn't learn Koran as quickly as the other children did. Finally, his Koran teacher became furious at his behavior and picked up a cane. He beat Abdul Jinah hard, marking his body with forty stripes*

7. Beliefs about weretigers among Malays were noted by European observers as early as the late eighteenth century (Marsden 1784). These skin-changers are believed to live in a community in the heart of the jungle, called Kandang Balok, where they hold court and in every way maintain a regular form of government. The name given to weretigers by east coast Malays (*hala*) is almost identical to the name given by Orang Asli (indigenous non-Islamic peoples in the interior regions of peninsular Malaysia) to their shamans (*halak, halaq*).

8. Pregnancy resulting from ingestion of semen is a frequent theme in the Malay shadow play (see Sweeney 1972).

9. Literally, "servant of adultery."

like the fur of a tiger. The teacher chased Abdul Jinah into the jungle, where he turned into a dangerous weretiger.

Angin Hala is difficult to express in socially accepted ways, unless its possessor is a fighter or occupies a social position that allows him to vent his aggression without fear of retaliation. Those with tigerish personalities may prove dangerous to others if they express their angin (as in ordinary wife-beating or, in extreme cases, running amok), or to themselves if they do not.

Angin Dewa Penchil is the heritage of those who are dissatisfied with their lives and their homes. They wander in foreign parts and dress and behave in a manner inappropriate to their station in life. Their archetype comes from a character in the Mak Yong, as told to me by Mat Daud bin Panjak, a Trengganu shaman:

> *Once there was a king called Dewa Penchil*[10] *who liked to dress in rough clothing and go out among the commoners. His behavior angered his wife's mother, who raised an army to chase Dewa Penchil out of the country. Before he fled, he tore a piece of* kain cindai[11] *in two, gave half to his wife and kept the other half. He fled to another land far from his kingdom and wandered for a long time, looking like a poor man and losing his kain cindai along the way. One day he sat down under a tree and heard the voice of a bird in the branches saying, "Your wife is being forced to marry another man, and your kingdom is in danger. Go back to your kingdom and kill your rival." As Dewa Penchil looked up at the bird, a suit of royal garments fell down, along with the lost kain cindai and a magical royal kris. He put on the clothes and hurried back to his kingdom, where he showed his wife the kain cindai to prove he was really her husband. With the magical kris he killed his rival and his traitorous mother-in-law and ruled his country in strength and in peace.*

Health problems associated with Angin Dewa Penchil appear to be rare among rural Malays. Perhaps the wandering urges of his person-

10. *Penchil* (*pencil* in the new orthography) carries the connotation of "detached from the main body, separated, strayed away, isolated, segregated."

11. *Kain cindai* is a silk cloth of reticulate pattern made by the tie-and-dye method, about five yards long and a yard wide, of such extremely fine texture that it can theoretically pass through a finger ring (Wilkinson 1959).

ality type are satisfied by the frequency with which Malay men resort to migratory labor to earn a living for their families (a pattern known as *pergi merantau mencari makan*, or traveling in search of a living, traditional to peninsular Malaysia and parts of Borneo; see, e.g., Freeman 1970).

Behavior inappropriate to one's station has been discouraged by Malay law and custom. In the past, it was a punishable offense for commoners to employ royal language when referring to themselves. Aside from legal sanctions against transgressing the prerogatives of royalty, commoners who dared to break the social barrier or disobey royal commands might expect to fall ill with an incurable skin disease (*kedal*),[12] or suffer in other respects from the curse (*ketulahan*) that accompanies the flouting of royal power (Mohd. Taib Osman 1976).

Rank has its privileges, it is true, but it also has its obligations. A surprising number of rural Malays, including some of the poorest, claim descent from royalty. Most express their nobility only during the preparations for the birth of their children. Since yellow is the color reserved for royalty, a yellow cloth must be spread above the head of a woman of royal descent in labor, its four corners attached to the four walls. An open umbrella, the symbol of noble rank, must be placed upon the outstretched cloth. Unless these measures are taken, the denial of her royal heritage may increase the difficulty of such a woman's labor and delivery.

To help me understand Angin Dewa Penchil as a personality type, Tok Daud compared the behavior of Australian hippies in Malaysia to Dewa Penchil's behavior in the beginning of the story. "They have $1,000 in their pockets," he said, "but you'd never know it, the way they dress in rags and try to bum rides."

People may be heir to one or several types of angin; for example, Toki Latip, the asthmatic puppetmaster discussed in chapter 6, had strong angin both for the shadow puppet theater and for *silat*, the Ma-

12. The Malay Annals (trans. Brown 1970) give two instances of *kedal* as a skin disease associated with offenses against royal dignity: (1) girls of humble birth who married the highborn Sang Seperba were stricken with kedal, as was (2) an emperor of China who disparaged the dignity of the Sultan of Malacca.

Sakit berangin in connection with Angin Dewa Penchil may be compared to the medieval Western concept of acedia in its relation to melancholy. A common meaning of acedia was neglect of the obligations of one's status or profession.

lay form of stylized self-defense. The strength of the Inner Winds can range from a mild breeze to gale force. These Winds, freely blowing or sublimated in everyday living in ways that satisfy both possessor and society, keep the individual healthy, and enrich his community. A person with Angin Dewa Muda may try his best to earn the love and admiration he so desperately needs. A man with Angin Hala may cover himself with glory on the playing field or battlefield. Powerful angin, though, if ignored or repressed, will make its effects felt in the mind and the body. The symptoms of sakit berangin include backaches, headaches, digestive problems, dizziness, asthma, depression, anxiety—in short, a wide range of what we call psychosomatic and affective disorders.[13] Asthma in particular represents a graphic example of repressed angin—Wind that is locked within, choking its possessor.

The Inner Winds of a patient in the Main Peteri who has been diagnosed as suffering from sakit berangin[14] must be allowed to express themselves, to be released from the confines of their corporeal prison, enabling the sufferer's mind and body to return to a healthy balance.

The band strikes up the appropriate music as the shaman retells the story of the angin's archetype. When the correct musical or literary cue is reached, the patient achieves trance, aided, as well, by the percussive sounds of the musicians and the rhythmic beating of the shaman's hands on the floor near the patient's body.[15] The essential differences between

13. Although symptoms of sakit berangin bear a great similarity to complaints reported by Kleinman's depressed Chinese informants (Kleinman 1980), the idiom is quite different. Malay theories concerning angin do not aim at somaticizing the experience, but, rather, locate the problem within the patient's personality. This emphasis differentiates Malay perceptions, as well, from Japanese cognition about depression as reported by Marsella (1977): external metaphors—clouds, rain, mist—are employed by Japanese, in contrast to the Malay internal metaphor of the Inner Wind. Marsella believes that "depression has far less crushing implications for the sense of self [in non-Western people] because the language/thinking process permits the experience to be coded and communicated in either somatic terms or in impersonal external referent terms" (1985:302). Not all folk healing, however, focuses "more on relations (with other people, or with supernatural entities) than with processes internal to the individual" (Marsella 1984:88). The Malay concept of sakit berangin, using internal referent terms, should provide a caveat to those who might be tempted to view all non-Western societies as the Other.

14. Although patients (and their neighbors) may suspect that they are suffering from unexpressed angin, the shaman's divination gives authentication to the diagnosis.

15. See also Needham (1962) and Lex (1979) on the relationship of percussion to altered states of consciousness.

the patient's trance and that of the shaman are (1) the patient's trance does not make him or her a conduit for hantu, but, rather, puts patients in touch with their inner being; and (2) shamans control the alterations of their own consciousness, while the patient's consciousness is controlled by the shaman.[16]

In shamanic ceremonies whose primary aim is to remove demonic influence from human sufferers, the patient's trance is "the peak moment [at which] the object of the demonic enters into direct communion with the subject" (Kapferer 1983:195). For the Malay patient, trance does not occur during the exorcistic parts of the Main Peteri. The communication achieved by trancing patients is not with the demonic, but with their own inner nature.

While in trance, if a patient has the angin for silat (the Malay art of self-defense), he will rise and perform its stylized moves and stances; if she has angin for Mak Yong, she will dance with the grace of a princess; Angin Hala will cause a trancing patient to roar and leap like a tiger. Patients are encouraged to act out the repressed portions of their personalities until their hearts are content and their angin refreshed. Coming out of trance, into the awareness of an enthusiastic, approving audience, the patient experiences a wonderful feeling of relaxation and satisfaction. Headaches and backaches have disappeared, and asthma sufferers find they can once more breathe freely.

Patients in trance feel the Inner Winds as experiential reality rather than merely metaphor. When I asked people what it felt like to be in trance, they couldn't, or wouldn't, answer. They told me that the only way I could know would be to experience it for myself. I avoided the issue for the better part of my stay, feeling uncomfortable with the lack of control that being placed in trance implied. Well into the second year of my research, while I was attending a Main Peteri as part of Pak Long's entourage, he motioned to me to sit down on the mat recently vacated by his patient. I thought that he wanted to do a short ritual for me, to release me from the dangers inherent in witnessing women give birth, a ritual he had often performed for my benefit at the close of Main Peteri. Instead, he proceeded to recite the story of

16. An interesting comparison can be made between Malay patients, whose trances are primarily controlled by the shaman, and patients of Puerto Rican Espiritistas (Koss 1975), who are expected to develop control over their own trances.

Dewa Muda (which he had deduced was my primary Inner Wind), accompanied by the orchestra and his own rhythmic pounding on the floor. My trust in him was strong enough now to allay my fears, and I allowed my consciousness to shift into an altered state. At the height of my trance, I felt the Wind blowing inside my chest with the force of a hurricane.

When I later described the feelings I had had while in trance to others who had been patients of Pak Long, they assured me that mine was a common experience. They also wondered at my surprise. One woman remarked, "Why did you think we call them Winds?"[17]

Western Winds?

Are Malay theories of the Inner Winds comparable in any way to contemporary Western theories of personality development, creativity, and frustration?

Mainstream Euroamerican psychological theorists, from Freud and Jung to those writing during the present decade, have emphasized the problematic and even dangerous nature of talent and creativity (usually in the arts, but occasionally extending to scientific fields) and the risks that they present to their possessors. Freud believed that creativity represents a considerable increase in psychic capacity which results from a dangerous predisposition to draw upon impulses from the id, that dark, otherwise inaccessible part of the personality, which intrude themselves on the ego (Freud 1949 [1905]). Jung denied the inevitable connection of psychopathology and creativity, but emphasized the vulnerability of the creator, who possesses "great gifts [which] are the fairest, and often the most dangerous, fruits on the tree of humanity. They hang on the weakest branches, which easily break" (Jung, quoted in Jacobi 1973:26). While Jung spoke about the fragility of the artistic personality which predisposes its possessor to possible psychological trauma, Rollo May did not hesitate to declare that "creativity is certainly associated with serious psychological problems" (May 1975:38)

17. My experience in trance reinforces my belief that "cultural ideas are constantly validated by the nature of subjective experience" (Obeyesekere 1981:113; Laderman 1981).

and, further, that "genius and psychosis are so close to each other"(May 1975:28) since "creativity and originality are associated with persons who do not fit into their culture" (May 1975:38). Secondary figures in the fields of psychology and psychiatry have said that "vulnerability . . . is indeed a requirement for the creative personality," a personality which is essentially narcissistic and even similar in structure and functioning to that of a schizophrenic (Fried, Bloomgarden, Lewis, Mermelstein, Spiegel, and Watts 1964:6). The creative person is thought to be a cultural misfit, afflicted with the burdens of loneliness, terror, never-ending restlessness and searching, frustration, depression, despair, suicidal risk, sexual difficulties, and interpersonal disharmonies (Slaff 1981:84).

This conception of artistic genius as concurrent with mental illness is so prevalent in contemporary Western society that Lionel Trilling has called it "one of the characteristic notions of our culture" (Trilling 1963:503). Art historians Rudolph and Margot Wittkower, in tracing the origins of this idea, have demonstrated its time- and culture-bound nature (Wittkower and Wittkower 1963). Until the High Renaissance, European artists were believed to be "born under Mercury" (as they still are in India), an astrological category that included merchants, watchmakers, organ-builders, and other artisans. Their chief characteristics were their shrewdness, industriousness, and devotion to duty. A shift in patronage to Saturn, the planetary influence of scholars, men of letters, and exalted creators, was accomplished by Renaissance artists as a conscious career move which helped them to attain higher social status. The saturnine temperament, however, was a mixed blessing since, according to humoral pathology, it was associated with a preponderance of black bile (melancholy) which, if not properly tempered, could produce depression, anxiety, and other conditions bordering on insanity. This association of creativity and melancholy in Western societies from the late fifteenth century on encouraged the notion that no outstanding intellectual or artistic achievement was possible unless its author was melancholic (Wittkower and Wittkower 1963:104).

Psychiatrists have noted that the burdens of creativity increase when the creative act is blocked. Blockage causes illness to the blocked artist or inappropriate behavior toward others due to stored quantities of inhibited aggression (Kubie 1958; Fried et al. 1964). The homology of genius and psychosis is considered particularly likely to surface whenever creators are deprived of the opportunity to exercise their gifts (Eissler 1967).

Western artists themselves bear witness to the psychic and physiological problems that occur when, for any reason, they are unable to practice their art. The clearest statement I have ever read comes from Raphael Soyer, a well-known New York painter, who recently died in his late eighties (Soyer 1986:16):

> I've painted for a very long time, but I don't get tired or bored by it. I love to do it. If I don't paint one day, I don't feel well physically or mentally. My eyes bother me when I don't paint. But when I paint a full day, I feel satisfied and everything seems to be OK. I would never stop, never retire. I can't see how people can retire; I don't understand that. My brother Moses died while he was painting. He was actually working on a painting, and the last words he said were to the model: "Phoebe, don't frown." Then he died. He worked to the very last minute.

Pak Long and his colleagues would understand Raphael Soyer's feelings immediately. It would be perfectly clear to them that Soyer was the possessor of an angin for painting of gale-force strength. They would not, however, agree with Freud, Jung, and others that creativity (read, "powerful angin") is dangerous in itself.

Angin is necessary for life—we all possess angin to a greater or lesser degree. It is only when our angin is not expressed, when our Inner Winds cannot blow freely, that problems may develop. The intensity of the problem depends upon the amount of unexpressed angin; therefore, possessors of strong angin are at greater risk than the person whose angin is weak, but *only if their strong angin is imprisoned within their breasts*. If it can be expressed in daily life, its possessors may lead healthier and more satisfying lives than the average and end their days like Raphael Soyer as successful, respected, venerable artists (or bomoh, or midwives, etc.). Malay bomoh would, therefore, question the validity of Freud's formulation but find Eissler's comments about the risk of psychopathology to creators deprived of an outlet for their creativity to be right on the mark.

I asked a number of psychiatrists of various theoretical persuasions to read an earlier version of this chapter. A follower of Karen Horney remarked on the correspondence he perceived between the Malay archetypes of Dewa Muda, Angin Hala, and Dewa Penchil, and the three major neurotic personality types of which Horney spoke: (1) the type that moves toward people; (2) the type that moves against people; and (3) the type that moves away from people (Horney 1945, 1950). The "moving toward people" type measures his own value in the currency of love, trying to win the affection of others and lean upon them. The type that moves against people is full of rage and suspicion of others whose hostility he takes for granted. He determines, consciously or unconsciously, to fight. The third personality type is emotionally detached, ever moving on to new people and new places, a wandering onlooker at life. My psychiatrist friend readily equated the "moving toward" type with Dewa Muda, the "moving against" with Abdul Jinah the weretiger, and the "moving away" with Dewa Penchil.

The proposed correspondence, although striking, is not perfect. The lack of congruence between the Western and Malay formulations arises once again in the area of normality versus psychopathology. Horney believed that these three personality types are manifestations of neurosis which overlay the "real self" (Horney 1950). Pak Long and his compatriots, however, would argue that they *are* the real self; a problem arises only when their needs are not met, or when their drives are manifested in inappropriate situations. The contemporary Western idea of the self as arising in social experience and developing in relation to the attitudes of others, is foreign to Malay thought. The theory of angin presupposes that the core of the self is essentially present at birth.

A higher degree of isomorphism can be found between the archetypes of the Main Peteri and the archetypes of Jungian theory. Both contend that the archetype is "an inherited mode of psychic functioning, corresponding to the inborn way in which the chick emerges from the egg, the bird builds its nest" (Jung 1976:ix). Malay shamans would certainly agree with Jung that neglected archetypes (read, "angin") "are the unfailing causes of neurotic and even psychotic disorders, behaving exactly like neglected or maltreated physical organs or organic functional systems" (Jung 1969:156). The Jungian archetype is an elementary poetic image, whose origins are deep within the collective unconscious of our species, beyond the reach of the individual ego (Jung

1958). Like angin, the archetype must find expression or the individual risks trauma:

> Owing to adverse personal circumstances or traumatic conflicts . . . an archetype may find no channel for the conveyance of meaning. . . . Conflicts between ego values and unacceptable drives, when seen as personal problems only, produce meaningless and hopeless suffering. It is by placing them in a wider transpersonal pattern . . . that the experiences of the archetypes gives a new impulse to the flow of psychic energy." (Jung, quoted in Whitmont 1969:84)

Whenever we are up against such conflict situations to which no rational solution seems possible, a symbolic experience can lead us beyond the impasse. The archetypal conflict can be lived as if it were a drama, the play of life or of the gods—in short, the type of drama exemplified by the Main Peteri.

Jung remarked that it is in fairy tales that one can best study the comparative anatomy of the psyche (Kiersey and Bates 1978); his follower, Marie-Louise Von Franz, has provided a key that can be used to translate the material of Malay archetypal stories in Jungian terms. She reminds us that a tiger in a story may represent human passions. "It is not the real tiger's greed that is represented, but our own tigerish greed" (Von Franz 1970:24).

The story of Dewa Muda lends itself most easily to Jungian analysis: The old man with the three humps who appears in Dewa Muda's dream is the Wise Old Man who represents the Self, the innermost nucleus of the psyche (Von Franz 1964:196). His three humps show him to be extraordinary, underlining his importance to the dreamer. When Dewa Muda gets lost in the forest, he has actually started on his journey into the unconscious. Awang, his servant, acts as psychopomp, his guide into the deeper realms of his psyche. The human spirit flies (on the Queen of Java's golden kite) in search of its other half—the anima, the feminine part of the male psyche. The father of the anima is often a jin or ogre in Islamic fairy tales (Von Franz 1970:81); Princess Ulana Mas is, in Jungian terms, unquestionably Dewa Muda's anima. She is his sister, his feminine half, lost to him forever. Forbidding the marriage of Ulana Mas and Dewa Muda denies the hero the unity he seeks with his feminine soul. His psyche fragmented, it is no wonder he goes mad.

To act as a healing force, the archetypal myth must be brought to the surface of a patient's consciousness. It "must be confronted with a full realization of its import in terms of personal impasses and problems; only then is there a channel for the new flow of life" (Whitmont 1969:84). This is an important part of the work of the Malay shaman.

Main Peteri and Psychotherapy

Some of the issues raised earlier concerning the relationship of shamanistic and psychiatric healing can now be addressed. Since shamans have been said to provide "remission without insight" or symptomatic relief, rather than a cure, in contrast to psychiatrists, who help patients to form a better self-image, which allows them to cope with the world (in effect, a cure), it would be valuable to examine what we mean by "cure."

Some of the Malay shaman's patients find it necessary to hold only one ceremony. The relief they experience is sufficient to preclude further treatment, and the problem that precipitated their illness is not one that regularly recurs. Such a patient was Siti Fatima, a young woman in the grip of severe postpartum depression after the birth of her first child. She cried all day, ignored her baby, and refused to nurse it. The cause of her sickness was divined as the Hantu Sawan, a spirit that attacks new mothers and babies. Her problem was located outside herself; she was not to blame for her behavior. The shaman's projection of her problems onto a culturally accepted external entity in the sight and hearing of her friends and family worked a kind of magic on this young mother. At the close of the Main Peteri, when the spirit had been exorcised, she smiled and cuddled her baby.

Malay shamans, themselves, may have recourse to Main Peteri to solve their problems. Pak Long Awang found himself in the position of patient when he was afflicted with a sudden painful and frightening illness (see chapter 8). During the course of the seance, it was revealed that his condition was due to the misguided anger of spirits he had recently exorcised from a patient. The patient's family had neglected to provide the spirits with promised offerings. Attributing her recovery to the treatment she received at a clinic, rather than to Pak Long's exorcism, they had held a feast to which the shaman was not invited. Their treatment of Pak Long amounted to public humiliation. His dramatic cure was due to the show of support he received from those present at the seance and the feeling that, having convinced the spirits that they were attacking the wrong person and should go after the real culprits (who had cheated them, as well as the shaman), he was once more in control.

Other patients benefit from having their troubles projected outside themselves, but need to have the experience repeated at frequent intervals. Pak Tahar had recently divorced his wife, leaving her furious and vindictive. A civil servant whose work involved writing and record keeping, he often found his "brain addled, his thoughts mixed up." A divination revealed that his former wife was sending spirits to torment him. An exorcism worked only temporarily, since she continued to persecute him by remote control.

Explanations of conditions involving unexpressed angin do not employ projective systems. Sufferers of sakit berangin must face the reality of their own personalities undisguised by symbols that locate their problems outside themselves. Those with powerful Angin Dewa Muda must understand that they long for the unattainable—they can never have enough love, admiration, and material comforts to satisfy their Wind. Those with Angin Hala must face the dark side of their personalities—face and accept. In trance, the angin is freed and refreshed. Repressed housewives with Angin Hala, afraid to express their Wind in daily life for fear of divorce, roar and show their teeth in trance (in fact, this may save a shaky marriage; see Kessler 1977); Mek Gemuk, a grotesquely fat woman with unrealizable angin for performing in the Mak Yong, rises in trance to dance once a year with the charm and grace of a leading lady. Understanding the basis of the illness and its treatment, we can understand why Mek Gemuk goes into an annual decline and needs to trance once a year, although she functions very well as a wife and merchant the rest of the time.

Malays do not conceive of this treatment as a "cure" since the drive known as angin is inherited and inborn, and, unless the life circumstances of patients change, they will always be at risk of accumulating too much unexpressed Wind. Although we, too, may not consider Mek Gemuk's treatment to be a cure, in the sense of ridding her forever of an affliction, it is comparable to the results obtained by clinical psychiatrists and psychiatric social workers who practice successful crisis intervention (and a good deal faster than most Western psychological treatments).

Western psychotherapy is supposed to differ from shamanistic treatments in that only the former is thought to provide patients with a learning experience that clarifies their problems and allows them to cope more successfully with reality. Having myself been analyzed by Pak Long as heiress to a strong Angin Dewa Muda and put into a refreshing trance to the sound of my archetype's story, I have learned to conceptualize my own drives for success and love in a way that clarifies my feelings and provides me with a better perspective. My husband, an artist considered by Pak Long to carry Angin Hala as well as strong angin for his profession, has been able to express both these drives in paintings of violence, a process psychoanalysts would call sublimation and shamans would refer to as allowing the Winds to blow freely.

A distinction between biomedical and nonbiomedical psychotherapies was stressed by Kiev when he said that "[t]he notion of individual susceptibility or vulnerability to stress which is heightened by the individual's failure to act autonomously . . . is quite central to psychiatric theory" (Kiev, quoted in Finkler 1985:181). Finkler considered this extremely salient, since this idea, central to biomedical theory, was not a feature of the nonbiomedical Mexican Spiritualist therapy that she studied. The Malay concept of angin, however, which incorporates the notion of individual susceptibility heightened by stressful life circumstances and lack of individual control within the theory of a nonbiomedical psychotherapy, points to the lack of universality of this distinction.

The Origins of the Myth

The foregoing discussion supports Lévi-Strauss's contention (1963) that the shaman's myth is received from collective tradition. His conclusion that psychoanalysis differs from shamanism in that the analysand presents an individual myth to the healer merits further consideration. There is convincing evidence that Western psychotherapeutic treatment flourishes only when patient and healer share the same cultural myths—contemporary myths that were formulated by the healers and have become part of the cultural assumptions of a significant portion of the society. Western therapists often assume that patients of a social class, race, or ethnic group other than their own will not benefit from psychotherapeutic methods and therefore are more likely to treat them with drug therapy (Horowitz 1982).

The Malay theory of personality and the theories of Freud and Jung are built upon different views of human development and relationship to the universe. Jung's archetypes find their match in Malay archetypes of the angin of personality, but Malay archetypes, although we may conceive of them as extending to the core of the unconscious, exist on the conscious level for Malay patients, healers, and members of their social milieu. Unlike Freud, the Malay healer is not constrained to reach backward through time and space to find a myth that illuminates the workings of the psyche. The stories of Dewa Muda and Abdul Jinah, and their implications for explaining personality, are common knowledge among east coast Malay peasants and fishermen, whereas the stories of Oedipus and Electra, which Freud used as archetypal myths, were not part of the cultural baggage of the Viennese man on the street at the turn of the century. The giants of psychoanalysis were powerful mythmakers. Their myths and symbols, derived from psychoanalytic theory, have become not only part of the shared assumptions of contemporary Western patients and healers but also part of popular culture.

The question of the "reality" and "truth" of Western psychotherapy, whether in and of itself or in comparison to healing methods of other cultures, has been a central problem for scholars of many disciplines. Prince, a pioneer in transcultural psychiatry, has concluded that shamanistic systems "have less truth value than Western psychoanalytically oriented theories" (Prince 1977:xv). Ryle, a post-Wittgensteinian philosopher who underwent a successful psychoanalysis, called Freud's teachings useful allegories (Ryle 1949). Garrison, an anthropologist who has worked with both psychiatrists and Puerto Rican Espiritistas, argues that the spirits of the Espiritistas serve an essentially conceptual function and that their existence is no more concrete than that of the ego, id, or superego (Garrison 1977).

The reality of neither the Western id, ego, superego constructs, nor the Malay concept of angin can be proven by objective means; their value is theoretical and clinical; neither is more nor less rational than the other. The superior "truth value" that Prince finds in Western psychotherapeutic methods is a statement of his belief in contemporary Western cultural assumptions regarding psychosexual development, rather than scientific fact. As he himself concedes, we still lack sufficient evaluation of outcomes of both Western and non-Western psychotherapies (Prince 1980:339). The difference between the Malay bomoh's view of the universe and our own should not blind us to the fact that the Malay shaman, working within the matrix of a spirit-raising seance, often achieves his results through conscious psychotherapy, built upon a consistent theory of personality, rather than as mere by-products of either magical activity or a socially sanctioned projective system.

The portion of the Main Peteri that attempts to heal the wounds of body and soul caused by thwarted angin is, to my knowledge, the sole example in the ethnographic record of an indigenous non-Western method of nonprojective psychotherapy existing within the context of a shamanistic seance. Can it be possible that the Malay theory and praxis I have discussed in these pages is an isolated island in an ocean of projective magic? Or might a fresh look at shamanistic rituals in other cultures reveal comparable approaches to knowledge of the human psyche and treatments of its wounds?

5

The Performance of Healing

Although it is problematic to insist upon our own categories and standards as constituting an unquestioned universal given, it is becoming increasingly evident that healing rituals can be judged, by standards applied to Western psychotherapies, to produce significant observable results. Healing rituals do more than merely label sicknesses, manipulate these labels, and apply new labels (cured, well) to the patient's condition (Kleinman 1980:372). Hypotheses regarding the mechanisms responsible for these results have clustered around two levels of human functioning: the psychological and the neurobiological.

One of the most powerful tools in any healer's armamentarium is the placebo effect, which triggers the body's ability to heal itself. Placebos (a term that usually refers to pharmacologically inert substances but can also refer to such treatments as injections of vitamins given merely to humor a patient) are used by contemporary Western physicians for such purposes as controlling postoperative pain, relieving anxiety, curing warts, and improving peptic ulcers (Frank 1974). The placebo effect is not necessarily limited to the administration of substances but may also include words and actions, such as occur in a shamanistic seance (e.g., Laderman 1983, 1987). The shaman, in engaging the mind and affecting the emotions of his patient, simultaneously initiates physiological changes.

The healing effects of shamanistic performance are, on one level, owing to the catharsis that can occur when a patient's unresolved emotional distress is reawakened and confronted in a dramatic context. For such healing to take place, aesthetic distance must be achieved. This is the balance point between feeling painful emotions that have been repressed in the past and reliving these feelings from a point of safety in the present. Aesthetic distance has been defined as "the simultaneous and equal experience of being both participant and observer" (Scheff 1979:60). At the heart of the concept is the idea of "proper" distance, neither an underdistancing, which would expose the patient to a painful emotional experience lacking objectivity, nor an overdistancing, which would intellectualize the experience and dilute its emotional content. In the West, aesthetic distance often occurs during a psychological counseling session, when a client, recounting a traumatic experience, is led to see his distress as viewed by an outside observer at the same time that he is feeling it from the inside. The theory of catharsis argues that unresolved emotional distress gives rise to rigid or neurotic patterns of behavior, and that abreaction, or discharge of negative affect resulting in catharsis, can dissipate these patterns (Scheff 1979).

Catharsis occurs when people are given "permission" to experience their feelings. This is especially important in a milieu—such as rural Malay society—where many emotions are regularly suppressed. Ritual, with its associated myths, provides a context that is both psychologically enabling and socially acceptable for repeated catharsis. Although Western psychotherapies rely strongly upon verbal recall for the production of abreaction, it is probable that sensory stimuli—the tastes, smells, music, dance, and drama associated with ritual—can have a similarly direct impact in discharging repressed emotions (Scheff 1979:76–77). Techniques of aesthetic distancing often rely upon a willing suspension of disbelief, and combine experiences of pleasure and pain, as evidenced by the interweaving of awesome scenes with comic episodes that not only relieve tension but also provide critical comments about status, class, religion, politics, and relations between the sexes.

A subjective sign of aesthetic distance is the patient's perception that the emotions that accompany abreaction, and their physical manifestations, are under control. Within the context of the Main Peteri, control rests with the tok 'teri. It is he who has the power to end the patient's trance, with its crying, laughing, dancing, shivering, and fighting. The patient's trust in the tok 'teri gives the healer implicit permission to provoke this emotional discharge and removes any fear the patient might otherwise have that this behavior will never end.

Emotional discharge under conditions of aesthetic distance is not the unpleasant experience it might be under ordinary circumstances. In fact, under optimal conditions, it is completely pleasant. For some, the pleasure may be overlaid with embarrassment. This was evident in the case of Mek Gemuk, the frustrated actress, who covered her smiling face with a cloth at the close of a seance to hide it from an audience that had witnessed her dancing entranced.

Optimal aesthetic distance in a shamanic ceremony occurs when "remembering" and "forgetting" are in harmonic balance. The linguistic references to this within this Main Peteri are revealing: the shaman is called the "man who forgets" (*orang lupa*), an active state, while the patient in trance is said to passively "not remember" (*tak ingat*). The shaman's trance is deliberate and controlled; the patient's altered state is evoked by and under the control of the shaman. A shaman in trance, Pak Long told me, is at once there and not there, aware and not aware. He "forgets" his own everyday persona, but remembers the shape of the drama, the order of performance, and the proper actions and expected behavior of the spirits whose personae he assumes. The shamanic trance, for an experienced healer, mixes seeming abandon with stylized control. It is not, however, simply a matter of emptying the shaman of his consciousness, or pushing it to one side, and allowing another persona to enter. There are levels of trance and levels of personal consciousness while in trace. During scenes when hantu or penggawa speak, the shaman's trance is light. He is aware of the spirits' presence, but it is he, not they, who speak. There is no question of fraud or mere role playing on the part of the shaman. He is the spirits' spokesman. He understands their characters, their behavior, their needs, and their demands, and he expresses them to their human audience. Only when a powerful genie appears does the shaman become deeply entranced. After returning to consciousness, he has no memory of the preceding moments. The separation between his own persona and that of the genie is complete. Pak Long, usually a modest man, listening with fascination to a genie's speech (using Pak Long's voice) on a tape I had made, remarked, "What a sly one he [the genie] is! How clever he is!"

A similar intertwining of states of awareness occurs during the patient's trance. Patients feel a separation between themselves and their physical bodies. My own trance was typical in this respect. Although I was conscious of the music, the smell of incense, and the faces of the people in the room, I seemed to be floating somewhere above the body that I knew was seated on the floor. Like the shaman, patients may combine "remembering" and "forgetting." They may "forget" themselves so far as to exhibit behavior that would be socially unacceptable under other circumstances, but "remember" themselves enough to be cognizant of their surroundings during trance and to recall their actions when the trance has ended.

The cathartic effects of abreaction in the healing of psychological trauma and psychosomatic pain have been attested to by many studies. Dramatic relief of asthma, in particular, has been observed following catharsis (French 1939; Doust and Leigh 1953; Weiner 1977): "The motor expressions of emotion, i.e., weeping, laughing, the acting out of anger . . . proved to reduce symptoms and remove the oxygen deprivation which characterized these patients" (Doust and Leigh 1953:304). The striking improvement of Toki Latip's asthma (chapter 6) following trances during which he fought with the shaman and manipulated puppets that had deep emotional significance for him bears witness to the healing catharsis of the Main Peteri.

The success of ritual trance in healing has been explained in neurobiological, as well as psychological, terms. Each of the human brain's two hemispheres is thought to control different functions: the left brain controlling speech, linear analytic thought, the sequential processing of information, and the assessment of the duration of temporal units; the right brain controlling spatial and tonal perceptions, recognition of patterns (including internal emotional patterns), and holistic thought. It is believed that the ability to assess duration of time is lacking in the right hemisphere (Lex 1979). Ornstein (1972) believes that ritual practices employing the rhythms of singing, chanting, clapping, and percussion instruments evoke and place into preeminence the right hemisphere's functions and inhibit those of the left hemisphere, accounting for the "timeless" quality of the trance experience.

Other parts of the central nervous system may also be stimulated by ritual performances. The sympathetic nervous system, excited by fear and awe, triggers the release of epinephrine and norepinephrine. Bombarding a patient with sustained fear-evoking stimuli may overload the sympathetic nervous system to the point that "flooding" takes place and rebound occurs, stimulating the parasympathetic nervous system. Parasympathetic nervous system stimulation results in pleasurable states, such as deep relaxation of the skeletal muscles and synchronization of cortical rhythms. Rituals, therefore, may heal not only through the temporary alleviation of stress but also because this "rebound" effect establishes a new balance of cortical integration (Lex 1979).

Percussive music, in particular, has been considered an important means of achieving transition to an altered state (e.g., Neher 1962; Needham 1962). The most effective rhythm, according to Neher, is four to seven beats per second, exactly the optimum frequency for pain relief through electrically stimulated acupuncture. This rhythm matches the EEG frequency of theta waves, produced by the brain most strongly during periods of deep meditation. It is also the rhythm of the drum beat at the height of the music that accompanies the trance in the Main Peteri.

A growing number of scientists, from biochemists and pharmacologists to psychiatrists and anthropologists, have speculated that another key to the shaman's success may be found in the biochemistry of endorphins, endogenous morphinelike substances that act on the nervous system and are generated in the human brain in response to pain, stress, or certain kinds of peak experiences. Given the proper cues, the brain may also generate other endogenous chemicals, as effective as Librium or Valium in their tranquilizing effects.

The healing effects of ritual, whether on a psychological or neurobiological level, take place within the context of a meaningful drama that engages the patient's mind, body, emotions, and, one might add, soul.

The Main Peteri as Ritual Drama

The Main Peteri, although its central purpose is the healing of human pain, is a form of theater, complete with heroes, villains, tension, comedy, stage, props, and audience. Like other forms of Southeast Asian theater, the shaman's seance uses music and dance as emphasis and counterpoint to the protagonists' words. The shaman and minduk, and their troupe of musicians, are accustomed to working together and are skilled in the basic patterns of the dramatic form of the seance. As Brandon has remarked about Southeast Asian theater in general, the troupe can produce a play "with no more special preparation than a jazz group needs to belt out a number"; it is only necessary to rearrange the standard parts of the genre, so no two patterns are exactly alike and none is totally different (Brandon 1972:155–156).

Performance of Main Peteri requires the establishment of a space set off from everyday uses. A structure may be built especially for the seance, or the shaman's or patient's home may be transformed by the arrangement of floor mats and the seating of the performers and audience. The props of the seance are often used in other types of ritual, since their symbolic value holds true for the total system. For example, the spirit feast offered in the Main Peteri contains the same ingredients as the feast offered to jungle spirits to placate them before their land is opened to agriculture. The double-slipknot palm frond "releasers" used to release victims of spirit attacks from danger are also used by midwives to release new mothers from the perils of childbirth. Patients are often bathed by the shaman at the close of the seance, to cleanse them of any remaining spiritual pollution. This ritually cleansing bath is also performed by patients themselves at the behest of bomoh who have treated them for "unusual" ailments; and midwives bathe new mothers, for similar reasons, at the close of the rituals of childbirth.

Some of the props are multivalent: the shaman places a loop of cord atop the offering to his spirit familiars. A similar loop of cord becomes a stand-in for the birth canal as a primapara passes through it at the finale of the *melenggang perut* (a ritual that takes place during the seventh month of pregnancy). It is also used at the end of the postpartum period, when a new mother and her child pass through the loop in a representation of rebirth into a new status. Another multivalent symbolic object is the *keras*, a dish containing money, raw rice, a coconut, and a loop of cord. The shucked coconut, with its suggestion of a face and hair, is a double of the patient's head in the context of the Main

Peteri. It becomes a stand-in for the uterus in the melenggang perut. Hard and round like her own pregnant womb, the coconut contains liquid and solid elements that mimic the fetus and amniotic fluid.

Within the shamanic ritual, the unsaid becomes the said, the intangible and inaudible take on form and sound, the chaotic becomes controlled. Spirits "borrow the voice of Adam"—they speak and sing, joke and complain, express their wishes, and agree to withdraw their harmful influence through the medium of the shaman. Normally present but unseen, they show their character through the shaman's movements and his tone of voice as he "carries" them in trance.

Concepts unexpressed in daily life come to the fore in the seance. Some are commonplace truisms of daily life that Malays assume are universally known and thus hardly worth discussing, such as the father's role in conception. Although I regularly assisted traditional midwives in delivering babies, it was not until I heard the minduk's song that I learned about the father's pregnancy. "For forty days and forty nights the baby rests within its father's womb," sings the minduk. "A single drop falls from the father's pen . . . thrust, then, into the mother's womb, enclosed there nine months and ten days." The text of the Main Peteri clarifies Malay beliefs about the nature of men and women: human beings possess an animal nature that makes us kin to the beasts, but we are unique among God's creations in possessing the rationality (akal) that makes us truly human and, in this respect, even closer to God than the angels. Men, however, have a greater amount of rationality than do women, in whom animal nature predominates. It makes sense, therefore, for a baby to begin life within its father's brain, the paternal womb, where it acquires rationality from a developed source. Understanding the father's role in the baby's prenatal development explains a good deal of the beliefs and behavior of Malays in connection with pregnancy and childbirth (see Laderman 1983 for an extended discussion).

Much of the symbolism of the Main Peteri centers around the mysteries of birth and sex. The patient's birth-sibling often appears at the seance, complaining of their unequal fates. Having begun in the mother's womb rather than the father's brain, the birth-sibling is not only lacking the air and fire that the baby takes in with its first breath but also lacks human rationality. The nature of the birth-sibling justifies the minduk's epithet: "Body of a beast with a human face . . . the true older brother."[1]

The disembodied spirits are kin to humanity in the same manner as the birth-sibling is kin to the patient. In one origin story, the spirits are said to have arisen from the afterbirths that accompanied the emergence of Adam and Eve.[2] The Yellow Genie and the Black Genie were formed from the debris of human childbirth; specifically, the Yellow Genie arose from the blood of parturition (yellow is often symbolic of blood in Malay magic) and the Black Genie arose from the placenta.

Supernatural beings connected with reproduction include beneficent as well as potentially dangerous entities. The Heavenly Midwives (*bidandari*), demigoddesses who live in Kayangan but come down to earth to assist mortal midwives (and occasionally women in childbirth, see Laderman 1983:132), are important figures in the seance.

Sex and other intimate bodily functions are not always serious matters in the ritual. Its humor tends to be broadly sexual and scatological. The names of many female spirits are graphic and uncomplimentary, unlike the awesome and powerful titles claimed by male spirits. While male spirits have such names as He Who Chastises as He Passes, and Mighty Hammer, female spirits are known as Mother Longbreasts, Miss Tits, the Moldy Old Maid, and the Old Maid Who Cannot Control Her Urination. Pak Long's penggawa, the Old Toddy Tapper (chapter 8), explains that it's a long time since he had a [toddy] container—his wife is old now. Miss Click-clack (Mek Ketuk-ketak), a spirit who appears in Mat Din's seance (chapter 8), is hot after a man—almost any man will do. The Mute Spirit (Hantu Bisu) is a favorite with audiences in Merchang. All he wants to do is to get laid, and he conveys his message by the universal symbol of a finger moving in and out of the circle made by the joined thumb and forefinger of his other hand.

Shamans themselves are teased about their supposed habit of apply-

1. Belief in the birth-sibling as an influential spiritual presence is widespread in Southeast Asia. See particularly Connor 1984.

2. The thought of Adam and Eve possessing afterbirths may be familiar to Westerners, whose most magnificent depiction of Adam (Michelangelo's ceiling of the Sistine Chapel) shows his umbilicus.

g their healing touch to pretty women's bosoms more often than they do to less attractive patients. They appear to take such teasing in good part. Sex, after all, is one of life's great pleasures, and what man would not take advantage of such an opportunity? Shamans believe that human woes, in fact, can sometimes be caused by unsatisfied sexual cravings and do their best to allow these feelings to be expressed in an atmosphere that does not threaten their possessor. Mat Daud bin Panjak, in his treatment of a young unmarried girl who laughed and cried for no apparent reason, put her into trance and urged her to act out her repressed feelings by singing to her, "What's the use of wearing pants? Get up and dance!"

Moments of humor in the seance may be reflections of a spirit's known character. For instance, Wak Long, one of the shaman's penggawa and a popular figure in the shadow play, claims to be a rich man. The minduk laughs at his claims, saying, "Oh, that's a good one! He even has debts piling up at the store . . . that's the kind of rich man he is." A sea spirit, asked to break off relations with his human associate, says that he will "row off."

More often, however, humorous episodes involving the spirits reveal the ways in which they are inferior to human beings. The hantu exemplify bad manners. They are noisy, threatening, greedy; they gobble up their feasts, grab their offerings, and show themselves to be not only lacking in a humoral sense but also in a cultural sense. They may behave like children, demanding bananas and stuffing the entire fruit into their mouths. Female spirits may act immodestly, like Miss Click-clack, who goes so far as to point out a man in the audience whom she would like to meet.

Many of the jokes that the minduk makes at the spirits' expense depend upon the hantu's lack of reasoning power. They do not understand the (often not very subtle) insults hurled at them. They are deficient in rationality (akal) and lack the knowledge essential to every human Malay. Even the Hantu Raya, the most feared spirit on the east coast, when pretending to be a pious Muslim, cannot recite more than the first line of the daily prayer. His ignorance amuses the audience while revealing his true identity.

The behavior of the hantu relegates them to a position outside the norms of polite human society, and the aim of the seance is to see that they return to the place where they belong in God's scheme (see Kapferer 1983:224 for similar material in Sri Lanka). Within their own sphere, the hantu's society is organized along much the same lines as human society. They have a hierarchy of rulers, headmen, assistant headmen, armies of soldiers, and servants. Their rulers may make demands on humanity, as well as on their ghostly subjects, similar to those of human rulers, for example, Hitam Seri Penakluk (the Black Conqueror), who rules the crossroads, "levies taxes and demands tribute."

Although human beings are placed in a relationship of superiority to hantu, the supernatural beings that appear during a seance are far from pathetic figures of fun, as Sri Lankan demons are described by Kapferer. Speaking of the dramatic seance, he says that the demons' howling and crying contribute to the destruction of any sense of awe which may have surrounded the demonic previously (Kapferer 1983:224). In contrast, the sea spirit who breaks off relations with Mat Din (chapter 8) remains a noble and tragic figure as he sings and sobs, "My prince, you have the heart to . . . All his words strike me to the quick. He wants to get rid of me, he wants to get rid of me."

Before either an exorcism or "moving the patient's Wind" can take place, the inner forces of the ritual pair and their patient must be invoked. The Four Sultans, Four Commanders, Four Warriors, and so forth who dwell within each of us must be awakened to the necessity of guarding their possessors. The body's own healers must be aroused: the minduk sings to "Awaken the drummers in the palace of bone, Awaken the fiddlers in the palace of flesh." The tok 'teri calls upon personified body parts to be on the alert, such as Sulung Kecil Penganjur Raja (the little firstborn advance guard of the king), representing the eyes, the first human attribute to develop in the fetus, and Awang Mahat (the elephant keeper), the nape of the neck.

The shaman's Winds must be moved so that he can become the spirits' vessel. The minduk's Bestirring Song opens "the gate of lust, the gate of passion, the gate of desire" and "the gate of law, the gate of faith, the gate of wisdom." The shaman's emotions and rationality must both be aroused before he can function effectively.

A recurrent theme of the Main Peteri is the necessity of order for the maintenance of physical and spiritual well-being—order within the human microcosm, within the body politic, and within the universe. The patient has lost his way: "I disembarked, not knowing to what place I had come . . . completely confused, totally lost." He must be helped to find his way home. Elements that have intruded into areas where they do not belong must be returned to their proper places. Courtesy and etiquette must be observed. Deference must be paid to personages to whom it is owing. The minduk's courtly speech when addressing dewa, his constant use of the term "*tuan hamba*" (which I translate as "sir," but which is literally closer to "master of this humble slave"), his reference to them as "foreign prince," are fitting treatment of exalted beings. As an earth spirit reminds the minduk, "We 'people of the earth' must be taken seriously, spoken to nicely, treated with courtesy."

Royal allusions abound in the seance. The shaman is called *inang*, literally the nurse of a royal child; the minduk is named *pengasuh*, the body servant and companion of a prince. Both the site of the seance and the patient's body are called "the palace." The body is the palace of the soul, its parts are like porches or verandahs. The mat upon which the patient sits is called the throne room, and his illness is often compared to a civil war, relating the disharmony of disease in the human body to disharmony in the body politic (see also Kessler 1977; Laderman 1981).

The minduk expresses the philosophy behind the seance when he ends by singing that "those born to be kings are content when they associate with kings; those born noble when they associate with nobles" and when he exhorts the genies to stay "with genies together in ranks, *mambang* with mambang together in ranks"—everyone must act as befits his place in society, and everything must be in its proper place for harmony to prevail.

Although the basic philosophy and dominant symbols of the Main Peteri represent values shared by many east coast Malays, conflicts in Malay society prevent it from expressing communal solidarity. Skepticism exists side by side with faith in a Malay village (see Firth 1974). Not all Malays believe in the shaman's divination. As the shaman Awang Jalal remarked (chapter 7), "People call it 'fortune-telling fakery.' They do it to annoy." A more serious problem is the discordance of basic elements of the seance with the tenets of Islam. Although all Main Peteri include fragments of Islamic prayer and references to Allah and Muhammad, the opposition of orthodox Muslims to the seance leads Tok Mamat to complain (chapter 6), "I don't know what to do about the injustice that we meet up with from pious folk." A striking example of religious discordance can be found in chapter 8 where Mat Din recites a charm. In the first two verses he says that nothing can compare with Muhammad and the Islamic Call to Prayer, and in the final verse he says that nothing can compare with Dewa Si Alam Tunggal, the chief deity of the non-Islamic abode of the gods. Pak Long unhesitatingly assures him that there is no problem with his continuing to use the charm. In a society in which folk beliefs conflict with a competing world religion, the power of ritual to unify a community becomes problematic.

The Main Peteri as Dramatic Form

Like a play, the Main Peteri is composed of a series of scenes within acts, often divided by intermissions. For example, in the seance I call "A Stifled Talent" (chapter 6), the first act sets the stage for the rest of the play. The spirits are invited to the seance; the inner forces and spirit familiars are invoked; and the first divination takes place, followed by an intermission. The second act consists of four scenes: in the first two scenes threatening spirits appear, raising the tension level of the participants and audience; the third visitation is a friendly one, easing the tension; and the fourth, although a dangerous spirit, quickly agrees to assist the patient. Since all the performers were also active in the shadow play, and since their patient was formerly a dalang, many of the persona who appear are characters from the wayang kulit.[3] After the second act, the participants change roles and a new shaman comes forward. The third act begins with a resetting of the stage and reinvocation of the inner forces, followed by a second divination. Then the patient is put into trance—a tense and exciting moment that brings release. Following his trance, there are five spirit visitations: the first two tension-producing fierce spirits and the last three friendly spirit familiars. The patient then trances for a second time, manipulating the puppets that had formed his life's center and attacked him for his negligence. The

3. The puppets of the shadow play are believed to be animated by their spirits (see Sweeney 1972).

release that comes with his trance prepares us for the final duet of the minduk and tok 'teri—an easing of the night's dramatic tension: "The waves have been put to rest by the strings of the Winds . . . one and all are at ease, each in his place in the palace."

Those who perform Main Peteri are individualists, each with his own history, training, and idiosyncracies. The reasons for holding a seance change from case to case. Certain conventions, however, appear to be basic to the genre, although the content can vary within categories. The minimal form of the Main Peteri, as illustrated by the abbreviated version done on an emergency basis for Pak Long Awang (see chapter 7), includes the following:

1. An invocation sung by the minduk as the prelude to the seance. In his introductory song, the minduk sends greetings to the ancestral teachers, healers, and saints, and awakens the healing powers within himself. He invokes the spirits of the place, mentioning their domains: the denizens of the earth, fields, village, orchards, water's edge, ocean, jungle, and heavenly abode (Kayangan). There is no list of denizens of the spirit world consistent from bomoh to bomoh. Each bomoh invokes the spirits most familiar to him and apologizes to those he has inadvertently omitted. The minduk accompanies himself on the three-stringed rebab, a spike-fiddle played with a bow. During the minduk's invocation, the audience usually mills about, paying little attention to his song, not because it is unimportant—it is a necessary prelude to the action of the seance—but because it is meant primarily for the ears of the invisible powers the minduk invokes, rather than those of his human audience.

2. At the end of the introductory song, the tok 'teri, having changed his clothes, seats himself before the minduk and listens intently while the minduk sings the Bestirring Song (*gerak angin*, literally "to move the Wind") that will assist the shaman in achieving trance. Toward the middle of the Bestirring Song, the shaman recites his incantation, calling on his inner resources and spirit familiars.

3. Having achieved trance, the shaman, in the persona of an internal force, has a conversation and shares a duet with the minduk.

4. The shaman then takes on the persona of an ancient and powerful bomoh, who sings a duet with the minduk and conducts a divination.

Main Peteri

5. Following the divination, the shaman and minduk sing a duet that talks about the changing nature of Dewa Muda. On the sea he is the Young Captain, on land the Young Prince, in heaven the Young Demigod.

6. The first moment of real tension arrives in the persona of the Assistant Headman of the Earth Spirits.

7. He is followed by another dangerous spirit, Anak Jin Serupa Muka (the Genie with the Look-alike Face). The tension of his presence is somewhat lessened by the insults he receives from the minduk, amusing to the audience, incomprehensible to the genie.

8. The third ghostly visitor arrives—in this case three spirit-brothers (although only one speaks through the agency of the shaman). The tension they engender quickly dissipates when they agree to help the patient.

9. After a break for tea, the Main Peteri resumes. The minduk and the shaman (in his own persona) sing a duet, "Let the Winds blow and open the way for the souls of former kings." All of the world is now at ease, everything is back in its proper place, as the seance comes to an end.

At each point of transition, and at the close of the seance, the musicians play a "traveling" tune, which becomes faster and louder, stopping suddenly as the shaman changes persona.

More elaborate Main Peteri are built upon this model, with appropriate changes to suit the circumstances, and variations to suit the training, temperaments, and moods of the performers. For example, in "Breaking Contracts with the Spirit World" (chapter 8), although the same bomoh acts as minduk as in "Seance for a Sick Shaman" (chapter 7), here he adds a long preliminary spoken invocation and expands the scope of his introductory song. There are many more spirit visitations, but the dramatic form follows the minimal model in building tension and periodically breaking it, either by alternating visitations of dangerous spirits with those of spirit familiars, or by presenting comic material in the presence of an otherwise awesome visitation. As Obeyesekere reminds us (1969), comedy in exorcism allows fear and terror to be laughed away.

Because this seance was held for the express purpose of breaking off relations with the spirit world, rather than to exorcise an attacking spirit or refresh a patient's Inner Winds, the theme of the final duet is "Who can release?" instead of "All are at ease, let the Winds blow freely."

Theater on the East Coast of Malaysia

The Main Peteri is closely related to two other major forms of Malay dramatic art that have flourished on the east coast of peninsular Malaysia: the Mak Yong dance theater and the wayang kulit shadow puppet theater. The three genres share much of their language, music, movement, themes, and world view. Practitioners of one form are often adept at one or both of the others. While Mak Yong and wayang kulit are performed primarily for their entertainment value, they employ elements of ritual as integral parts of their performance (in fact, a dalang may use the same invocation to the spirits before a performance of the shadow play as he uses in his function as a Main Peteri bomoh), and include within their scope dramas used primarily for healing or spiritual cleansing. This blending of the sacred and profane is not surprising. We have similar examples in the Western world in ancient Greek drama, in medieval musical dramas like The Play of Daniel, and in the passion plays still held in Oberammergau. As Sweeney reminds us (1987:133), "the differentiation between entertainment and what is not entertainment (didactic, magico-religious, etc.) is a relatively new development."

The most important of all wayang kulit rituals are those called *berjamu* (feasting), performed for the propitiation of spirits. The basic form of berjamu follows that of the Main Peteri. Unlike other wayang performances, which employ only the dalang and his assistants, the berjamu requires as well the presence of a minduk, who leads the orchestra and plays the three-stringed rebab (otherwise used only in the seance). In the berjamu, the dalang, after achieving trance, engages in dialogues with the minduk in the same manner as the shaman in the seance, and the idiom of their language is often that of the Main Peteri (Sweeney 1972:278).

Mak Yong performances done for reasons of health include the *semah angin* (offering to the Winds), meant to prepare student performers for their graduation and to adjust their humoral well-being thereafter, and *sambut* (catching) or *memanggil* (calling) *semangat*, performed to strengthen or recall the vital spirit. In addition, the Mak Yong can combine with the shaman's seance to produce a special genre known as Mak Yong-Main Peteri (or Puteri). A patient diagnosed as suffering from an unrealized identification with a Mak Yong character is given the opportunity of performing in the Mak Yong as a means of curing his *sakit berangin* (Ghulam-Sarwar 1976:256). In a typical Mak Yong-Main Peteri performance, a patient might assume the role of the hero, Pak Yong, while the bomoh takes the role of his clown-assistant, Peran. This genre appears to be the type of performance witnessed by Kessler (1977). He describes the seance of a woman with Angin Hala who acted out the part of a warrior and beat up the officiating shaman, thereby alleviating the feeling of powerlessness she suffered in everyday life.

So strong is the actors' belief in the power of even ordinary performances of Mak Yong that enactment of certain roles, especially that of Dewa Muda, entails not only dramatic rehearsal but psychological and spiritual preparation as well. In the drama of Dewa Muda, the part of Peran Tua (the old clown-assistant to the prince) is played by a bomoh, who recites all the incantations and conducts all the necessary rituals. Before the portion of the play in which Dewa Muda and his Peran enter the forest, the bomoh must ask the spirits for their protection and offer them a feast. His actions are vital to the safety of the performers: They are not merely play-acting, they *become* the characters. Although the performance of a Mak Yong drama may take place on several succeeding nights, the action of any night can never end at a place in which one of the characters is in danger, lest the actor's welfare be put in jeopardy.

This strong identification between the actors and their roles benefits the players as well as increasing their risks. Actors rarely suffer from sakit berangin since their performances allow their Winds to blow, and the appreciation of their audiences flatters (*memujuk*) the players' Winds and keeps them content (Ghulam-Sarwar 1976: *passim*).

The Music of Healing

Apart from performances and ceremonial occasions, I never heard my Malay neighbors play any musical instrument and rarely heard them whistle or sing. On one memorable day, the voice of a man reached my ears as I walked by the house where he cantillated his prayers. Although I spent a good deal of time with mothers and their babies, I never heard a lullaby. Music is not part of the school curriculum, but before the day's instruction begins the children sing the National Anthem. None of the children in my son's class appeared to agree on the melody, although they sang together loudly and enthusiastically. We had no idea of the tune its composer had intended until we found it in a book.

But although it is not an everyday occurrence, music is important in the fabric of Malay life. Performances of wayang kulit and *dikir barat* (male group singing taking two forms: praises to Allah, and profane joking songs) cannot be imagined without music. Music accompanies the stylized movements of silat, the Malay martial art. The musical prelude of the Mak Yong not only sets the stage for the performance but also helps the actors prepare themselves psychologically before the play begins.

Music, both vocal and instrumental, is also an integral part of the healing seance. As other students of Malayo-Indonesian culture have indicated (e.g., Errington 1975; Siegel 1979), the mere sound (*bunyi*) of a beautiful voice is considered to produce an effect upon its listeners. The importance of the voice was brought home to me forcefully during the course of a Main Peteri. Several ritual specialists, including a young novice, took turns putting patients into trance. The novice was signally unsuccessful. Clients explained to me later that there was nothing wrong with what he said, the difficulty lay in his unmelodious voice which jarred the ears and prevented the harmonious state of mind and body that allows one to trance. Although, as Errington remarks, ideally sound, meaning, and effect can be thought of as an inseparable whole (the word *bunyi* encompassing the concepts of sound, melody, meaning, content, and purport), in practical terms each aspect can be judged and found satisfying or wanting.

The music of the Main Peteri conducts the participants into the realm of the sacred. Although the tok 'teri seemingly ignores the minduk's introductory song, its sound permeates the air, preparing the ritual partners for their encounters with the supernatural. The minduk's duets with the tok 'teri, both in his own persona and in the personae of other beings, are in the form of a dialogue with musical overlaps that attest to the interactive harmony of their partnership. While the vocal mu shows the relationship between people (or between people and spirits), the instrumental interludes function as transitions into an altered state. They occur as the shaman changes from one persona to the next, when a patient is helped into and out of trance, and at the close of the seance. Often the transition music is "traveling music" (*lagu berjalan*, as it is known in the wayang kulit), played as participants travel from one level of awareness to another.

Much has been written about the power of music, particularly rhythmic percussive sound, to induce trance (e.g., Needham 1967; Neher 1962; Lex 1979), but it seems clear that, by itself, music cannot alter the consciousness of those who are neither sensitized to it nor expectant of its results (Rouget 1980; Blacking 1985; Roseman 1988). The audience at a seance hears the same sounds as the shaman and his patient, but rarely does anyone go into trance who is not meant to do so. Very infrequently, a member of the audience may react to the music. I witnessed this only twice in the many dozens of times I attended a seance. On each occasion, an unmarried young woman unexpectedly achieved trance. One was the divorced older sister of Mat Daud's young patient. When he sang, "What's the use of wearing pants? Get up and dance!" his patient only shivered "like a bird in the rain," but her sister rose to dance with the handsome shaman. The other accidental trancer was a young woman who had had an abortive affair with the apprentice shaman who was assisting at the night's seance. People commented later that her emotions had overflowed at the sight of him, but since his wife was also present, the young woman had no way to express her feelings other than to thrash about in violent trance. Some people who are particularly sensitive to certain kinds of musical cues, such as Sapiah, who was *berangin* to perform in the Mak Yong, avoid attending Main Peteri for fear of losing control.[4]

The choice of music used in the seance rests, to a large extent, with individual performers and their troupes. In some troupes (e.g., the one that treated Toki Latip; see chapter 6), the roles are, to some extent, interchangeable in the manner of a Javanese gamelan. Performers take

4. Sapiah was so strongly berangin for the Mak Yong that, although she loved to hear the music on my tape recorder, she could not bear to listen to it for more than a few moments for fear of going into trance.

turns acting as minduk and tok 'teri and playing various instruments. In other troupes (see chapters 7 and 8), the roles are constant.

Mat Daud bin Panjak begins the seance with Lagu Kijang Mas Tuah (Lucky Golden Barking-Deer Tune). He uses Lagu Pandan Wangi (Aromatic Pandanus Tune) to move the shaman's Wind, Lagu Pak Yong Muda (the tune of the hero of the Mak Yong) to send praises to his Grandsire, and Lagu Sedayung (Oar or Boat Pole Tune) to call his penggawa. He does the divination to the tune of Lagu Wak Tanda Raja (Tune of the Old Man With Tokens of Royalty), and puts his patient into trance with Lagu Mengambul (Swinging Back and Forth; Submerging and Emerging Tune). If it is necessary to evoke the Wind of the Weretiger (Angin Hala), he plays Lagu Kecubung (Datura Tune). The seance ends with Lagu Mengulit (Lullaby).

Many of these tunes are also used in the Mak Yong, where they perform different but related functions. Lagu Kijang Mas is traveling music for characters in the Mak Yong who are going from one location to another. In the Main Peteri, it accompanies travel from everyday life to a sacred space. In the Mak Yong, Lagu Pandan Wangi is played during scenes of lamentation. In the seance it is used to heighten the emotions of the shaman—to move his Wind. Lagu Pak Yong Muda is the tune that introduces the hero of the Mak Yong, a royal personage, full of *sakti* (magical power, like mana). The same tune accompanies the shaman's praises to the Grandsire, an even more powerful being. Lagu Sedayung, played in the Mak Yong during magical situations, is used by the shaman to call his spirit familiars. Lagu Mengambul, in the Mak Yong, accompanies the transmission of messages. In the Main Peteri, that music sends a message to the patient's inner core, enabling him to trance. Lagu Mengulit, played during gentle and delicate moments in the Mak Yong, ends the seance by soothing the Winds that have blown that night, setting spirit and mortal at ease.

The troupe of players who came from Kelantan to heal a sick puppet master (chapter 6) were themselves performers in the shadow play as well as in the Main Peteri. The music they used in the seance, with few exceptions, were familiar tunes of the wayang kulit and Mak Yong, often slightly adapted to fit the changed circumstances and modified band. The first duet, sung to the tune of Sedayung Cepat, sets the stage in much the same manner that this tune sets the stage in performances of Mak Yong, situating the participants in relation to the earth, village, fields, and jungle, sending greetings to the Grandsire and asking for blessings on the night's proceedings. The transition music they played to assist the shaman in achieving trance was Barat Cepat, used in both the shadow play and the Mak Yong to accompany fast scene changes. During the shaman's trance the music intensified: the rebab played two repeated notes, the gong cycles (*gongan*) became shorter, the reiterative patterns less varied. Everything funneled down as the shaman took on a new persona. After the first transition, the eight-beat cycle expanded to sixteen beats as the music changed to Seri Rama Berjalan (Rama walking), a tune that accompanies the movement of refined characters in the shadow play. The action had moved to the realm of Semar, the holy clown whose humble, ugly aspect conceals his godhood. The first persona to appear, Little Prince Flower Play of Times Past (a personification of the performers' Wind) sang a duet with the minduk to the music of Sedayung Mak Yong, a tune of magical power (sakti), used again when the shaman invoked his patient's Inner Winds. Lagu Bertabuh (Beating Tune), used to set the stage on the second and subsequent nights of a Mak Yong performance, introduced the second shaman who replaced the initial tok 'teri. While Latip, in trance, fought the shaman, the band played Gendang Silat, the music that traditionally accompanies the performance of the martial art. Lagu Pak Dogol was heard while the dalang, once more in trance, manipulated the Pak Dogol puppet. Sedayung Pak Yong, the signature tune of the most important and powerful character of the dance-drama, was reserved for the divination and the invocation of the Heavenly Midwives. Lagu Berkhabar (Giving News Tune) was sung by the tok 'teri in the persona of Princess Zohor, who told of the abduction of her sister, the patient's semangat. It occurred again at the close of the ceremony, when the minduk and tok 'teri informed their audience that everything was returned to its proper place and "the waves have been put to rest by the strings of the Winds."

The music of the Main Peteri punctuates and reinforces the words and action of the drama, and helps to shape its form by means of rhythm, tonal range, and pitch center.[5] Songs start with a compressed

5. I owe the information on the technical aspects of the music of the Main Peteri to Marina Roseman who, at my request, transcribed and analyzed the music and collaborated with me in its interpretation. Patricia Matusky's extensive knowledge of east coast

tonal range, and then widen in range as the section repeats, pressing the limits with stresses, ornamentations, and elaborations much like the process of elaborated repetitions found in the European Baroque tradition. During the course of the ceremony, the tendencies found in individual songs are replicated in the overall shape of the seance, as the pitch center rises, the rhythms intensify, then finally ease down. The rhythm often identifies the genre, such as Lagu Berjalan (traveling music), while the melody points to specifics (e.g., which character is traveling).

In "Breaking Contracts with the Spirit World" (chapter 8), the music of the minduk's introductory song is repeated four times during the course of the night: when the minduk sings the Bestirring Song that moves the shaman's Wind; when he sings a duet with Awang Mindung Pengasuh (a benevolent character in the story of Dewa Muda); with Pak Deh (Pak Dogol, one of the tok 'teri's penggawa); and with the shaman in his own persona—always during scenes that are unthreatening in themselves or ease the tension of a preceding scene. The quarter-note pulse of the music is interrupted by rests and marked by syncopation, reducing the driving quality exemplified by the constant repeated rhythmic figures found in the instrumental transition music.[6] The melody of the minduk's introductory song, in this seance, begins at a tonal center of D, with a low point of B and a high point of F and progresses to an ambitus or tonal range with a low point of B flat and a high point around G as the song increases in intensity and melodic elaboration.

The song of Mek Bunga (Miss Flower) is set to old-fashioned dance music, used in the Mak Yong and wayang kulit for the hokey dances of comic characters. Its tonal center is raised approximately a whole step higher than that of the preceding music (centering between D♯ and E,[7]

Malay music, particularly in relation to the shadow play, which she kindly shared with me, was invaluable.

6. Rouget (1985) lists acceleration, stresses (sforzandi), and syncopation as musical traits generally associated with trance. Syncopation in particular is supposed to disorient the hearer, who expects to hear a regular beat and loses his place or step when the expected beat is missed. As Rouget stresses, however, the music of trance can take many forms, depending upon cultural expectations. His thesis is supported by the lack of syncopation that characterizes Malay shamanistic transition music.

7. The tonal center in this song rose from closer to D♯ in the beginning, to closer to E. The tones can only be approximated, using the standard Western notational system for

with a low point of C♯ and a high of F), as befits a high and girlish voice.

The plaintive song of the sea spirit, who cries as he sings, "He wants to get rid of me," is repeated later by Nenek Betara Guru, who sobs, "Mat Din really wants to abandon me." The tonal center, which had dropped after Mek Bunga's song, rises again to F when the sea spirit sings, both accompanying and contributing to a rise in emotional intensity, a technique well known to musicians of many cultures. The rhythms of the preceding music change here to a continuous and driving sixteenth-note drum beat, without the syncopation that marks the permutations of the minduk's introductory song. Increasing the intensity of the beat in relation to the other music of the seance, and keeping it constant, intensifies the message of the words and melody. The extent to which language is transformed by music constitutes the ritual reframing of reality through sound (Basso 1984; Roseman 1986). Sung music expands the parameters of speech, but the spirits' sobbing goes beyond both spoken language and music.[8]

The instrumental music that accompanies the shaman's trance not only marks a transition to a new persona; it is also a transition from sung speech to the shaman's inarticulate cries of "Eiii, aiii" as he goes from the solidity of one persona into wordless chaos before the shift to a new persona is complete. The transition takes place as the oscillating two-note figure in the lowest part of the tonal range accelerates and comes to a crescendo.

The seance ends with a new tune as the minduk and the shaman, in the persona of King Potent Cure, sing a lovely duet whose slower tempo and narrowed pitch range prepare us to leave ritual time and space. The syncopation, and the play of three beats against two, are more marked here than in any of the other songs. The tonal center has returned to D from its high point of E, attained by the sobbing spirit, and the rhythm once again moves in stately quarter-note beats, rather than the driving sixteenth-note beat of the song of the forsaken spirit. Each beat of King

---

music. My use of the terms, "quarter-note, eighth-note, sixteenth-note" also refers to Western notational conventions, rather than Malay traditions.

8. As Frith (1981:35) remarks, in connection with American popular songs, it is the inarticulate, rather than the articulate, that carries the greatest intensity of feeling. People measure the depth of their emotions by their very inability to find words to express them.

Potent Cure's song has a longer duration than the beat in any music that has come before. The seance has slowed down and soon all will be at rest.

Movement in the Main Peteri

Even more than music, dance in rural Malaysia is usually the province of professionals and ritual specialists. Although I attended many weddings, circumcision parties, and celebrations of all kinds, the only dancing I observed was on public ceremonial occasions, such as the birthday celebration of the Sultan of Trengganu in the state capital, Kuala Trengganu, where there were performances of Mak Yong, *Menora* (a Thai-influenced musical drama), and *rodat* (danced by a line of young men chanting in Arabic, to the accompaniment of tambourine-drums played by older men, often including a teacher of Koran).

In the village, I witnessed one performance of silat, the Malay martial art that incorporates many dancelike movements, held by the village men as a special treat for me shortly before I left for home. Every year, professional players and dancers were invited to perform at the three-day annual *Main Pantai* (festivities at the seashore). Actresses from the Mak Yong troupe took turns performing as *joget* girls, dancing alongside daring young village men. The dancers never touched one another, but the experience of men and women moving their bodies to music, facing one another, was considered terribly exciting and verging on the scandalous (particularly in the case of men who were already married). Actresses in the Mak Yong usually dance with slow circling movements, while the male players have more complicated and stylized dances that incorporate steps (*langkah*) and turns (*kirat*) often named after the characters they are meant to portray. Rough or brutal characters move with large, sudden, and violent gestures, while noble characters use smaller and more delicate movements. The hand gestures of the Mak Yong, such as the fluttering of held-out fingers, denote nobility of character but do not themselves have specific meanings, with the exception of those done in the section called *Menghadap Rebab* (Salutations to the Spike Fiddle).

The Menghadap Rebab is the most elaborate part of the Mak Yong, both in its music and its dance. The ritual serves the dual functions of paying respect to the rebab and its attendant spirits and preparing the actresses spiritually and psychologically for the roles they are about to play. Each arm movement in this section has a meaningful name, such as *tangan sembah guru* (obeisances to the teacher), *tangan susun sirih* (arranging the ingredients of the betel quid), *tangan burung terbang* (flying bird), and *tangan sawah mengorak lingkaran* (rice fields unwinding their curves). The body postures are called *liuk ke kiri, liuk ke kanan* (bend to the left, bend to the right) (Ghulam-Sarwar 1976:131–132).

All three genres, wayang kulit, Mak Yong, and Main Peteri, include many scenes of traveling. The music that accompanies walking movements in the shadow play accounts for fourteen pieces in the musical repertoire (Matusky 1980:181). Mak Yong players take mincing, circling steps as they pretend to travel from one location to another. The same movements, punctuated by head whirling, accompany the shaman's transition to another persona as he rises and dances in trance.

As in the Mak Yong, not all the gestures and movements in the Main Peteri have specific symbolic content. Persona can be identified by their movements and postures, as well as by their voices and speech, as the shaman portrays them with dramatic gestures and expressive characterizations. The truth of his interpretation is vital to the success of his treatment: he is not merely an actor who must convince his audience; he is the embodiment of entities who are present and real. Human beings who ordinarily can only feel the effect of invisible spirits upon their bodies, visualize them in the seance through the efforts of the tok 'teri. Jin arrive with sudden, violent thrusts and crouch threateningly before the minduk. Strong but benevolent characters, such as Hanuman the White Monkey (one of the shaman's spirit familiars), make large, heroic gestures. The gentle penggawa, Mek Bunga, announces her arrival by feminine, flirtatious wiggles, which Tok Daud compares to sifting rice, winnowing it up and down. Offerings, on other occasions merely left in strategic places for the spirits, are actually eaten by them before the onlookers' eyes. A hantu childishly stuffs his mouth with bananas; the Yellow Genie who guards a mountain top swoops down upon a raw egg and sucks it dry.

The movements made by the shaman as he first goes into trance on any particular night are invariable: he seats himself cross-legged before the minduk. Toward the middle of the Bestirring Song, after the shaman has begun his incantation, a tremor starts in one foot, going up through his leg and torso until it reaches his head, which begins to shake and whirl faster and faster until trance is achieved, indicated by the cessation of shaking as the shaman claps his palms together overhead. The tok 'teri's initial head-shaking marks the division between his ordinary actions and the shamanic behavior that his minduk and the audience have now been signaled to expect during the rest of the night's work. Successive trances are faster and less strenuous, often requiring only a few moments of head-shaking for one spirit to exit and another to take its place. The seance ends with a final series of head-whirlings and shakings, marking the transition of the shaman back into everyday life. When the music has ceased and his head has stopped shaking, the tok 'teri wipes his face, stretches, and speaks once more in his own voice. The drama has come to an end as decisively as though a curtain had fallen.

Spoken dialogues are always done in a seated position; duets may be sung either while the ritual pair is seated or while the shaman dances (the minduk never leaves his seat). The shaman's dance is slow and stately, with small circling steps in the manner of Mak Yong actresses. His dance, like theirs, is marked by bending to the left, swaying to the right (*liuk ke kiri, longlai ke kanan*), like the dance in Menghadap Rebab. His bending, swaying body, like a branch waving in the breeze, attests to the blowing of his Inner Winds, stirred into life by the minduk's song.

The shaman's gestures communicate their meaning to his spirit audience as well as to the mortal onlookers. When he points his hand, palm facing inward, to the sky, it bids the spirits to stay calm. An arm outstretched and bent at the elbow, palm outward and fingers lightly raised, asks for protection and favor from the Original Teacher (*guru asal*). When the dancing shaman closes his fist with the thumb outside and brings it up to his mouth or to his temple, he is recalling his magical knowledge (*ingat ilmu*). He joins the little fingers of both hands and lifts them slowly from chest height to his chin as he mentally recites a spell (*baca ilmu*). Lowering one arm behind him, hand brought back and palm up, and the other arm elevated obliquely, palm down, sends a call to his penggawa. Extending his arms horizontally, the hand of one arm pointing down and the other up, or raising one hand with the fingers bent, the other hand flat on his knee, announces the approach of a spirit. Raising a hand with the index finger extended and the other fingers folded salutes the spirits and asks them to accept his apology (usually on behalf of a patient).[9]

From time to time, the tok 'teri dips his hand into the water, to which perfume or sweet-smelling flowers have been added, and rubs it on his face and neck to cleanse himself of the spirits' hot vapor. The more powerful spirits, such as the Hantu Raya or the jin, manifest themselves in the form of a virulent heat that is particularly oppressive to the shaman's face. When the tok 'teri dances before his patient in the persona of a spirit who has agreed to be helpful, he often takes hold of the patient's head or shoulders, sometimes violently, pulling the oppressive vapor from the patient's body into his own hands. He then claps them together, forcing the vapor to escape into the air and dissipate.

The patient's trance in the Main Peteri, unlike those described by Kapferer (1983) for Sri Lanka and Epton (1966) for dervishes, does not develop out of the dance, but precedes it. The patient's trance neither marks a transformation into a demonic self, as in Sri Lanka, nor brings the trancer divine intoxication, as it does for whirling dervishes. The Malay patient's trance transforms him by opening the gates to his inner self. His Winds show their mighty nature in his vigorous head-whirling at the height of trance, and their gentle strength as he dances, bending and swaying to their inner breeze. The patient's dance is usually a pas de deux with the tok 'teri, as when Mek Gemuk danced the role of a Mak Yong actress with Pak Long Awang, or when Toki Latip performed the dancelike movements of silat with Tok Mamat. Occasionally, a member of the audience, having achieved trance, electrifies the audience with uncontrolled violent movements, or joins the shaman in a sedate dance. On one occasion, the participation of an onlooker made the difference between a partial cure and a successful treatment. Mat Daud bin Panjak had been trying to get his patient to rise and dance, entranced, for three nights, but she only sat "shivering like a bird in the rain," while her sister (who was not a patient) danced with the shaman.

9. I showed the photographs reproduced in Cuisinier's book (1936) to several Malay shamans, and they agreed that her interpretations of the meaning of the gestures in the seance were correct.

On the third night, an old friend of the family arrived: a famous Mak Yong actress who sprang up when she saw the shaman's unsuccessful struggle and pulled the entranced young girl to her feet. To the tune of Lagu Mengambul they danced—the shaman, the actress, the young patient, and her older sister—until the patient's Wind was refreshed in spite of herself, and her cure was complete.

PLATES

(Left to right) Carol Laderman, Pak Long Awang (the shaman), and Yusof bin Hassan (the author's field assistant).

Pak Long, in trance, engages in a dialogue with Pak Daud, his *minduk*.

A shaman recites a protective spell as he prepares to achieve trance.

A candlelight divination.

A divination using popped rice.

Mek Gemuk rises from her mat in trance.

Mek Gemuk, in trance, dances the part of a Mak Yong princess with Pak Long.

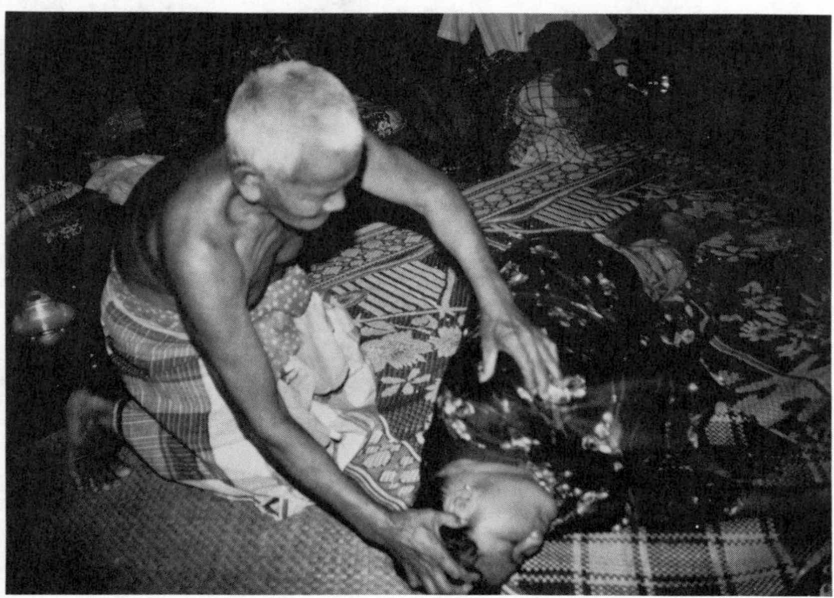

Her trance over, Mek Gemuk falls to the floor. Pak Long assists her in regaining normal consciousness.

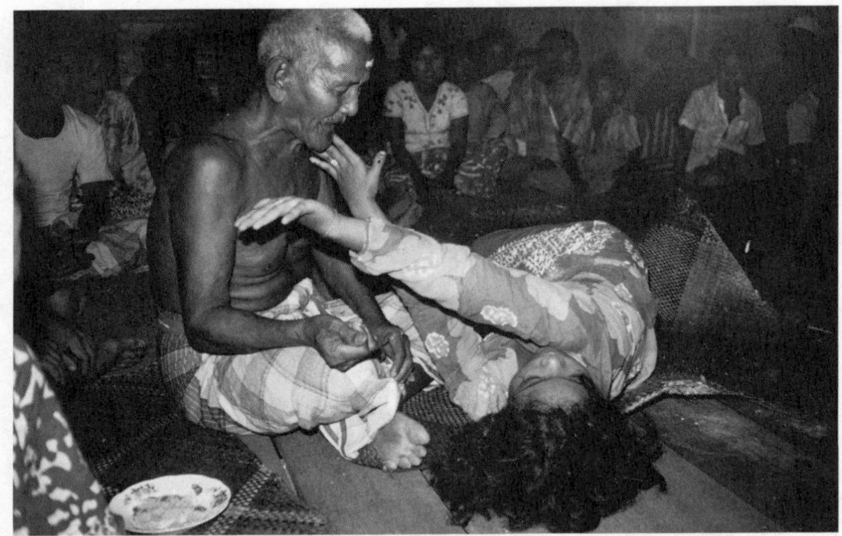

A member of the audience, her emotions overflowing at the sight of her illicit lover, has gone into trance. Pak Long recites a calming spell and prepares to throw protective rice.

Pak Long instructs a student in his school for shamans.

An apprentice shaman attempts to move a patient's Wind, but his ugly voice does not allow her to achieve trance.

Raja Ngah dances behind Toki Latip. The people in the back and on the sidelines are members of the audience.

Toki Latip, in trance, fights *silat*-style with Tok Mamat.

Toki Latip's trance gives the sickly old man enough strength to worry the hefty shaman, as they perform *silat*.

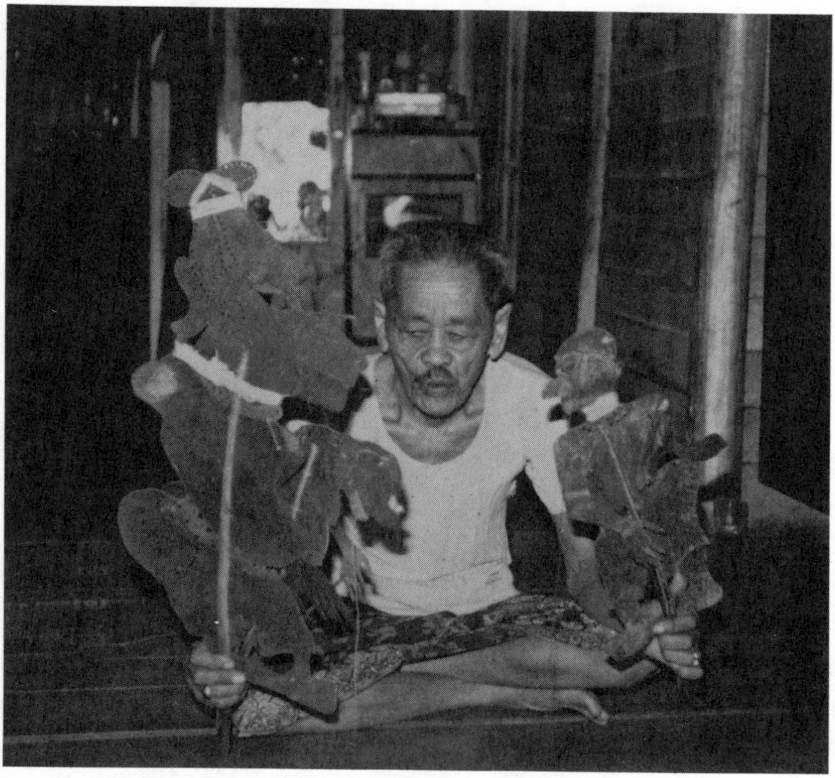

Toki Latip, in trance, manipulates his shadow puppets.

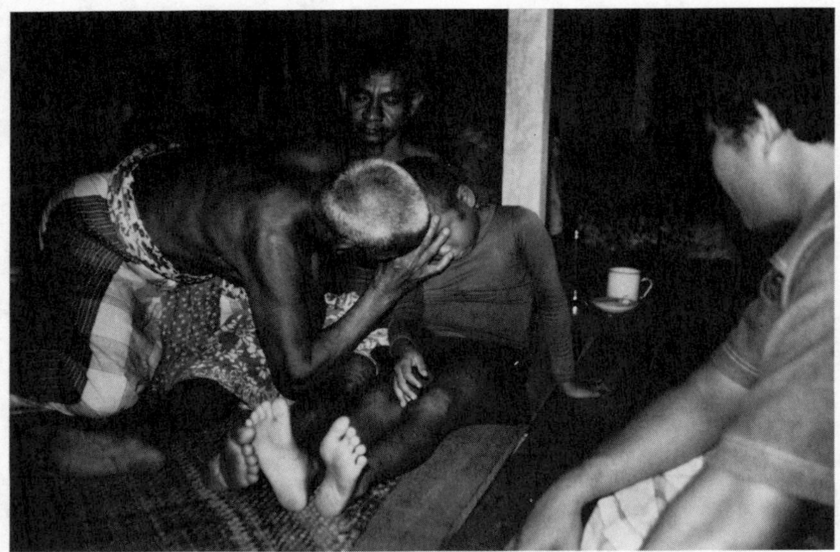

Pak Long, in the persona of a spirit, grabs the head of Mat Din's son in an effort to remove evil influences.

Offerings for a spirit farm—animals, people, sea creatures, and kitchen utensils—made of rice flour and water by Pak Long.

At the close of the ceremony, Pak Long places a spot of *tepung tawar* (neutralizing rice paste) on the foreheads of his troupe to protect them against the airy heat of the spirits.

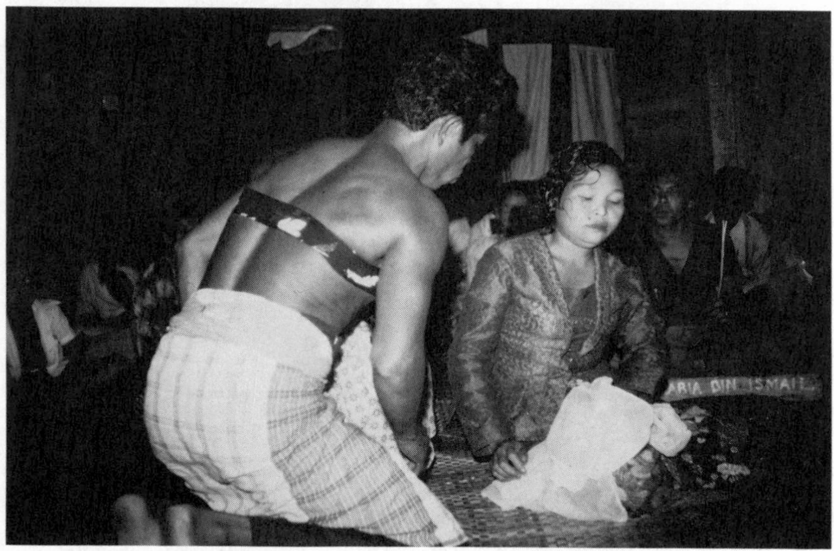

Pak Daud bin Mat treats the sister of his patient, who unexpectedly left her place in the audience and went into trance.

The shaman and his patient's sister are joined by a famous Mak Yong actress. Together they induced the ailing younger sister, already in trance (not shown here) to join them in a healing dance that completed her cure.

Pak Long releases the author, her son, husband, and field assistant from spiritual dangers.

PART II

Ritual Dramas of Healing

Part II consists of transcriptions of three seances taped during their performance and translated by the author. Each of these ritual dramas is preceded by an explanation of the circumstances surrounding its occurrence and a summary of the action. The primary aim of the first seance, which I have called "A Stifled Talent," was to relieve the suffering caused by frustration of a puppet master's creative impulses (Inner Winds). The second seance ("Seance for a Sick Shaman") combined the exorcism of unsatisfied spirits with the strengthening of the shaman-patient's Winds. The third ("Breaking Contracts with the Spirit World") was held solely to exorcise spirits who were tormenting the neighborhood, and did not involve the Inner Winds.

The interpretations found in the annotations that accompany these transcriptions, unless specified by the author's initials in brackets, by citations, or otherwise made clear by their context, are those of ritual practitioners commenting on their own speech.

Italicized material within brackets in the body of the texts are comments by the author, intended to provide the reader with clues as to the action of the dramas.

6

A Stifled Talent

Pak Latip (or Toki ["Grandpa"] Latip, as he was known in the village) had been a famous dalang of the shadow play, a profession requiring stamina, memory, and creativity. A dalang manipulates and provides the voices for all the puppets in performances lasting three, and sometimes many more, hours. As old age approached and his faculties began to wane, Toki Latip decided to retire from the shadow play and stay home, assisting his wife in her little food and sundries shop. Soon after retiring, however, he was afflicted with severe asthma. He grew thin, sallow, and weak. His health declined to the point where, for three years before I came to live in the village, he was housebound, unable even to walk around the kampung. He had tried to treat his asthma in the past, both by incantations and herbal remedies, and by medicine which he had received at a clinic in Kota Baru, the capital of Kelantan. He was particularly enthusiastic about the clinic's medicine, praising it for making him look healthy and making his face plumper. Before I left for a visit to Kota Baru, Toki Latip asked me to get a refill on his prescription. (It was understood that I would pay for it, since he had taught me several incantations and was giving my son lessons on the rebab.) The doctor refused to refill the prescription without seeing the patient, since it turned out to be cortisone, a potentially dangerous steroid given to asthma patients under close medical supervision. Cortisone frequently has the side effect of producing a "moon face" in the user, which Toki Latip had mistaken for a sign of health.

When I returned without the cortisone, Toki Latip was disappointed but he did not despair. There was still a path back to health that he had not yet taken. Alexander Alland, Jr., my dissertation advisor from Columbia University, had come to Merchang with his wife, Sonia, for a short visit. He had brought a movie camera and was particularly interested in filming Main Peteri. The showman in Toki Latip was aroused at the prospect of appearing in a film. He agreed to play the hanging gong at a seance held for Pak Su Weng, a sick bomoh who was being treated by Pak Long Awang and Tok Daud, on the understanding that I would drive him there and back, since he was too weak to walk the few hundred yards to Pak Long's house, where the seance was to be held. The evening's entertainment refreshed Toki Latip, who said that he hadn't felt so well since he gave up the puppet stage. He refused to be treated, however, by any of the local shamans. His was a hard case, he believed, amenable only to treatment by famous specialists. The only ones who could help him were Mamat bin Damit, Raja Ngah bin Raja Kecil, and Raja Hussein bin Tuan Bongsu, renowned Kelantanese bomoh. Despite their regal titles, the latter two receive the bulk of their income from farming and the selling of chickens at the local market. Many Malays use a title, such as raja or tengku, before their names; they are often mere honorifics that do not confer any political power on their possessors.

They were all active and respected participants in the wayang kulit as well as in the Main Peteri, and would therefore be *sesuai* (in harmony) with Latip, a prime consideration, since Malays believe that unless the patient and healer are in harmony, no amount of expertise will effect a satisfactory cure.

Latip had not called on their services before, since the expense of transporting the team, over the above the usual expenses of the Main Peteri, seemed to him prohibitive. He was unusually careful with his money, even when it came to his health (his wife characterized him as "stingy"). He was very enthusiastic, however, in his acceptance of Alex Alland's offer to underwrite the expenses (which came to M$125, the better part of a month's income for most of the families in Merchang). I sent my field assistant, Yusof bin Hassan, in my car, to bring the team and their paraphernalia to Merchang. It must have been a tight fit, since Tok Mamat made a point of complaining about the transportation during that night's seance.

On the night of the Main Peteri, a crowd of well over a hundred people gathered, some finding room on the floor inside the shop-house and others thronging outside. Toki Latip's neighbors had removed the wooden boards and door at the front of his shop-house, opening it up like a stage and ensuring that the audience would have a good view.

The company included the three famous bomoh from Kelantan, who took turns being tok 'teri, tok minduk, and instrumentalist: Tok Mamat, a strong, heavyset man in his late forties, who had previously been in the police force; Raja Ngah, slender, elegant, with a shock of wavy white hair; and Raja Hussein, somewhat younger, compact and muscular, whose black hair had not yet begun to grow gray. They were assisted by musicians who played on two hanging gongs (*tetawak*), two floor gongs (*canang*), two double-headed horizontal drums (*gendang*), a Malay oboe (serunai), and a three-stringed spike-fiddle (rebab). Although Toki Latip was pale and drawn, coughed frequently, and breathed with difficulty, he was encouraged to play the gendang and canang during the first half hour or so of the Main. Patients' performances are ordinarily limited to the times during the seance when they are in trance, but in Latip's case the opportunity to perform the kind of music that had been an intimate part of his life when he was a dalang was part of the therapeutic process—it refreshed his angin, so long denied.

After eating a festive meal cooked for the performers by Latip's wife, Tok Mamat placed the dish containing the *nasi guru* (an offering for the bomoh's familiar spirits, consisting of a betel quid, raw rice, cooked rice, a few coins, and a hard-boiled egg with the top removed) in a palm-leaf holder and hung it from the rafters. Dishes containing raw rice mixed with little pieces of turmeric, popped rice (*bertih*), perfumed water, and benzoin (*kemenyan*) were placed atop the woven pandanus mats spread on the floor along the far side of the house. A pillow, covered with Latip's most beautiful batik pillow case, was placed behind the dishes. Raja Ngah lit the kemenyan and censed himself and his rebab. He passed the incense dish to Tok Mamat, who censed himself and passed it on to Raja Hussein; before the performance began all the performers and their instruments had been censed, and short protective spells had been recited over them.

The performance began with a long incantation recited by Tok Mamat. While he spoke, people kept arriving and greeting their friends. I had never seen such a large crowd at a Main Peteri held by local bomoh. Most of the audience had not been present at any of the previous seances I had attended. The atmosphere reminded me of Mak Yong and wayang kulit performances held during the Main Pantai, a yearly celebration featuring visiting performers from Kelantan, widely attended by Merchang villagers. During Tok Mamat's invocation, the audience spoke in low tones and their conversations were brief, since everyone wanted to hear the famous visitors.

The musicians arranged their instruments along the far side of the room. Tok Mamat seated himself near them, sitting cross-legged on a mat. His incantation started with a request to Allah for protection and an invocation of the angels, prophets, and holy men of Islam, both in Arabic and Malay. The bomoh then proceeded to invoke the denizens of the unseen world in turn: the earth spirits, the spirits of the kampung, the fields, the swamp, the river, the lake, the streams, and the jungle. His jampi was followed by a duet with the minduk (more accurately, a sung conversation with musical overlaps), reiterating much of the import of the spoken incantation. At Tok Mamat's signal, "Ah, chap . . . ," the band began to play the music that assists the shaman in his transition to an altered state. The music grew faster and louder as the shaman's limbs began to twitch. The movement was carried through his body until his head was shaking violently and he had achieved trance. The band stopped playing and a dialogue between the tok 'teri and the minduk followed. This procedure was followed between each visitation, in an abbreviated form. The music of transition accompanied the exit of each spirit as the shaman achieved trance and took on a new persona.

The first persona to speak (and sing) through the agency of the shaman was Radin Kecil Dahulu Permainan Bunga (Little Prince Flower Play of Times Past), a protective inner force of the performers and a personification of their Inner Wind. After a brief visitation from a spirit who claimed to be a descendant of Persanta (one of the manifestations of the entity who also appears in the shadow play as Pak Dogol and Sang Yang—or Si Alam—Tunggal), Persanta himself arrived, also briefly, followed by Wak Kedi Bomoh (The Old Bomoh from the Siamese Monastery), who presided over a divination. Three handfuls of popped rice were placed on a pillow. Each pile was counted out in pairs of grains: earth, air, fire, and water. The count ended on fire, air, and earth. Latip's sickness was diagnosed as due to the fierce fire of someone's wrath; an attack by the earth spirits; and a problem with his Inner Winds. Since retiring from the puppet stage, his performer's Wind was no longer being expressed. Furthermore, the spirits of his puppets were furious at the cavalier way he had forsaken them, selling nearly all of them and neglecting to hold the requisite ritual to prepare them for this change. The precipitating cause of Latip's problem was that he was startled and fell, breaching his body's "gates" and leaving him open to spirit attacks. There was also a suggestion (the allusion to the bidandari, or Celestial Midwives) that his envious birth-brother (the placenta) was adding to his problems.

A number of earth spirits appeared and agreed to restore Latip's health in return for offerings. After the visitation of Hulubalang Babi Garang (Captain Fierce Pig), Tok Mamat complained about how crowded it was in my car during his trip from Kelantan, how uncomfortable his false teeth felt, and how it was about time for another bomoh to take his place as tok 'teri and let him have a rest.

The second tok 'teri, Raja Ngah, after reciting his protective jampi and singing a duet with the minduk, assumed the persona of Tuan Kecil Radin Bertimbang Gambar (Dear Little Prince of "Pictures," i.e., shadow puppets), who related the tale of how he had been lost and how he discovered the identity of his true father (a story line reminiscent of Dewa Muda in the Mak Yong). The next persona to arrive was Wak Long, one of the major comic characters of the wayang kulit; a clown-god whom Pak Dogol made from his own body dirt to be his companion. Wak Long complained about the unceremonious treatment he and his fellow puppets received at Latip's hands when he retired and revealed that he and his offended companions had contributed to Latip's illness. Persanta (a manifestation of Pak Dogol) in particular had been making him ill. Latip had not sold the Pak Dogol and Wak Long puppets when he sold the others, but kept them wrapped up in his bedroom. According to the various bomoh and dalang I spoke to later, the physical presence of these puppets, since they were not being employed in the shadow play and were not receiving regular offerings, was highly dangerous.

A second divination implicated Latip's birth-brother (the afterbirth

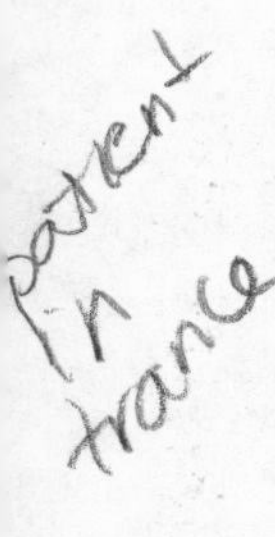

that emerged when he did) as a cause of his illness. The ritual pair agreed that it was time to invoke Latip's Winds, to put him into trance and allow him to express his pent-up emotions. Angin Cik Salim Pendekar, the Wind of the silat master, was invoked. Latip entered trance to the tune of Gendang Silat, the music that traditionally accompanies silat exhibitions, and fought with Tok Mamat. After leaving the trance state, Latip sat down again on the mat in front of the ritual pair. The tok 'teri assumed the persona of a member of the ghostly family of Sang Kala. He said that certain claims must be met in return for Latip's release from illness.

The next persona was that of a spirit who pretended to be a pious Muslim, calling himself Wak Haji Putih Kopiah Lembek (The Old White Pilgrim with the Soft Cap, a crocheted white cap that Muslim men wear). He was really the Hantu Raya (Mighty Spirit), the most feared of all hantu on the east coast. His true identity was revealed when he showed his ignorance of Islamic daily prayer and when he mentioned Daeng Dalit, known to be the Hantu Raya's father. The spirit demanded offerings, including a white chicken and some banners. Latip agreed, and asked when his health would be restored and what sign he could expect to receive as a harbinger of the end of his sickness. The spirit said that in seven days Latip would be able to run down to the seaside (about a half mile from his house). He warned Latip that if he went back on his word and didn't produce the promised offerings, he would come back to seek revenge. Latip warned the spirit, in turn, that should he give offerings and still remain ill, he would take his offerings back.

The Hantu Raya left, after shaking hands on the bargain with Latip, and was replaced by Anak Kera Gantih (Hanuman the White Monkey as a child), a spirit familiar (penggawa) of the tok 'teri. He asked whether they would like to exchange Latip's "asthma fruit" for something else. He advised calling on Cik Amat (another of the tok 'teri's familiar spirits). He was succeeded by Princess Zohor, who spoke of her vanished sister, Princess Flower (the patient's semangat). She asked for the help of the Heavenly Midwives. Another penggawa, Awang Malas Mati (Awang Loathe to Die), suggested that they invoke more of Latip's Winds. The minduk commented that the Tiger Wind (Angin Hala) had not yet appeared. They sang of the "birth-brother" and his unhappiness at the unequal treatment accorded him by his parents (Latip's mother and father). "Your father doesn't love you, your mother doesn't cherish you," sang the minduk. "The sky is your roof, the earth is your pillow," alluding to the burial of the placenta in a coconut shell coffin.

The ritual practitioners attempted to invoke the Tiger Wind but it did not appear since it was not intrinsic to Latip's personality. They then put Latip once more into trance. He performed silat in trance and almost succeeded in throwing Tok Mamat (almost twice Latip's weight) to the floor. After Latip emerged from trance, they called upon Persanta to descend and allow Latip to perform once more as a dalang. As the band played music appropriate to the wayang kulit, Latip once more achieved trance. The minduk handed the puppets of Pak Dogol and Wak Long to Latip, who manipulated them with grace and assurance.

The Main Peteri ended with all the forces that had been invoked put to rest and returned to their origins. The minduk sang, "The waves have been put to rest by the strings of the Winds"—the unexpressed emotions, the Winds of Desire that had festered in Latip's breast, had been tamed by the music of the Main Peteri.

When the ceremony was over, Latip's condition was visibly improved. His color was better, his wheezing had stopped, and he was able to breathe normally. His Winds were once more blowing freely within his breast. Seven days later, I saw him bicycling down to the seashore.

In the transcription of the seance that follows, tok 'teri is abbreviated as *T* and minduk is abbreviated as *M*. The first tok 'teri was Tok Mamat; the first minduk was Raja Ngah. After the visitation of the spirit pig, Hulubalang Babi Garang, Tok Mamat left his role as tok 'teri and Raja Ngah took his place. Raja Hussein assumed the part of chief minduk (*M*) at this point, and Tok Mamat occasionally acted as auxilliary minduk (*M2*).

A STIFLED TALENT

Shaman's Incantation

[Recited loudly and rapidly by Tok Mamat as the musicians tuned up and latecomers to the audience arrived and greeted their neighbors.

By the end of the incantation, the audience has settled down and listens in a silence unusual for Main Peteri, occasionally interrupted by conversations in lowered voices. The shaman's appeals to Allah, Muhammad, and the holy people of Islam, and his incorporation of Arabic prayer is typical of Malay magic, which synthesizes Islam with echoes of Malaya's Hindu past (dewa, and wayang kulit characters derived from the Hindu epic, the Ramayana), and invocations of nature spirits.]

TOK 'TERI: The drummers are seven, the fiddlers are five.[1] Let no one double obstructions. Let no one cover and oppress. Let no one set traps and snares upon this verandah, within this palace.[2] Oh Allah, oh Allah, oh God, oh God, oh my Creator. I ask that my incantations and holy words be launched with safety, with powerful magic and pious chants. I ask to stand together with the myriads of shaikhs, holy men of high degree, so that I may be a physician. Adam asks to open the proceedings.[3]

(I take refuge in Allah from Satan the Stoned One, in the name of Allah the Loving and Merciful. In the name of Allah who is everlasting, mighty and knowing.)[4] Allah is powerful, Muhammad Ahmad is blessed, the followers of the Prophet Muhammad are blessed in the name of Allah, in His mercy. Muhammad appeals to the Four Shaikhs, the Seven Saints. I ask that it may come to pass. I ask that my healing be effective and my prayers fulfilled with the blessings of Al-Fatihah.[5] (I

1. The seven drummers are the seven body parts (*tujuh anggota*): the chest, the shoulders and arms, the forehead, the stomach, the thighs, the legs and feet, the ears and head; the five fiddlers are the five senses and the five obligatory Islamic daily prayers. Sweeney (personal communication) says that this is a common formula for the wayang orchestra. (See Cuisinier 1936:20–26; Gimlette 1971 [1915]; and Winstedt 1922 for other interpretations of the numbers five and seven in Malay symbolism.)

2. The Main Peteri abounds in royal allusions. The palace refers both to the house in which the ceremony is taking place, and to the human body, the palace of the soul. The porches of the palace are often metaphors for body parts; the throne room is the mat on which the patient sits. The patient's illness is often compared to a civil war, relating metaphorically the disharmony considered to be the cause of disease in the human body to disharmony in the body politic (see also Kessler 1977; Laderman 1981).

3. The ritual practitioners of the Main Peteri often refer to themselves as "Adam" (in the sense of humanity versus the unseen spirits, as when they say that the spirits "borrow the voice of Adam" during the ceremony), and call themselves and their patients "Adam's grandchildren" (*cucu* Adam).

4. Words within parentheses originally spoken in Arabic.

5. Al-Fatihah is the first chapter of the Koran.

take refuge in Allah from Satan the Stoned One. A revelation warns us all, as our fathers were warned, that we must understand there is no God but Allah, the straight path,)[6] while we appeal to our eternal and majestic Prophet, and to Grandsire Haji Ajar, the sage, Wak Pusat and Wak Semar, no ordinary image, that image named Semar Kala the Eldest Brother.[7] Hey Semar Toten[8] of the black rock, Semar Toten of the red rock, Semar Toten of the fiery moss, Semar Toten Baginda Ali,[9] Semar, the body's companion, you hear "bisik" and I hear "risik",[10] while the Angel Gabriel stands, may peace be with him, Michael, may peace be with him, and Israfel, may peace be with him. I want to invoke peace and to stand alongside the Recording Angels,[11] the seven angels, the Prophets David, Joseph, sixth the Prophet Jesus, seventh the Prophet Moses, eighth the Prophet Muhammad, the caretaker of mankind, of whom I ask for refuge in Allah, to whom I pray with three prayers. The first prayer is for the angels, the second prayer is for the father, the third prayer is for the mother.

I call upon Him, I call upon Him, oh Omar, oh Osman, oh Abu Bakar, oh Recording Angels, oh Night of Power when the triumphant Koran was revealed, to him, Ali Jabar. Oh My Guide, oh Pole Star, oh my soul, oh Sang Beri, Sang Bera, Seh Talut.[12] I want to cast all evil

6. Words within parentheses originally spoken in Arabic.

7. Semar is both servant and eldest brother since, as a character in the shadow play, he is the highest of the gods (in the position of an older brother), who descends to earth, takes on a plebian aspect, and becomes the servant of Rama (see Sweeney 1972).

8. According to Tok Mamat, *toten* is a Javanese word, part of Semar's name. The word is possibly "*tonton*," a show or performance (tonton or nonton wayang = to watch a shadow play; Horne 1974), alluding to Semar's place in the shadow play.

9. Baginda Ali (Ali the Blessed) is the title usually reserved for Muhammad's son-in-law. Here and in the following sentences, Semar, of the Hindu Javenese Panji tales, is being identified with Islam [CL].

10. "*Bisik*" and "*risik*" are ritual utterances.

11. *Kiraman katibin*, the Recording Angels, attend each human being; one records good deeds, the other evil.

12. Ali, Osman, Omar, and Abu Bakar were Companions of the Prophet. The Night of Power (Malay, *lailatul*; Arabic, *lailat al-kadar*) may occur on any night of the latter part of Ramadan. On that night, lucky people who observe portents, such as trees bowing down, can make a wish that is likely to come true. Seh Talut = King Saul. Ali Jabar might once have been Al-Jabar (the constellation Orion), since the name appears in association with the Pole Star, another heavenly guide; in passing down the ritual over the ages, such changes are likely to have occurred and the original meaning to have been forgotten. Rituals are learned by rote, and questions are discouraged as discourteous, leading to

influences out of the body and then stand alone beneath the tree Sumerbadalum.[13] The scribes of Islam are Islam's pious heritage.

The naming is over, Allah's gates are opened by the seven angels of the earth's realm. Allah's earth, the gates of earth, receives a thousand names, a thousand creations, a thousand tricks, a thousand temperaments. Hey, Black Jin of the earth, imp of the earth, Black Thundering Albino of the earth's surface, Black Jin Who Threatens the Earth, Scolding Jin, a black army of jin in the earth, pelesit[14] of the earth, Dalang[15] Swooping Eagle, King of Ogres, Grandsire Sang Bogar, you hold audience where the ground gives rise to a towering anthill.[16] Accept, please, this yellow rice, pancakes, popped rice, a drop of water, a quid of betel.[17] Accept it, one and all, whether small or large, old or young, male or female, I don't mention letters, I don't change names. Each of you accept, one and all.

The tale of the earth's denizens is over, now I go to the edge of the village in the shadow of the orchards to seek audience with Grandsire Sang Gana, king of the village. Hey, Dewa[18] Light, hey, Little Praying Mantis,[19] pelesit who walks by night, small and pampered, small and sly. This is the place of the Black Jin, Pak Leh the Mighty, Black Rhinoceros of the village. If you are descended from kings, accept. Hear what I say, listen to my tale. Please let there be no treachery, injustice,

---

frequent idiosyncratic individual interpretations. I was often told that had I been a Malay seeking to learn incantations, and so forth, my many questions would have been resented and I would have been rejected as a student [CL].

13. Sumerbadalum is the name of a tree in the tale of Dewa Muda, from the Mak Yong.

14. A *pelesit* is a familiar spirit conjured up by women to make them more attractive to men. It can be dangerous, particularly to young children, causing weeping and illness. (See also McHugh 1959:64–73; Skeat 1972[1900]:330–331; Laderman 1983:111.)

15. A *dalang* is the puppet master of the shadow play, who manipulates and provides voices for all the characters. The meaning is often extended in the Main Peteri to mean "someone of power" [CL].

16. A large anthill is considered a prime location for spirit abodes.

17. These are ingredients of many spirit offerings.

18. *Dewa* are the gods who inhabit *Kayangan*, the heaven of the shadow play (in contrast to *syurga*, the Islamic heaven).

19. Budak Kecil Belalang Kacung (Little Praying Mantis) is one of the many names of the Hantu Raya (Mighty Spirit). The Hantu Raya, most feared of all spirits on the east coast, are members of a royal family whose power is great but whose range is limited. Each is rajah of his own territory and does not travel beyond the confines of his parish. (See also McHugh 1959:35–38; Laderman 1983:60, 125.)

envious looks, or attacks on the body of Pak Tip, the person in this house, on this verandah. Jin, don't cause coughing, asthma, gasping for breath, phlegm in the throat, unsteadiness of gait.[20] Listen to my story, listen to my tale, listen while I ask you sweetly and coax you for health. Accept, one and all, yellow rice, pancakes, popped rice, a drop of water, a quid of betel. Hear me, big or small, old or young, even if I don't know the letters to call you by name.

The tale of the village is over, now I emerge in the open fields for an audience with Princess Golden Guava.[21] Hey, Languishing Snail, Shady Tree, Fledgling Bird, Miss Sweet Orange, Miss Herb of the Fields, forces of He Who Chastises as He Passes, Dewa Distant Light, Heavy Ambush, Be and It Was, Then Cut it Down, Commander Dangerous War Due to Evil Influences, Jin Dancing Sunbeam, who levies taxes and demands tribute, a share of rice for the king, rice cooked in coconut milk, the produce of the world. Here, now, each of you, accept and receive yellow rice, pancakes, popped rice, a drop of water, a betel quid. Hey, Jin Omen, who collects fees and offerings, speak to Endeng Mambang,[22] care for Endeng and feed him. Accept my offerings, one and all. Each of you accept, large and small, young and old. I don't change the letters when I speak your names.[23]

The tale of the open fields is over, now I land near the long swamp, the wide river, the lake, the streams. I seek audience now with Sir Persistent Whirlwind, Grandsire Redoubles Himself. Hey! Treacherous One Who Casts His Net, Red-Eyed One with Curling Hair and Balding Tail. Each of you accept and receive yellow rice, pancakes, popped rice, a drop of water, a betel quid. Accept them, one and all.

The tale now is over, where next shall I land? I land in the pristine

20. Pak Tip (Latip, sometimes referred to as Tok Tip, Cik Tip) had been suffering from severe asthmatic attacks for three years previous to this Main Peteri; those are his symptoms.

21. This and the following are names of spirits of the fields.

22. *Mambang* are invisible spirits that can be identified by their works: if one discovers unexplainable bruises on one's body, or is very tired but unable to sleep, it is due to a mambang sucking one's blood. Endeng Mambang is, I was told, the Siamese name of this particular spirit, which is interesting in light of the fact that the name Endeng is also the name of one of the servants of Maharisi Mata Api, a major character in the shadow play who lives in a Siamese temple. See n. 63 [CL].

23. Not "changing the letters" means that the bomoh is being honest and straightforward with the spirits.

jungle and seek audience with Grandsire Yellow Turban, Green Shirt, Red Hat, Commander Keling-keling Bani, Anak Kera Gantih, Anak Kera Beleh, Wak Patih Dalang, Wak Peran Muda, Peran Tua.[24] Each of you accept, one and all, you warriors from the land where the sun sets, from the place where the sun rises, you people from the river's mouth, you sons of the lands upstream.[25]

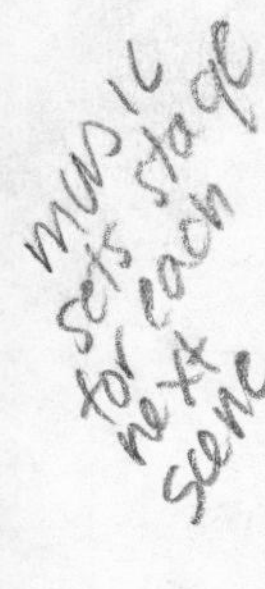

[The audience has become hushed, but is rarely completely silent. Conversations in low tones occasionally occur, particularly during the spoken part of the seance, as people comment on the action. Tok Mamat looks at the crowd with a satisfied air and says, "Ah." The minduk begins to play his rebab. After the shaman exclaims, "Hey, ah" the other instruments join in, playing LAGU BARAT CEPAT, the music of transition. They stop after a few moments. The tok 'teri has not yet changed persona. He and the minduk sing a reprise of the incantation's content, to the tune of LAGU SEDAYUNG CEPAT, the music that sets the stage for the performance to come.]

T: May these proceedings be blessed. We send greetings to our friends.

M: Come and send greetings to our friends, send a greeting to our grandsire.[26]

T: The first greeting goes to the grandsire, the second to the teacher. Seven teachers will become twelve.[27]

24. *Wak* means "uncle," or "old-timer." Peran Hutan is the forest clown in the shadow play who claims to come from a long line (Peran Hutan the Older, Peran Hutan the Younger, etc.; see Sweeney 1972).

25. These are the main Malay directional divisions. The place where the sun rises is, of course, the east, the land where it sets, the west; the distinction between people living at the river's mouth and those of the lands upstream was particularly vital economically and politically speaking, since the one who commanded the river's mouth controlled trade with the outside and could tax products going into and out of the interior.

26. Although *nenek* (which I have translated as grandsire) means "grandmother" in standard Malay, it is not used with that meaning on the east coast. The common usage in Trengganu is *tok* for grandmother and *toki* for grandfather. Nenek in the Main Peteri means both "ancestor" and "powerful lord." Translating the word as "grandsire" combines both its meanings of progenitor and ruler. The grandsire to whom the greeting is sent is Nenek Betara Guru, the Great Teacher. See Skeat 1972 [1900]:81–91, and Wilkinson 1959:132, for identification of Betara Guru with Siva, an identification which does not exist on the village level.

27. Tok Mamat explains that this means that the ceremonies will assure an increase in all that is good.

M: Seven teachers will become twelve. Two remedies are one, the teacher's one white remedy.[28]

T: The teacher has prayed at the foot of Alif. Alif stands in the shadow of Ba.[29] All is complete.

M: All is complete to the seventh day, to the eighth night while we visit the teacher, the teacher-dalang.

T: The king, late reclining, descends, face down toward earth; the crown prince awakens and runs. Swiftly he steps to the flower garden and asks which things he may kick away. He asks the seven holy wise men, he asks the elders, whoever they may be.

M: Seven holy elders, guardians of the faith, be alert one and all.

T: Be alert one and all. Seh Talut, scourge of our enemies, we ask for your help here and now.

M: Seh, in whichever bay you're reposing, wherever you are, I call on you.

T: I ask you to shower us again with compassion, with magical chants, with holy knowledge, with mystical knowledge, with pious chants.

M: Rid the body of all evil influences.

T: Rid the body of all evil influences, the body's many obstructions. The fiddlers are five, the minduk is one, the shaman is one.

M: The minduk is one, the shaman is one.

T: My brother takes a shortcut, he does indeed, descending to the seventh earth for an audience with Grandsire Kohor,[30] Commander Writes All Day.

M: [*indistinct*]

T: A thousand names, a thousand changes of form, there a ruler of spirits, here a ruler of spirits, a company forty strong, with seven imps.

M: I ask you to be on the alert, one and all; I don't mention letters, I don't change names.

28. The white remedy (*penawar*—neutralizer of harmful influences both material and spiritual) refers to the *nasi guru* (teacher's rice) that forms part of the offering hung from the rafters before the Main Peteri begins.

29. Alif (the first letter of the Arabic alphabet) stands for Allah, Ba (the second letter) for Muhammad.

30. *Kohor* means "decrease" (become slower or quieter, depending upon the context) [CL]. The phrase commonly used for "shortcut" is, literally, "cut across the cape, pass the river's curve."

T: The tale of the seven earths is told, now I ascend to the edge of the village to seek audience with Grandsire Sang Gana of the village's edge.

M: To seek audience with the ruler at the edge of the village, Sang Gana who lives at the village's edge.

T: At the edge of the village, in the shadow of the groves, that's where the King of Birds is, the Winged Steed.[31] Let all hear my story, let all hear my tale.

M: Listen to the story, listen to the tale, listen one and listen all.

T: Now the tale of the village's edge in the shadow of the groves is over, so we go to seek audience in the open fields.

M: We go to seek audience in the open fields.

T: The open fields, stretching as far as the eye can see, I travel through the fields to seek audience with Grandsire Hukum,[32] the king of the fields.

M: Grandsire Hukum, the king of the fields, listen one and listen all.

T: Everyone listen to the story, to the tale. The tale of the open fields is over. Who will inherit this vast domain?

M: The king of the fields has a vast domain, seven fields, and eight palaces.

T: Everyone listen to the story, to the tale. Now I land in the thick pristine jungle.

M: To the thick pristine jungle to seek audience with the shaikhs of the jungle.

T: Everyone listen to the story, to the tale, since I am going to see the new holy people, the old holy people.

M: Don't mention letters, don't change any names.

T: Ah, chap. . . .[33]

[At the shaman's signal, the band strikes up LAGU BARAT CEPAT, the "traveling music" that facilitates the tok 'teri's travel to another level of awareness. Seated before the minduk, the tok 'teri commences the head-shaking that signals trance. The shaman does not assume another

31. The Winged Steed (Borak) bore Muhammad on his visit to heaven.

32. *Hukum* means legal decision, usually of punishment [CL].

33. Ah, chap (or ah, saa) is a signal to the orchestra to commence playing the music that assists the shaman in achieving trance and changing his persona [CL].

persona here, but has traveled farther from the everyday world into sacred space. During the music the ritual pair speak:]

T: Everyone listen as my tale unfolds.

M: Listen one and listen all.

[The serunai enters, and the music changes to LAGU SERI RAMA BERJALAN, used in the wayang kulit to accompany the travels of particularly refined characters. When the instrumental music ends, the tok 'teri begins a short incantation:]

T: I take refuge in Allah from Satan the Stoned One, in the name of Allah the Loving and Merciful.[34] It's no ordinary image, it's the image of Semar, the eldest brother. Hey, Semar, with a black stone, Semar, with a red stone, Semar, I come before you "hidu" supported by "hidu",[35] you support "bisik" and I support "risik" while we stand alongside the angels Gabriel, may peace be with him, Michael, may peace be with him, Israfel, may peace be with him, and Israel, may peace be with him.

[Toward the middle of the shaman's jampi, the minduk takes up his rebab and begins to sing an unidentified tune, 32 beat, form G (see Matusky 1980), not in Wayang repertoire, probably not in Mak Yong repertoire, may be Main Peteri only.]

M: [*sung*] I lay my prayers down at the foot of Alif, in the shadow of Ba, while we meet and complete our reckoning.

T: To the seventh day, to the eighth night.

M: To the seventh day, to the eighth night.

T: Oh, watch over us, ancient gods.

M: Watch over me as I recite my spells.

T: Oh, King of the Mountain, oh Nik Si Khabar, alert and intelligent godlike being.

M: During the time that Awang[36] speaks.

T: [*spoken*] May the speech that descends from without be sweet within.

M: [*sung*] Cause the spirits to appear in the country's villages.

34. Spoken in Arabic.

35. *Hidu . . . hidu*, is said by the shaman, Tok Mamat, to be a Javanese expression meaning "to assist in healing." Not listed in Horne 1974.

36. Besides being a common masculine name, Awang is a nickname given to boys in the same sense as the American "Sonny." Awang thus can stand for men in general [CL].

T: [*spoken in declamatory style*] Being incarnate, heritage of Islam, angel father, mother first pilgrim.[37]

M: [*sung*] Descending from without, sweet within, sprung from Islam's heritage.

T: [*sung*] Heritage of Islam, angel father, mother first pilgrim.

M: Ah.

T: The father is invisible in the Garden of Eden.

M: Ah.

T: The mother disappeared into Jeddah[38] long ago. The child is waiting in the wastelands.[39] Oh, put your clothes on and descend.

M: The child waits in the wastelands, at the bolted door of the earth. The child raises Grandsire White Bird.[40]

T: They glide through the air, bathed by the wind.

M: The white bird glides through the air, bathed by the wind atop the anthill of the inverted wise man, from the line of Melur Merang Kesokma.[41]

T: Oh, from the line of Melur Merang Kesokma.

M: Ah.

T: We ask you to shower us with compassion . . .

M: Ah.

T: . . . one minduk, younger brother of one shaman, seven drummers, five fiddlers.

M: [*sung*] Watch over the minduk atop the white tree. Watch over the shaman upon the dais.[42]

37. The father and mother are really Adam and Eve.

38. According to Islamic legend, Eve was hurled from Eden to Jeddah, the port of Mecca (Wilkinson 1908:30).

39. Tok Mamat explains that *tanah mati* (wasteland) in this context means graveyard. He said it was because the child had not yet gone on a pilgrimage to Mecca and so was not fully alive in a religious sense.

40. The White Bird is a metaphor for the vital spirit, the *semangat*. For references on the bird-like character of semangat, see Skeat 1972 [1900]:587; Wilkinson 1959:1053 [CL].

41. *Titis . . . kesokma* (line of . . . Kesokma) is a stock phrase of the shadow play meaning "all the past history," "the whole story." *Titis* also refers to incarnation, and *sokma* is the Malay term for the soul of metempsychosis. Dewa Kesokma is a character in the shadow play (Sweeney 1972). According to Pak Daud, the whole phrase means that the wise man is the descendant of gods. His upside-down state refers to his special powers, making him different from ordinary people.

42. The white tree is the spinal column; the dais is the head.

T: [*spoken during minduk's song*] Watch over us, Young Warrior Laleng,[43] keep a watchful eye on this company.

M: [*sung*] The many players here assembled.

T: Watch over us, friends, watch over us, penggawa,[44] beloved friends, devoted penggawa.

M: [*spoken*] Continue.

T: [*sung*] Crowded together, sleeve to sleeve, like fish on a string.

M: Watch over us, ancestral gods, gods of our heritage.

T: Princely gods in the palace by night.

M: I beg of you, watch over me.

T: [*spoken*] Continue.

M: [*sung*] Let the angel see that my prayers reach his ruler.

T: [*spoken*] Ah, chap!

[The instrumentalists play the transition music, LAGU BARAT CEPAT. The music increases in speed and intensity as the shaman whirls his head and rises to dance in trance. During the transition, he receives a new persona, Radin Kecil Dahulu Permainan Bunga (Little Prince Flower Play of Times Past) a protective inner force of the ritual performers and a personification of their Player's Wind.]

T: [*spoken*] While grandsire . . .

M: My lord, while you . . .

T: It seems . . .

M: . . . feel compassion for the leader who slipped from the loving hands of his father, from his mother's affection.

T: Oh, very true, pengasuh.[45]

43. Raja Muda Laleng is the hero of a Mak Yong play, and the archetype of an Inner Wind (that of an idler). See Sheppard 1974, bk. 1.

44. *Penggawa* are the shaman's personal spirit familiars who protect him during the ritual and act as messengers and guides for the other spirits summoned to the seance. The term's most common usage outside of the ritual refers to the subdistrict headman who mediates between villagers and the state political apparatus, just as the shaman's penggawa mediate between the human and spirit worlds [CL]. See Kessler 1977:322 for a discussion of the political symbolism of the Main Peteri.

45. *Pengasuh* refers to the caretaker or guardian of a child; a nursemaid; usually the attendant of young royalty. Awang Pengasuh is the comic companion of the prince-hero in Mak Yong plays (see Wilkinson 1959:577). In the context of the Main Peteri, pengasuh refers to the minduk, who acts as guardian of the tok 'teri (whose own title recalls that of royalty, i.e., *peteri*, *tuan 'teri*, "princess").

M: The bird, whether big or small, the firstborn bird, all ivory and onyx, is like a severed palm blossom; the pengasuh enfolds you within his embrace. Oh, magpie, clever reciter, oh, thrush, clever converser, oh, hummingbird, clever narrator.[46]

T: Oh, very true, my younger brother [*chuckles*].

M: If your younger brother should come in the morning, tell him the tale in the morning. If he should come in the evening, tell him the tale in the evening. Please, sir, kindly peck out the word. I call on your first peck to tell us good things, and your second to tell us the news.

T: Very true, younger brother.

M: Please, sir, you received a new name and you changed your character. What is your name and what is your title? Who is it that comes before me?

T: Yes, indeed.

M: Right.

T: When I awoke, my younger brother was fast asleep . . .

M: Yes, indeed.

T: . . . while I opened the seven shutters . . .

M: Right.

T: . . . the nine back doors, while I seized the government's wireless within the four walls of the five palaces.[47]

M: Oh, right.

T: So I was facing upstream, just as my brother was.

M: Yes.

T: My minduk leaned against the white tree.

M: Right.

T: My shaman relaxed upon the dais. My players leaned against the shade tree. [*drumbeat emphasis*]

M: True.

46. The bird is the patient's *semangat* (vital spirit); "like a severed palm-blossom" means that the patient is ill, his spirit has been severed from his body.

47. The seven windows are the seven body parts. The nine back doors are the orifices of the body. The four walls are the four elements, earth, air, fire, and water, of which the Universe is composed. The five palaces are the five senses. The use of the word *wireless* (*wayales*, or as it is pronounced on the east coast, *wayalih*), lends a modern note to this loose recounting of a story akin to that of Dewa Muda. The minduk, shaman, and players mentioned in the succeeding lines are internal healing forces of the body. The white tree is the human backbone.

T: I faced upstream, I faced downstream. There were hordes of people within the throne room, small and large, old and young, men and women, females and males . . .

M: Yes, indeed.

T: . . . while I took a new name and changed my character, and my title became Little Prince Flower Play of Times Past; I'm the bird's caretaker now, my brother. Your elder brother cares for you day and night. Well now, that bird ascended on high to the gates of heaven; the dalang rode down and descended to earth, right in the middle of a very vast field.

M: True.

T: The Jati Jawa tree[48] has many lovely leaves, one shoot, and two boughs. A branch on the left has been trampled on this side. The branch on the left now is drooping. A branch on the right has been trampled. The branch on the right now is drooping. The shoot has been trampled. I fear that the shoot will be chopped down. My speech is becoming confused, my behavior is going awry.

M: Yes, indeed.

T: Oh, ho, ho [*chuckles*], what kind of doings are these?

M: Ah, when the pengasuh greets you and calls you by your pet name, tonight . . .

T: Yes?

M: . . . he wants to urge you to be aware of what's going on in the father's house, on the mother's land, as you firm up the inner fortress and strengthen the outer fortress. Don't allow jin to enter uninvited, don't let *bayu*[49] come in and take shelter.

T: In the body of the inang,[50] in the dark and gloomy night.

M: Bring a light and place it here to illuminate the entrance to every lane and valley; [*drum beat emphasis*] in the wink of an eye someone

48. The bird represents semangat. The patient is compared to the Jawa Jati tree (associated with Dewa Muda), which is suffering from injuries.

49. *Bayu* are disembodied spirits associated with the wind and akin to mambang; in fact the Mambang Bayu is considered to be equivalent in power to the Hantu Raya (Mighty Spirit), but is spoken about less often.

50. The *inang* (a word that usually means the female equivalent of pengasuh: nurse or governess of a princess) referred to here and elsewhere in Main Peteri is the shaman himself, the caretaker of both spirits and patient.

can enter the land of four palaces, the true body, the principal world,[51] to rob and steal.

T: The principal world?

M: Yes. [*drum flourish, joined by rebab*]

T: Well now, my brother, I have arranged the twelve kings in nine rows.[52]

M: Yes.

T: While one stands guard alongside the father, while two stand guard alongside the patient, your elder brother counts thirty verses within . . .

M: Ah, yes, indeed.

T: . . . twenty attributes without.[53] During this time, no one will double obstructions, no one will cover and oppress, set traps or snares on the palace verandah.

M: Oh, tonight we'll invoke the souls of former kings, we will ask our magical, powerful Grandsire for his blessings.

T: True.

M: His throat is black, his bone is unique, his tongue is glib and his spittle is salty;[54] he makes wishes come true, requests be fulfilled.

T: Right. I've talked a lot about this kind of thing, I've said he'll command wondrous magic—that's the kind of person Grandsire is.

51. This is a clear statement of the basis of the Main Peteri, and of much of Malay magic and philosophy: the body is the microcosm and the universe is the macrocosm; one can be equated with the other.

52. The twelve kings are protective forces within the human body; the nine rows are body orifices.

53. According to Raja Ngah, "thirty verses" refers to the number of chapters in the Koran, and "twenty attributes" are the outward signs of humanity. [The number of chapters in the Koran are actually 114; the 20 attributes are the attributes of God according to Islamic doctrine. Alluding to them as the attributes of humanity, while it illustrates the concept of microcosm and macrocosm, also brings this Main Peteri concept close to the association of self with God for which Sufism has been condemned, as in the case of the famous al-Hallaj, whose utterance "I am God," meaning self-extinction in the contemplation of God's Unity, cost him his life (Naguib al-Attas 1963:9).] [CL].

54. These are the attributes of the man of power. "Salty" speech is convincing speech. Possessors of a "salty mouth" (*mulut masin*) are believed to influence events—if they say that something will occur, it will. Before a newborn baby is allowed to feed, its grandmother (or other relative) touches its mouth with gold, sweetness, and salt (the *belah mulut*, or "opening the mouth ceremony") so it will be rich, its life will be sweet, and it will be an effective speaker [CL] (cf. Sweeney 1987:146).

[*Rebab starts to play*] Well, we'll hear the same tune again today. When we visit our ancient Grandsire, our first teacher, we won't find him asleep, he won't be sleeping in his room, because we have to treat our Pak Tip in the room.

M: Right.

T: But I can't go on any longer. [*coughs*] Give me a glass.

[He drinks some water. The drum joins the rebab, followed by the other instruments, to play LAGU SEDAYUNG MAK YONG, a tune of magical power, as the ritual pair sing.]

T: Awang, arise from your heavy sleep. Don't you want to take part in the seance tonight?

M: Ei . . .

T: [*spoken aside*] I just can't manage.

M: When I thought it in my mind, when I felt it in my heart, when I weighed it in my body, I almost felt like flying [drum flourishes].

T: [*spoken*] Right.

M: [*sung*] The princess's voice sounds within the room.

T: [*sung*] Ei, while I stand, recalling my body, father . . .

M: [*spoken*] Yes, indeed.

T: [*sung*] . . . I don't want to walk, recalling my mother's body.

M: [*spoken*] Aha!

T: [*sung*] When mother isn't angry, father isn't, either . . .

M: [*spoken*] True.

T: [*sung*] *. . . on the palace verandah.*

M: In the time of the father, Arak Temarak.

T: [*spoken*] Oh, yes, my father's name is Arak Temarak.

M: [*sung*] The mother's name is Siti Nur Ziarah.[55]

T: [*spoken*] Yes, indeed.

M: [*sung*] Father meditates by the waters of Babylon; Mother meditates [*indistinct*]

T: I beg of you, mother, remember to toss down to me . . .

M: [*spoken*] She will!

T: [*sung*] . . . bouquets of golden flowers, bouquets of silver flowers.

M: [*spoken*] Yes, indeed.

55. Arak Temarak and Siti Nur Ziarah might be glossed as The Predecessor and Lady Light of Visitation [CL].

T: [*sung*] Of course I ask, on behalf of the patient, that misfortune should depart.

M: We ask that misfortune depart when the mother causes clear water to come down and fill the glass, water clear as glass, a cup to drink.

T: [*spoken*] Ah, continue.

M: [*sung*] Fine powder and coarse powder, too,[56] so his body may be released from all evil influences.

T: [*spoken*] Ah, it can happen.

[A short instrumental interlude of LAGU SEDAYUNG MAK YONG, a tune of magical power.]

T: [*spoken*] Well, we made important requests, more or less, no? If they haven't been granted yet, we just have to try asking again. Pious folk would like us to follow a different road. But this is the way we are, we ask to follow this road. Well, I can't just hang around here, brother, I want to invoke some more friends.

M: You want to do it now.

T: Invoke one penggawa, or, better yet, two.

M: Yes, indeed.

T: Three would be even better than two.

M: If you please, sir, the day is good, the moment has come, the time has arrived. [*rebab enters*]

T: I don't know what to do about the injustice that we meet up with from pious folk.[57]

[The band joins in to play LAGU SEDAYUNG MAK YONG.]

T: [*spoken*] That's good. [*sung*] I'm trying to invoke Cik Tip's friends, his many friends and numerous penggawa. Where have they disappeared to?

M: [*sung*] Awang turns to the back, to the left and the right . . .

T: Eiii!

56. These are included among the ingredients traditionally used in the neutralization of evil influences; they are *beluru* or *luring* (*Entada saponin*), a woody climber whose bark is used as soap; *sintuk* (*Cinnamomum*), whose bark is used for washing hair, fine powder, coarse powder; and the juice of *limau kesturi* (*Citrus microcarpa*, the musk lime), all mixed with water and poured over the patient.

57. Tok Mamat is talking about opposition of the Islamic hierarchy and some pious co-religionists to the Main Peteri, on the grounds that it incorporates "Hindu" doctrine and leads to the worship of spirits, a contention that bomoh stoutly deny.

M: . . . he dances and sways through the throne room.

T: Dancing and swaying through the throne room like a jungle fowl waiting to fight a rival, you frolic in the wind like an owlet. Bayu are waiting lined up in ranks for their orders to march, for the time they can stride, one foot after the other. Be on guard, one and all.

M: Like a bird waiting to fly. Be on guard, one and all.

T: [*spoken*] Ah, chap. . . .

[LAGU BARAT CEPAT, the music of transition, is played. The shaman trances, dancing in the style of the Mak Yong. The minduk and shaman cry out during the music, "Ah, hey! Ya!" When the music stops, the shaman has taken on the persona of a manifestation of Pak Dogol; see Footnote 58.]

M: [*spoken*] One disappears and another takes his place, emerging with a rush in spite of obstacles, confused and heedless, walking a little and running a lot, receiving a new name and changing his character. Who has come to the palace throne room?

T: That's right, grandson, I'm a descendant of Gerga Jiwa of the shadow play.[58]

M: Yes, indeed.

T: He who invokes the great god Indera.[59]

M: Yes, indeed.

T: True.

M: When I invoke Grandsire . . . [*he hesitates*]

T: The god. [*provided like a cue*]

M: . . . the great god Miraba.[60] [*rebab plays briefly*]

T: Good, you want to ask Grandsire to stand guard atop these original foundations.

M: Yes, indeed.

T: I fear there are all kinds of evil influences here.

M: Yes, indeed.

58. Gerga Jiwa is a soubriquet of Kakak Persanta (in other guises, Pak Dogol and Dewa Si Alam Tunggal, also known as Sang Yang Tunggal). *Jiwa* means soul, and *gerga* may be related to the Javenese *gereg* (to herd livestock), so the sense of Gerga Jiwa may be given as "Caretaker of the Soul" [CL].

59. Indera (Indra of the Hindu pantheon) is one of the high gods of Kayangan (the abode of the gods) mentioned in the shadow play (see Sweeney 1972:90, 97).

60. Miraba is one of the sons of Rawana, the villain of the shadow play (Sweeney 1972:247–248).

T: Jin Pari, with her evil influences, treachery, oppression, and envy, has been peering into the palace verandah.

M: True.

T: I ask Grandsire to leap atop the mat created from the first picture, the first word,[61] while we travel on. Hey, hey, chap!

[The band plays the music of transition, LAGU BARAT CEPAT. The shaman trances and takes on the persona of Persanta, another manifestation of Pak Dogol.]

M: [*spoken*] Who's here now?

T: I have a name and I have a title. One disappears and another takes his place.

M: Right.

T: Grandson, I'm Big Brother Persanta,[62] in person. What is your pleasure, grandson?

M: It's like this, sir.

T: Yes, indeed.

M: I ask you to pit your exalted strength, your exalted forces, against every person whatsoever.

T: Very well.

M: I fear that thieving jin and mambang[63] have struck your servant; we have to put a name to them while you, sir, guard the house.

T: The palace verandah?

M: Yes, indeed.

T: You called on Big Brother Persanta; that's me, in person.

M: Good.

T: I fear that Captain Poison and Captain Seafish[64] are about. I'll ask Grandsire to guard us from the front courtyard.

M: Yes, indeed.

61. Mats laid on the floor are an integral part of the Main Peteri. The most attractive mats available are used, and they are arranged in a manner that allows the participants to sit, and dance, upon them. The "first picture, the first word" means that the Main Peteri existed from the beginning of Creation.

62. Persanta (or Prasanta) is another name for Pak Dogol (identified with Semar, see Sweeney 1972:224), who is really Dewa Si Alam Tunggal (also known as Sang Yang Tunggal), the ruler of Kayangan. In the form of Pak Dogol, he has taken on an ugly humble appearance and become the servant of Seri Rama, the hero of the shadow play.

63. See n. 22.

64. These captains are sea spirits.

T: Big and small, old and young, men and women, females and males, let no one cause an uproar, disturbance, or confusion. Well, sir, Grandsire . . . Big Brother Persanta will leap atop the original mat, the first creation of its kind.

[While the band plays LAGU BARAT CEPAT, the shaman changes from a vigorous and energetic persona to that of an old man: Wak Kedi Bomoh, the Old Bomoh from the Siamese Monastery.]

T: [*spoken*] The Old Bomoh's here.

M: There are lots of old bomoh.

T: The Old Bomoh from the Siamese Monastery.[65]

M: Oh, is that so, uncle?

T: I came here all dripping with sweat.

M: Oh, is that so, uncle?

T: Yes, indeed. I descended, I leaped down, mouth and phallus of a bomoh, the original phallus.

M: He descended with the original mouth and phallus. Everything is ready, the flower bud is waiting,[66] hoping to unfold.

T: True. Well, we can speak of Brother Tip's attributes; we can speak about Tip, well, in the matter of Tip, one can see or one cannot, one can look or one cannot, at which sickness is afflicting him, who has snatched him, who has slandered him, [*rebab begins*] ah, I can see, no matter where. If it is due to his Wind, which Wind?[67] [*singing, LAGU*

65. Wak Kedi Bomoh, the Old Bomoh from the Siamese Monastery, is Maharisi Mata Api (the Sage with the Eye of Fire), the foster father of Siti Dewi, heroine of the shadow play. He is identified with Siva in the literature, but not on the local level. *Kedi* (Thai, *kuti*) means monks' sleeping quarters (Sweeney 1972:344). The shaman assumes this persona for the purpose of conducting a divination [CL].

66. "The flower bud" refers to the popped rice, which expands when subjected to dry heat, like a flower in bloom. The metaphor of unfolding is extended to the message encoded within the piles of rice, which will inform the ritual practitioners of the diagnosis and prognosis. While the shaman is in the persona of Wak Kedi Bomoh or its equivalent, he places three handfuls of popped rice upon a pillow. Each pile is then counted out in units of two grains each, representing earth, air, fire, and water. The divination is based upon a consideration of where the counts ended [CL].

67. If the count ends on air, the diagnosis involves the patient's Inner Wind: his drives, needs, talents, and character. According to the Malay theory of personality, each of us is born with one or more Winds of varying strengths. If this Wind can be expressed its possessor will be healthy and happy, but if it is repressed and allowed to build up inside one's body it can cause a variety of conditions, most of which are similar to the Western categories of psychosomatic illnesses and affective disorders [CL].

SEDAYUNG MAK YONG, slowed down to accommodate the many words of the song, while he places three handfuls of popped rice on a cushion] Oh, I am patient, enoh, enoh, enoh,[68] as I call on one fold to light this gloomy darkness. [*spoken, as the music continues*] What sickness has afflicted Pak Tip, who has seized him, from what direction have these influences come?

M: [*sung*] Enoh, enoh, open the message, one fold within the gloomy darkness.

T: Two folds show a grayish haze, enoh. Two folds show a grayish haze, enoh, enoh, noh, noh. With three folds we can now see clearly. [*spoken, as the music continues*] What sickness has afflicted him, who has seized him, who has slandered him? I seek answer in the divination, *sekun* or *raksi, janji* or *temuan*?[69]

M: [*sung*] Enoh, enoh, will it be janji or temuan?

T: [*sung*] Please be kind when you visit, enoh. Flower bud, be kind when you visit, enoh. Enoh, enoh, enoh, what sickness, what slander? We have finished the count.

M: Enoh, enoh, who has seized him, who has slandered him, enoh, enoh?

[Music ends. They count out the grains of popped rice. There is much discussion in the audience as the divination proceeds. Pak Long Awang, in the audience, voices his approval of the proceedings, nodding his head and saying, "Um hmm!"]

T: [*spoken; in a low conversational tone meant for the other ritual specialist*] Fire is in the middle, that one's Earth. That Fire's pretty fierce. This one's Wind. This one's Earth. There's not much Earth. [*changes to loud declamatory tone*] Well, now, his Wind's in short supply; now, this is how it happened in the first place; he would like to be able to come and go but he quickly gets out of breath.[70]

M: Hmm.

T: It felt like a needle was sticking into his leg.

M: That's so.

T: Ah.

68. *Enoh, enoh* is equivalent to tralala.

69. The "folds" are piles of popped rice. *Sekun, raksi, janji, temuan* (harmony, good luck, promises, meetings) refer to the prognosis given in the popped rice divination [CL].

70. A reference to Latip's asthma.

M: That's how it was at first.

T: That's how it started. Well, sores that you get from the dirt can be treated, but I figure it this way: it's because he used to give lots of offerings to the spirits in those days, I heard tell. It was his friends who accosted him, don't you agree?[71] Concerning Wind, don't even try to guess. Wind certainly enters into this. [*Murmurs of agreement from Latip's wife and others in the audience.*]

M: He exercised his Wind each and every day.[72]

T: Well, about the Wind just now, well, if you want to know about it, that's OK. Well, all right, it's come out, that first group, just now. Besides that, did Tip fall down or get so startled[73] that he almost fell down?

M: One or the other?

T: One or the other.

MAN IN AUDIENCE: Oh, I could tell you . . .

T: Ah, that's the second part of the case. When he fell down, his soul flew off, his spirit fled. That's all there is to it. If you want to ask me to speak about his Winds up to now, I can whisper about it. It's only then that we can speak about Tip.

M: Well, we can take a look in the great book of the Heavenly Midwives.[74]

71. "Sores that you get from the dirt" refers to *kudis* (scabies), a skin condition actually caused by itch mites, but believed by rural Malays to be due to dirt. It is contrasted with Latip's condition, difficult to treat, which was caused by the unceremonious manner in which he disposed of his shadow puppets. It was to their spirits that he used to give offerings; they are the friends who accosted him and made him ill [CL].

72. He "exercised his Wind" by performing in the shadow play.

73. An important underlying cause of many illnesses, according to Malay medical theory, is being startled, which can result in vital spirit (semangat) leaving the body. Thus depleted, the body is prey to influences that would otherwise not affect it [CL].

74. The Bidandari were explicitly identified with the Seven Heavenly Midwives, regularly invoked by traditional Malay midwives and thought to aid laboring women when all human help has failed. Their name has had an interesting evolution since its Sanskrit beginnings. The original word, *bidadari*, refers to the beautiful nymphs of Indra's heaven. Addition of the letter "n" has brought the word closer to the world of the rural Malay; the Indian temptresses have become heavenly village midwives (bidan) (Laderman 1983:132). The reason they are mentioned here is that there is a suspicion that some of Latip's troubles were caused by his envious birth-brother, the placenta and debris of childbirth. These incomplete siblings, lacking the breath of life (and thus, two of the essential elements: fire and air), are mirror images of the disembodied spirits (hantu) and

T: Oh, the Heavenly Midwives, hah, hah.

M: It's their sort of thing.

T: It could be. It's also very much a case of the denizens of the earth. It also could be because he wants to perform the shadow play, but he parted from it on bad terms a long time ago. Oh, you have to be on the alert. But don't tell him that I mean the whole thing hinges on the shadow play. The divination fell to Thursday and Sunday, that means the denizens of the earth.[75] [*A baby starts crying and is hushed and rocked back to sleep.*] Later on we'll chew on it some more. Well, that's the advice of at least two of us.

M: That's it.

T: Let's drink first, all right? [*laughs*] We need a drink because we're all sweaty. [*rebab plays a few notes*]

[The action stops for a short while; drinks are served. The audience discusses the outcome of the divination. The anthropologist asks the shaman, "Earth—does that mean earth spirits?" "Yes, it's earth spirits." "What about fire?" "It's because he was startled and fell." "And air?" "That's the Wind inside himself." Turning toward the minduk, the shaman says, "She wants to know everything. That's fine." The seance resumes.]

T: [*spoken*] If you're someone of good family, listen here. As it was in the beginning, those of the same heritage, the same ancestry, the same type, all the descendants, down through the ages. [*sung to the tune of LAGU BERTABUH MAK YONG, used in the Mak Yong to set the stage for the second night and succeeding performances, and used here to set the stage for the second tok 'teri, soon to take Tok Mamat's place*] Two war-chiefs, brother, are in your palace; awake and hear my tale.[76]

M: [*sung*] Whether of knives or of needles.

---

are subsumed under the category of spirits. Disembodied spirits, composed only of fire and air and lacking the earth and water of which Adam's body was made, are also thought of as being in a quasi-sibling relationship with humanity. All of these incomplete beings tend to envy their more fortunate human siblings and sometimes find ways to vent their spleen [CL].

75. This refers to another method of divination, using days of the week, to point to the category of spirit responsible for making trouble. Those implicated here are the earth spirits [CL].

76. The two war-chiefs are the minduk and the tok 'teri.

T: [*spoken during minduk's singing of above line*] If you are a descendant of holy men, if you are a descendant of vanished worthies.

M: [*sung*] You look within.

T: [*sung*] Iiii.

M: I go straight to the heavenly village and enter.

[An inaudible discussion begins between the shaman and the players, as the minduk sings the preceding line.]

T: [*sung*] Listen, brother, to the story he tells.

M: I feel it's a serious matter; I enter and leave a request.

T: Everyone listen to the tale that he tells. The older brother leaves a request with the younger brother, his body all aching. His body is suffering, he is in torment.[77] Listen to my story, listen to my tale; it comes down through the line of descent, through the ages.

M: If you are really and truly a man of good heritage [*drum flourish*], if your background is fine . . .

T: [*spoken*] Hey, hey, hey, mmm . . .

M: . . . if the father's inheritance has come down to you through your family line, then you are truly a man of good family and fine heritage.

T: Listen to my story, listen to what I say about the family line as I take up the tale.

M: [*spoken*] That's true.

T: [*sung*] In the family of a noble, I take up the tale of nobility; in the family of a king, I take up the tale of brothers, Andera Raja and Raja Andera,[78] prince of players, noble king.

M: If he's a prince, he's the prince of players.

T: [*spoken*] That's true.

M: [*sung*] He's King Generosity Overflowing. He's no one to fool around with, so you'd better wake up at once.

T: I want to open the gates of Faith, the gates of Love, the gates of Sensation, the gates of the Winds. [*The rhythm speeds up, the music sounds fuller.*] It's so sweet to hear this. Be on guard, oh warrior, within

77. This is a reference to the sibling relationship of the patient and his placenta.

78. For a recounting of the story of Dewa Andera and Andera Dewa from the Mak Yong, see Sheppard 1974:40–48.

the five chapels,[79] atop the foundation made of old iron. The warrior stands all alone [*the rest of the sentence is inaudible, covered by the minduk's song*].

M: If the four warriors stand on guard, with Commander Ali,[80] Excited Ali, when they hold each other's hands, they can cast away harm with the tips of their fingers.[81] This is a very serious matter.

T: Guard the soul of the little god, Dewa Muda,[82] in the land of Java. His father's name is Raja Andera, his mother's name is Princess Hidden Moon.

M: Yes, his mother is Hidden Moon. He sleeps on the seven verandahs of the five palaces.[83] I hope he is safely dreaming.

T: You may tell us his story, about how he became wise though still young.

M: True.

T: True it is, my brother.

M: Your mother wants you to eat the golden deer,[84] the magical deer of the forest. If you don't hunt the golden deer, the country will be plundered, the country will be oppressed. As surely as fire devours cotton, the nation will be in an uproar.

T: Let us hold a conference within the seven rooms. Each of you

79. The five chapels are the five senses. The warrior is one of the body's own forces. The iron is human bone.

80. Ali is the Prophet's son-in-law.

81. During the ceremony, the shaman makes casting-out movements with his hands, after touching the patient [CL].

82. Dewa Muda, a version of whose story from the Mak Yong can be found in Sheppard 1974:21–39, is the archetype for a personality type (characterized by Malays as Inner Wind) which has a strong need for material comforts, love, and admiration and becomes ill if these needs are not satisfied. The name of the queen of Java in this story is Si Lindung Bulan (Hidden Moon). The king's name is not mentioned, but Raja (or Dewa) Andera is the hero of another Mak Yong story.

83. The seven verandahs are the seven body parts, the five palaces are the five senses. The meaning of this statement is that the Inner Wind, Angin Dewa Muda, dwells within the human heart, and its possessor, unless he is fortunate enough to be able to express and satisfy this Wind, is better off if his Wind is "sleeping."

84. The golden deer does not appear in the Sheppard version of the story of Dewa Muda, but east coast shamans and minduk consider it an integral part of the tale, some insisting it was a golden deer (*rusa*), others that it was a golden mousedeer (*pelanduk*) [CL].

listen to what I say, each of you listen to my tale. If you are descended from the Seven Tigers,[85] listen to my story, one and all.

M: Oh yes, if you're a Tiger, a Tiger young or old, if you have the heritage of Tigers, if your hide is covered with forty black stripes, wake up and listen.

[The band plays LAGU BARAT CEPAT, the music of transition, as the shaman returns to his own persona.]

T: [*spoken, as rebab plays*] Well, I figure it this way. We've made our requests, more or less. Well, if we intend to arouse him right away, how should we go about treating him? We'll treat him first, we'll catch one of his tormenters, the one we suspect. We'll hold discussions, but we won't let it go at that. [*The rebab is joined by the band: sung to the tune of LAGU BERTABUH MAK YONG, music for the second tok 'teri.*] Follow along on the road of duty, Awang, Keeper of the Bird.

M: Be on your guard, one and all.

T: Yes, sway to the right in the throne room, like a decoy awaiting the foe . . .

M: Like a decoy awaiting the foe. I don't mention letters, I don't change names.

T: [*spoken*] Ah, chap! Hey!

[As the band plays LAGU BARAT CEPAT, the shaman changes to the persona of Grandsire Dahar Berasa Ribu,[86] an earth spirit.]

M: [*spoken*] Hey there, who are you, sir?

T: You must be addressing me. I've received a new name and changed my character.

M: Is that so?

T: My name is, and my title is . . .

M: Truly?

85. The *Hala* (weretiger) is another Inner Wind, or basic personality type. It can be particularly difficult for the possessor if unexpressed, or for others if expressed, but can be used to advantage by warriors, silat masters (experts in the Malay art of stylized, dancelike self-defense) and people who can vent their aggression without fear of retaliation. It is interesting to note that *hala* (or some variation of the word) is the term for shaman in a number of aboriginal languages, and that the ability of some people to turn into tigers is a widespread belief in Southeast Asia [CL].

86. Nenek Dahar Berasa Ribu can be glossed as Grandsire Who Dines Upon a Thousand Tastes, *dahar* being the High Javanese word used for the dining of royalty [CL].

T: . . . Grandsire Dahar Berasa Ribu from the gates of the earth.

M: Is that right?

T: Oh, yes indeed.

M: I'd like to ask you a few friendly questions now.

T: Very well.

M: I want to ask your swaying self why you are pursuing a claim . . .

T: Hey, my dear physician/dalang . . .

M: Right.

T: . . . you want to ask about those with seven attributes . . .

M: True.

T: . . . in one body?[87]

M: Right.

T: In the past, my dear physician/dalang . . .

M: True.

T: . . . I often partook of the mother's feasts, the father's preparations, under Inu's playhouse, under Semar's stage,[88] my dear physician. [*rebab is briefly heard*] Nowadays no one is serving me, nobody cares.

M: Is that so?

T: Yes, indeed.

M: I heard that your friends don't want to associate with you now.

T: Yes, indeed.

M: I fear that your palace guards, the sons of your body, were pursuing your claim concerning the mother's feasts and the father's preparations, sir.

T: Ah, yes, indeed. You would like me to have a word with them . . .

M: Oh, right.

T: . . . one and all, the whole crew of forty-four spirit soldiers, the great mighty pack of them from the earth's realm, my dear physician/dalang.

M: Yes, that's so, sir.

87. "Those with seven attributes in one body" are human beings.

88. Inu's playhouse, Semar's stage refers to the patient's previous occupation as master of the shadow play. Inu is the Prince of Koripan, whose stories and character have been intermingled with those of Seri Rama, the hero of the Kelantanese shadow play. Semar, Inu's servant, is identified with Pak Dogol, the servant of Seri Rama.

T: Well, I'll put an end to the discussion and go on my way. The day is good, the moment has come.

M: Hey! Ah, chap!

[The band plays LAGU BARAT CEPAT, as the shaman assumes the persona of Anak Dewa Tiga Bertukar, the God with Three Aspects. In this aspect, he is identified as an earth spirit by his statement that he is now calling himself Black Beetle: Black is the color of the earth spirits.]

M: [*spoken*] Who's there now, sir?

T: Are you addressing me?

M: Yes, I am.

T: I am the God with Three Aspects. When I appear before you, I call myself Black Beetle. I change my ways and behavior when I'm among those with seven attributes in one body.

M: Is that so?

T: What do you want to talk to me about?

M: I do want to talk to you, sir.

T: Very well.

M: I would like to make sure that the promises previously made to you will be kept.

T: Very well.

M: Sir, you are thirsty, parched, hungry, ravenous. You would like to get a little taste, at least a sniff.

T: Yes, indeed.

M: Then make him well as he was in times past before he was startled, afraid, afflicted by noxious influences by dark of night and light of day.

T: You mean I can't leave any noxious influences behind?

M: That's just what I mean.

T: I can't leave evil influences of any kind?

M: That's right.

T: You want to pay the judgment . . .

M: Right.

T: . . . and redeem the fine?

M: Yes, indeed.

T: With all your heart and soul?

M: Oh, yes.

T: In the way that the mother and father used to serve me my feasts?

M: Oh, yes, indeed.

T: Hey, when will that be, physician?

M: Hey, as soon his health returns according to ancient custom. You mustn't bring asthma to the fortress gates, to the palace courtyard.

T: Is that right, sir?

M: It is.

T: Well now, if I have a word with them, one and all . . .

M: Right.

T: . . . the whole crew of forty-four spirit soldiers . . .

M: Yes, indeed.

T: . . . that closely packed crowd . . .

M: Right.

T: . . . and let them know that they mustn't bring coughing, sobbing, asthma, and throat clearing . . .

M: Right.

T: . . . will you give me my due then?

M: That's right, sir.

T: Hey, now, it's like this, physician. I'm not going to trouble myself about it; if you really and truly mean to give it to me, three days from now I will send you an omen.

M: Is that right?

T: When are you going to give it to me?

M: On the seventh day and the eighth night, if his health returns according to ancient custom.

T: Hey, if it's seven days and eight nights, it will never be finished.

M: That's right.

T: Seven days and eight nights, seven nights and eight days, ai, in that way it never will be finished.[89]

M: If it isn't finished, that's OK too.

89. The spirit is afraid that he will not receive his promised offerings soon after Latip has regained his health since the minduk has implied that there will be a waiting period of at least several days to make sure the changes are lasting. The "seven days and eight nights" are not meant to be an exact measure but merely an indication that it will be sometime in the future. As it turned out, Latip never did give the spirits their offerings. His miserliness got the better of him: he wouldn't part with his own money either to grant the spirits their due or to employ bomoh to refresh his frustrated angin periodically. After enjoying a year or so of returned vitality, his asthma returned and he died three years later.

T: [*angry and suspicious*] What? You mean you won't give it to me?

M: Let him regain his health.

T: I'll restore his health as it was in the past, according to ancient custom.

M: Yes indeed.

T: Very well, dear physician/dalang, I'm going to invoke the Winds he inherited from his parents . . .

M: Oh, yes, indeed.

T: . . . that have descended to him through all the generations.

M: Oh, yes.

T: Don't stay in your cozy nest and hang around the nooks and crannies of your home, or you won't be able to carry any offerings to me out in the fields. Ah, hey!

[The band plays LAGU BARAT CEPAT, as the shaman changes to the persona of the black Borak Raja Burung Sewah Rajawali, the Winged Steed, the Eagle, King of Birds.]

T: [*spoken*] Here I am before you, physician.

M: Right.

T: I'm the very black King of Birds, the Eagle, the Winged Steed. I swoop down upon the seven souls,[90] the five spirits.

M: The third spirit?

T: Yes indeed, my dear physician.

M: Allow me to meet you and ask you for health, since seven souls and five spirits are in danger of being taken, sir.

T: Very well.

M: Now the bird will be joined with its shadow,[91] it's best that you take back . . .

T: You want me to enter through the twelve doors of the one room. Make sure that no one causes nightmares to occur.

M: Quite right.

90. Tok Mamat said people have only one soul (roh) and that talking about seven souls is just a figure of speech, but there is some indication that at one time there was a Malayo-Indonesian belief in seven souls (see, e.g., Skeat 1972 [1900], particularly p. 50; Cuisinier 1951:205). Cuisinier relates the Malay notion of multiplicity of souls to the Batak belief in seven *tondi.* The third tondi (which might be the equivalent of *semangat ketiga*) is characterized as hostile in nature and able to leave the body (Cuisinier 1951:200).

91. The spirit will be joined with the body.

T: No one shall cause him to get thin and dried up. You want me to take it all back, do you?

M: Right.

T: Ha! I'll cut the conversation and put an end to the discussion, aii . . .

[As the band plays LAGU BARAT CEPAT, the tok 'teri dances, shaking his head and exclaiming, "Hey! Hey! Ah, hey!" He changes his persona to Hulubalang Babi Garang, Captain Fierce Pig, a spirit from the jungle's edge. The only pigs in a Malay village are wild pigs who lay waste to villagers' gardens planted near the jungle. They add nothing positive to the Malay's cultural ecology, since Muslims are forbidden to eat the flesh of pigs. When the music stops, the minduk speaks:]

M: Who's that?

T: I'm Captain Fierce Pig, who's always rooting around the building with three spaces . . .[92]

M: Right.

T: . . . compartments, three compartments. What's on your mind? Huh, huh. [*meant to sound like a pig's oink*] I'm about to root around the rajah's village right now, that's the absolute truth.

M: The rajah's palace, do you really mean that?

T: Yes, the rajah's palace, huh, huh [*oink*].

M: Do you think you can manage to do it?

T: I sure do. Why, just now . . .

M: Just now you came to see me, didn't you?

T: Yes, I did. You want to plead with me and coax me to restore his health. You want me to remove all treachery, injustice, and envious stares that make him thin and dried up, make him cough, make him sob, make it hard for him to breathe, and make him keep clearing his throat.

M: It can't continue like that.

T: No, it can't. It can't continue like that.

M: It can't go on like that anymore.

T: Oh, they were bluffing. We entertain them from nightfall to dawn, and they just stick us all in one car.

M: This is just fooling around . . . it's not . . . it's an imitation howdah.

92. The building is the human body; the three spaces are inside the head, inside the chest, inside the belly.

T: A howdah, a howdah coming from . . . oh, now, I can't squeeze into the car.[93]

M: What's the trouble?

T: Well, now, I'll spread the word to one and all, to the company of spirit soldiers in the open fields stretching as far as the eye can see, in the middle of the four crossroads with three branches. The rude jin, the jin who collects wages, the jin who gets tips, I'll kick the whole lot of them. Ah, hey!

[As the band plays LAGU SERI RAMA BERJALAN, "traveling music" for refined characters, the shaman dances near the patient, clapping his hands together and making casting-out motions. When the music ends, Tok Mamat speaks:]

T: I'm Awang Scissors in the Barrel of the Gun; the rajah looks up to the "heavens."[94] Oh, I can't "cut" the speech anymore, I just put these teeth in. I want to yank them out right away. If they were the original "scissors,"[95] it wouldn't matter. Well, now, while we are thinking it over, why don't we change the "pictures?"[96] That would certainly feel good.

M: There are plenty of "pictures" here now.

T: We'll change two.[97]

[Raja Ngah, who had taken the part of the minduk, prepares to take over as tok 'teri, in place of Tok Mamat, who needs a rest. Raja Ngah

93. The complaint about the "imitation howdah" is really about my car. The whole company of ritual practitioners, including the very plump tok 'teri, was imported from Kelantan to Trengganu, squeezed into my car.

94. Tok Mamat is making a pun on the word *langit,* which can mean "the sky or heavens" or "the roof of the mouth."

95. That is, if these were my own teeth (which "cut" the sounds into words), rather than a set of false teeth.

96. "Pictures" refers to the ritual practitioners, comparing them to the "pictures" of the shadow play (as the puppets are commonly called).

97. Tok Mamat goes on to say he is sweating and out of breath. The music starts up again as a new bomoh censes himself and recites his invocation, and a new minduk replaces the last one and takes up the rebab. The following section was sung by two minduk (Raja Hussein = M; Tok Mamat = M2) at the same time as the new tok 'teri (Raja Ngah) recited an invocation to help himself achieve trance. It was impossible to hear everything clearly in this section, since both voices were often speaking together. I was not able to transcribe these particular bomohs' incantations, since such information is usually passed on only to trusted followers, and I was not on the same footing with them as I was with Trengganu bomoh [CL].

recites a protective jampi (which I was unable to hear over the music), while Tok Mamat sings a duet with Raja Hussein, who will now assume the minduk's role. They sing to the tune of LAGU SEDAYUNG MAK YONG, a tune of magical power.]

M (Raja Hussein): If you would send greetings, join me in sending greetings, we would stand together as witnesses. One greeting would travel to the Grandsire, two greetings to the teacher.

M2 (Tok Mamat): Seven teachers and one inang will become twelve in all, five, four, three. Two look just alike, one is white, the teacher's white charm.

M: When he's really awake, the inang bends to the left and sways to the right.

M2: The seven teachers have become twelve. I turn my body into a weapon.[98] Twelve white stones, a black charm.

M: Guard the country while our friend sleeps. I want to arouse the princess. The king is asleep, wake him up within the seven palaces, in the room where he lies.

M2: He lies in the room, the seven rooms. If the door is locked tight, we must open the lock; if it's shut with a bolt, we must open the bolt. If the road has been closed, we must open the road. Nine roads and twelve gates;[99] the king will beckon, the gods will sleep.

[Transition music, LAGU BARAT CEPAT, is played. Raja Ngah, the second tok 'teri, trances and, dancing, assumes the persona of Tuan Kecil Radin Bertimang Gambar, Dear Little Prince of "Pictures" (a word also used to describe the shadow puppets), a personification of the tok 'teri's Wind for performing in the shadow play.] [Spoken]

M (Raja Hussein): You wait patiently near the mango tree, the layang tree, the ratna plant encircling the ru tree's waist.[100]

T (Raja Ngah): Quite so, pengasuh.

98. The phrase used here, *senjata pakaian*, means to make one's body into an invulnerable weapon, so that, for example, the hand becomes like a knife and can cut through wood. Heroes of romance, such as Hang Tuah, were believed to have magical means of hardening their bodies (*kebal kulit*) to make them impenetrable to weapons and so slippery (*kebal minyak*) that weapons will glance off.

99. The nine roads are the eyes, ears, nostrils, mouth, anus, and the opening of the urethral canal; the twelve gates are the aforementioned plus navel, palms, and fontanelle.

100. The ru tree (casuarina) is often used metaphorically to connote sexual love, since its leaves are considered to resemble pubic hair [CL].

M: Yes, indeed.

T: Ah, while the "picture" of the steed serves up the meal, the Hovering White Light of Desire climbs the tree at Kuala Kubu.

M: Yes, indeed.

T: The sky unfolds, making Java and all its works vanish. The Winds, Lisu and Lisi, confer and agree; quiet Winds they are, not at all like the Winds Soh the Hot-tempered, Semar the Hot-tempered.

M: Oh, very true.

T: My name now is Dear Little Prince of "Pictures" from the Land of Grassy Beaches, along the Strand of Blooming Palms.

M: That's right. [*drum beats*]

T: I came straight from the cape at the river's mouth; I leaped into my little junk, my golden barge.[101]

M: Yes, indeed.

T: I sailed for two times seven days and two times seven nights upon that junk until I reached the coarse sands at the harbor's edge.

M: Yes, indeed.

T: Well, where was that—a place with three islands and a harbor? I disembarked, not knowing to what place I had come.

M: Yes, you stared at the islands but could not see them; you stared at the land but could not see the sands.

T: That's right.

M: You were completely confused, you were totally lost.

T: That's right.

M: Yes, your servant spoke four times to the princess, sir.

T: Yes, he did.

M: When you instruct the inang, you inform his *jinjang*.[102]

T: Exactly.

M: I fear that jin may enter uninvited, that mambang may come seeking shelter with the inang. [*rebab begins*]

101. This is a story very similar to that of Dewa Muda, involving a prince who becomes lost, discovers that his parentage is other than he believed, uses a golden means of transportation (in this case a boat rather than a kite), and so forth. I have found no written version of this story. The word *gambar* in this person's name (Radin Kecil Bertimang Gambar), which I translated as "pictures," could have been translated as "puppets," since the puppets used in the shadow play are referred to as gambar [CL].

102. The "princess" spoken to could also be the "shaman" since both are called *'teri* [CL]. Jinjang is another term for familiar spirit.

T: Cease your suspicions, lay aside your cares.

M: Very well, sir.

T: In this direction lies the Rich Land of Grassy Beaches, the Strand of Blooming Palms.

M: Yes, indeed.

T: Our friend has remembered that his true father is really a bomoh.

M: Exactly so. Oh, true.

[The rebab is joined by a drum. Then the other instruments come in as the tok 'teri and minduk sing LAGU SEDAYUNG MAK YONG, magical music. The tune starts very slowly, a typical convention in the Mak Yong when there is a lot of text to sing during each beat. The later speeding up of the duet is due to a textual consideration, as well as contributing to a building up of emotion.]

T: I awake with a start from a heavy sleep. I arise and go to awaken the pengasuh.

M: When you woke with a start from a heavy sleep, what was it troubling you, what misfortune? You could hear a voice cry but could not see the speaker—where was it coming from, who made the sound?

T: I thought of my father, my true father, my real mother. Family ties, ties of religion, ties of white, they pursue me forever.

M: When Awang remembered his true father . . .

T: [*spoken*] When Awang woke up he came straightaway.

M: [*sung*] . . . his real father.

T: [*spoken*] Yes, the real one, very true, pengasuh.

M: [*sung*] The father's name is Ali Akbar.

T: [*spoken*]That's right.

M: [*sung*] The mother's name is Siti Mak Lamah.[103] Ask the mother to let her child receive his heritage into his hands.

T: When I awoke I was all alone. I went straight to the city to sit on the lap, the lap of my father.

M: In the ancestral home, the first stable, the stable and horses which must be passed before one arrives and speaks to the royal father.

T: [*spoken*] Oh, we cut across the cape, we pass the river's curve. [*Sung to the tune of LAGU BERTABUH, the tune of the second tok 'teri.*] I want to change the subject. What drum is that whose sound comes straight from the pengasuh's rooms?

103. Ali Akbar and Siti Mak Lamah are really Adam and Eve.

M: Hey? Wake up, one and all.

[The band begins to play LAGU BARAT CEPAT, the music of transition. The minduk and tok 'teri's voices (as given below) are heard through the music.]

T: Look toward the left, look toward the right, then go straight in the proper direction.

M: Awaken four, five, one and all.

T: The king arises, he writes on the left hand, he writes on the right, he goes straight in the proper direction.

M: Awake, one and all.

[To the tune of LAGU BARAT CEPAT, the shaman assumes the persona of Wak Long, an important comic character in the shadow play. He is very angry at Toki Latip.]

M: [*spoken*] Who's that? One disappears and another takes his place.

T: Mr. Long.[104]

M: Mr. Long?

T: Mr. Long has arrived.

M: The friend of the inang.

T: His penggawa.

M: You eat your fill and then you sit still. Oh, that's how it is, Mr. Long.

T: What's up? The painting isn't over, the bellowing hasn't died down, the film is still being played out.

M: The film about Mr. Long has just begun.

T: It has?

M: I've been waiting. I want to give the inang some instructions, too, while I give instructions I can . . . our little brother, Tip . . .

T: Our little brother, Tip? This is how things stand with our little brother, Tip. I haven't done a proper divination yet, but that's all right, I'll take a look at the candle now. I'll see whether or not it's possible to divine anything regarding the man who used to be called "dalang." Well, I'm Mr. Long. I always used to have a ticket for the evening show. But now, he doesn't throw anything at all to us "pictures."

104. Mr. Long (Cik Long) is Wak Long, Pak Dogol's sidekick (in the shadow play), created out of Pak Dogol's body dirt (the dead skin that comes off with a vigorous toweling after washing). See n. 61.

M: That's true. [*drum beats*]

T: He left all kinds of evil behind.

M: That's so.

T: Well, to sum it all up, sometimes he wants us, sometimes he doesn't.

M: That's true.

T: That's the reason the "pictures" have blocked him. They were ones who had ties of love to the family of Dewa Sang Yang Tunggal.

M: True.

T: It's Brother Persanta from the shadow play who's been making him ill.

M: True. [*drum beats*]

T: The Players want to continue the Play, sir.

M: True.

T: It's the cause of misfortune and turmoil.

M: True.

T: Oh, once he wanted the "pictures," another time he didn't and rejected them. Tip rejected them. [*rebab begins*]

M: Was that his intention from the beginning? [*indistinct*]

T: One day he wanted us, the next day he wanted us, another day he didn't, and the following day he didn't.

M: You mean he didn't speak to you about it?

T: Yes, yes, yes, yes, yes.

M: Ah, that's it, Mr. Long.

T: Well, he doesn't feast me, he doesn't want me for a companion, I don't know where he chased Pak Dogol to, he never spoke to me about it. Well, to make a long story short, I don't feel like being his healer.[105] I don't feel like treating Tok Tip.

M: Hah, look at it this way. If you notice anything that needs kicking, get it and kick it away. We'll try to move his Wind now.

[Popped rice is again placed upon the pillow by the tok 'teri for a second divination, while the tok 'teri and minduk sing LAGU SEDAYUNG PAK YONG, the signature tune of the hero of the Mak Yong, a personage of great magical power.]

105. Wak Long resents the unceremonious way in which he and his fellow puppets were disposed of by Pak Tip.

T: Blessed am I as I climb up the mountain and send a greeting to my fellows.

M: One greeting travels to the seven teachers, the place where the princess has left her mark.

T: We are looking for harmony, for harmony and good fortune, for promises, for promises and meetings . . .

M: Ah, ah.

T: . . . from the seven verses; I don't want more, I won't take less.

M: Everything is now complete. We don't want more, we won't take less.

T: The flower bud came forth from the land of China[106] into the palms of the first pengasuh.

M: If you plant it, plant the rice in the soil of Kelantan; King of Roots, it sits in state.

T: We look for harmony and good fortune in our divination.

M: Ay, ay, ay!

T: The day is good, the time is right.

M: I ask you to remember, remember what's been said. Everything's counted out completely now.

T: Everything's counted out completely now, the seventh day, the eighth night, everything is complete.

M: Enough has been done, it now is complete.

T: Ah, hey!

M: It's now in force by means of the original invocation. The flower bud's accustomed to come ashore and descend into the house.

T: The flowery brothers, children of Princess Kebayan Bunga, are made of sepal and flower bud.

M: Flowers, don't wither away. Flowers, don't drop from your stems, flowers, just follow along in line, you promised us a visit.

T: He sleeps neither by day nor by night; not by day nor by night can he rest. Things that are asked for shall be obtained.

M: Ah, things that are asked for shall be obtained, enough has been done, it now is complete.

T: [*spoken, agreeing*] Oh, lah.

M: [*in a low voice, to the other ritual practitioners*] It's already been

106. The flowerbud, that is, rice, originated in China.

counted, we've looked long enough. Water, there's not much water here. There is some cold water, though.[107] [laughs] Fire, there is some fire, not a lot. We've already looked, we've already done it.

T: Ah, we have harmony and good fortune, more or less, now.

M: Ah, hah, hah.

T: [*in a declamatory voice to the audience, while rebab and drums softly play*] I feel pity and sympathy because the younger brother is suffering as much as the older brother; they share the same origin.[108] The day is good, the time is right, we'll speak some more of this tonight. [*sung to the tune of LAGU SEDAYUNG MAK YONG (fast tempo)*] Invoke the storied ones. Look to the shore where the birds are flying, I'll run there and enter; I'll run to the laps of my father and mother.

M: [*spoken*] Ah, harmony and good fortune. Harmony is there, good fortune as well. [*sung*] Oh, listen to what I have to say, I leave a request, I place my trust, upon the palace verandah right now.

T: When I look at father, my heart fills with pity, when I look at father upon the rolled drapery, I sympathize.

M: His body is in torment, the tears roll down his cheeks. I leave a request, I place my trust. Those on the palace verandah are descended from noble families.

T: The younger brother lives in the palace; he enters the palace verandah, in the village, in the land. He looks to the right, he looks to the left, he begins to sway to the music.

M: He leaves and travels through the land, seeking his fate. Bad luck and misfortune on the palace verandah. [*speaking*] Let him go into trance; if he has the Wind to play silat, then let him play silat. [*singing*] Yes, if his ancestor was Budak Kecil Seri Permainan,[109] I invoke the original Players, I invoke the original dalang—let the dalang emerge.

107. The minduk is making a joke—the "cold water" is a glass of water set beside him in case he wants to drink and has nothing to do with the divination.

108. The younger brother is Latip; the older brother is the placenta and debris of childbirth that emerged when Latip was born. "Siblings" of this sort exhibit the same kind of mixed feelings that human brothers and sisters feel toward one another. The sibling rivalry that they feel is exacerbated by the unequal portions that fall to the human and his "sibling." The human receives his parents' love and inheritance, whereas his "sibling" receives only the half coconut shell and white cloth used as its coffin and winding sheet (see Laderman 1983: *passim*).

109. Budak Kecil Seri Permainan (the Noble Young Performer) refers to the Wind for performing in the shadow play.

T: If he has the Wind of a bomoh, I'll invoke it in bomoh style, here on the palace verandah.

M: Let no one speak, let all sit still and be on the alert, all who share the mother's heritage, the family line.

T: Oh, listen well to my story. The day is good, the time is right to cause the original Players to descend.

M: Yes, listen well to the tale, descendants of Budak Kecil Seri Permainan, of Cik Salim Pendekar,[110] it's time now to come to your friend Tok Tip, Tip, Tip, Tip, Tip, Tip, Tip. Come along!

[The band plays GENDANG SILAT, the music that accompanies exhibitions of martial arts. It stops for a moment while the ritual pair speak:]

T: I call upon my penggawa, those brave and fierce people to whom I make requests, to go on a mission.

M: Do you want to ask them to do something?

T: I want to ask them to become bomoh, to become physicians.

M: Quite so.

T: I want to ask them to come near us, the physicians and healers, and on no account to loiter on the roads or piers.

M: No, they shouldn't loiter there.

[LAGU BARAT CEPAT, the music of transition, is played, changing to GENDANG SILAT as Latip, in trance, rises from the floor and fights with the shaman silat-style. When the music stops, Latip sinks down, out of trance, and is helped up by friends. The tok 'teri has assumed another persona, that of Sang Kala, the spokesman for a family of fierce spirits. The ritual pair speak:]

M: Who has crossed the picket fence to come before the physician/*panglima*/dalang?[111]

T: So, tok dalang.

M: Right.

T: Most illustrious dalang.

110. Cik Salim Pendekar (Mr. Salim the Champion) is the legendary originator of silat, the traditional Malay art of self-defense. Invoking him and playing the music performed at silat matches puts those who, like Latip, possess the Wind for silat, into trance. While in trance, Latip, who had been in a weakened condition for several years, got up and fought the shaman, using the stylized stances and motions of silat.

111. *Panglima* (commander, warrior) has been added to the minduk's titles, since he now confronts a very powerful spirit.

M: True.

T: I represent the powerful ones of these parts, Sang Kala Upstream, Sang Kala Downstream . . .

M: Sang Kala Who Endures, Sang Kala the Large.[112] Hey, you've caused suffering by your unjust actions to the one with seven attributes and one spirit. What kind of sickness have you caused, what kind of treachery have you performed?

T: Hey! I did it by means of malevolent influences.

M: That's true.

T: You won't get rid of us with noise and drumming, but quietly, in private . . .

M: Just so!

T: . . . because I am making claims on behalf of the spirit armies of Sang Kala Upstream, Sang Kala Downstream, Sang Kala Who Endures, Sang Kala the Large, sir.

M: Oh, yes, indeed.

T: Aha hey! [*Drums and serunai blast point the exclamation.*]

M: Those who cause false steps and misunderstandings,[113] their children and grandchildren, can't cause unjust suffering now if you and I can have a serious discussion.

T: Just so, sir!

M: The gods named The Four Sultans will release us from . . .

T: True.

M: . . . for whatever reason . . .

T: Yes, indeed.

M: . . . Sang Kala Upstream, Sang Kala Downstream, Sang Kala Who Endures, Sang Kala the Large, far, far away.

T: Very true.

M: They won't be able to obstruct us . . .

T: True.

112. Besides being a family of earth spirits, Kala is associated with an important (and bloodthirsty) character in a performance given for the feasting of the spirits of the shadow play puppets. Sweeney (1972:278) notes that this ritual is similar in form to the Main Peteri: the dalang, in trance, requires the presence of a minduk skilled in the Main Peteri, who plays the rebab used in the seance, but not in the shadow play.

113. "False steps and misunderstandings" carries the connotation of missing one's stroke at silat as well as stepping into trouble; the play on words is due to the phonetic closeness of silat and *silap* (to make an unintentional mistake).

M: . . . those Sang Kala, whatever their names may be.

T: Oh, true.

M: Well now, I want whoever can release us from evil to cut it off at the source.

T: Hey! Brother Persanta can do the whole thing for us.

M: Brother Persanta is an incarnation of Dewa Sang Yang Tunggal. [*Serunai begins to play.*]

T: Oh, if you please, the day is good, the time has come, ah, hey!

[The band strikes up LAGU SERI RAMA BERJALAN, refined traveling music. During the music, the minduk says, "Release the body from all evil influences. Don't allow any of them to take effect, including kuwung.*"*[114] *The music changes to LAGU BARAT CEPAT. The tok 'teri says, "Hey! Hey! Let there be no mistakes or misunderstandings. I want to continue the discussion." As the music of transition continues, the shaman assumes the persona of an old man who claims to be a pious Muslim, but is in reality the Mighty Spirit, the Hantu Raya who is the spirit most feared on the east coast of Malaysia. Notwithstanding his power, the hantu is still a fit subject for mockery.]*

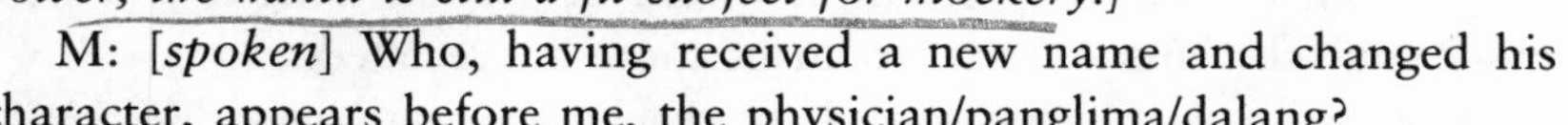

M: [*spoken*] Who, having received a new name and changed his character, appears before me, the physician/panglima/dalang?

T: [*wearily*] Ah, that's so.

M: Yes, indeed.

T: Oh, alas, alas, ah me.

M: Hah, hah, hah.

T: Alas, alas, ah me.

M: Oh, who are you, huh?

T: Alas.

M: Who is it?

T: [*portentously*] Take heed, take heed of my wordies.[115]

M: Hah, Allah!

T: Take heed, take heed of my wordies.

SOMEONE IN THE AUDIENCE: What did he say?

114. Of the many kinds of evil influences talked about by Malays (*cending, seroko, carar, kuwung, badi, etc.*) kuwung is among the most serious and difficult to neutralize.

115. Saying *kecekanan*, a nongrammatical word derived from *kecek* (small talk, chat), renders the spirit's speech ludicrous rather than portentous. I have added another syllable in English (wordies) to preserve the form and the feeling of the Malay.

M: [*joking*] Pour out, pour out the water.

T: Hah!

M: [*laughs*] Who is it, huh?

T: Wak Haji Putih.

M: Oh, Kopiah Lembek.[116]

T: I rule these parts.

M: [*agreeing*] Oh, haha, hah, hah.

T: Early this morning they made a clearing in the forest.

M: Oh, haha, hah, hah.

T: It sounded as though they were having a big noisy party at the foot of the hill.

M: [*laughs*] Hah, hah, hah. Oh, I'll bet it was noisy.

T: Huh?

M: You were invited, Wak Haji.

T: I was?

M: Hah, I'm going there now, Wak Haji Kopiah Lembek.

T: If there's a feast, I'll go there myself.

M: Oh, I'd like you to. Oh, it would be a good thing if you went there yourself; your speech would be more appreciated.

SOMEONE FROM THE AUDIENCE: Is he teaching Koran around here?

M: Are you teaching Koran these days?

T: Well, that's something! Long ago, around these parts, Da'eng Dalit[117] made a clearing near the pool in the forest around here. I'm Uncle White Turban.

M: Oh.

M2 (TOK MAMAT): Can you say your prayers all by yourself?

T: Hey! La'illaha illa'lah, la'illaha illa'lah![118]

M2: Hey, hey, hey, hey, wait a minute, I want to ask you something.

T: Allah!

M2: Have you been studying here a long time?

116. Wak Haji Putih Kopiah Lembek means the Venerable Pilgrim with the Soft Cap (worn by pious Muslim men, particularly those who have gone on the haj). Here the spirit gives away his true identity: he is not a pious Muslim, he is the Hantu Raya (Mighty Spirit).

117. Da'eng Dalit is the Hantu Raya's father. Da'eng is a Bugis title of nobility.

118. The hantu shows his nonhuman origin by his inability to recite more than the first line of the prayer.

T: Not so long as all that; I just happen to look old and weary.

M: Well, hasn't he said he only wants twenty-four hours?

M2: Hah, hah, hah.

T: They'd take as long as they could, that bunch.

M: Only as long as was promised.

T: Twenty-four hours.

M: Hah, hah, Raja Adil.[119]

T: Raja Adil was a great teacher.

M: He certainly was. Who said longer than twenty-four hours?

T: Huh?

M: I'm asking only for twenty-four hours, that's all.

T: I'll be waiting for four full moons, I bet.

M2: Four months is a long time.

M: Oh, four of them will celebrate.[120]

M2: They can celebrate, others will be the winners.

T: I'm the ruler of the people upstream.

M: Oh, yes, that's certainly true.

T: So, what's up, huh?

M: Well, I ask you to return to your people upstream, Muhammad's people whose prayers are constant.

T: The fruit of numbness had just fallen to the ground.

M2: Go away.

M: I'm asking you, how about it?

LATIP'S WIFE: Will you leave? Will you leave?

T: I was just about to leave.

M: Ah, just about to. Ha, chap, hey!

[Very brief music, LAGU BARAT CEPAT; tok 'teri stops the music with a gesture.]

M: What does he want now?

M2: He wants to pursue some more claims.

M: The argument's gone on long enough. We asked you to leave, so why don't you leave?

M2: Well, since you're here, what do you want?

M: What do you want, Grandsire?

119. Raja Adil = The Just King. The minduk is mocking the spirit's "generosity."

120. He is making a pun on "*bulan pernama raya*" (the full moon) and "*rayakan*" (to celebrate).

T: Everything.

M: What do you mean, everything?

T: Hmm, hmm, I'm getting tired of this.

M: Talk about something else. Other things I understand; I don't know anything about this sort of thing.

T: I don't want just anything. I used to get a white chicken, and I want a banner. [*The rest of the sentence is indistinct.*]

M2: That's very little to ask, Grandsire; little and thin, just like your mouth. [*laughs*]

M: It makes no difference whether your requests are heavy or light, sharp or dull, poisonous or bland, hard or soft.

T: I think those guys are lying. [*general laughter*]

M: Hey!

M2: He's a hard case. We traveled a long way to come to Gong Kasim.

M: We came here to ask questions. [*They can scarcely contain their laughter.*]

M2: It was a long way.

T: Did you come from far away to hit and run, I ask you?

M: It's not like that at all.

T: All right, let things be as they were before, let health return.

Man in audience: [*approvingly*] Ah, hah, hah.

M: If his health returns the way it was before, we'll invite you to fill up your belly until it's swollen.

T: Well, if his asthma disappears and his health and strength return according to ancient custom, then I ask you, when will it be? Are you going to give me what I want?

Latip: I will.

M1: Oh, let his health return.

M2: They say you don't want much.

T: [*complaining*] Well, will you give it to me or not?

M2: [*disgusted*] Oooh, Allah!

Latip: What's he asking for?

T: Are you going to give it to me?

M: He will.

Latip: I will.

T: Has he asked what he should give?

LATIP: What should I give; what do you want?

T: One long banner, two long banners.

M: One or two long banners.

LATIP: I'll give him one or two banners. [*drum beats*]

M: Two of them. Ah, two of us here want to sleep. Can he stand to . . .

LATIP: That's no lie.

M2: Can he stand to sit near the window in the evening, near the window in the morning, near his own window, even?[121] [*serunai blast*]

M: Hey! This is what he said. He's the representative . . .

M2: He's our member of parliament.[122]

M: He says that once the patient feels strong and healthy, you'll have to go look for another stomach.[123]

T: How will I receive the representative's offerings? I can see he's a son of Kelantan [*indistinct*].

M2: Oh, my Gawd! [*laughs*]

M: Did he come yet?

T: Come from where?

M2: Ah, he came.

T: What are you talking about?

M: He came from Kelantan.

T: Well, that's far away. If I restore the health of my petitioner, should I send for news to this village?[124]

M2: Who knows?

M: Who knows?

T: That's how I feel.

M: You can't ask beforehand, you can't do that.

T: Are you going to give me what I ask for?

121. This is a thinly veiled bawdy insult: "his own window" refers to his buttocks. The allusion is carried further in a later exchange (see n. 125).

122. Not necessarily a member of parliament, he could be called a representative of any of various political bodies. For a discussion of political allusions in the Main Peteri, see Kessler 1977.

123. That is, you'll receive so many offerings of food that they won't fit into one stomach.

124. Since the ritual practitioners came from Kelantan and the patient lived in Trengganu, the spirit wanted to know where he should go to send for news or pursue claims [CL].

LATIP: I will!

M2: What will you give?

T: Ask him. I'm going home.

LATIP: When will you send me a sign?

M2: When will you restore his health?

LATIP: How long will it be before my health is restored?

T: After seven evenings I believe he'll be able to run down to the seaside over yonder.

M2: Seven evenings.

LATIP: As soon as I'm well, I'll definitely give it to you.

M2: He's willing to sit there with his knees up, near the hole in the window, as he speaks. [*laughter; serunai blast*][125]

M: Let's see how it goes, first.

M2: Let's see how it goes, first.

LATIP: How many *katis*[126] will we two have to carry?

T: If you don't give me anything, after I've restored your health and you are strong and rosy-cheeked, if you don't give me anything, then I'll come back again.

LATIP: It would be hard on me if I gave it to you and I was still sick anyhow; what good would that be? If I don't get well, I'm going to ask you to give back everything I gave you.

T: Oh, that's OK. Give me your hand. [*They shake hands.*]

M2: Hey!

[Transition music, LAGU BARAT CEPAT; speaking through music, the minduk says, "Who is that?" The shaman has taken on the person of Anak Kera Gantih, Hanuman the White Monkey as a child (one of the shaman's familiar spirits). He is gentle and childlike, and speaks in a high-pitched little voice.]

M: Who is it, eh?

T: [*in a high small voice*] I'm Anak Kera Gantih. [*soft laughter in audience*]

M: [*laughs and speaks in an indulgent way, as one would to a cute child*] Oh, my, I just called you over.

125. The "hole in the window" is Latip's anus, which was supposedly revealed by his immodest manner of sitting. The laughter that the audience indulged in here was decidedly "dirty laughter" [CL].

126. *Kati* is a unit of weight measurement (one kati = 1.3 lbs.).

T: I am Anak Kera Gantih.

M: Huh?

T: I am Anak Kera Gantih.

M: Oh, Anak Kera Gantih, Anak Kera Beleh,[127] why have you tagged along?

T: Huh?

M: You can't do that.

T: I'm looking for fruits.

M: For various fruits?

T: Fruits of many different kinds. I'm looking for asthma fruit, I'm looking for coughing fruit, too.

GONG PLAYER: Hey!

LATIP: There's plenty of coughing fruit here. [*audience laughter*]

M: We don't want it. Well, now, I'd like to hear the future prophesized; we don't want asthma, we don't want coughs.

LATIP: Don't give me any more.

M: No, we don't want it. It's OK if you want it, it's your share.

T: You want to exchange[128] it?

M: Yes.

T: You want to exchange the coughing fruit for something else?

M: Yes, we do.

T: You want to exchange the asthma fruit for something else?

M: Yes, we do.

T: There's no use talking to me about it. You'll have to speak to Cik Amat,[129] the king's retainer, who supports him day and night.

M: Well, as far as that goes . . . [*drum beats*]

T: It's not my responsibility.

M: Oh, now we can discuss anything at all. If you don't spin your thread[130] like that, it's all right, it doesn't matter among dalang.

127. This visitation is from one of the shaman's familiar spirits, Hanuman Kera Putih (the White Monkey), the monkey son of Seri Rama and Siti Dewi in the shadow play. Anak Kera Gantih and Anak Kera Beleh are names used by Hanuman in his childhood (see Sweeney 1972).

128. There is a play on words here between the monkey's name (Gantih) and *ganti*, meaning "to exchange."

129. Cik Amat is another of the shaman's familiar spirits.

130. Another play on words: *gantih* means "to spin thread." The meaning here is "if you don't want to do it."

T: Everyone's a dalang here. [*drum beats*]

[Sung to the tune of LAGU SEDAYUNG MAK YONG:]

T: I've been daydreaming. I've been thinking in my heart, all alone.

M: Hey, wake up, brother, I'll shake you till you wake. Brother of mine on the palace verandah, you come from a good and honorable line. Hear my story, hear my tale.

T: Hear the story. I want to enter a country . . .

M: True.

T: . . . a country called Weeding the Flower Garden.[131] If the flower is received along the way, all will receive it.

M: Blessings on the flower as it blooms, the flower with seven petals. The first petal makes the flower bloom, the second petal is called the Antidote Stone.

T: Sway to the left, sway to the right, go straight to the father's room, to the mother's room, and awaken them. I want to hear news of the vanished princess.[132] Where has she gone to, where disappeared?

M: If there are three petals, the flower is called Marble; if four, it's called Starburst of Sapphires. If there are five petals, it's called Yellow Stone, if six, it's the same thing.

T: My sister was abandoned far from the courtyard, the courtyard of the palace. Where has my sister vanished?

M: Hear my story, hear my tale. The body's flower follows its form. Flower, don't fall from your stem.

T: Ah, saa . . .

[The shaman dances to the music of transition, LAGU BARAT CEPAT, shaking his head as he changes to a gentle feminine persona, Princess Zohor, who speaks of the theft of Latip's semangat, personified as her sister, Princess Flower.]

M: [*spoken*] Who are you?

T: [*sung to the tune of LAGU BERKABAR ("Giving News Tune"), in a pained and wailing voice*] Oh, father, the pain is shooting through me. My name is Princess Zohor.[133]

131. The flower is a metaphor for the human spirit; weeding the flower garden is caring for the spirit.

132. The princess is another metaphor for the human spirit, which is said to have fled or been taken from the patient. This becomes even more evident when, shortly, she is referred to as a flower with seven petals, a delicate replica of the human seven body parts.

133. Zohor is the Islamic afternoon prayer.

M: [*sung*] If your body's all bruised, may your body be healed; I send you my love, it's a serious matter.

T: Oh, father, where has my sister vanished? Where has she disappeared? My sister's name is Princess Flower, where has she gone, where has she vanished?

M: I don't know where she vanished, no one told me where Flower disappeared.

T: [*spoken*] I am Princess Zohor, father. While you sit, sad and compassionate, the flower with seven petals is being eaten away, father. My sister, Princess Flowerbud, has vanished, who knows where, stolen out of her cradle and taken away, by whom I don't know. [*Murmurs from the audience, discussing the significance of this news. The rebab continues to play softly, and the drum is softly beaten.*]

M: Very true.

T: They say she was taken by the one called Make the Baby Laugh, that it is certain she was taken away from the top of the main mast[134] by his forces. Day and night she sits, her face pale, her body close to dying.

M: Very true.

T: She's just skin and bones.

M: Very true. If you won't help her, she'll remain in pain and suffering.

T: Ah, that's so, father.

M: Yes, it is.

T: That's how it is with Princess Flowerbud.

M: Yes, indeed.

T: They say she is definitely atop the main mast. I want to get her, but she's out of reach. I want to pluck her down, but I fear I might fall.

M: Yes, indeed.

T: I will follow the troops down the true road to the land and sea of Malaya, father.

M: Yes, indeed. [*drum beat emphasis*]

T: [*sung to the tune of LAGU SERI RAMA BERJALAN (refined traveling music), as the tok 'teri slowly dances. The words are those of*

134. When a baby laughs and there is no apparent stimulus, Malays say that his "sibling," the placenta, is playing with him. As we have seen, the "sibling" is not always beneficent [CL]. The "main mast" is the human backbone, the top of the main mast is the head. The patient's semangat was stolen out of his body.

Seri Rama's song from the shadow play, sung here in eight-beat wayang style with ornaments] I'm thinking as I walk, I'm thinking as I walk. [*As the music continues in a long instrumental interlude, the tok 'teri says to Latip, "Don't be shy."*]

T: [*spoken*] Ah, that's it, father.

M: Oh, yes, indeed.

T: Well, when I was following my sister . . .

M: Yes, that's true.

T: . . . she had already arrived at the tip of the tongue of land at the river's mouth.

M: Yes, indeed.

T: Well, I wanted to reach the lake across the ocean of Malaya and ask for help from the white elephant with nine tusks[135] who lives across the sea from Malaya. [*rebab begins*]

M: Yes, indeed.

T: To ask him to extend his trunk from there to here.

M: Among those whose body hair is upside down, whose tongue is clever, whose spittle is salty, things that are asked for will occur, things desired will be obtained. [*murmured audience discussion*]

T: That's right, father.

M: Yes, indeed.

T: Let us ask the white elephant with nine tusks across the sea from Malaya to manifest itself.

M: Yes, indeed.

[Sung to the tune of LAGU SEDAYUNG PAK YONG, signature tune of the personage of greatest magical power in the Mak Yong.]

T: I ask the Heavenly Midwives, eternally beautiful, I ask them to descend upon the white elephant.

M: They are truly magical, wonderful beings, whose body hair is upside down, whose tongues are clever, whose spittle is salty.

135. A white elephant with nine tusks appears in a dream to the Raja Besar, father of the Conch-Shell Prince, in the Mak Yong play, "Anak Raja Gondang" (see Ghulam-Sarwar 1976:339). The white elephant here symbolizes the sweating and subsequent cooling down of the patient. Its nine tusks are the body orifices through which the body can rid itself of impurities. [The elephant is later credited with seven tusks which then refer to the seven body parts.]

T: Among the forces of the gods, things desired can be obtained, because they are beautiful, magical beings.

M: Dalang from these parts, dalang from elsewhere, we pay our respects.

T: I want to welcome the teacher from the seven curves in the road into the palace. I want to guard the white elephant in the land of Malaya.

M: The seven teachers stride, the elephant is white.

T: The seven teachers stride, step towards the white elephant.

M: The white elephant with nine tusks.

T: I ask the gods to descend and imbue us with their power, the original gods, the gods of beginning.

M: Original gods, beautiful Heavenly Midwives. What is asked for will occur, things desired can be obtained.

T: I still can't reach the flower to pluck it down. It's blowing in the wind.

M: Let the wind blow it from the mainland.

T: What is asked for will occur, things desired can be obtained.

M: Blow from the mainland, from the mainland.

T: Ah, cik, ha saa!

[Transition music—LAGU BARAT CEPAT.]

T: [*spoken*] Here I am, father.

M: Yes, indeed.

T: My younger sister who was here has gone home already.

M: That's true.

T: Her face and body both are pale.

M: True.

T: It's because I have not yet restored her to health; I must restore her to health and strength, along with my inang.

M: Oh, yes, indeed.

T: There have been errors and misunderstandings. I light incense and ask the highest of gods to restore my sister's health.

M: We'll proceed in this way, with bouquets of gold and bouquets of silver, with *sintuk, beluru* vine, limes, fine powder, and coarse powder.[136]

136. See n. 56.

T: Oh, is that so?

M: Yes. If you please, the day is good, the time has come.

[Music of transition, LAGU BARAT CEPAT. Shaman dances near patient, changing persona to Awang Malas Mati (Awang Loathe to Die), one of his penggawa. They discuss the necessity of invoking Latip's Winds, and sing of his birth-sibling.]

M: [*spoken*] Who are you, sir?

T: Oh, you want to know, do you?

M: Right.

T: I'm Awang Loathe to Die.[137]

M: Is that so?

T: I'm carrying a sword and a torch.

M: That's true.

T: Since I have friends, my chest is four yards wide; since I have friends, my torch is lit with five flames.

M: True. [*rebab begins*]

T: Well, this servant of the Most High wants nothing other than one sharp blade.

M: True.

T: The one I already gave orders about.

M: Hmm.

T: Well, when I gave those orders to my friend and beckoned to the penggawa's envoy, from which side did he wave?

M: Ah, from no side whatsoever, if you're referring to Tip over there.

T: I am.

M: Oh. Which Winds are you talking about?

T: Which Winds does he bear? Which Wind was it just now? He has a warehouse full.

M: He has a warehouse full of heroic Winds. We'll play them out to his heart's content.

T: If they want to emerge, let them do so with grace. If they want to arise, let them do so sweetly.

M: The Tiger Wind hasn't appeared yet, has it? Play on, we haven't

137. Awang Malas Mati (Awang Loathe to Die) is another of the shaman's familiar spirits. *Malas* here carries no connotation of laziness, but, rather, refers to unwillingness.

seen the Tiger Wind as yet.[138] Oh, play on. If he wants to fight silat, the feast is ready.

T: Oh, that's delightful!

[Sung to the tune of LAGU SERI RAMA BERJALAN ("traveling music")]

T: Climb upon the tail of the Wind.

M: He was brave, but he suffered injustice. [*speaking*] Body of a beast with a human face, he is the genuine older brother.

T: [*sung*] He rested in the original womb.[139]

M: [*spoken*] True.

T: [*sung*] The same path, the same origin.

M: [*spoken*] Real older brother, true older brother.

T: [*sung*] Wake from your sleep on the palace verandah.

M: The true, genuine older brother. Your father doesn't love you, your mother doesn't cherish you. Long ago you sat atop the thorny palm for forty days, thrown there by the Seven Midwives. To what place did you fall? To the four roads with three branches, the sky for your roof, the earth for your pillow.[140] You mustn't take revenge against your younger brother, you really should not.

T: You are a descendant of a noble line.

M: You ascended the skies to the seventh heaven.[141] Your name is Dewa Berma Jaya, brother of the Green Horse.[142] Body of a beast, with a human face. You descended to earth in the guise of the Great Tiger. [*spoken*] Oh, in the guise of the Great Tiger, Harimau Besar Serjan Kilat.[143]

138. Even though Latip has already performed silat while in trance, this was in response to a Wind specific to silat, Angin Cik Salim Pendekar. The Wind of the Tiger had not yet been invoked.

139. That is, the placental "sibling," only partly human.

140. A reference to the burial of the placenta; see Laderman 1983:158.

141. The heavens, the earth, and hell are believed to be composed of seven layers each (corresponding in macrocosm to the human seven body parts). The seventh heaven is the highest (see also Wilkinson 1959:310, 896).

142. Latip's "birth-sibling" is being equated with the afterbirth of Seri Rama, which turned into the Green Horse (Sweeney 1972:138). "Body of a beast with a human face" shows its dual nature: of human origin but not fully human [CL].

143. The Great Tiger (Harimau Besar Serjan Kilat Sejalur Wangi) is an important character in the ritual drama of the shadow play (Sweeney 1972:285), as well as personifying Angin Hala. *Turun sarung*, which I have translated as "descended . . . in the guise

T: [*sung*] In the past, I ate yellow rice, . . .

M: [*spoken*] True.

T: [*sung*] . . . roast chicken, seven kinds of wheat, pancakes, popped rice, seven measures of sugarcane.

M: [*spoken*] Seven kinds of wheat, a measure of popped rice, seven sugarcanes, limes, coarse powder and fine.

T: [*sung*] Coarse powder and fine, along with seven candles.

M: [*spoken*] Seven candles. [*sung*] Oh, Seven Tiger Spirits with forty stripes, seven macaques, seven tender shoots. Make haste, be swift, the day is good, the season is charming.

T: [*sung*] The day is good, the season is charming.

M: [*spoken*] Be on guard from above.

T: [*indistinct*]

M: [*sung*] Guard the "releasers";[144] if you are hungry you can have a taste, you can have a smell of yellow rice, roast chicken, seven kinds of wheat, along with seven candles.

T: Seven kinds of grain, roast chicken, along with seven candles. Open the four gates.

M: I beg of you, be kind, open the gates with kindness, the time has arrived. Don't let anyone sleep on the palace verandah.

T: [*indistinct*] Open the gates, open the windows.

M: [*indistinct*] Your mother's name is Lady Fatimah,[145] if your family's good and your background is fine.

T: Oh, yes.

M: The heir to the Main Peteri, upon the palace verandah.

T: True heir on the palace verandah, if you're thirsty and parched, if you're hungry and starving, bristle your fur. You are brave and strong and quick to anger.

---

of," actually means to assume a form by climbing into it physically (as into an envelope), a common occurrence in the shadow play.

144. "Releasers" are made of two strips of palm frond tied together in a double slipknot, used to release a patient from a state of danger. They are held before a patient while the ritual practitioner recites an incantation, ending with "1,2,3,4,5,6,7, you are released," at which time the ends of the "releaser" are pulled apart.

145. According to one origin story, the first patient to be cured by the Main Peteri was Fatimah, the daughter of the Prophet. Her husband, Ali, was assisted in the cure by the Companions of the Prophet [CL].

M: Dodododo.[146]

T: Hey!

[During the following song, the ritual partners encourage Latip to trance, invoking the Wind of the Weretiger, but to no effect, since he does not possess this Wind. The other members of the troupe add encouragement, joining in with shouts of "Hey! Ah!"]

M: Dodododo, heir of the Seven Tigers, seven tigers with forty stripes, servants of The Great Tiger, dodododo, dodododo. [*spoken*] Oh, stupid one, you are the Tiger's child. [*sung*] Dodododo. Open the windows, open the doors, your origins are good, your background is fine. Dodododo, if you are hungry and starving, dodododo, let no one bar your way. Your mother's name's Black Meriam, the Tiger's keeper, one of the troops of the Seven Holy Steeds, dododo. The story of the Seven Tigers is over, now I want to recall the story of Princess Zali, the adopted daughter of Dewa Penchil,[147] of the line of Hang Jebat, Hang Tuah, Hang Lekiu, Kasturi, who could turn their bodies into weapons,[148] creators of four stances and nine steps for silat. Umar Umaya,[149] the first, the original silat master, whose father and mother both were fighters. Be alert, tiger spirit, when you leap, tiger, tiger, tiger spirit, tiger spirit, great tiger spirit. Great Tiger, Sergeant Lightning, Fragrant Striped One, lash your tail, unsheath your claws, whet your fangs. Hear my story, hear my tale, listen, listen one and all. Let no one disturb the peace. All of you, of the same origins, from the same family line, all you heirs, hear my story, hear my tale. Let no one hold vain memories. If you are truly an heir of Budak Seri Permainan, the King of Players, I invoke the original players. Let no one lose his way. Let no one quarrel or fight. I call upon the nine silat masters, King Ali and Hang Kasturi, who could turn their bodies into weapons, awake, awake. Hear my story, hear my tale. Our heritage and origins are truly fine. Heirs of Hang Jebat, Hang Likir, Hang Likiu, who knew how to turn their bodies into weapons. Father and mother both were

146. Supposed to mimic tiger noises.

147. Dewa Penchil is the hero of a rarely performed Mak Yong story and the archetype of a basic personality type.

148. These are all heroic characters in the Malay epic, Hikayat Hang Tuah.

149. Umar Umaya is a cunning, Ulysses-like figure in the Hikayat Hamza (Wilkinson 1959:1265).

fighters. Who governs silat gayung? Umar Umaya, the first, the original fighter of silat. Let no one who can't remain silent try to create stances and steps for silat. Commander Ali, Excited Ali. Ah, Tip, Tip, Tip, Tip.

[Latip goes into trance, influenced by the invocation of the Wind of the silat masters. In trance, he fights the shaman, while the band plays GENDANG SILAT. During the fight, the shaman recites invocations to the Wind of the Silat Masters, and calls on them to protect Latip. The music ends; soft laughter and appreciative conversation take place in the audience while the performers rest. People comment on the energy shown by Latip, whose asthma usually made him easily fatigued. Tok Mamat says that they really did good work tonight. The music begins again, LAGU SERI RAMA BERJALAN.]

T: [*spoken*] If you call on others, they won't descend. Only the Winds of wayang kulit and silat have descended. After this we'll have to let him do a shadow play. It has to be tonight, because that's why we've come. Let him content his heart. It's eleven o'clock already. [*He motions for someone to hand him a dish containing a glowing ember of benzoin to cense the puppets.*] That's enough fighting for him. If he wants to fling himself on the ground, that's OK. That's enough fighting, fighting is painful. If we're dealing with a sickness that makes people fight all the time, I don't want any part of it.

[LAGU SERI RAMA BERJALAN (expanded); Latip, in trance, is handed the puppets of Pak Dogol and Wak Long.]

T: Guard us, Black Semar; guard us, King Ali.

M: Ask him, go on and ask him.

T: Hey, Semar, why have you brought sickness to our dear dalang? When you descend, cast away all kinds of poison so that his ailing body may be healed. You give me the power when you descend to earth, the mortals' abode.

M: Oh, descend, Brother Persanta.

T: You can't let this situation continue.

M: Oh, descend upon Pak Tip.

[LAGU SERI RAMA BERJALAN; Latip manipulates the puppets as in the shadow play. The tok 'teri recites jampi which cannot be heard clearly through the music.]

T: [*speaking in a low voice to minduk*] Allah! Give us another one, won't you?

M: Which tune would you like?

T: It doesn't matter which.

[Music starts up again with LAGU PAK DOGOL, the signature tune of the Pak Dogol puppet. The tok 'teri, muttering jampi over Latip, helps him to come out of trance; the puppets are put away. The music stops while the players confer softly, then the ritual pair sing a duet to the tune of LAGU SEDAYUNG, a tune of magical power.]

M: Oh, which tune shall I play? Your origins are good, your heritage is fine. Restore your servant to health. [*spoken during tok 'teri's song*] Take pity because of our serene prayers, and see that no one causes him terror and confusion. Take pity, calm his thoughts, for the sake of the first kings, descendants of gods. Surely our origins are good, we are heirs of Ali the Invulnerable. Since hordes of jin are seeking revenge upon the twelve dalang, let the gods protect them, carry them carefully in a litter, in their hands.

T: [*sung*] As in the beginning, if you travel, leave a request, place your trust.

Pak Long: [*spoken aside to me in the audience*] He's instructing the gods.

T: [*sung*] Fine origins, heritage . . .

M: [*sung*] The king will arise, the gods will emerge. Surely we are on good terms with those of the seventh heaven, the vast myriads of gods, the enormous hordes, who've released us from evil since the beginning of time. [*spoken during tok 'teri's song*] Try to hear me, friendly, exalted gods of the line of Sang Semaris, friend of Samad,[150] Grandsire, Sang Alam Dewa Tunggal, descend. May the scent of gods pervade the air.

T: [*sung*] Descend, oh gods, and be worshipped; let the flowers descend, two flowery brothers, a pound of flowers, two pounds, a ton, two tons.[151]

M: [*spoken*] Allah! We must call upon a ton or two of friends, call forth an abundance of golden adornments. We must call our friends [*indistinct*] from the forces of Si Alam Tunggal.

150. Semaris (Chemuras) is Turas in the Panji cycle, the companion of Semar, and thus equivalent to Wak Long in the Wayang Siam; Samad is the Patani equivalent of Wak Long (Sweeney 1972:42, 224).

151. Actually, one or two kati, one or two *pekmor* (keti = 100,000 and peku = 1,000 in Javanese).

T: [*sung*] Oh, Grandsire from the domain of Dewa Si Alam Tunggal in the highest heaven, strew down bouquets of gold and silver flowers. Sintuk, beluru vine, limes, fine powder, already on the table, coarse powder, too, to render harmless ten kinds of danger.[152]

M: [*sung*] Ten kinds of danger, oh, people of the seventh heaven, descend and kick away noxious influences.

T: [*spoken*] Troops of Si Alam Tunggal.

M: [*sung*] Descend and sweep away all noxious influences from the body.

T: [*sung*] Cast out poisons and noxious influences and make our dear dalang well again, oh Youngest Dalang, Middle Dalang, Old Dalang, Young Dalang, let the whole line of dalang descend. [*Spoken aside*] You who were born dalang, we surely want you to allow the Wind of the dalang to descend upon our friend. Descend and free him from whatever noxious influences there are, because of your shared heritage.

M: Descend, cast out evil.

T: Strew down bouquets of gold and silver flowers, strew down limes. Guard this living, breathing child, return the dalang to health. Look with favor on the youngest child of the tuan 'teri, twelve in one.[153] [*spoken*] Be careful to see that those born to be kings associate with kings, those born gods associate with gods, those born warriors associate with warriors, those born nobles associate with nobles. The king sleeps deeply beneath his covers; when he bathes he wets himself thoroughly; he is in good health on the palace verandah. The noble's at ease to sleep deeply. [*sung*] It's time to obey the call to rest, to sleep soundly, to wet

152. The danger specified here is *carar*. I was told of two specific types. The most common occurs only in midwives, who run the risk of impaired eyesight as a result of their having witnessed the mystery of birth. To avoid carar, they must regularly release themselves from this danger during the postpartum ceremony, which also takes the new mother and child through the final stage in this rite of passage (Laderman 1983:205). Another type of carar is no longer a problem, since it was associated with tooth-filing, a practice that died out within the last twenty to twenty-five years [CL].

153. "Twelve in one" because within the one body are twelve protective forces (see n. 62), and, as well, the body is made up of seven parts and five senses, twelve in all.

154. *Tersenang Sini*, which I have translated as I Am At Ease Here, means both to be at ease and to have come out of trance. The shaman's aim, during this long speech, is to protect himself from the spirits who have appeared during the seance while making sure that everything returns to its proper place in the scheme of things.

ourselves thoroughly when we bathe upon the seven verandahs. The commander of gods called I Am At Ease Here[154] is now at ease, the king is at ease from his labors, the king is at ease in his throne room, the noble's at ease in the throne room. [*the music stops; spoken*] Under no circumstances may you cause destruction by dark of night or light of day. Why is it that those born to be kings are content when they associate with kings, when those born nobles associate with nobles? When the waves have died down, the Winds are at rest, the company of The Intruder, the company of Fear and Trembling, Confusion and Stupidity, Hidden Message of Annihilation, the noxious influences from the earth I just mentioned, all are at rest. It isn't I who repel them. If arisen from the skin, let the skin be at ease, if arisen from the body hairs, let the body hairs be at ease, if arisen from the flesh, let the flesh be at ease, if arisen from the blood, let the blood be at ease. Let this happen because of the two physicians, the one servant. Release us from all noxious influences, release us in the Name of God, my guardian, God and all His holy saints who descend to neutralize harm. [*indistinct*] Guard me, Awang Mindung Pengasuh,[155] along with the other ancient supernatural beings, throughout the day and night, because of the requests I make, because of the trust I place. [*sung to the music of LAGU BERKABAR ("Giving News Tune")*] Commanders at ease with commanders, nobles at ease with nobles.

M: The waves have died down, the waves are at rest. Why have the waves died down, why are the Winds at rest?

T: The warrior is at ease, the noble is at ease, at ease in the king's throne room, the nobleman's Winds are at ease in his body. Why should the minduk call you to tell you the news?

M: The minduk's name is Fruit of White Waters. The princess on the dais will be a bride by midday. The waves have been put to rest by the strings of the Winds.[156]

---

to protect himself from the spirits who have appeared during the seance while making sure that everything returns to its proper place in the scheme of things.

155. Awang Mindung Pengasuh, mentioned in the preceding paragraph, is the full name for the *Peran* (servant-attendant) in the Mak Yong.

156. Allusions to White or Foamy Waters are common in birth incantations (e.g., Laderman 1983:141); they are appropriate in this context since much of the symbolism of the Main Peteri involves childbirth itself and, by extension, rebirth away from a state

T: The great waves have returned to their kin, the pengasuh has returned to his fellows, the princess has returned to her tree.[157] One and all are at ease, each in his place in the palace.

[Transition music—LAGU BARAT CEPAT. The shaman whirls his head in trance for the final time, returning to his own persona. When the music ends, he stretches his limbs and smiles. Latip's color has heightened, his breathing is unlabored. Latip's wife and her friends serve coffee and cookies.]

---

of danger. "Princess" and "bride" could also have been translated as "shaman" and "minduk," since the terms carry both meanings. The waves put to rest are Latip's emotions and angin; the "strings of the Winds" (*tali angin*) that have put them to rest are the strings of the minduk's spike fiddle.

157. The "tree" is the human backbone, the home of the internal 'teri (princess and shaman), the body's healer that we all possess within ourselves.

7

Seance for a Sick Shaman

Late one Friday afternoon, my son, Michael, and a group of children came running down the hill from Kg. Padang Pauh, where Michael had been studying martial arts. They told me that Pak Long was very sick, that he was calling for me and needed me to come right away. As I hurried up the hill I saw crowds of people standing around Pak Long, who lay on the ground gasping for breath. They urged me to do something, fast—Pak Long was dying. He appeared to be in great pain, unable to move, and clutching at his chest. Several neighbors helped him into my car, and we drove to the hospital in Kuala Trengganu. Since it was the Islamic sabbath, the hospital had only a skeleton staff on duty. A resident examined him but failed to discover the source of his pain. No one was available to perform more sophisticated tests. The symptoms, including pains that traveled throughout Pak Long's body (usually associated by rural Malays with illnesses that have some degree of spirit involvement), didn't add up to any syndrome recognized by the resident. He gave Pak Long an injection of vitamin B, a popular procedure in both the hospital and at local private clinics when nothing else comes to the medical mind. It is given, and works, primarily as a placebo.

Pak Long did appear to feel better after the shot. The doctor suggested he stay overnight at the hospital and be subjected to laboratory tests the following morning, but said that if he preferred, he could go home and come back to the hospital the next day. Pak Long chose to go home.

Night was falling as we drove back. After we left Kuala Trengganu, Pak Long's sense of well-being began to diminish and his pains started to return. The closer we got to home, the more intense were his pains. When we got as far as Tok Daud's house in a neighboring kampung, Pak Long asked me urgently to stop and pick up his friend and ritual partner. When we arrived at Padang Pauh, Pak Long seemed almost as ill as when we had left. His next door neighbor, Pakcik Din, said he believed the sickness had started when Pak Long passed by the graveyard on his way home from the mosque. Pak Long lay on a floor mat while Tok Daud recited jampi over him. When he didn't respond after forty minutes of incantations, Tok Daud said it was time to have an emergency Main Peteri. My assistant, Yusof, drove to Kg. Gong Balai, a nearby kampung, and roused Awang Jalal, a bomoh accomplished in Main Peteri, from his sleep. It was midnight by the time the company was assembled in Pak Long's house: Awang Jalal as tok 'teri, Tok Daud as minduk and rebab player, Ali playing the *rebana* (a hand-held drum with parchment stretched over one side), and his wife, Cik Mas, playing an overturned pot, which substituted for the *canang* (floor gongs). The audience was unusually small for this impromptu seance: only Mak Long (Pak Long's wife), my assistant, Yusof, and myself.

The *nasi guru* was prepared and hung from the rafters; the instruments were censed; Tok Daud recited a short jampi over his rebab. Pak Long was too weak to sit up, so he lay on the mat in front of the performers, a pillow beneath his head. Mak Long prepared a plate of raw rice with chopped turmeric, one of popped rice, a bowl of perfumed water, and a dish of *kemenyan* (benzoin lit for incense), all of which she arranged on the mat. Tok Daud took up his rebab and sang the song of greeting, calling on the benevolent forces of the body and briefly recounting the story of Creation and birth before he invoked the spirits of the earth, the village, the plains, and the jungle. When he finished, Awang Jalal, who had changed into a clean sarong, sat down in front of Tok Daud. As Tok Daud sang the Bestirring Song (Gerak Angin), Awang Jalal censed his body and prepared to go into trance. The Bestirring Song, meant to evoke the Wind of the tok 'teri, praised these powerful hereditary elements of his personality which originate in the sex act. At about the midpoint of the Bestirring Song, and forming a kind of counterpoint to it, Awang Jalal began to recite an incantation meant to strengthen and protect him during the coming seance. As he approached trance, the music of the band became faster and louder, and his head and body shaking became more violent. The music stopped, and the first spirit visitation took place.

It was Radin Kecil Mulia Maharaja (His Small Majesty), one of the body's protective forces. After a dialogue and duet with the minduk, he was replaced by Seri Mas Raja Bomoh (Golden King of Bomoh), who presided over the popped-rice divination. The divination revealed that Pak Long's illness was caused by earth spirits who had been angered when offerings that had been promised to them were not forthcoming. After he was startled by a sudden fall, which left the protective "gates" of his person momentarily open, the spirits took the opportunity to launch their attack.

Following the divination, a spirit claiming to be the assistant *penghulu* (headman) of the earth's realm illuminated the problem further. About a week before, Pak Long and Awang Jalal had participated in a Main Bagih (similar to Main Peteri but lacking instrumentalists) for a young woman visiting her parents in Gong Balai (a nearby kampung). After three months of pregnancy, her bowels had closed for almost a week. This caused severe abdominal pains that did not respond to treatment at the hospital in Kuantan, Pahang, where she ordinarily lived with her husband, a hotel manager. The seance had been a disturbing experience for Pak Long. The family, recently arrived from Pahang, understood neither the theory behind the performance nor the etiquette expected of its sponsors. Although Pak Long waited patiently for some time after his arrival and preliminary examination of the patient, who lay groaning and clutching at her belly, the usual pre-performance feast was not provided. The spirit offering had not been prepared, and the pinang branch, used by the shaman to brush away evil influences, had not been plucked. For the first time in his practice, Pak Long was forced to instruct his clients as to the basic ingredients he would need in his seance and to wait while they boiled an egg and some rice, and popped other grains of rice over dry heat. When the performance was about to begin, I remarked on the absence of perfumed water, which Pak Long asked them to fetch. Pak Long's rapid head-shaking as he achieved trance was greeted with laughter. When the performance was over, neither cakes nor coffee were offered. The young woman's father handed the outraged Pak Long only $2.00 as his fee, which he had to share with Awang Jalal, who had acted as minduk.

The patient's tormentors, who borrowed Pak Long's voice when they appeared at the seance, included earth spirits and a particularly powerful jin, Datuk Minyak (Sir Oil), sent by a bomoh employed by enemies of her husband. The spirits, finding the husband healthy, attacked his more vulnerable wife. During the course of the Main Peteri, these spirits were promised a number of offerings if they would consent to restore the woman's health. Datuk Minyak, said to take on human form in order to rape or kill before disappearing to view, was particularly insistent, holding up first one hand, then the other, then both feet, to show how much money he demanded. Pak Long commented later that he had sensed an unpleasant oiliness when Datuk Minyak appeared.

The patient's husband, skeptical of the value of the seance, took his wife to a private clinic in Kuala Trengganu the following day. When she recovered, the family attributed her cure to the clinic's medicine rather than to Pak Long's seance. They not only neglected to give the promised spirit-offerings but also held a feast (*kenduri*) to which most of their neighbors were invited and did not invite Pak Long.

An earth spirit, appearing during the emergency seance for Pak Long, revealed that he had attacked him because he considered it Pak Long's responsibility to see that the offerings were made. The minduk explained that Pak Long was only acting as an intermediary for the patient and her family. He was joined by members of the audience (including myself), who advised the spirit to seek redress from the family in Gong Balai.

When Pak Long heard the divination and the earth spirit's explanation of his illness, he sat up, his pale face became suffused with color, and his eyes lost their dull heaviness. When the next spirit visitor arrived, making further claims, Pak Long felt strong enough to try to persuade him to follow the first to Gong Balai.

The last ghostly visitors, three brothers, agreed to assist in removing all evil influences from Pak Long. The Main Peteri ended with a duet celebrating the end of chaos and sickness, and the return of peace and harmony. The spirits had returned to their origins, and all was again in its proper place in the universe.

After the final music, marking the transition from ritual time and space to the world of everyday life, had died down, Mak Long brought out tea and plates of cookies. Pak Long rose from his mat and stuffed several bills into Awang Jalal's and Tok Daud's shirt pockets, despite their protestations. He, for one, would see that decency and decorum prevailed and that his physicians were paid their due.

Pak Long's pains were gone. We did not return to the hospital the next day. By morning, he was able to resume his work as tobacco farmer and bomoh. His ungrateful patient and her husband had gone home to Kuantan soon after their feast, and we heard nothing further about them.

The following is a transcription of the ritual:

SEANCE FOR A SICK SHAMAN

[Pak Long, ashen-faced and breathing shallowly, lay on a mat near Tok Daud, who played the rebab and sang an invocation meant to awaken the spirits, both internal and external, that would assist at the seance and to ask for divine blessings on the night's work. He was joined by Ali, playing the hand drum, and Cik Mas, who hit an overturned pot with a stick. While Tok Daud sang, Awang Jalal changed into a clean sarong and tied two sashes tightly around his waist:]

Minduk's Introductory Song

Oh, let the rites now begin with a greeting to my kinsman.
One greeting goes to the Grandsire,
One greeting I send at this time.
Grandsire, don't let problems double,
Oppress and cover and fill up the spaces.
Grandsire and god within the king's palace,

And I, as well, within the palace,
As I try to awaken my minduk.[1]
Awaken, old minduk, young minduk,
Awaken, old tok 'teri, young tok 'teri,
Together with the seven drummers and five fiddlers,
Twelve in one.[2]
Each of you awake.
The white minduk awakens the shaman upon the royal dais,
Awakens the drummers in the palace of bone,
Awakens the fiddlers in the palace of flesh.[3]
The minduk awakes and the waves dance[4]
To the beat of the royal band.[5]
Ah, the fiddlers awaken the sleepy gongs.[6]
One awakes while all speak,
Wakens with the original Player,
The original Player of the earliest Play,[7]
Each of them awakens.

1. As Tok Daud explained, all of us have a minduk, a tok 'teri, and many other forces inside own bodies. They can be aroused by the minduk's song. They work with the bomoh to heal the patient. When the patient is in harmony with himself and the universe, his body can heal itself.

The microcosm-macrocosm identification is a constant of the world view presented in the Main Peteri; its language must be understood as referring at the same time to the universe outside and the world with the body [CL]. (See also Cuisinier 1936; n. 151, chap. 6.)

2. "Twelve in one" because of seven body parts plus five senses. See n. 1, chap. 6.

3. The royal dais is the human head, the palace of flesh and bone is the human body.

4. The dancing waves refer to the style of dancing used in the Main Peteri (very similar to the style of the Mak Yong) and to the emotions the participants feel during the ceremony.

5. The royal band (*nobat*) is not only the most treasured part of a Malay ruler's regalia but is also essential to his investiture, since Malay rulers are installed to the sound of its music rather than crowned. (See Sheppard 1972 for further information on the nobat). The comparison of the Main Peteri musicians to the musicians of the nobat continues the use of royal allusions previously noted [CL].

6. The gongs mentioned are *canang*, which are not hanging gongs but floor gongs. Overturned kitchen pans are often substituted [CL].

7. According to Pak Long Awang (a shaman who is the patient in this Main Peteri), and Awang Jalal, the tok 'teri, *gebiah*, which I have translated as "Play," is a generic term for all spirit-raising seances, including Main Bagih, Main Peteri, Main Berhantu, and so forth. See, however, Cuisinier 1936:74–83; Gimlette 1971 [1915]:76–77 for discussions of gebiah as a specific genre.

We cut across the cape, we pass the river's curve[8]
And invoke each of the seven teachers,
The sixth, fifth, or seventh, they're all the same age,
The fourth and the fifth ones look alike.[9]
Three vanish and two appear, two vanish and one appears,
The white sovereign remedy of the master,[10]
The white stone that is not powder.
Then the pious sages will pray
While the master observes
As he runs straight up to the seventh layer of heaven
Then soars right down to the seventh layer of earth.[11]
Last of all teachers and first of all teachers,[12]
Of a long line,
Who meditates within the glassy pool
Of earthly beads.[13]
The first of his names is Prince of the Koran,
The second, Sincerity, the third, Kumar Hakim,[14]

8. A common formula, meaning "to take a shortcut, or to make a long story short."

9. The seven teachers are really the seven body parts. It is no wonder that they are all the same age since they are all part of the same body.

10. Three refers to the offering of rice, money, and betel quid placed in the hanging tray before the start of the Main Peteri. Two refers to the two types of spirit helpers who receive the offering: Nenek Betara Guru and the penggawa (the shaman's familiar spirits). One refers to the name of the offering, nasi guru (the teacher's rice).

11. *Tujuh petala langit, tujuh petala bumi* are the seven strata of earth and sky. Although Wilkinson (1959:896) gives an elaborate description of each stratum and its inhabitants, Tok Daud was sure only that the *dewa* (gods) live in the upper heaven, human beings live on the first layer of the earth, and some of the earth spirits live on lower levels.

12. "Last of all teachers . . ." is reminiscent of the description of Muhammad as having been the last prophet, in his bodily manifestation, and the first, in his spirit (*Nur* Muhammad) [CL].

13. The glassy pool refers to the eyes, the beads to the pupils. The eyes are the first human attribute that develops in the child before it is born.

14. Kumar Hakim was the first bomoh. His knowledge was so deep and his treatments so effective that while he practiced no one died. Allah could not allow this, so he placed Kumar Hakim in a cave and sealed up the entrance. Before he was incarcerated, Kumar Hakim passed on some of his knowledge to his apprentices. Each time knowledge is passed from master to apprentice a bit is lost in transmission. That is why the world is in the sorry state we find it in today. (This was related to me first by Pak Long Awang, and I heard essentially the same story from several other bomoh.)

Hakim, which means learned man or judge, became the name generally used for the practitioner of Islamic medicine in medieval times and is still used in India to refer to

The fourth of his names is King, Radiant King.
Grandsire comes down to earth and becomes Beramah the
Invisible,
He comes down to earth and starts on a journey
To the white-peaked mountain, to practice austerities,
Under the sky which has not yet been sundered.[15]
He asks for burned incense, for mats to be spread[16]
When he comes down to earth once more.
The first of his names is Prince of the Koran,
The second, Sincerity, the third, Kumar Hakim,
The fourth of his names is Radiant King.
I invoke the Sky Father, the Earth Mother.
The Father's name was Nur Allah,
The Mother's name was Nur Ahut[17]
When the angel held them in his hands.
Just forty days in the father's womb,[18]
A full forty days in the father's womb.
Then from the tip, in that time long ago,
Fell a drop, a mere dot.
Then it was thrust in the mother's womb.

---

practitioners of Unani medicine (literally, "Greek," but actually Islamic, which developed out of Greek medical theory), in contrast to *vaid*, or practitioner of Ayurvedic (traditional Indian) medicine (Leslie 1976).

15. The earth and sky had not yet been separated; before Creation.

16. These are two of the necessary conditions for the performance of Main Peteri. Mats of the finest quality possessed by the owner of the house in which the ceremony is to take place are spread on the floor. Incense fumes, thought to attract spirits by their dry heat and fragrance (see Laderman 1983:57), are used by the shaman to perfume his body prior to trancing [CL].

17. Nur Allah means the Light of God. No one could tell me the meaning of Nur Ahut or why the Earth Mother is called by that name. I suspect that it may have originally been Nur Ahadiat (Divine Light of Beginning) and was shortened as it passed down by rote from master to apprentice [CL].

18. The word used here, *kandungan*, is the same word ordinarily used for a woman's womb. East coast Malays believe that while both sexes possess rationality and animal nature, men have more of the former and women more of the latter. It is, therefore, appropriate for a baby to begin life in its father's brain, where it receives rationality from a highly developed source. The father is believed to be pregnant for forty days before the mother achieves that state; indeed many couples "remember" the husband's food cravings preceding those of the wife (Laderman 1983:74–77).

The mother is pregnant nine months and ten days.
May the child be safe in the womb.
May it suffer no harm, no attack, no disaster,
Father, let there be no misfortune, Mother, no attack or harm.
May the child be a healer, may he be a physician.[19]
The Father's tale over, where next shall we land?
We land in the earth's realm for an audience with the Earth
  Jin.
Imps of the soil, earth spirits, earth goblins,
Forces of His Highness Light of the Bottom,
From the bottom of the earth,
His Highness Light of Speech, from the middle of the earth,
His Highness Thundrous Light, from the realm of the earth,
Black Turas, Senu.[20]
Hear me, hear me, I leave a request, I place my trust.
May no errors enter into our discussion
With the spirit armies of the king in the earth.
I will not change names,
Each letter remains.[21]
Hear me, hear me, one and all.
The tale of the earth's realm is over, where next shall we
  land?

19. I have translated bomoh as healer and tabib as physician. *Tabib* has the connotation of physician of Arabic medicine, in contrast to *bomoh*, a native Malay practitioner; however, for the village Malays involved in the Main Peteri there appears to be no true distinction.

20. Senu usually refers to Bisenu or Bersenu (Vishnu), and occasionally to another high god (i.e., Dewa Senu is a descent of Betera Guru in one play recorded by Sweeney 1972:182). Turas is the companion of Semar, a servant of Prince Panji, who created Turas from his own body dirt. Semar himself is an incarnation of Si Alam Tunggal (or Sang Yang Tunggal), the chief dewa of *Kayangan*, the abode of the gods. In one version of the shadow play, however, Semar is identified with Ijazil, the angel who refused to bow down to Adam and was cursed and changed into a devil. In his pique he burnt himself and half of Kayangan (Sweeney 1972:179–180). The blackness of the Semar and Turas puppets is echoed here by the blackness associated with the earth spirits [CL].

21. When I asked about the significance of these lines I was told that many Malay men, when they leave their villages temporarily to work elsewhere, give false names to their new employers and acquaintances. If they should happen to get into trouble and have to leave, it will then be harder to trace them. The minduk is saying that he is being completely honest and will not try to hoodwink the spirits.

We land at the edge of the village,
And seek audience with Nenek Sang Gana,
The headman and goad of the village and groves.
Two colors, by the dark of the moon,
The jin descends and releases The Yellow Lord Who Asks to
  Fly,
Young Beramah Yellow Essence of Flying,[22]
His Ethereal Majesty Beramah the Soarer,
The Essence of Flying, the Young Glider,
Called Western Lightning when the time is ripe.
I make a request, I place my trust
In each of you servants and sons of the king
At the edge of the village.
Oh, hear me one and hear me all.
Let no error enter into the discussion
With all of the servants and sons of the king
At the edge of the village.
Oh listen, I ask one and all to hear.
Where next will we land?
In the open plains, to seek audience with Nenek Raja Hakim,
The king of the plains, the prince of the jungle,
Raja Bali[23] of the plains, the sultan of the plains.
Seven spinsters and widows[24] are there, if we count them.
I ask you to hear me, one and all.
I make a request, I place my trust.

22. Yellow is the royal color in Southeast Asia, as purple was in Europe. In view of the complaint of Islamic orthodoxy that the ceremony is a holdover from the Malays' Hindu past, it is interesting to note that a jin, a supernatural being from the Arabic tradition, releases one of the chief deities of the Hindu pantheon (Brahma).

23. Raja Bali is a major figure in the shadow play cycle (Sweeney 1972).

24. Although *bujang* (which I have translated as spinster) can carry the meaning of "servant," it more often refers to a currently unmarried person of either sex, whether never married, widowed, or divorced. *Janda* (which I have translated as widow) refers to a previously married but currently single person, due either to death or divorce. The spirit bujang of this section may be etymologically related to *bajang*, a term used in other Malay states, but not in Kelantan and Trengganu, for spirits that afflict pregnant women and young children (Skeat 1972[1900]:321–315; McHugh 1959:72–75; Colson 1971). These spirit bujang and janda are not associated with obstetric problems but are, rather, spirits of the fields [CL].

Let no one step over the line.[25]
Let no one leave his territory,
None of you men of the king of the plains.
Hear me, hear me, one and all.
This tale now is over.
Next we land in the jungle, where the shade trees grow densely,
To seek audience with the Black One, descended bodily,
With the Yellow One who oversees destiny.
Black One, from whence did you spring?
Yellow One, where do you roam?[26]
The forces of Beramah the Invisible come, his descendants arrive.
I ask you, please hear me, hear me new holy ones,
New holy ones, old holy ones,
Worshipped holy ones, holy ones not worshipped.

[Toward the end of the Prelude, the tok 'teri sat down in front of the minduk, his legs crossed in tailor style, and prepared to achieve trance. At the close of the Prelude, the band played the transition music that accompanies travel in the seance, into sacred space, within the self, or during the act of changing personae. Then the minduk began a reprise of the same music as that of the Prelude. This time, however, it accompanied the Bestirring Song, which moves the tok 'teri's Winds and assists him in achieving trance. Toward the middle of the Bestirring Song, the shaman began his spoken incantation, calling on his familiar spirits to protect him during the seance.]

25. Tok Daud says that this means that spirits should stay where they belong and not interfere with humanity. Sweeney (personal communication) comments that the original idea is that of a magic circle drawn on the ground, for example, *baris Laksamana* in the Rama tale.

26. The world of the spirits and the world of the spirit made flesh are linked through the identification of disembodied spirits with the by-products of the birth process. Spirits are not only creatures of the earth, the fields, the sea, the jungle, but originate within ourselves as well. Tok Daud explains (and all of the other ritual specialists I spoke to confirm) that each time a baby is born, three siblings come into being: the child, the afterbirth (the black kinsman), and the blood spilled in parturition (the yellow kinsman—yellow being a frequent substitute for red in Malay symbolic thought [see Laderman 1983:99, 242]).

Minduk's Bestirring Song[27]

Ah, I utter the name of God with one Alif.[28]
Alif stands at the gates of Heaven.
I spread a welcome at the gates of Earth.
Ninety holy prayers I recite,
And then I will open the pent-up Wind.
Wind as small as a sesame seed,
Wind as small as a mustard seed,
Wind called a golden bouquet of flowers,
Wind called a silver bouquet of flowers,
When it emerges, three brothers strong,
A family of four companions.[29]
The first is called Angin Lahar Ahmad,
The second is called Angin Umara,
The third is called Angin Nur Jila,
The fourth is called Angin Nur Zila.
They arose long ago, in the earliest times.
The Winds put forward the father's secret.
The Winds still receive the prayers of the past.
The Winds emerge from the tip of eternity![30]
They descend, through the father, to his posterity,

27. *Gerak angin*, the name given to this section by the ritual practitioners, means "bestirring the [shaman's] Wind." Human talents, drives, needs, and desires are characterized as Winds, the airy component of the four elements that make up the human body (and the rest of the universe). It is believed that without the proper angin, no amount of training will make a person a successful healer, midwife, puppet master, singer, dancer, and so forth. The minduk's song, the shaman's incantations, the censing of his body with benzoin fumes, and so forth encourage his angin to flow and allow him to achieve trance [CL]. Compare this section with Gimlette 1971 [1915]:279; Winstedt 1951:75.

28. See n. 29, chap. 6.

29. The four companions are earth, air, fire, and water. Angin Lahar Ahmad (sometimes called Angin Al-Ahmad; *lahar* means lava) is a hot red Wind of anger that can cause strokes and madness. Angin Umara carries *nafsu jahat* (wicked desires). Tok Daud could not characterize Angin Nur Jila and Angin Nur Zila; he had learned their names but had either not learned more about them or had forgotten.

30. The phrase I have translated as "the tip of eternity" is *hujung kadim* in the original Malay. Hujung means tip; kadim can mean the eternal, the future, and people of the same descent, depending upon context. Tok Daud comments that all of these meanings apply here, since *hujung kadim* means the tip of the penis. All human characteristics, the

Along with the welcome Winds of the mother.
The father has chosen forty days,
The mother was pregnant for nine months.
The father's name is Ali Akbar,
The mother's name is Siti Halmah,[31]
The child's name is Wise One is Born.
The Wind is lit with five rays of light,
It stands and recites six magical words.
The Wind comes out with seven claps of thunder.[32]
The Wind comes out of a handful of earth,
A drop of water, a tongue of flame, a puff of air.
Earth, let there be no oppression.
Water, let there be no floods.
Fire, let there be no scorching.
Wind, let there be no great sin.
Let us talk about families of men loyal and true
And the time they descended to earth.
Brother Persanta Gerga Jiwa,
Brother is he to Radin Pati,[33]
True princes are they.
Each of you, wake up and meet face-to-face
Near the seven gates, every one of them vanished.
The gate to the lane, each gate to the valley,
[The shaman begins his incantation here.]

---

way we look and the ways in which we behave, are inherited through the seminal fluid and the female sexual secretions. This has been true from the beginning and will continue into the future.

31. Ali Akbar is Adam, Siti Halmah is Eve.

32. The five radiances are the five senses. The six magic words are the four cardinal directions plus up and down. The seven claps of thunder correspond to the seven body parts.

33. Radin Pati is one of the names of the hero of the Panji tales. Persanta is his servant. Panji and Seri Rama, the hero of the shadow play, have taken on each other's characteristics and have become closely identified, as have Persanta, Semar, and Pak Dogol, the heroes' servants. According to the ritual specialists, the servant is really the great god, Si Alam Tunggal, in disguise [CL]. Gerga Jiwa is the name of one of Rama's arrows (Cuisinier 1936:193). For further information, see Sweeney 1972:210, 224; Knappert 1980:102; Skeat 1972 [1900]:584; see also n. 62, chap. 6.

The gate of lust, the gate of passion, the gate of desire,[34]
The gate that shuts off elemental desire,
The swaying together.[35]
Awake, budding flower.
The gate of law, the gate of faith, the gate of wisdom.
Open the gate with a key,
Open the latch of the gate,
Golden gate, latched from without,
Locked from within.
Gate fastened shut with Muhammad's needle,
Before the jeweled gate where the spirits stay,
Spirits of the pores, spirits of the skin.[36]
Oh, call upon each and every king
To open the way for the Wind Lahar Ahmad.
Wind that stands with one strong faith.
Original kings, royal by nature,
Warrior gods of the royal line,
Winds of our family, winds of our heritage,
Now I open the way for the friendly Winds.
Winds of the father's line, Winds of the mother's,
Winds that interpret our very souls.
Let the father's Winds wake, the Winds of the father.
Let the father's friendly Winds emerge out of his semen.
Powerful Winds, the Winds show their power,
Pervasive Winds, Winds penetrating,
Awake to raise and put forward your king.
Hear me, each and every one.
The young warrior, the old warrior,

34. *Matekat*, although it derives from *itikad* (faith, purpose), has taken on the meaning of sexual desire in Main Peteri and wayang kulit. *Sir hawa matekat cita rasa*, a string of words that all connote desire, is a common wayang formula (Sweeney, personal communication).

35. *Di wadi mani manikam* are the four elements of seminal fluid which together make up what I have translated as "elemental desire." Di creates earth, wadi creates water, mani creates fire, manikam creates air. The "swaying together" is the sex act.

36. Every part of the body has its attendant spirit.

The fruit[37] of the father from ages past.
The Wind receives the ancestral heritage,
The seed of the father, the stock of the mother,
And awakes within the bright, clear glass.[38]
Then it moves within the mother, then it moves and
starts to fly.
Awaken and raise the Winds of the Four Kings.
Awaken and raise the Winds of the Four Commanders.
Awaken and raise the Winds of the Four Guardians.
Awaken and raise the Winds of the Four Heroes.
Awaken old warrior, awaken young warrior,
Awaken old warrior with the first of the kings,
May trouble not increase nor pile up upon us.
Awake, Muhammad's white warrior, as you did
In the days you were close to the White Stone,
The White Stone, the Black Remedy.[39]
A warrior steps upon old steel,
A warrior leans upon new steel,
The warriors carry new steel
From the earth, from the Pillars of Heaven.[40]
Wake up at once, may friends and penggawa.[41]
Where have you vanished, invisible ones?
Now let us go and awaken the inang.[42]

37. *Buah ayah* (fruit of the father) = *buah pelir ayah* (the father's testicles, the seat of his fruitfulness).

38. The "clear glass" are the eyes.

39. The White Stone is the "teacher's rice," hung from the rafters of the structure in which the seance is taking place. The Black Remedy is the areca nut, part of the betel quid included in many spirit offerings.

40. Steel and iron are used not only as symbols of strength, but are actually employed to strengthen people's *semangat* (vitality, spirit). For instance, during the *lenggang perut*, a ceremony performed by the midwife for a woman during her first pregnancy, the midwife lightly touches her patient's skin with a razor blade or knife. After the baby has been born, his grandmother receives him on her lap, upon which a knife or scissors has already been placed (Laderman 1983:89, 157).

The Pillars of Heaven (*tiang aras*), a term used for the human backbone (according to all of the ritual specialist I spoke to), has been part of Malay mystic nomenclature for at least 150 years. For an early citation, see Newbold 1839:351–352.

41. See n. 44, chap. 6.

42. See n. 50, chap. 6.

Awake along with two penggawa,
Awake one and all.
Awaken, White Crow, steed of the gods![43]
Practice austerities up on the mountains,
The Hill of Intimacy, the Flaming Mountain,[44]
In the forest near Mount Heap of Bones.[45]
I bid you awake with all haste and speed.

The Shaman's Incantation

[Toward the middle of the Bestirring Song, the tok 'teri, having previously censed himself with benzoin fumes and washed his hands and face with perfumed water, began to recite his incantation. Since it was impossible for me to hear every word clearly in the background of the minduk's much louder song, I recorded it separately on the following day.]

T: Peace be with you. I want to send prayerful greetings to the Divine Teacher, to awake him so he may glide down to earth. While the Grandsire issues his pious commands, his wonderful knowledge, to the shaman and the minduk, may he guard the shaman's Wind as it emerges straight from the heavens down to the earth. I ask for assistance in raising it properly. Bless the awakening of all who sleep deeply, including Hanuman Ikan,[46] invisible here, lost to view there. Rouse him to carry all of the Winds, the spirits who escort the Winds. For what reason do I now ask to open the four gates, the gates of beginning, the gates

43. The White Crow is mentioned as a character in the shadow play, associated with Garuda Tarbuni (Sweeney 1972:150–151). Calling it the steed of the gods relates the crow further to Garuda, the steed of Vishnu. Tok Daud, however, did not mention any of these references. The White Crow, he said, is the human soul (*roh*).

44. Bukit Berapik Gunung Berapi is a place-name found in some versions of the shadow play (see Sweeney 1972:144, 160). According to Tok Daud, it signifies two separate places, one cold (Bukit Berapik), the other hot (Gunung Berapi, the flaming mountain or volcano). (See Laderman 1983:35–72 for a discussion of the significance of hot and cold in the Malay symbolic universe.)

45. Mount Heap of Bones is the human head atop the human skeleton.

46. Hanuman Ikan (the Fish), the son of Hanuman the White Monkey and the Fish Princess in the shadow play, is one of the shaman's spirit familiars.

that are latched? The Wind sways the original king, the hereditary king, of good ancestry, of fine family. Twelve warriors of the king,[47] gods who set the world in motion, awake and hear me one and all, at this time, at this moment. Four gods, gods of our heritage, seven gods, descendants of gods, I want to receive my father's inheritance, my mother's inheritance. I want to speak of the Wind's descent through the family line since, without it, I, the inang, would be left with a heedless heart.[48] Awake, gods of our heritage, gods of our origins. I want to raise the seven gods, the legendary gods from the stories of gods, the tales of the seven gods.[49]

I awaken you sweetly, invoke you with care. Winds awake at this time, at this moment. Dewa Kecil Derma Jaya,[50] Dewa Andera and Andera Dewa,[51] awake and bring each of the Winds to the center of Inu's and Turas's stage.[52] I awaken you sweetly, invoke you with care, Dewa Penchil, Dewa Semar, gods together with Dewa Muda.[53] Awaken sweetly, appear to view. I want to speak to the Queen of Java, to awaken her sweetly, invoke her with care.

I will speak now of other matters. Awake, oh twelve famous Winds, four heroes, four guardians, awake, old warrior, sole warrior, warrior taking a fighting stance, awake. Remember Hang Jebat, remember Hang

47. A reference to the forces of the body. The number twelve denotes the seven body parts plus the five senses. See n. 1, chap. 6.

48. The drive and talent to be a shaman are considered to have been inherited and are called the bomoh's *angin* (Wind). Without angin, we would all be uncaring husks of flesh [CL].

49. The stories of the shadow play and the Mak Yong are used in the Main Peteri to represent archetypal personalities. To put a patient into trance, the shaman often recites excerpts from the story that best fits the patient's character, or calls upon the archetype to the accompaniment of appropriate music.

50. Dewa Derma is one of the names of a god who rules a portion of Kayangan (see Sweeney 1972: *passim*).

51. Dewa Andera and Andera Dewa are characters in a Mak Yong play (see Sheppard 1974:40–48).

52. The center of Inu's and Turas's stage ordinarily refers to the shadow play, but here the reference is to the place in which the Main Peteri is held. It is interesting to note that the most important of the wayang kulit rituals, the *berjamu* (feasting the spirits of the puppets), requires the presence of a minduk as well as a dalang (puppet master). The dalang performs the berjamu while in trance. The berjamu features a play within a play, in which the Turas puppet acts as dalang (Sweeney 1972:281).

53. See notes 7, 62, 81, and 145, chap. 6.

Tuah.[54] Awake, old warrior, young warrior. Remember the first silat masters, Umar, Osman, Umayah,[55] at this time, at this moment, the originators of silat, fighters through and through. Make no mistake, it's no trivial matter. Awake as I speak to each of my many friends, my numerous penggawa, to whom I beckon, to whom I call for a discussion in the palace courtyard. My friend, Wak Tanda Raja, Awang Jiding, I say, at this time, at this moment, Awang Mahat, the elephant driver,[56] I call upon you, at this time, at this moment. Awake, Mother White Swallow,[57] awake sweetly and flap your wings. Forces of Semar Lengah, Semar Lengan. Let no one go back and forth at this time, at this moment. Ah hey! Protect me from every sort of evil.

[At the end of the Bestirring Song, the minduk and tok 'teri cried "Ah, hah!" giving the band the signal to begin the music of transition. The shaman's foot started to shake, and the movement traveled up his body to his head, which whirled vigorously as the shaman achieved trance. When the music ended, the shaman had taken on the persona of Radin Kecil Mulia Maharaja, His Small Majesty, one of the body's protective inner forces.]

M: [*spoken*] One king with two names[58] who takes pity on the favorite child of Nerajit,[59] from which bay does this fragrant person

54. Hang Tuah is the quintessential hero of Malay legend and Hang Jebat is one of his companions.

55. Umar and Osman (two of the Companions of the Prophet) are being confused or equated with Umar Umayah (see n. 144, chap. 6). Silat masters are considered to have inherited Angin Umayah or Angin Cik Salim Pendekar [CL].

56. Wak Tanda Raja (Old Man with Regal Tokens) is the spirit of a divining bomoh. While in this persona, the tok 'teri performs the divination. In Main Peteri conducted by other ritual specialists the spirit bomoh is sometimes called Maharisi Mata Api (Sage with a Fiery Eye), or Wak Kedi Bomoh (Old Healer from the Siamese Monastery). See n. 64, chap. 6 [CL].

Awang Jiding is the pulse; Awang Kasim (sometimes called Awang Kasim Gila) refers to the eyes of the shaman as he goes into trance; Awang Mahat is the nape of the neck, the center from which the shaman shakes his head in trance. The elephant (the word used is *beram*, a literary word for elephant; however, Tok Daud said it was a rutting elephant) stands for the emotions, which must be under the shaman's control as an elephant is under the control of his driver.

57. Mother White Swallow is the human spirit (semangat).

58. "One king with two names" means that the shaman has taken on a second persona; he is "carrying" a spirit.

59. Nerajit is one of Mahraja Wana's sons in the shadow play (Sweeney 1972:94). Tok Daud identifies him only as a dewa.

come, bending to the left and swaying to the right, shaking his head until he's out of breath, running and flying to the palace courtyard? Who is being carried by the inang?

T: [*spoken*] Is that so, sir?

M: Yes.

T: I was furious when the sound of your voice, pengasuh,[60] swirling toward the palace verandah, awakened me.

M: Oh, indeed.

T: Someone new has bobbed up dancing there in the palace.

M: Ah, true.

T: The sound of the ghostly royal band entered the seven verandahs, the five castles, the one palace.[61]

M: Ah, quite true.

T: I left in great haste, confused and heedless, running and swaying to the left, to the right, toward the sound of the band, to you, Grandsire, to the shadow of Ba[62] where the mats have been spread.

M: Ah, yes, indeed.

T: I receive a new name and change my character.

M: Ah, yes, indeed.

T: I'm called Radin Kecil Mulia Maharaja.[63] I've been keeping an eye on the inang and his *jinjang*.[64] Why all the haste, why the confusion?

M: I can tell you politely why I called you, Little Prince.

T: Oh, yes, quite true.

M: You make the inang bend to the left and sway to the right, cause him to shake his head till he's past caring, in the courtyard of the palace.

T: Oh, yes, indeed.

60. See n. 45, chap. 6.

61. The seven verandahs are the seven body parts; the five castles, the senses; the one palace, the human body.

62. See n. 29, chap. 6.

63. He is one of the forces of the body.

64. *Jinjang* is not only the attachment of the shaman and his familiar spirits (penggawa), but is also a word that means "person who escorts the king's herald." Its double meaning carries forward the royal references used in the Main Peteri.

M: Now when I instruct the inang, I inform his jinjang. Let no one be forgetful, let no one make mistakes. Guard well the fortress within, strengthen the outer barriers.[65]

T: Do you want me to, pengasuh?

M: Oh, yes.

T: I'll instruct the inang and inform his jinjang while I guard the four outer walls of the palace, the two worlds facing this village.[66]

M: Oh, yes.

T: I guard the right, the left, behind, before, above, below—I guard the four outer walls, the corners of the world, seven corners, eight villages.

M: Ah, yes, indeed.

T: Also, I frighten all seven jin, five imps, jin of four types, devils of four sorts, who would cheat and lie to the inang in the palace.

M: Oh, that's true.

T: From the very beginning, before Creation was complete, I guarded the four outer walls, [*indistinct*] caverns, the two bends in the river, the fortress of excrement, the gateway to wisdom, sir.[67]

M: Ah, yes, indeed.

T: When I guard from below, I become a foundation; when I guard from above I become a shelter. I've been guarding my friends from behind since the beginning.

M: Oh, yes, that's true.

T: Ah, we've been idling away the herald's time.

M: That's my good fortune. Sweet is the story you tell, the news that you bring; nothing is false, more truth is revealed. You make it easy to give you our offerings.

[His Small Majesty sings a duet with the minduk.]

T: [*sung*] The sounds of drumming have reached our Grandsire, the pengasuh's invocation has reached our Grandsire. [*spoken in an undertone during minduk's song*] Early ancestor, first teacher, keep your

65. "The fortress within" and "the outer barriers" are the inner defenses of the body and its outer protections against spirit invasion, often achieved by means of *pengunci* ("locking" charms).

66. The two worlds: the external universe (the macrocosm) and the universe within our bodies (the microcosm).

67. A marvelous description of the human condition [CL]!

promise, let no traces be left behind.[68] Grandsire, don't deceive me. I ask you to travel straight down the proper road.

M: [*sung*] Ei, I ask you, early ancestor, first teacher, Grandsire, don't double our problems. Grandsire, please don't deceive me.

T: [*sung*] In the time of our early ancestor, in the time of the first teacher, Grandsire, whom we greatly honor tonight, was called . . .

M: Ei.

T: . . . our teacher was called . . .

M: Ah.

T: . . . The Player Who Stands in the Night, who stands and speaks twice, three times, five times, and never is silent. [*spoken during minduk's song*] The first speech is for all souls, the second is for the breath of life, the third is for all bodies, the fourth is for those of noble descent. Don't forsake the body, body do not abandon the soul. Soul, don't abandon the body before its time has come.

M: I want to recite three prayers. The first lifts the soul to the breast, the second lifts the breath of life.

T: [*spoken*] Yes, indeed.

M: [*sung*] The third lifts the vital force, the true feelings. If your feelings are beautiful, they make you feel good.

T: [*sung*] In those times long ago, Grandsire didn't trick or cheat, Grandsire didn't let problems weigh us down.

M: Ah.

T: I ask the teacher to shower our souls with peace tonight.

M: Ei, I want to take on the task of the healer. Grandsire, I want to be entrusted, entrusted with your secrets. Your child will be a physician and healer.

T: [*speech during minduk's song unclear*] [*sung*] Our friends, the five old warriors, four royal healers, ancient ancestors, invisible souls, kings long vanished, great men of the past, descend tonight to the inang so that he may become a healer.

M: Awake, old ancestral warriors. Awake, my king, invisible soul. Awake, hallowed dead. Awake with great haste and speed.

T: [*speech during minduk's song unclear*] Hah!

[Transition music begins—Tok 'teri speaks during music: "Eiiii.

68. No traces of any noxious influence, like the vapor of genies.

Guard me, my many friends and numerous penggawa. Hear me, one and all." When the music has ended, the shaman has received the persona of Seri Mas Raja Bomoh, the Golden King of Bomoh, who presides over the divination.]

M: [*spoken*] Ah, you emerge with a rush, swaying, confused and heedless, receiving a new name and changing your character. One person has gone and another has taken his place. Who are you?

T: [*spoken*] Indeed, pengasuh?

M: Oh, yes.

T: The grandchild leaves and the widow appears. The younger brother leaves and the older one appears, the older brother leaves and the younger takes his place. That's how it is when I receive a new name and change my character. Let's take a shortcut.

M: Yes.

T: Ah, they call me the Old Warrior, and by now I'm really old.

M: Yes, you certainly are old.

T: I'm the Golden King of Bomoh, an ancient ancestor, an invisible soul, a vanished king.

M: Ah, be alert tonight, sir. Be alert, golden warrior king of bomoh, ancient ancestor, invisible soul, king of long ago.

T: Oh, yes indeed.

M: Now when I instruct the inang, I inform his jinjang. Let no one be forgetful, let no one make mistakes. Guard the inner fortress firmly, and strengthen the outer barriers.

T: Just so, pengasuh.

M: Yes.

T: You would like me to guard the four outer walls, the five palaces, the two worlds, to come before the principal world, the true body. Do not worry, lay aside your cares, your life will not come to an end tonight.

M: Oh, that's true.

T: I don't know about tomorrow or the next day.

M: Oh, about that, what can anyone do? May the inang . . .

T: As I just now said, what can anyone do? I'd like to leave soon, it's getting late . . .

M: Yes. Tonight no trouble or harm will befall. Tonight I put my trust in you, foreign prince, in the courtyard of the palace. I plea for help to become a healer and aid this fevered body.

T: You can certainly ask me for help, and I'll give it to you in my own way. I can't do it as others would.

M: Well, that's the way he is.

T: All has been kindly prepared, sir, because of the signals we recently requested from the Main 'teri. The first may be called the Flower's Child, the second is named the Yellow Child[69] because the third wants to search for sweet jasmine. I cannot search for that jasmine. Now I must say I can't stay here much longer. I say that we go look at the divination.

[sung]

T: Staunch and firm, within this rite, I awaken the flowerbud. The flowerbud is sleeping, I shake it awake.

M: Ah, wake up, flowerbud, we want you to awaken. Wake up, we will shake you awake.

T: The bomoh's flowerbud comes out of China[70] when it awakes.

M: When it comes out of the country of China, it soars aloft and becomes a bomoh.

T: The flowerbud will become a shelter. It falls, then it becomes a bomoh. The minduk lifts it, the great king listens.

M: The flowerbud falls to the palms of Fatimah.[71] Who plants the flower? Lady Fatimah plants the flower.

T: Friends are waiting. The name of the root is King Who Sits Below, illustrious king. Everyone listen to what I say.

M: The name of the stem is Standing King. The name of the leaf is the Sword of Ali.[72] The name of the shoot is Arrow Gandewat.[73]

T: When our friend falls to earth, Flower's Child is its name. It soars straight up from the seventh layer of earth to the seventh layer of

69. The Flower's Child is the popped rice used in one kind of divination; the Yellow Child is the flame of the candle used in another.

70. The bomoh's flowerbud came from China because that is where rice originated (at least according to Tok Daud and Awang Jalal).

71. Fatimah was the daughter of Muhammad.

72. Ali was Fatimah's husband.

73. The Arrow Gandewat (originally the umbilical cord of Seri Rama), belongs to the hero of the Malay shadow play and the Ramayana, the Hindu epic upon which it is based, where he is identified as one of the incarnations of Vishnu (see Sweeney 1972). The personification of the parts of the rice plant clearly illustrate the Islamic-nonIslamic mix of the elements in the Main Peteri [CL].

heaven, then straightaway goes back down to earth. Three flowery brothers, four companions.[74]

M: Three flowery brothers seek harmony and auspicious omens.

T: The flowerbud seeks harmony and auspicious omens. The physician looks at the flower and sees a compass to guide him in worldly divination.

M: There's no need to speak of its origins longer, no need to speak of its source.

T: The flowerbud's not given to lying and cheating.[75] Where does it fall? Into the four nations.[76] The flowerbud sees within the Main 'teri.

M: Flowerbud, don't step over the line, don't leave your territory. Let there be no lies.

T: The flowerbud has descended to earth. It brings peace to the earth, then it soars aloft downstream from the village, it climbs on high above the village.

M: If he was stricken in the fields, show us the fields, let us know if harmony can be restored.

T: Flowerbud, the right amount's counted out.

M: Ah, as in times past, I ask you to show me the place it occurred, to shed true light on the matter for me.

[During the duet, the tok 'teri places three handfuls of popped rice on a pillow. When the music ends, the ritual partners count out the grains, two by two, reciting "earth, air, fire, and water." The divination is based upon the element that ends the count for each pile. It reveals that Pak Long's sickness was caused by misguided spirits who were angry at not having been given promised offerings. They attacked him when his vitality was at a low ebb, due to his being startled. His Inner Winds had also suffered because of his chagrin at not being invited to a feast of thanksgiving held by a patient's family.]

74. Three flowery brothers are the three piles of popped rice used in the divination. Four companions are the elements: earth, air, fire, and water. The shaman places the three piles of rice upon a pillow and proceeds to count each pile in units of two grains, counting out earth for the first two grains, air for the next two, fire, and then water. The divination is based upon the way the count falls for each of the three piles. The distribution of the rice is thought to be influenced by the spirit of the Golden King of Bomohs whose persona the shaman has taken on during the divination [CL].

75. The phrase used is *golok Sunda mata dua*: literally, a double-edged Sundanese sword; figuratively, a double-crosser.

76. The four nations are the four elements—earth, air, fire, and water.

[spoken]

T: There's the sign.

M: It certainly is.

T: Not much Earth, not much there, what else? The Wind is low, too, because his Wind is weak, isn't it? There's plenty of fire. Well, that's how it usually is. [*laughs*] Well now, that's the main thing Sister Light shows.[77]

M: Yes, indeed.

T: People call it "fortunetelling fakery."

M: They say it to annoy.

T: They want to annoy us. I don't know why they want to annoy us. [*laughs*] This divination provides us with a compass. It already has.

M: I don't know how it does it.

T: I don't, either. Well now, he was startled a bit.[78]

M: Before he was stricken?

T: Before he was stricken.

M: You can't ask him, he's sleeping.

T: He's sleeping very soundly. [*laughs*] His sickness started when he was struck hard. First he became dizzy, it started in his head. After that it got much worse; he was unable to catch his breath, ha! It suddenly came on like great waves. There is, as well, a case brought by a claimant.

M: Oh, yes.

T: The claimant is one of the denizens of the realm of the earth. That claimant had, perhaps, been made a promise that was never meant to be fulfilled. Did he go to the one who made the promise? That sickness was meant for someone else and given to us. They said they would do it, but they dawdled around. [*minduk laughs*] Ah, that's how it was. He started to sulk a little. That's how "people" of his sort behave. He said to himself he was furious. People gave him promises, showed him two, three, those clever, crafty people.[79] Their stomachs are content, we

77. *Kakak nur* (big brother or sister light) is a term more often used in candle divination.

78. One of the tenets of Malay medical theory is that being startled causes the semangat (or, rather, some of it) to leave the body, weakening it and making it vulnerable to sickness, particularly spirit-induced ailments (see also Endicott 1970:50).

79. They were holding up two and then three fingers, to show the extent of the offerings they proposed to make to the spirits.

just sit around. They eat the meat, we just get the sauce. Well now, I can't just stay here and doze. There's work to be done, let's get to work.

M: If you please, sir, if you please. The day is good, the moment is right, the time has come.

T: [*sung*] Oh, Hidden Flower,[80] if the Winds are good and the season is fine I will leave a request and place my trust. [*speech unclear during minduk's song*]

M: Oh, if you please, sir, oh, Hidden Flower.

T: [*sung*] Tempers are heating up at this time, at this moment.

M: While I leave a request, I place my trust.

T: Each of you hear me, one and all. Don't behave badly, all behave well, don't act in unpleasant ways.

M: Listen to my story, listen to my tale. Let no one make light of our origins.

T: Climb up the mountain, oh noble of good family. Wake up, shake yourself awake, I want to leave a request. [*speech unclear during minduk's song*]

M: Forty days within the father, the father's seed, the mother's stock. Everyone listen to what I recount, listen well to the story, the tale.

T: Everyone listen while I leave a request and place my trust in the four gods within one god, the ancestral gods, the original gods, the invisible souls of kings.

M: Awake, ancestral gods, original gods, hereditary eternal gods. Gods who will see that our royal band does not . . .

T: Gods who bring our inheritance, let us have a pleasant discussion. Don't behave badly. Don't cause such fright that we tremble. Play fair with us. Listen to Awang's[81] pleas. Everyone listen. Change your bad ways for good.

M: Oh, speak truly of the hereditary eternal gods, the gods inherited in any manner whatsoever. Oh gods, oh charming flowers of the Wind, the Wind unfolds the lovely gods.

T: Let one and all listen to what I say. Let no one bear grudges or angry feelings toward Awang tonight. Tomorrow he will be healthy and

80. Hidden Flower (Si Lindung Bunga) is one of the shaman's familiar spirits.

81. Awang is the name of both the presiding shaman and his patient; it also stands for males in general (see n. 36, chap. 6).

strong. If he's well by tomorrow, there'll be laughing and feasting for all in the palace throne room.

M: As in times past, when you're on the sea you are called the Young Captain. When you come on land you are called the Crown Prince.

T: [*spoken*] That's true.

M: [*sung*] When you fly up to heaven you are called little Dewa Muda.

T: [*sung*] Let one and all listen to what I say, all the invisible souls, all my many friends, numerous penggawa. I want to awaken each one of you so that your younger brother may draw each of the seven jin into the discussion and ask them if some mistake has been made. [*speech during minduk's song unclear*]

M: Wake up at once, if you're sleeping, wake up. I want to shake you, to shake you awake. I'm not furious, not even angry, I don't want to restrain you, or chase you, or hit you, oh no!

T: I want to end by asking the seven jin and seven imps if they brought any errors into the discussion. The minduk wants to awake you, to shake you awake. [*speech during minduk's song unclear*]

M: Wake up for a while. I want to hold a discussion in the courtyard of the palace. I want to awaken each of my many friends and numerous penggawa.

T: [*spoken*] Ah, ha!

[Transition music. Through the music the minduk speaks: "Where will we land? In the earth's realm, to seek audience with the denizens of the earth. The king's warrior's vapor arrives, changing the atmosphere."[82] The shaman has taken on the persona of an earth spirit.]

T: [*spoken*] I'm the assistant headman of the earth's realm, physician.

M: [*spoken*] Oh my, the assistant headman of the earth's realm, sir.

T: Hish!

M: Are you the one who governs all the bays and hills inhabited by the people of this area?

T: Yes, I am.

82. The atmosphere changes because the spirit's vapor adds heat and air. Spirits are composed of only air and fire and lack earth and water. They often afflict their victims by blowing on their backs, thereby disturbing their humoral balance.

M: I can tell you politely, headman, why I summoned you. I want to ask some questions pertaining to this ceremony.

T: What do you want to ask, physician?

M: Has anyone, whether of high birth or low, made a mistake regarding the body and soul of Pak Long?

T: Indeed, physician?

M: Yes.

T: Because I haven't caused any trouble whatsoever.

M: Really?

T: Toward him, ha! Why shouldn't I have confronted him? That's really a good one!

M: What do you mean, that's a good one? What did he do to you?

T: What?

M: What did he do to you, headman?

T: He didn't do anything. I've been thinking that, not too long from now, I'm going to squeeze him, I'm really going to squeeze him.

M: What do you mean, how could you think of doing that?

T: That tightwad there, he won't be able to tell so many lies anymore. He's pretty clever.

M: What lies are you talking about?

T: Oh, he was certainly ready to take on the responsibility. I was minding my own business, and he took it upon himself to make promises.

M: He made promises?

T: He certainly did.

M: Try to think straight about this, who is really to blame? I figure it this way, he's a good guy, he was only acting as their spokesman. It's not his property that's in question.

T: Huh, that's right. There was feasting and laughing and carrying on around our way, and I didn't get even a crumb. [*minduk laughs*] Was I supposed to take some or not?

M: Ah, look at it this way, sir. A long time ago . . .

T: Are you trying to say that he didn't promise?

M: I don't know. I don't remember.

T: Over yonder there were noisy crowds.

M: Ah, over yonder.

T: I was the only one left out.

M: Oh, clever!

T: Go ask Yusof about what was going on there that day.[83] That kid didn't reach him. I don't remember his name. When he reached him, he turned back and went home again.

M: Who's that. I don't know him.

T: It's that kid, I don't remember his name.

MAK LONG (PAK LONG'S WIFE): It's that couple over in Gong Balai.

YUSOF: They're the ones.

M: Did they do it or not?

YUSOF: They didn't do it.

M: They didn't do it? I bet they didn't fulfill the vows they made.

MAK LONG: They were the ones who should have fulfilled the vows made by the bomoh. It was solely their responsibility.

PAK LONG: [*his eyes have brightened and his face is less pale*] They didn't do what they should have done, and I took the consequences.

M: Ah, just think it over, it's their property.

CAROL: It's their fault.

M: Right.

ALI (THE DRUMMER): It's their fault.

M: I figure it this way, the property doesn't belong to the bomoh. When they give some to him, then he can give it to you.

T: When will that be?

CAROL: Go ask them!

M: Go make your claim to them. When they tell you, that's when it will be.

ALI: Go ahead and make your claim to them.

T: I'll go make my claim, but I'll signal[84] first.

M: Huh?

T: I'll signal first.

ALI: How will he signal?

MAK LONG: He'll signal first?

M: Oh yes, I understand what that means, signal first. [*laughs*] He just recently gave a signal.

T: I gave a signal.

83. Yusof was my field assistant.

84. The signal the spirit is talking about is the illness he will cause to announce his displeasure.

M: A signal, ha, ha, he just signaled.

T: Don't think I'm joking. When the bomoh slipped a little, I quickly gave him a sneak punch.

M: If that's how it is, listen to this. Ask directions, go back to them and make your claim. Go away from here.

T: All right, I promise. I'll go quietly and ask them, I'll do a job on them, I'll ask them.

M: Now, I guess . . . I don't know . . .

T: I'm going to throttle those people who used Pak Long.

M: [*laughs*] Oh, yes. I don't know about that, it's up to him.

T: Oh, I can do it. I won't take long. I'll give it to them good. I'll run over there and let their monkey loose,[85] just for a reminder.

MAK LONG: That's a good idea.

M: Well now, here's how things stand, sir. We have already had our discussion tonight. I don't claim to be clever, to be knowledgeable or wise, to be an expert in any way, oh no. I just want to find out if there has been some mistake, some mistake that hasn't been corrected, some nasty error, some misstep. I ask now for peace, for all quarrels to end, and for you to return to your home, sir.

T: Is that right?

M: Yes!

T: Since you ask me so nicely, I'll go home.

M: Yes!

T: We "people of the earth" must be taken seriously, spoken to nicely, treated with courtesy.

M: Yes!

T: Ha! Now, if you please, the day is good, the time is ripe.

[Transition music. Through the music the minduk says: "Hey, a vapor emerges changing the atmosphere." The shaman has taken on the persona of an entity who does not want to give his name. He turns out to be Anak Jin Serupa Muka, the Genie with the Look-alike Face.]

M: [*spoken*] Hey! Your vapor emerged, changing the atmosphere, swaying, confused and heedless. You receive a new name and you change your character. What is your name and what is your title, who is this who comes here to meet me? Hmmm?

85. The family in Gong Balai derived most of their income from a macaque, trained to harvest coconuts.

T: Are you speaking to me, physician?

M: What is your name and what is your title? Hmm?

T: I was going about my business, not bothering anybody.

M: He was minding his own business when people called him.

T: They showed me five, ten, fifteen, twenty. [*He holds up one hand, two hands, adds one foot then the other to illustrate how much money the people in Gong Balai supposedly offered him to return the woman to health.*]

M: That's a lot. What is your name and what is your title, sir?

PAK LONG: [*raising his head from the pillow, the color flooding back into his face*] Go! Go ask the people in Gong Balai. They're the ones who made the promise.

T: I bet those two didn't pay a proper fee.[86] I'm going back to their place.

M: Now that's great! We all think so.

PAK LONG: [*sitting up*] That's fine.

YUSOF: Ask them down there if they want to give you anything.

M: Well, I still don't know your name.

T: Well, I want to say that they tried to flatter me. I want to say that they made an agreement with me, a strong, firm agreement. Then, all of a sudden, they broke their promise to me. They broke their promise and didn't pay me. I'm going to let their monkey loose. Now I have to choose, right?

M: Right.

T: Oh, there's no use my staying here with you, physician. People call me to be gone.

M: What is your name and what is your title, sir, you who have brought error into the discussion . . .

T: Oh my.

M: . . . with Tok Awang here.[87]

T: Oh, there he goes, asking me again. My name and my title are . . .

M: Yes?

T: They call me, heh, ooh ah lah, I don't want to tell you.

86. They were, in fact, very stingy. They neither provided the obligatory meal for the tok 'teri and his entourage, nor did they pay a reasonable fee for their services.

87. Tok Awang here refers to the patient, Pak Long Awang.

M: Why not?

T: I don't care to say; I feel like going home.

M: Oh, you can't act like that. I want to speak to you, but how can I? I don't know your name. Everyone has a name.

MAK LONG: He doesn't want to give his name.

T: They call me the Jin with the Look-alike Face.

M: Oh my.

T: I was chased down to earth. I agreed to seek audience with Black Semar Who Rolls Up the Earth.

M: Oh my, the Jin with the Asshole Face.[88] [*laughs, drumbeat emphasis*]

T: Hey, I'm one of two brothers.

M: Oh my.

T: We levy taxes and demand tribute. I'm accustomed to receiving gifts and payments for my services.

M: Oh, yes, indeed, a brave and handsome supernatural apostate we have here, a supernatural apostate who was born a god but was cursed.

T: Hish!

M: Hish! [*drumbeat emphasis*] You were cast down from heaven when you made a pact with Black Semar Who Rolls Up the Earth.

T: Hey, since I tread the earth now . . .

M: Yes, that's true.

T: . . . I've made a pact with the Seven Ogres of the earth's realm.

M: Oh, that's true, sir. Tonight you'd better have a discussion with me. I ask you to remove your vapor. Clear the atmosphere of every stifling vapor from the body and soul of Tok Awang, sir. If you please, sir. The day is good, the time is ripe.

T: Hah!

[Transition music. The ritual pair make inarticulate cries as the shaman assumes the persona of three ghostly brothers, Mambang Indera Waki, Mambang Indera Wayang, and Mambang Indera Waya.]

M: [*spoken*] What friend is this, now, who emerges with a rush, swaying, confused and heedless, sir?

88. The minduk is mocking this annoying spirit, who doesn't respond to the insult, by using a word that sounds like his name (Anak Jin *Serupa* Muka; Anak Jin *Sejubur* Muka) but means something quite different.

T: Is that so?

M: Yes.

T: I receive a new name and I change my character.

M: Yes.

T: I'm called the first friend, the original friend.

M: Hmm.

T: A friend who makes claims.

M: Yes.

T: Whom they call Mambang[89] Indera Waki, Mambang Indera Wayang, Mambang Indera Waya. We are three brother-companions.

M: Oh, may I speak politely to all three together, all three in a row, you who descend upon the inang? I want to ask you, if there is any trace of jin vapor, poisonous vapor, mambang vapor, or bayu[90] vapor, to kick it far away, release us completely, cast it on high.

T: Ah, is that what you want, sir?

M: Yes.

T: We'll do it as best we can, my friend. Don't worry, lay aside your cares, your earthly days are not yet at an end. We will thoroughly kick away every jin, the vapor of seven jin, five imps, four kinds of jin, four sorts of devils.

M: Oh yes, that's right! [*aside, in a lowered voice: I'm getting pretty dry in my throat. Let's stop soon for a drink.*]

T: [*sung*] I ask for help from all four sides. [*spoken*] Four outer walls, five palaces, a tranquil body, one world.[91] I ask for help, both early and late, to kick away the mambang's vapor.

M: [*sung*] Oh, guard the four sides of the palace verandah. Let each one be on the alert.

T: [*sung*] Think of the body's destiny, its fate upon the verandah, the verandah of the palace. Kick away each and every mambang vapor from the seven corners.

M: [*sung*] Oh, kick away thoroughly each trace of the vapor of jin, poison, mambang, bayu from the inang's person . . .

T: [*spoken*] Yes, that's right.

M: [*sung*] Kick it away completely, push it away till it's gone, cast it far on high, far away from the inang.

89. See n. 22, chap. 6.

90. See n. 49, chap. 6.

91. "Four outer walls . . . one world" = the human body.

[The music stops while everyone has tea. Pak Long Awang discusses the night's developments with the ritual pair; others join in. He is still a little weak, but his expression of peace, instead of the worried look he previously had, shows his satisfaction with the diagnosis. Awang Jalal, the shaman, has resumed his own persona, which he keeps during the following song:]

T: [*sung*] Each of the souls of long-gone kings, one and all, have vanished.

M: [*sung*] We've made requests and placed our trust in each of the company.

T: Each of you listen to what I say: let all live in friendship through all generations. Hear my story, hear my tale.

M: Down the family line through all generations, turning up now here, now there, upon the palace verandah. Wind, don't drive us away, make us gasp for breath, swell up or be nauseated upon the palace verandah, in the village within the country.

T: Each of you listen, let the Winds blow and open the way for the souls of former kings.

M: Oh, listen as I tell my story, tell my tale. Let no one step across the line or leave the territory.

T: Hear what I say on the palace verandah, the seven verandahs of the first of the kings, the original god, listen well, all in the family line, warriors and kings of our ancestors. Let all friends form ranks, each god and each king, each man of good family, let all form ranks with their friends.

M: Ah, original king, truly first of the kings, I ask you to rest, each of you stop your work.

T: All of you on the palace verandah, all be at rest, don't be angry at Awang.

M: Ah, all of the gods together with gods, pengasuh together with pengasuh, warriors together with warriors, kings together with kings.

T: Let no one bear grudges or anger toward Awang.

M: I ask you, friends, one and all, be at ease. The king can depend on the gods now at ease.

T: A man by himself, a man all alone. He has no brothers, he has no sisters. If his friends do not help him, who will?

M: Ah, each of you hear me, all you many friends and numerous penggawa. Hear me, one and all. The king is at ease within the old fortress, upon the high ivory dais.

T: Everyone listen, one among all. Let there be no fury or anger upon the palace verandah, or any porch or in any room, as we meet the crown prince.

M: The king, at ease upon the tall ivory dais, listens to the first king upon the muslin sofa above the carpet. He listens well to three prayers, he does not stir but remains at his ease. Friends at ease with friends, penggawa at ease with penggawa, warriors at ease with warriors, kings at ease with kings, gods at ease with gods, upon the palace verandah.

[The band strikes up the final transition music, ending the seance and returning the participants to the space and time of everyday life and the cookies and coffee served by Mak Long.]

8

Breaking Contracts with the Spirit World

Mat Din had entered into many contracts with spirits and demigods to increase his luck in fishing and farming, to preserve him from enemies, and to increase life's satisfactions in every way. Things went well for Mat Din, but after several good years he became complacent, careless, and neglectful of his obligations to the spirits. He failed to give them the regular offerings he had promised them in return for their help. Since he was not keeping his end of the bargain, they withdrew their support and, angered, struck out. His family was the first to suffer from his negligence. His children were sick more often than seemed normal, and one young son was not growing up the way he should. He wandered aimlessly about, made silly faces, and urinated wherever he chose. People called him "crazy" (*gila*).

The problem spread to neighboring households. Many of the children fell ill, or had frightening dreams. Mat Din's worried neighbors insisted that he deal with the situation. The wrathful spirits had to be summoned to a seance where they could be cajoled and appeased, and Mat Din would have to formally break the contracts he had made with the spirits.

The monsoon had just begun a few days before the night of Mat Din's Main Peteri. I picked up Pak Long Awang and Ali, the drummer, and we drove through sheets of rain to Serating, a nearby kampung where Tok Daud, the minduk, and Mat Din lived. Mat Din had lit several pressure lanterns, which cast a pale yellow light around his large front room. His wife had prepared a kenduri for the performers (and the anthropologist) of large plates of rice, a bowl of curried chicken, and a platter of spicy fried fish. After we finished eating, Tok Daud wove a palm frond holder for the plate containing the *nasi guru* (teacher's rice), consisting of a boiled egg, a handful of popped rice, a dollop of glutinous rice, a betel quid, 20 cents, and a coil of raw twine, which people in vulnerable states of health often use during rituals of release, passing it over their bodies and emerging in symbolic rebirth (see Laderman 1983:89, 206). Hung from the rafters, the nasi guru attracts the shaman's spirit familiars to the seance. They perch there invisibly, waiting their turn to be summoned for the night's work.

Mat Din's wife spread out their most beautiful mats and placed a pillow covered with a batik cloth on top of the central mat. In front of the pillow, she placed the usual ingredients of the seance: a dish of popped rice, a dish of raw rice mixed with pieces of turmeric, a bowl of perfumed water in which a sprig of jasmine floated, and a dish of *kemenyan* (benzoin).

This Main Peteri demanded far more elaborate preparations than usual. The spirits with whom Mat Din had formed long and intimate associations would not be willing to break their ties without the proper recompense. Pak Long and Tok Daud, assisted by some of Mat Din's neighbors, assembled the following:

1. *Pulut kuning* (glutinous rice colored yellow—the royal color).

2. Little cakes (*'teri mandi*) made with glutinous rice. The name is rich in allusions, tok 'teri being the title of the shaman, and *mandi* (bathing) the final step in the night's proceedings, which would wash away the dangers inherent in the ritual.

3. Six hard-boiled eggs, including one with seven pins stuck into it.

4. *Dadar kuah* (pancakes with custard sauce). This forms part of the spirit offering traditional to many serious and risky undertakings, such as opening the jungle to agriculture.

5. Fried corn, millet, and beans, mixed with salt.

6. Popped rice (*bertih*). Raw rice is the quintessential fruit of the earth. Grown in water, it represents the ultimate in earthy and watery qualities and, thus, has the capacity to repel the airy, fiery spirits. Popping rice grains over dry heat tempers their earthy and watery nature, making them attractive, rather than repellent, to the spirits.

7. Cold water for the spirits to drink, poured into clam shells.

8. Limes (often used in cleansing ceremonies).
9. A handful of small stones.
10. Coins.
11. "Releasers"—strands of palm frond tied into double slipknots.
12. A coconut with one end struck off. Home-rolled cigarettes and betel quids were stuck into deep gashes made in a zigzag pattern around the outside.
13. A nail hammered into a piece of wood.
14. Rice-flour dough fashioned by Pak Long into figurines shaped like people, horses, water buffalos, cows, chickens, ducks, crabs, skates, kitchen utensils.
15. A letter addressed to the hantu, telling them that a farm would be waiting for them complete with animals, servants, kitchen implements, food, cigarettes, and betel quids. The letter went on to say that when the fried corn, beans, and rice sprout, when the stones take root, when the nails come out of the wood, when the pins fall out of the egg, and when the clam shells have babies, then, and only then, can they return to Mat Din's house.

Pak Long lit the kemenyan, said an incantation, and censed his face, hands, and feet with its sweet-smelling fumes, passing the dish three times around his body. He recited a short incantation over the popped rice and put a handful under the pillow. He said a short prayer in Arabic over the raw rice, asking God's protection from Satan (*A'uzu billahi min ash-shaitani*, etc.), and threw the rice to the four cardinal directions, up to the ceiling, and down to the floor, to neutralize the spirits' airy heat with its earthy and watery qualities.

Pak Long washed his face and rinsed his mouth with the perfumed water to make himself more attractive to the benevolent spirits. He recited an incantation over the trays of offerings, then moved aside while Tok Daud censed them. Tok Daud said a short prayer over his rebab, censed it, and threw a handful of bertih at it. Ali rubbed his hand drum with bertih and sat back against the wall. Since Cik Mas, Ali's wife who usually played on the overturned pot, was not there, a neighbor agreed to take her place. An audience of about thirty friends and neighbors had gathered in Mat Din's large front room, and the performers were now ready to begin the seance.

While Tok Daud recited his invocation and sang his introductory song, Pak Long smoked a cigarette and chatted with friends. Tok Daud's strong voice soared over the stirrings and soft conversations of the audience and the driving downpour of the monsoon.

The minduk's long incantation invited the spirits to the feast. After sending greetings to the teachers and bomoh of ancient times and recounting the story of Creation and human birth, he invoked the spirits of the earth, the village, the forest, the plain, and all the spirits who would help serve the feast. He followed his incantation with a song asking for an audience with the spirit-rulers of each domain, while Pak Long, the tok 'teri, changed into a clean sarong. He tied two sashes tightly about his waist, to guard against the embarrassment of having his sarong fall down during his coming exertions. Pak Long stubbed out his cigarette and seated himself cross-legged in front of Tok Daud, listening intently to the minduk's Bestirring Song (Gerak Angin, literally "to move the Wind"), which would prepare him to "forget" himself and take on the personae of a series of ghostly entities.

Toward the middle of the Bestirring Song, Pak Long began the recitation of his protective jampi, calling upon his familiar spirits, Mek Bunga and Mek Sekuntum Melur (Miss Flower and Miss Jasmine Bud, ancestresses of Pak Long who have become orang ghaib, "invisible people"); and Wak Long, Pak Dogol, Dewa Si Alam Tunggal, Hanuman Kera Putih (the White Monkey), and his sons, Hanuman Ikan (Fish Hanuman) and Hanuman Bongsu (Youngest Hanuman), all of whom he had acquired while performing in the wayang kulit, to join the protective forces of his body in guarding him during the seance. At the end of his jampi, the music rose to crescendo, marking the shaman's transition into receptivity to spiritual visitation.

The first spirit to visit was Awang Mindung Pengasuh, one of the body's protective forces whose name is that of Dewa Muda's servant in the Mak Yong drama. He was followed by Wak Kedi Bomoh, The Sage from the Siamese Monastery (a character in the shadow play, who often presides over divinations), who agreed to help in the proceedings. The next to arrive was an earth spirit who protested his innocence. The minduk told him to go back and send someone else. He also instructed Mat Din to take off his shirt, change his seat, and put his legs together, the better to receive treatment.

The next spirit to arrive was Pak Deh (Pak Dogol), the tok 'teri's spirit familiar, who agreed to help him. He was succeeded by Hitam Seri Penakluk (Illustrious Black Conqueror), a powerful spirit who rules the crossroads. The minduk coaxed him into "removing his hot vapor and lowering the temperature" that oppressed Mat Din. He was followed by a spirit from the outskirts of the village, one of the followers of Sang Raya Tujuh (The Seven Mighty Spirits), who also accepted the offerings and agreed to leave. He advised the minduk to call upon the father of all *polong* (a dangerous type of spirit harbored by men for personal gain) if he wanted to continue the discussion.

The next to appear was Mek Bunga (Miss Flower), Pak Long Awang's favorite penggawa, who signals her presence with her high girlish voice and flirtatious movements that Tok Daud compares to sifting and winnowing rice. She sang a short duet with the minduk before she left and was replaced by one of the spirits (who did not give his name) who had made compacts with Mat Din. He asked whether Mat Din was willing to give him offerings or whether he would like to get rid of him. Mat Din replied that he would like to get rid of the spirit.

Pak Long Awang, returning to his own persona, reminded Mat Din that he had also kept a polong and some sea spirits and asked him to remember every other deal he had made with the supernatural. Mat Din admitted that he had been lax in giving spirits the necessary offerings. He showed Pak Long some papers with drawings and spells written on them and asked him to annul their power. Pak Long called for some beeswax candles to use in a divination, but none had been prepared. Since no other type of candle would do, the divination was dispensed with.

At Pak Long's urging, Mat Din revealed the names of his "kept" spirits: Panglima Hitam and Panglima Garang (The Black Commander and the Fierce Commander, sea spirits); Jin Tanah, Jembalang Tanah (earth spirits); dewa (demigods), all the way up to Nenek Betara Guru (Grandsire Powerful Teacher), the ruler of Kayangan; the whole lineage of the Wayang Jawa (a form of the shadow play that is practically extinct). The tok 'teri then announced that he would bring the polong created by magical pictures and spells to the seance.

One of the Polong Tujuh (Seven Polong) arrived, and the minduk invited him to the kenduri. Before accepting the offerings, the polong engaged the minduk in a bargaining session for the life and health of Mat Din. He left and was replaced by Mek Ketuk-ketak (Miss Click-clack), a female spirit who lusts after men—almost any man will do. She was followed by Hanuman Ikan (Fish Hanuman), a spirit familiar who offered to round up any other spirits with whom Mat Din had associated. A sea spirit appeared. He was very unhappy to hear that Mat Din wanted to break off their friendship; he sobbed as he sang "His words strike me to the quick—he wants to get rid of me." Tok Jerambang (Old Will-o-the-Wisp), a sea spirit who helped Mat Din catch fish, arrived and was told to "row off," that is, to return to his place of origin and never return again to Mat Din.

Pak Deh (Pak Dogol, another spirit familiar), the next arrival, was sent to summon Nenek Betara Guru (one of the chief dewa) to the seance. The minduk informed Betara Guru that Mat Din would like to break off relations with him. He agreed, adding that since Mat Din's house is "dirty, filthy, stinking, rotten, putrid" it would not be fitting for such a high god to associate with him. His feelings were hurt, however, and he wept as he sang "Mat Din really wants to abandon me." After the brief reappearance of Wak Long, Pak Dogol's comic sidekick, who traded jokes with the minduk, Pak Long Awang asked Mat Din who else should be summoned. He replied that all the spirits he had trafficked with had already appeared.

"Now it is time," said Pak Long, "to travel to the dense forest for an audience with Budak Kecil" (Sonny Boy), a fierce jungle spirit whose name belies his power. He, too, was one of Mat Din's associates, but he now accepted the offer of a kenduri (feast) in exchange for breaking off relations. He was followed by two other spirits: Wak Tok Juara Mikat (The Old Expert Birdcatcher), who helped Mat Din in the hunt, and Sultan Ahmad, who protected him from enemies.

The next to arrive was Tok Nyadap (The Old Toddy Tapper), a familiar spirit Pak Long had acquired in the days when he earned his living tapping the sweet sap of palm trees (toddy). Tok Nyadap is a jolly old character, fond of making bawdy jokes; in one, he compared his wife to a toddy container. He asked Mat Din whether there were any other spirits he should summon. Mat Din replied that "it's all finished . . . I don't have a single worry left. What remains is the magic I studied.

I want to know if there's anything dangerous in the things I studied with my teacher. I want to recite them."

Mat Din recited three jampi; after each he asked Pak Long whether it was all right to continue using them. Pak Long assured him that there was no problem. Since all the spirits had been invited to the feast, and all the spells had been approved for future use, the time had come to put the offerings in the underbrush. They had to be placed far from human habitation, to avoid the possibility that a child might unwittingly step on or dirty the spirits' farm. Several men in the audience volunteered to carry out the offerings. Pak Long advised them as to the proper procedure: "Well now, when you hammer the nails in firmly, you must say, 'Should these nails fall out, only then can you return; should these nails not fall out, then you can never return.' Remember this well. You also have to say this, 'If the corn, millet, and beans don't grow, then you must wait here.' " He told the men to hurry and not keep the spirits waiting. Sang Raya (the Mighty Spirit) grows quickly impatient and must not be treated lightly.

After they left, the Main Peteri continued. Raja Hanuman Kera Putih (the White Monkey), one of Pak Long's penggawa, was sent to summon Sang Raya Uban (The Mighty Gray Spirit). The minduk explained to the Great Gray Spirit that Mat Din was giving him a farm, with ducks and chickens, cows and water buffalos, goats and sheep, and all kinds of kitchen utensils (made of rice flour and water), and asked him to go wait there until the corn and millet grew. Since they had previously been fried, which killed the germ, they would never sprout.

After Sang Raya Uban left, Anak Raja Mahatawar (Prince Potent Cure) appeared, along with his brother-god, Anak Raja Segunung Tawar (Prince Mountain of Remedies). They are dewa who have the power to release those who have taken part in the Main Peteri from the dangers of dealing with the spirit world. Pak Long placed a spot of *tepung tawar* ("neutralizing rice paste" made from rice flour and water—a potent antidote to dangerous spiritual "heat") on the forehead of each of the family members and each of the members of the Main Peteri troupe. He placed some on each of the *pelepas*, the palm frond "releasers" that had been prepared earlier. Pak Long and Tok Daud passed among their patients, singing. As Pak Long recited "One, two, three, four, five, six, seven, you are released," he pulled the ends of the pelepas, undoing the double slipknots. Then Pak Long cut up some limes, adding them to two pails of water, and passed the dish with the smoking kemenyan around each pail three times. He bathed Mat Din and two of his sons with the water; then he picked up some raw rice and threw it in the four cardinal directions and up toward the ceiling, to disperse any remaining spirits by the repellent force of the earthy and watery elements of the rice.

The Main Peteri was not quite over. The minduk and tok 'teri had to recite the words that embody the ceremony's aim: "Kings with kings, gods with gods, courtiers with courtiers, nobles with nobles, warriors with warriors, familiar spirits with familiar spirits." With everything once more in its proper place and the Cosmos in harmony, the little band struck up the transition music a final time, returning the participants to the space and time of everyday reality as the Main Peteri ended.

Mat Din's neighbors seemed quite satisfied. Henceforth, if their children became ill or suffered from nightmares, it had to be due to other causes—Mat Din was not to blame. The behavior of Mat Din's retarded, and otherwise peculiar, young son, however, did not improve in the slightest. This could not be attributed to any shortcomings on the part of Pak Long and Tok Daud. As Pak Long told me, the damage had already been done long before and was beyond repair, but it didn't hurt to try.

The following is a transcription of the seance.

BREAKING CONTRACTS WITH THE SPIRIT WORLD

[While the minduk recites his invocation to the spirits, inviting them to attend the seance and accept the offerings, conversations, held in a normal tone of voice, in the audience and among the players, continue. The invocation is meant for the invisible audience, and not for the mortals. The minduk speaks swiftly in a loud voice, but the only human being listening carefully to every word is the anthropologist.]

Minduk's Invocation [*spoken*]

I invoke the seven teachers, one by one, 1,2,3,4,5,6,7.[1]
Three vanish and two appear, two vanish and one appears.[2]
The white one is named White Teacher, White Stone Teacher is his name,
The sage of the world.
The teacher calls upon God, as he lifts his face to heaven and then quickly looks down.
He looks straight up to heaven, he looks straight down to earth.
Grandsire White Shaikh was born in religious seclusion in the glassy pool.[3]
The first of his names is Prince of the Koran,
The second, Sincerity, the third, Datuk Kumar Hakim,[4]
The fourth is Radiant Shadetree.
Nenek Bersenu became Beramah the Invisible[5]
In that long ago time when he mediated atop the white throne under the locked-up sky,[6]
When he practiced asceticism, Great Storehouse of Wisdom.
I ask that bad influences be removed, that I be shown
Whoever is untrue, whoever is unknown,
If Adam is a healer, then he will be at peace.
Yellow rice, pancakes, popped rice, a coconut, a betel quid, a drop of water[7]
For all the jin, wherever they may be,

1. See n. 1, chap. 6.

2. Tok Daud said that "one appears" refers to the one God; however, in the next sentence he connects the one (the White Rock Teacher) to the nasi guru (teacher's rice), the offering that is placed in a hanging receptacle before the performance begins. The friendly familiar spirits are supposed to perch atop the nasi guru.

3. The glassy pool is the eyes, the beads are the colored portion. See n. 13, chap. 7.

4. See n. 14, chap. 7.

5. The equation of Nenek Bersenu and Beramah with Vishnu and Brahma of the Hindu pantheon is not made on the village level.

6. The locked-up sky (*langit*) refers both to the time before Creation and to the cloth (often called *langit-langit* or *lelangit*) which is hung from the ceiling over the area in which the Main Peteri takes place to represent the sky.

7. This is a listing of some of the offerings that will actually be given to the spirits.

Who made agreements long ago and later caused such commotion.
Now the time has come, the season has come, the moment has come.
Receive, one and all, the mother's feasts, the father's offerings, the grandsire's gifts:
Yellow rice, pancakes, popped rice, a coconut, a betel quid, a drop of water.
I invoke, besides, the Sky Father and the Earth Mother.
Nallah Nur Ahut[8] was the mother's name when the angel held her in his hands.
Forty days within the father's womb, full forty days within the father's womb.[9]
A single drop falls from the father's pen,[10] Point is its name.
Thrust, then, into the mother's womb, enclosed there nine months and ten days.
May the child be safe in the womb.
Let him suffer no ruin, destruction, attack.
All danger to the mother brings misfortune to the child.
Father must release the child from harm, Mother helps to cast it away.
May bad luck, misfortune, calamity, and slander all be cast away
By Mother the Physician, by Adam the Healer.
I bid you, one and all, accept our offerings.
Finished with the Father's Tale, I continue, wherever I land.
I land in the depths of the earth for an audience with the Earth Jin,

8. During other seances, the Sky Father was named Nur Allah (Light of God), and the Earth Mother was named Nur Ahut. Here the mother receives a version of both names (Nur Allah becoming Nallah). See n. 17, chap. 7.

9. See n. 18, chap. 7.

10. *Kalam* refers to the Divine Pen that writes in the Book of Fate (see Wilkinson 1959:497) and is also a euphemism for the penis. The identification of human reproduction with divine creation, and the identification of the human body (the microcosm) with the universe (macrocosm) are major themes in Malay magic (see, for example, Cuisinier 1936; Laderman 1981, 1983). The theme of conception and gestation is on one level universal to humankind and its well-being, but "the child in the womb" also refers specifically to the patient, and secondarily, to the performers in the seance.

The Earth Imp, the Spirit of the Soil, the Soil Imp, the troops of the earth's triumphant headman.
Triumphant Light from the veins of the earth, Triumphant Craftsman from the earth's horizon,
Prophet Habar from the earth's shell, Light of Speech from the center of the earth,
Booming Bezoar from the depths of the earth,
Whose troops are these?
Hey, there, Soaring Bezoar, Dancing Bezoar, Bezoar's Footstep, Frothy Bezoar, Bedewed Bezoar,
As we land in the halls of the White Jin, the earth's shadow.
We land again on earth and who do we meet?
Hey, Majestic Point from the depths of the earth,
Majestic Shaker from the earth's shell,
Majestic Thunder from the earth's realm,
Friends of Black Turas.[11]
I seek an audience with Black Turas in the kingdom of the earth
Because our brother was ensnared while he meditated at the spit of land in Tanah Daha Gegelang Sari.
One sole *nibung* palm in a field of *culak* trees; healing water from the dragon's tip.[12]
Each of you, accept, one and all, the mother's feasts, the father's offerings, the grandsire's gifts:

11. Turas, the servant of Semar, is black since he was created from Semar's body dirt (the flakes of dead skin that rub off after bathing). Semar was burned black upon God's decree because he refused to do obeisance to Adam (see Sweeney 1972:179–180). Here and further along, Semar and Turas are identified with the earth spirits.

12. Daha, a medieval Javanese state (Tanah Daha Gegelang Sari = Land of Daha Encircled by Flowers), was the home of Princess Chandra Kirana, heroine of the Panji Cycle (Wilkinson 1959:247). To be ensnared means to have been made ill by a spirit. The lone *nibung* palm is really the nose. The plain of *culak* trees is the space between the nose and the mouth. The healing water is saliva. The dragon is the digestive system (Tok Daud actually referred to *tali perut*, or intestines), and its tip is the tongue. It is interesting to note that the root of the nibung is boiled for fever (Gimlette and Thomson 1971:172), and the leaves of the *culak* tree are used medicinally by Malays as a poultice and also internally for fever, colic, and so forth (Burkill 1966:408). A spit, or tongue, of land is considered a prime gathering place for spirits and a dangerous place on which to build a human habitation.

Yellow rice, pancakes, popped rice, a coconut, a betel quid, a drop of water,
For every jin, no matter which, who made agreements in the past,
Only now it is voiced, I invoke you.
Now the time has come, the season has come, the moment has come.
Come, one and all, accept the offerings.
I call on you, friends and followers of Seri Penakluk, his brother Seri Penaklik and Wak Panglima Muda,
Who rule the banks and bays of all these parts.
Born sons of gods, companions of jin,
Confronted by evil, were cursed and cast down to the darkness of earth.
May I, the physician and healer, greet Black Semar who rolls up the earth and a piece of the sunset,
Hey, Semar Point, Swaying Semar, Semar Who Sweeps Heaven and Earth,
Semar Who Catches the Earth, Semar Who Upends the Earth.
Semar Who Gives Life to the Earth, Semar Who Shuts Up the Earth.
Hey, Lone Helmsman of the earth's realm,
I ask for, I plead for health.
I bid you accept, one and all, the mother's feasts, the father's offerings, the grandsire's gifts:
Yellow rice, pancakes, popped rice, a coconut, a betel quid, a drop of water.
Whoever I have called, whoever I invoked, whoever has made agreements long ago,
Now the time has come, each moment of time.
Accept the offerings, one and all.
Tomorrow or the next day, or any day to come,
Don't return to ask for more.
Remove all harm from these banks, from these bays.
Each of you listen, one and all, black-skinned friend with seven followers,

Yellow one with a clever tongue,
Eight tongues in nine besmirched heads above a pockmarked chest,
White-tipped fur above your feet, white-tipped tail, bracelets round your ankles, seven hairy moles, seven followers,
Whose troops are these?
The Seven Ogres, the Playful Ogre, the Ogre called Lampagar, the Sturdy Ogre, warrior called Green Fly.
Seven Ogres, Earth Ogre, Water Ogre, Fire Ogre, Phlegm Ogre, ogres all.
Hey, Old Man Who Spins Heaven and Earth,
Mother Faithful Flycatcher, practicing austerities,
Friend of the Four-headed Monkey
In the back of the world, in the heart of the earth.
Pelesit of the earth, *putarranggas* of the earth, *polong* of the earth,[13] feasting in the earth,
Whose troops are these?
Old Man of the Jungle, Awang the Pole Turner,
Our friend, Black Jin Road Blocker, Black Jin Stake Wedger.
You always have blocked all the roads, all the piers.
Now I bid you accept, one and all, the mother's feasts, the father's offerings, the grandsire's gifts:
Yellow rice, pancakes, popped rice, a coconut, a betel quid, a drop of water.
For those I have mentioned, for those who replied.
Excuses, evasions there were in the past, now the time has come, the season has come.
I bid you, one and all, accept.
Each of you listen, one and all, 1,444 spirits,[14]
Followers of the king from the depths of the earth.

13. *Pelesit* and *polong* are familiar spirits, the former employed by women and the latter by men (see also McHugh 1959:64–74; Skeat 1972 [1900]:329–331). *Putarranggas* are dangerous spirits. Wilkinson (1959:945) gives "*bota ranggas*" and *jin patah ranggas*" and calls them "evil spirits of the brushwood." See also n. 14, chap. 6.

14. The number of *jisi* (spirit troops) mentioned in the version of the *berjamu* (feasting the spirits of the shadow play puppets) given by Sweeney (1972:280) is different only in one figure (1,044 vs. 1,444).

I don't change names, I don't weigh letters.[15]
I have finished this tale, and continue, wherever I may land.
I land at the edge of the village, in the shelter of the groves.
With whom will I have an audience?
Nenek Sang Gana Seri Naga Ulit, Dewa Nur Lak Juna,[16] reknowed in the village.
The Yellow Jin's essence flies—yellow essence, yellow shadow, yellow turban, flying shadow.
Hey, Beramah, Majestic Soaring Essence,
Whose troops are these?
Black Jin Thunder and Lightning from the West, black warning in the village.
Red Jin of the sheltering groves, the Spinning, Rolling Jin, brother of the Yellow One.
Whose troops are these?
The Tiger Spirit,[17] the imp of the village, the Royal Spirit, the imp of the groves.
Hidden tribe stretched out in darkness, ruling spirit of the village, house-friend.
Hey, Winged Steed, Great Eagle, you crash against our doors.
Whose troops are these?
Hey, great elephant whose driver is stupid, crazed elephant whose driver's a fool,[18]
Accept, one and all, the mother's feasts, the father's offerings, the grandsire's gifts:
Yellow rice, pancakes, popped rice, a coconut, a betel quid, a drop of water.
For those I have mentioned, for those I invoked.

15. The minduk is assuring the spirits that he intends to play fair with them. See n. 20, chap. 7.

16. Tok Daud said that Nenek Sang Gana Seri Naga Ulit was the *penghulu* (headman) of Sang Raya, the Mighty Spirit, considered to be the most powerful and dangerous of all. Lak Juna is one of the sons of Seri Rama (see Sweeney 1972).

17. The *Hala*, tiger spirit or weretiger, is also (and primarily) used as a category for basic personality type in that part of the traditional Malay medical system which deals with *penyakit angin*.

18. Our emotions are compared to powerful animals. If we act like a foolish elephant driver and don't control them wisely they can cause as much harm as a crazed elephant.

Excuses, evasions there were in the past, but the time has come, the season has come, the moment has come.
Accept, one and all, friends and followers of the Black Jin Who Assaults Five Times.
Whose troops are these?
Troops of the village headman, Noble Awang, Great Weapon, Mighty Pak Deh,
Great One, Mighty Reverser, Mighty Hammer, Mighty Traveler, Companion called Awang Sultan Suleiman,
Bringer of Catastrophe, Hammerer of Flesh.
Whose troops are these?
Great Awang from the village center, boastful, invisible presence,
Noisy Awang, Noble Awang, our friends the Seven Mighty Spirits.
Mighty Red Spirit, Mighty Blue Spirit, Mighty Green Spirit, Mighty Purple Spirit, Mighty Yellow Spirit, Mighty White Spirit,
Your father was Sang Berit, your mother Sang Bronah, your child Sang Limpah
When you emerged from the afterbirths of Lord Adam and Lady Eve.[19]
Accept, one and all, the mother's feasts, the father's offerings, the grandsire's gifts:
Pancakes, popped rice, a cigarette, betel quid, a drop of water.
Tomorrow or the next day, or any day to come, don't return to ask for more.
Hear me, hear me, one and all,
Accept, one and all.

19. One of the origin myths of the disembodied spirits is that they arose from the afterbirths of Adam and Eve. Afterbirths of all human beings are subsumed under the category of spirits, since both are lacking two of the four universal elements. Disembodied spirits are composed entirely of air and fire, while afterbirths, having never breathed, are composed of only earth and water. They have the power of afflicting their human siblings and may do so out of envy of their "brothers'" happier lot (see Laderman 1983:201). The ritual practitioners did not perceive any discrepancy between the story of the creation of Adam from earth and water, the creation of Eve from his rib, and the presence of afterbirths. God can proceed with the creation of his creatures in any way he sees fit.

Little sister, Miss Yellow, calls on the village palace by night.
Good-looking, fine featured, she's yellow, too.
Yellow is her power and yellow's her flaw.
Miss Scabies, as I've said, visits jin over yonder.[20]
I enumerate now Jin Jisim, Jin Jiring, Jin Jiha,[21]
Accept, one and all,
You hunters in the forest at the edge of the village,
Noisy invisible throng in the village.
Pak Wah's throng of hidden stalkers.
Hey, Sparrow, two Sparrows, forty Crows, all standing alone.[22]
Lone Monkey, Lone Ape, Lone Gibbon, standing alone in a row.
Each of you accept, one and all, your spirit armies at the village's edge.
I don't change names, I don't weigh letters.
I want to end that tale.
I land now on the vast open plain, stretching as far as the eye can see.
With whom shall I seek an audience?
Nenek Raja Hakim, crown prince of the jungle, of the open plains, stretching as far as the eye can see.
Troops of the Seven Royal Princesses from the open plains, stretching as far as the eye can see,
Three retinues have they:

20. Mek Kuning, the younger sister of Jin Kuning, the Yellow Genie, emerged, as he did, from the by-products of childbirth; specifically, the Yellow Genie arose from the blood spilled during childbirth (yellow is often symbolic of blood in Malay magic; see Laderman 1983:99, 228, 243) and the Black Genie from the placenta. In the words of Pak Long, the tok 'teri, "*Jin Kuning keluar sok uri, beradik Jin Hitam, sedarah sedaging, sama jalan jadi dengan manusia.*" (The Yellow Genie arose from the afterbirth, as did the Black Genie, his brother. They are our blood brothers, one blood, one flesh, who came down the same road as humanity [the mother's birth canal—CL] to be born.) They are not the implacable enemies of their human siblings, and, indeed may act as guardians (*jaga roh kita* "watch over our souls").

21. All of the spirits in this section are found in the jungle. *Jiring* and *jiha* are names of trees. *Jisim*, however, means "the body," reminding us again of the dual nature of the world, the interdependence of events within and without the human body.

22. These are not real birds, but names of spirits.

The Seven Spinsters and the Nine Divorcees.[23]
Hey, My Lady Fire, Miss Soaked-in-Water, Miss Adulteress, Single for a Year, the Moldy Old Maid, the Champion of Spinsters,
You are champion of all the mambang,[24] you are champion of all these hills, you are the winner of every quarrel.
Accept, one and all, the mother's feasts, the father's offerings.
I invoke, among the lords of the plains, stretching as far as the eye can see,
Captain Maddened Buffalo and his brother Captain Golden Pig.
Their keeper is a crazy old Chinese.[25]
They emerged, it is said, from the seven mountains and nine caves.[26]
They emerged from Budak Kecil,[27] the praying mantis, the wide-chested, mischievous one with red eyes.
Each of you accept, one and all.
I have finished the tale of the vast open plains, and I want to continue my invocation.
Where will I land this time?
Where the shady trees harbor armies of spirits.
No one is waiting, no one comes near the trees, black and yellow,
While the guardian's[28] beacon lights the way.

23. Although *bujang* and *janda* can refer to a currently unmarried person of either sex, it is clear that these are female spirits of the fields [CL]. See n. 25, chap. 7.

24. See n. 22, chap. 6.

25. For material on Kerbau Amuk (Maddened Buffalo) as a character in the wayang kulit, see Sweeney 1972. In the context of the Main Peteri, he and his swinish brother, Babi Bermas (Golden Pig), are symbolic of human emotions that, if not carefully guarded, can run amuck (see n. 18). *Topek* is a racial slur used by east coast Malays to refer to an elderly Chinese (not considered by Malays to be the best guardian of the emotions). It may be related to *topekong*, an image or picture used in a Chinese shrine [CL].

26. The seven mountains are the seven parts of the human body. The nine caves are its orifices. The vast open plains is a metaphor for the human breast, as well as being an actual place where humans step and spirits live.

27. Budak Kecil's name (Sonny Boy) belies the nature of this fierce jungle spirit.

28. *Gembala* is generally used to mean the caretaker of animals. The black-and-yellow color of the trees repeats the colors of the black and yellow genies, humanity's siblings.

Whose troops are these?
It's the place where the ghostly tormentors all live:
Mother Longbreasts, Mother Wailer, Miss Tits, Sliding Princess, troops of the Seven Pari.[29]
Each of you come to me, one and all,
I will give every jin the mother's feasts, the father's offerings.
I present them to you as a token of love.
I ask you, I plead with you, move yourselves.
Each of you hear me, one and all, at this time, at this moment.
Each of you accept, one and all.
Throngs of ancient saints, new saints, dead saints, living saints, worshipped saints, saints unworshipped in these parts.
Each of you accept, one and all.
Whose troops are these?
Datuk Red Cap, White Syed,[30] hear me, friends.
Each of you accept, one and all, you seven warriors strong as granite.
With whom shall I seek an audience?
The Seven Royal Princesses, hey, Miss More-and-More, Miss Double-the-Days,
Accept, one and all.
Troops of the Seven Royal Princesses, the captain's troops, men like mountains, strong as granite.
Accept, one and all.
Captain Laleng, smoldering yellow stone, troops from the mountains, strong as granite,
Accept, one and all.
Now I invoke the time long past when great men strode the earth,
Men from tall mountains, strong as granite, from these banks, from these bays.
Whose troops are these?

29. *Pari* are female spirits of the rivers and hills.

30. The cap (*kopiah*) refers to the soft headhugging cap worn by Muslims. *Syed* is a title given to reputed male descendants of Muhammad (Wilkinson 1959; Iskandar 1970).

The troops of Princess Sadung.[31]
Each of you accept, one and all.
Troops of Wak Selamat Muda.
Each of you, hear me, one and all, accept one and all.
I give you these offerings to coax you, to plead for health.
I ask you to hear me, one and all, to accept, one and all,
Troops of Captain Moving Rock, Captain Traveling Rock, warriors all.
Hey, tall mountains, granite rocks, troops of the mountain top's Lone Striding Jin,
Each of you hear me, one and all, accept, one and all, one kati for a hundred twenty thousand.[32]
Who, then, will serve the feast but the Seven Experts?
Who makes the request? The Oldest Expert makes the request.
Who does the Job? The Younger Expert does the job.
Who finishes the job? The Youngest Expert finishes the job.
Who serves the feast but Mak Babu Kalang Dermi[33] and her sister, The Black Servant.

31. Princess Sadung is the subject of numerous tales. Skeat (1972) writes of her as the princess who ruled over Alang-ka-suka, rejecting all suitors. Sheppard (1961) writes that her beauty was so extraordinary that the King of Siam ordered his men to take her from her husband by force and deliver her to his court. She refused to marry him and, spitting at him in disdain, caused an ulcer to appear on his chest, which would not heal until he sent Puteri Sadung back to her husband in Kelantan. Her husband, refusing to believe that she had remained faithful, struck her. She retaliated by stabbing him to death, proclaiming his younger brother king in his place, and retiring to Ulu Kelantan. Rentse (1934:44) believes Puteri Sadung to have been a historical person, the "Queen of the Sakai"(aborigines). According to Cuisinier (1936:82), Puteri Sadung was the adopted daughter of Queen Che' Siti of Tanah Serendah Sakebun Bunga (Kelantan); and that Che' Siti is also the symbol for the Inner Winds. Tok Daud says only that Puteri Sadung "*jaga padang*" (she is the guardian spirit of the fields).

32. Tok Daud commented that, since spirits don't really eat the offerings but only receive their essence, one *kati* (1.3 lbs.) would suffice for 120,000 spirits. He is unaware that *seketi* = 100,000 (see also Sweeney 1972:304, 340, where a dalang speaks of the number of *dewa* as "sekati dua laksa" which would equal 120,000) [CL].

33. According to Pak Long, Mak Babu Kalang Dermi is the wife of Si Alam Tunggal, the sister of Nenek Betara Guru, and the mother of Semar. See Sweeney 1972 for her role in the ritual drama of the shadow play, in which she serves food. The word, *bujang*, in her sister's name (Mak Bujang Hitam), refers here to "servant," rather than unmarried person.

Original servitors, servants by breeding, serving jin with jin,
together in ranks, mambang with mambang, together in ranks,
Then kings and kings, together in ranks, dewa with dewa, together in ranks.
Who, then, sends the feast round but Miss Champion of Servants?
That is your nature, that is your breeding, to serve up the feast
If the jins stay together in ranks.
When you send round the feast, see that friendships aren't smashed past repair or ground into dust.
Who, then, lifts up the feast . . . takes charge of the kitchenware but the Lone Helmsman Jin from within the earth's realm?
That is your nature, that is your breeding, when you do it play fair and don't misbehave.
Jin with jin, together in ranks, mambang with mambang, together in ranks, bayu[34] with bayu, together in ranks,
Kings with kings, together in ranks, dewa with dewa, together in ranks.
Who, then, lifts up the feast but Father Dalang Yahudi,[35] Dalang Yahuda,
Dalang of all souls, he lifts up the feast,
Dalang Kelongan Lokek, Dalang Kelubangan, three brother dalang lift up the feast.
Dalang Suruh Wati-wati, holy one just like a mountain, he lifts up the feast.
They don't lead us falsely, hidden in darkness, oh no.
They are dalang by breeding, dalang by nature, dalang of standing, experienced dalang.

34. See n. 49, chap. 6.

35. Dalang Yahudi means Jewish puppet master. One of the origin stories of the Main Peteri (which was told to me by Tok Daud) credits (or, rather, discredits) the Jews as the originators, as well as linking its origins to the foundations of Islam.

Take, for example, Dalang Wan Mustafa,[36] accustomed to inviting throngs of jin, hordes of imps,
Along with his brother, Semar; yes, yes, my brother, Semar.
Semar, where is your spirit troop, forty-four strong, from the ends of the earth?
Brother, please appear.
Brother, which ones don't appear?
Brother, please appear.
Perhaps our brother's men at the edge of the village haven't heard.
Brother, please appear.
Where are you on the open plains, that you don't appear?
Brother, please appear, come from the open plains, stretching as far as the eye can see, covering all of the world.
If you're up on the granite mountain's peak, why won't you appear, why can't I reach you?
It isn't I who asks; 1, 3, 5, 7 dalang perform the release.[37]

[When the invocation was over, Tok Daud was offered some tea, which he drank while relaxing and chatting. Then the drummer and pot-player took their places near Tok Daud. He picked up his rebab and, accompanied by the percussionists, sang his introductory song, which echoed, condensed, and embroidered on the invocation, and set the stage for the Bestirring Song that would follow. Conversations in the audience continued for awhile and then died down.]

Minduk's Introductory Song

I utter the name of God with one Alif.[38]
Alif stands at the foot of Heaven.
Mother spreads a welcome at the gates of Earth.
I weigh my words before I speak

36. *Mustafa* (chosen) is an epithet often applied to Muhammad, God's Chosen (Wilkinson 1959:791).

37. It is typical of Malay magic that the speaker disclaims any power in his own right and, instead, locates the power and intention in the original dalang, the original teachers, the heavenly midwives, and so forth [CL].

38. See n. 29, chap. 6.

Because I want to awaken the sleepers.
The minduk is sleeping, I'll shake him awake.
Wake up, old minduk, young minduk,
Awake with the Royal Princesses in the palace courtyard.
Each of you awake.
Wake up, minduk, at the white tree;[39]
Wake up, princess from Mount Setom.[40]
I bid you awaken, one and all,
All who lie in heavy slumber.[41]
The minduk awakes and attracts the flowerbud.[42]
The musicians awake, tired still.
Each of them awakens.
I'll shake the sleepy cymbals[43] awake,
The first of the players, the first of the plays,
The first of the incense I surely will wake.
I bid the sleepers, one and all, awake, inang[44] and musicians,
So I may speak of my own slumbers.
Seven teachers, all of one age, all alike,[45]
People with five souls,[46] oh, sleep no longer.
Two disappear and one emerges,
The white one, the teacher's potent cure,

39. The white tree is the human spine. The minduk at the white tree is part of the healing forces within the human body which must be awakened to assist in effecting a cure.

40. Gimlette (1971 [1915]:86) says, "The mountain Setong is said to be the head of the Peteri." Sweeney (1972:345) comments that *setom* means "to metamorphose." The mountain, in the symbolism of the Main Peteri, stands for the human head. The changing quality of the princess's (peteri) "mountain" is an apt metaphor for the arrival and departure of the many spirit visitations that take place through the agency of the tok 'teri [CL].

41. All of the body's own forces, those of the tok 'teri and his patient, need to be awakened.

42. The flowerbud refers to the piles of popped rice that will be used in the divination.

43. The floor cymbals (canang) are often replaced by an overturned pot played by striking it with a piece of wood [CL].

44. See n. 50, chap. 6.

45. See n. 9, chap. 7.

46. "Five souls" means the five senses.

The white granite rock is shining here.[47]
I speak of the teacher, the sage of the world,
Who soars aloft straight to the seventh heaven,[48]
Then soars down to earth, to the seventh layer.
The original teacher, a teacher by nature, who hails from a long and ancient line,
Meditates in seclusion in the glassy pool of earthly beads.[49]
I have told my tale honestly, put things in order.
It is best to invoke our mother now.
Nur Allah the father's name, Nur Ahut the mother's,
When the angel held them in his hands.
Forty days within the father's womb,
Full forty days within the father's womb,
Then thrust into the mother's womb.
The mother bears the child nine months and ten days.
Let the child be safe in the womb.
Let him suffer no ruin, destruction, attack,
So the child may become, may become a physician,
And Adam become, become a healer,[50]
Here, in his father's castle courtyard.
Where do we land?
In the depths of the earth for an audience with the ruler,
The Earth Imp, Black Ruler of the earth's realm.
Black Conquerer of the earth's realm.
Each of you awake, listen, you nine,
I have a request, I place it in trust.
May no errors enter into our discussion.
I ask that you hear me, one and all.
Let no one step across the line,[51]
Let there be no treason in the earth's realm.
The earth's tale now finished, where shall we land?
At the edge of the village, in the shadow of the groves,

47. See n. 28, chap. 6.
48. See n. 11, chap. 7.
49. See n. 13, chap. 7.
50. See n. 3, chap. 6.
51. See n. 26, chap. 7.

For an audience with Nenek Sang Gana before we meet the Village Imp.
Hear me, hear me, I leave a request, I place it in trust.
May no errors enter into our discussion at the edge of the village,
All you sons and daughters of the ruler at the village's edge,
Let the physician return to the grandsire.
I ask you to hear me, one and all.
The tale of the edge of the village now over, where shall we land?
On the vast open plain of Raja Hakim, hidden from view on the plain,
And all of his subjects and children on the vast open plain.
May no errors enter into our discussion.
Now I finish the tale of the vast open plain, stretching as far as the eye can see.
Should we land at the feet of the saints, the new saints,
Mother Longbreasts is the saint who rules here.
Datuk Yellow Turban, Green Turban, Blue Turban, White Turban,
These are the saints who are found in these parts.
May no errors enter into our discussion.
The elders are good, strong as granite, each one.
Black rocks, yellow rocks, smoldering rocks.
Hey, Lone Striding Jin, from what center do you come?
May no errors enter into our discussion.
Each of you listen to what I say, hear my story, hear my tale.
Hear me, great spirits, hear one and all.
If two hear my story, go back and tell three.
Ah, oh, old dalang, may no errors enter into our discussion.
Hear me, hear me, one and all.
[Transition music, during which Tok Daud says:]
I'll say seven prayers to Dalang Yahudi, Yahuda,
Dalang Semar who commands the heavens.
Be serene, holy guardians, like the betrothed of a holy line.
They do not lead us falsely, the dalang's voices, dalang by nature, original dalang.

Oh, dalang who lives in the fire, Dalang Semar,
Best of all dalang, who brings healing herbs.[52]
Oh, Wan Mustafa, who watches over the multitudes.

[Toward the end of the introductory song, Pak Long snuffed out his cigarette and changed his clothes. He took off his sweater and shirt and slipped a clean sarong (provided by Mat Din) over his head, letting his old sarong drop to the floor. He added two sashes, tying them tightly around his waist to make sure his sarong wouldn't fall during his exertions, an important step since he didn't hold with wearing underpants. He sat down cross-legged in front of Tok Daud and listened intently, as the minduk sang the Bestirring Song that would arouse Pak Long's angin and allow him to trance:]

Bestirring Song

Ah, I utter the name of God with one Alif.
Alif stands at the gates of Heaven,
The tribe spreads a welcome at the gates of Earth.
After they spread it their prayers will begin,
In order to open the blocked gates of Wind.
Wind as small as a sesame seed,
Wind as small as a mustard seed.
Wind called a golden bouquet of flowers,
Wind called a silvery bouquet of flowers,
As it emerges when we invoke it.
Family of four brothers,[53]
The first named Angin Al-Ahmad,
The second named Angin Umara,
The third named Angin Nur Pila,
The fourth named Angin Nur Jila.
They arose long ago, in the earliest times.
The Winds hold the father's secret,
They receive it still.

52. Semar has a dual nature. Although he was burnt in the fire for his arrogance toward Adam (see n. 20, chap. 7), he can yet be persuaded to help mankind [CL].

53. The four brothers are Earth, Air, Fire, and Water, the four elements of which the Universe, and humanity, is made. See n. 29, chap. 7.

Told to the mother,
The Wind emerges from the tip of eternity!
Down through the generations
By the choice of the father.
The Wind is tended by the mother.
The father stays forty days in his room,
The mother is pregnant for nine months.
[The tok 'teri begins his incantation here.]
The father's name is Ali Akbar,
The mother's name is Siti Halmah,[54]
The child's name is Magical Wise One.
The Wind glows with five rays of light.[55]
It stands and recites six magical words.
The Wind glows from seven holy books.
The Wind rules over a handful of earth, a drop of water,
A drop of water, a tongue of flame.
Earth, do not cause us to rot and to crumble.
Water, do not make us choke down our sobs.
Fire, do not make us heat up with fever.
A puff of Wind watches over the whole world.
The Wind emerged from a split betel-nut.[56]
The Wind is shut up in the land of Java.
It will land on the soil of Java.
The Wind will take on its original godhood,
When the Wind lands on the soil of Malaya.
Then it will become a most beautiful princess,
One of good family, one of fine ancestry.
That tale truly ended, another commences.
I want to invoke now Brother Persanta.[57]
Brother Persanta slides down from above.

54. Ali Akbar is Adam and Siti Halmah is Eve.

55. The "five rays of light" are the five daily prayers of Islam.

56. Tok Daud explains that all angin comes originally from Adam and Eve, who were once one but were split to make two people.

57. Persanta is another name for Pak Dogol, one of the shaman's familiar spirits. See n. 62, chap. 6.

Two brothers study the Main Peteri,[58]
Then they can recite it.
Let no danger come to the two brothers, raise them,
Then they will be inang.
Hear me, listen while I invoke you,
If you would be dalang in the village,
At the same time you travel, invoking the spirits.
Seven bonds have come to be weighed,
Four bonds we have to the Koran victorious,
Bonds, bonds to the father's season.
Our mother's legacy, bonds of royal color.[59]
Aii, I am alone, alone,
Wei, wei, I am alone.
Everyone else is deep in slumber.
If I want to awaken the kings and the dewa
Of good ancestry, of fine family,
I speak of his source and the king springs awake
Out of his slumbers on the palace verandah,
On the little dais of Tanjung Laleng,
While Raja Laleng keeps saying his prayers.[60]
Raja Laleng is being wed upon the gauzy muslin mattress
That sits on the carpet above the dais.
Someone is meditating atop the canopy
Hanging over the yellow mattress.[61]

58. The "two brothers" are the minduk and tok 'teri.

59. Seven ties are the seven body parts; four ties are the four elements. The ties of the mother and father (or our ties to our ancestors) are the angin that they have passed down to their descendants.

60. Dewa Laleng is one of the archetypal Inner Winds. In the words of Mat Daud bin Panjak (see Appendix A), "If one falls heir to Dewa Laleng, he doesn't want to work . . . he wants to play chess, he wants to play games, he wants to gamble, drink, steal other people's belongings." *Ratib*, which I have translated as "prayers," does not refer to the five obligatory daily prayers, but rather to a mystic exercise based on the repetition of a religious formula such as Allah Akbar (God is Great): "The formula is repeated slowly at first so as to allow the mind to think out what it means and suggests; then the repetition becomes louder and more rapid so as to divert the mystic's attention from the illusive world around him and enable him to realize and enjoy the celestial truths in this formula" (Wilkinson 1959:952).

61. The mattress is yellow since that is the color reserved for Malay royalty. The canopy (*lelangit*) is hung from the ceiling on the occasion of a Main Peteri. The shaman's

Awake from slumber on the palace verandah.
Awake, Four Royal Winds, Four Heroes,[62] I invoke you,
Four Champions, Four Warriors.
Awake, old warrior, young warrior,
Little warrior, youngest warrior, all of you awake.
Awake, old warrior, captain of the king,
Awake, little warrior, lone helmsman,
White warrior, loyal to Muhammad.
The flower vase still lacks a foundation.
The white rock has not yet turned green.[63]
The warrior treads on the old steel,
The warrior reclines on the new steel.
The warrior is sheltered below the locked sky,
Till the sky opens up, then below white umbrellas.[64]
The pillar becomes the Throne of God.[65]
The warrior awakes in the silver betel box,
In the golden bowl, in the dish of pure gold.[66]
Guard well the tips, the tips of the fingers,
Guard as the sickness leaves through the hands' palms.[67]
Guard along with the Fearsome Commander.[68]
Ali[69] says that all should awake.

---

friendly familiar spirits may perch atop the canopy. The shaman's patient is often referred to as royalty; the house in which his cure is taking place is called the palace [CL].

62. All of these kings and heroes are personifications of the forces within the human body (as I was told by both minduk and tok 'teri). They come in groups of four because of the four-fold nature of the Universe (earth, air, fire, and water).

63. The white rock has not yet turned green because the time that is being spoken of in this section is so long ago that the moss that grew there later has not yet had a chance to grow on it.

64. The locked sky refers to the time before Creation. White umbrellas are the sign and prerogative of royalty (see also Wilkinson 1959:927).

65. Tok Daud says that the pillar (tiang aras) is the human backbone, which becomes the Throne of God when we pray. *Arash* (Arabic) is God's Throne of Glory (Wilkinson 1959:44). See n. 40, chap. 7.

66. Tok Daud explains that the silver betel box is the body; the golden bowl is the skull, which contains the brain.

67. Malays believe that sickness leaves the body by way of the hands and feet [CL].

68. The Fearsome Commander (Panglima Garang) is a powerful sea spirit.

69. Ali does not refer here to the Prophet's son-in-law. It is the name of a Wind—Baginda (King) Ali. At first the Winds are tired and sleepy, but as the minduk arouses them they awake and roar with the strength of a typhoon.

Ali is tired, and so are they all.
Ali roars, thunderous Ali,
Ali the hero, heroic Ali.
Awake, along with the vicious rhinoceros,
The cruel tiger with a vicious face.[70]
Awake, one and all.
Awake, all you friends, throngs of penggawa,[71]
Loving friends, affectionate spirits.
Awake as you've done from the earliest times,
Rouse yourselves from your slumbers.
Your name is Great Tiger, Hulubalang Rimau Besar Serjan Kilat.[72]

[At about the middle of the Bestirring Song, Pak Long began to recite the following incantation:]

Shaman's Incantation[73]

T:[74] Peace be with you. I want to send greetings now to the troops and battalions of these parts, the courtiers of the Earth Jin, the imps of the earth, the jin of the soil, the imps of the soil, the pelesit of the soil, the putaranggas of the soil, the polong of the soil, the retinue of the ruler of this place. I am not here just to amuse myself, but because I want to be a healer and physician at this time, at this moment. Let no one be nasty, let no one be angry at Pak Long. I call on my many penggawa, my numerous friends. I want to awaken them, I want to awaken the fine heritage that descends to me from my father and mother. I want to awaken Sulung Kecil Penganjur Raja, together with Awang Mahat, the Elephant Keeper, together with Awang Kasim Gila.[75] Awake, together

70. The "vicious rhinoceros" stands for strong negative emotions; the "cruel tiger" is Angin Hala. See n. 84, chap. 6 and n. 25 this chapter.

71. See n. 44, chap. 6.

72. See notes 84, 141, chap. 6.

73. Since it was impossible for me to hear every word of Pak Long's incantation clearly in the background of the minduk's song, I asked him to recite it for me the following day.

74. The tok 'teri was Pak Long Awang (the patient in chap. 7).

75. Sulung Kecil Penganjur Raja are the eyes, the first human attribute that develops

with the four heroes, the four guardians, the four warriors, the four nobles.[76] The four warriors guard from above and become a shelter; they guard from below and become a foundation; they guard from before and become a crown; they guard from behind and become the inang's palisade. Guard me, all my many friends, my myriads of penggawa. One and all are deeply sleeping.

I want to continue the discussion. I want to awaken Wak Long, together with Pak Deh.[77] Awake, Pak Deh, you of fine ancestry, and come quickly to the inang. I want to awaken others, wherever I may land. I travel to awaken my many friends and penggawa. Awake one and all, together with Dewa Si Alam Tunggal,[78] four angels, four friends of the inang. Guard above, guard below, guard behind, guard before.

I want to go further, wherever I may land. I land in the original byre of the weretigers.[79] I want to awaken the family of seven weretigers in their original byre. The *hala* is the heritage of the father and the mother. The weretigers live in the original byre. Who is the weretigers' keeper? The Black Servant is their keeper; she follows behind a tiger cub. Stride, stride thrice. Jump, jump thrice. Then jump into the inang's lap, bringing pious prayer from Allah's castle to the inang.

I travel on, wherever I may land. I travel to Dewa Si Alam Tunggal, heritage of my father and mother. I awaken him together with four

---

in a baby. That explains his name [the little firstborn advance guard of the king—CL]. Awang Mahat the Elephant Keeper is the nape of the neck. Even though an elephant is large, a person can control it; even though commerce with spirits can be dangerous to a tok 'teri, his knowledge and penggawa protect him. [The nape of the neck is the center from which the characteristic headshaking in trance proceeds—CL.] Awang Kasim Gila [gila = crazy] are the shaman's eyes as he goes into trance.

76. The four heroes and so forth are the forces of the body—four to correspond to the four elements.

77. Pak Deh is Pak Dogol, one of the shaman's spirit familiars. Wak Long (another one of Pak Long's familiars) is Pak Dogol's sidekick, whom he created out of his own body dirt.

78. Although Si Alam Tunggal, Pak Dogol, and Persanta are the same entity in different guises, they are treated as separate in the Main Peteri and make separate appearances in the seance [CL].

79. Hala can refer variously to tiger spirits, to men who can change themselves into tigers, and to a Wind, or personality type. The weretigers are believed to live in enclosures or villages in the heart of the jungle, a belief noted by Marsden in 1784 (p. 253), still current on the east coast of Malaysia. See notes 84, 141, chap. 6.

angels, I awaken him together with four friends. I travel on, wherever I may land. I meet my older brother, Persanta, a god without doubt, who has soared swiftly down to the abode of mortals.

I travel on, wherever I may land. I reach a country with a king. Now I awaken the tiny god, Dewa Muda,[80] the young god who lives in the Land of Java, whose father is the king of Java, whose mother's name is Princess Hidden Moon. Swiftly descend to the inang. The inang calls you, the minduk beckons. Awake, together with your servant, Awang Mindung Pengasuh, who cares for the body and soul of the inang. Five times day and night[81] come quickly, don't slow down when you're called, when you're beckoned. Awake one and all.

I want to awake others, wherever they may be. I travel on, and shake Miss Flower awake, meditating atop Star Mountain. Swiftly, Miss Flower, descend to the inang. Awake, Miss Jasmine Bud.[82] Awake at this time, at this moment. Truly our heritage is fine. I want to assume my parents' heritage.

I land wherever I may land. I travel to the Mountain of Magical Blue Caves for an audience with Raja Hanuman[83] who meditates atop the

80. Angin Dewa Muda is the most prevalent form of angin, and the sicknesses brought on by its frustration constitute a large part of the shaman's practice. As a personality type, Angin Dewa Muda characterizes people with strong needs to be admired and coddled, to eat dainty foods, dress in attractive clothing, be surrounded by sweet smells, and in general, to be spoiled.

Pak Long, the shaman reciting this incantation, believes that he has three strong Inner Winds: Angin Hala, Angin Dewa Muda, and the Bomoh's Angin. He remains healthy, since all of them are satisfied by his performance in Main Peteri: Angin Bomoh, because he is treating patients; Angin Hala, because he takes on the personae of violent genies and powerful spirits such as Hanuman; and Angin Dewa Muda, because he is treated to a special meal before the performance and tea and cakes after; he is surrounded by sweet smells of flowers, perfume, and incense; he dresses in a new sarong, and is the object of admiration [CL].

81. An echo of the five daily prayers [CL].

82. Miss Jasmine Bud (Mek Sekuntum Melur) and Miss Flower (Mek Bunga) are two of the shaman's familiar spirits. Miss Flower is a member of Pak Long's family who, several generations back, was stolen from her cradle by the *orang bunyian*, invisible but audible spirits, who took her up to Bukit Bintang, a hilltop in Kelantan famous as a dwelling place of spirits. There she became an *orang ghaib* (invisible person). Pak Long finds her help especially valuable in the performance of love magic [CL].

83. Hanuman the White Monkey (Hanuman Kera Putih) and his sons, Hanuman Ikan (Fish Hanuman) and Hanuman Bongsu (Youngest Hanuman), were acquired as familiar spirits by Pak Long when he performed in the shadow play.

Mountain of Magical Blue Caves. Come swiftly to the inang. I travel on, wherever it may lead. I reach the middle of the ocean where the magic mango tree grows amid five mango trees where three ridges emerge from the sandbank. Awake, Raja Hanuman Ikan, grandson of Sang Sepit the King of Dragons. Truly our heritage is fine. Come swiftly to the inang. I reach the place of rushing winds and blue clouds where Raja Hanuman Bongsu meditates amid the rushing winds. Awake and quickly come to the inang. Don't be reluctant to be called, don't make me beckon long.

I travel on, wherever I may land. I reach the cape at the river's mouth for an audience with Captain Maddened Buffalo.[84] Truly our parents' heritage is fine. Come quickly, don't stop and stare. Let no one look with anger upon the inang.

[As he recited the incantation, Pak Long's foot began to tremble. The movement was carried through his body to his head. When it reached his head, he signaled to the musicians to begin the music of transition, shouting "Ah, saaaa!" Through the music, the shaman and minduk shouted "Eh, eh! Ahhh, ahhh! Hei hei, ah hei!" (inarticulate cries that accompany each transition during the seance). As the music accelerated, the shaman's head shook and rolled faster and faster, his arms thrust out violently. Finally, he threw a handful of popped rice and clapped his hands above his head, alerting the musicians that he had achieved trance and a new persona. He is now Awang Mindung Pengasuh, one of the protective forces of the body, who acts as caretaker to the person, just as his namesake in the Mak Yong acts as servant and councillor to Dewa Muda. When the music stopped, the tok 'teri knelt before the minduk and commenced a dialogue:]

M: [*spoken*] One king with two names[85] who takes pity on our favorite child, from which flowerbud[86] have you emerged; what spirit are you?

T: Yes, indeed.

M: From which bay has this jasmine blossom come, bending to the

84. Pak Long says that here the Maddened Water Buffalo (Kerbau Amuk) refers specifically to the afterbirth.

85. One king with two names—because the tok 'teri now carries two personae, his own and that of the visiting spirit.

86. The flower symbolism, which continues in the succeeding paragraph, is meant to be flattering to the spirit visitor.

left and swaying to the right, shaking your head till you're out of breath, running and gliding until you arrive at the courtyard of the palace?

T: True, sir.

M: Who are you, sir, who receives a new name and changes his character? What are you called, what is your title, you who are carried by the inang?

T: Ah, is that so, sir?

M: Yes.

T: Yes, I receive a new name and I change my character. I imitate the behavior of devils and demons.[87]

M: Yes.

T: Here is my name and my title, sir. I am Awang Mindung Pengasuh. I watch over the soul and the spirit of my inang throughout the day and the night, sir.

M: Oh my.

T: It's true, sir.

M: Be on guard, Awang Mindung Pengasuh, man of ancient times, early days.

T: Right.

M: You are older than the father, older than the mother, as old as the village hut and the nation, the palace and its verandah.[88]

T: Ah, yes, that's true, sir.

M: Ah, you come to the inang in the courtyard of the palace as he goes into trance.

T: Yes, that's so.

M: Now creep up the mountain and sway toward the fields.[89] When I instruct the inang, I inform his jinjang.[90] Let no one be forgetful, let no one make mistakes. Guard the inner fortress closely; guard and strengthen the outer gates.[91]

87. The tok 'teri explains that, during the performance, he does not *become* a devil or spirit, but merely imitates their behavior. Several ritual practitioners emphasized this point very strongly during our conversations and felt that religious Muslims who objected to the performance misunderstood the distinction.

88. He is, in fact, as old as the creation of humanity, since he is one of the body's own protective forces (*dalam badan kita*).

89. The mountain is the head, the fields are the chest.

90. See n. 65, chap. 7.

91. He is speaking about the human body. Spells recited by Malays to protect them from harm are known as *pagar* (fences) [CL].

T: Ah, how sweet it is to hear this tale, my prince, that you have told me. Nothing is false, it's entirely true.

T: Cease your worries, lay aside your cares. I watch over my inang to the seventh night, to the eighth day. No harm whatsoever will come to my inang.

M: Ah, yes, that's so.

T: I agree, sir.

M: Ah, the way you tell the story, the way you recount the tale, is sweet to my ears. Nothing is false, it's entirely true.

T: I agree, yes, it's true.

M: I trust in you, oh foreign king; I ask you now for your help and assistance.

T: Right, sir. Cease your suspicions, lay aside your cares, I can help you to the best of my ability, in a rough-and-ready fashion, but you'd better call Wak Kedi Bomoh,[92] my prince.

M: Ah, yes, that's so.

T: Right.

M: Ah, now then, sir, I will speak to all our many friends, our throngs of penggawa, our loving friends, affectionate penggawa, at this time, at this moment.

T: [sung] If you please, sir, I will speak to our grandsire. I'll ask Grandsire Adam to act as a healer, become a physician.

M: Ei, then I'll go pay my respects to my earliest grandsire . . .

T: Ah.

M: . . . my first teacher. Grandsire, don't let our troubles increase.

T: Ah, yes, that's true.

M: Second, don't let problems pile up and crush us.

T: Ah, where is Adam over yonder? There Adam tills the soil, over yonder he plants his farm, disturbs the soil. I ask that he become, that Adam become a healer.

M: Ei, while we paid our respects to our grandsire . . .

T: Ah.

M: . . . we visited each room of our many friends and had an audience with the king.

T: True.

92. See n. 64, chap. 6.

M: We have many friends and throngs of penggawa, plenty of loving, affectionate friends. Be alert, be on guard, one and all.

T: Guard my body. The Little Dewa[93] is calling, is waving.

M: Ei.

T: In this place, through the night, no disaster will come, in this place where the multitudes sit and wait.

M: Ei.

T: Ah, saa, ah, saa . . .

[Transition music. The shaman, shaking his head, signals the exit of one persona and the entrance of another, Wak Kedi Bomoh, the Sage from the Siamese Monastery, a character from the shadow play, who often presides over divinations. In this case, however, he merely visits to give advice about how to proceed in the seance.]

M: [*spoken*] When one disappears and is changed for another, the older brother vanishes and the younger turns up . . .

T: Yes, sir.

M: . . . emerging with a rush, arms waving and body swaying, confused and heedless, to meet with the inang in the palace courtyard.

T: Yes, that's so.

M: Ah, what is your name and what is your title?

T: Me, sir? I can receive a new name and change my character. My name and my title is Wak Kedi-kedi Bomoh. I was meditating in solitude in the Golden Monastery of the Seven Temples, with the Forty Idols in the Pillars of the Shrines and the Yellow Banners, sir.

M: Oh my.

T: Why the great hurry, my prince?

M: I can tell you politely, Bomoh Kedi, the youngest in the monastery, who emerged from the Seven Temples and the Golden Monastery, from the temple of the Great Sage Eye of Fire[94] with the Forty Idols in the Pillars of the Shrines and the Yellow Banners, sir.

T: Yes, that's so.

M: Ah, you can meet with the inang in the palace courtyard. Tonight, when I instruct the inang, I inform his jinjang. Let no one be

93. The Little Dewa is Dewa Muda.

94. The eye of fire derives from Siva's third eye, which he uses for destruction [CL]. This interpretation is not current on the village level.

forgetful, let no one make mistakes regarding the inang and his jinjang.

T: Cease your suspicions, lay aside your cares. I watch over my inang to the seventh night, the eighth day. My inang shall suffer no damage or harm.

M: Oh, yes.

T: Yes, indeed.

M: May the inang not suffer attack and destruction tonight.

T: Right.

M: I trust in you, foreign prince, and ask you to help and assist us by acting as a physician and healer.

T: Oh, you may ask, sir, but don't depend too much on me—I'm an old man and my eyes are growing dim, my son.

M: Yes, that's so.

T: Yes, indeed.

M: This is the way things are, uncle . . .

T: Right.

M: None of us is truly wise, none of us is truly clever, none can be sure that his wish will be granted . . .

T: Yes, indeed.

M: . . . because we are only mortals.

T: That's right.

M: We can only carry our pleas to God, to the foot of Alif in the shadow of Ba.[95]

T: We must ask Him.

M: Oh, yes, indeed.

T: If He grants our plea, we'll take it home to our children.

M: Oh, how extraordinary.

T: If He doesn't grant our plea, that's it as far as we're concerned.

M: We must ask elsewhere.[96]

T: Go ask at another house and come back if they give it to you. Ah, if you please, sir.

M: [*to Mat Din*] Do you want to have that boy treated?

MAT DIN: Yes, I do.

95. See n. 29, chap. 6.

96. This comment, and the one that follows, would be considered, at best, extremely problematic by orthodox Muslims [CL].

T: Now this is the way things are, sir.

M: Yes?

T: Since things are calm here, I'll descend to the earth, to the wastelands,[97] for an audience with the Earth Jin, the Earth Imp, sir.

M: Ah, then, if you please, sir, if you please. The day is good, the moment is right, the time has come.

T: I can't delay longer, taking part in this drama. I'll descend to the earth, to the wastelands. Ah, saa . . .

[Transition music; the tok 'teri dances briefly, then kneels on one knee in a threatening position with a fierce expression on his face. He speaks now in the persona of an earth spirit.]

M: Hey there, just now you emerged with a rush, arms waving and body swaying, confused and heedless . . .

T: Right.

M: . . . to meet with the physician.

T: Right.

M: What is your name, what is your title, what are you called?

T: Me, my prince?

M: Yes.

T: I'm one of an army of putarranggas and pelesit from the earth, that's who I am.

M: Oh, my, the troops of the Earth Jin, the Earth Imp . . .

T: Right, sir.

M: . . . ghosts of the earth, imps of the earth . . .

T: Ei.

M: . . . pelesit of the earth, putarrangas of the earth, those who receive offerings.

T: Right, sir.

M: I can't tell you politely why I summoned you.

T: Right.

M: Tonight I offer you a feast with yellow rice, pancakes, popped rice, a coconut, a betel quid, a drop of water . . .

T: Right.

97. *Tanah yang mati*, which I have translated as "wastelands," is land that was once but is no longer under cultivation [CL]. Pak Long remarked that it was a prime gathering place for spirits.

M: . . . because I want to ask a favor of you, sir.

T: Oh, is that so, sir?

M: Yes.

T: Hey! I wasn't the one who happened to ensnare him.[98]

M: Is that so?

T: That's right. I was only an innocent bystander.

M: Right, yes, sure, he was only an innocent bystander.

T: That's right.

M: It's beyond me who this "person from the earth" is; I can't recall who he is tonight.

T: Yes, that's true, that's right. (I feel stuffed even though I only ate a little rice.[99])

M: Ah, yes, indeed.

T: Right.

M: Well, it's this way, sir. Since you are not the one who brought error to the discussion, sir, perhaps it's time for you to go home.

T: Yes, I will.

M: Go back and send someone else here, sir. Let them all know that if anyone has made a mistake . . .

T: All right.

M: . . . he should come and see me. I want to confer with him.

T: All right, it's no trouble, you can do it. I'll spread the word to every road and pier, sir.

M: [*aside to Mat Din*] Take off your shirt. Sit back there toward the left.

T: Look, see to it that his legs are together.[100] [*He gives some popped rice to Mat Din and his "crazy" son to eat; the son has to be coaxed but finally eats some.*]

M: Put your legs together, hm, hm, hm. Move to the left, ah, finally his legs are together.

T: May I go home now to speak to my ruler?

98. See n. 12.

99. The tok 'teri is talking in his own persona in this aside.

100. It is important for a patient in the process of being treated during the Main Peteri to sit with his legs together, feet facing the doorway. A space is cleared between the patient and the doorway. None of the onlookers may sit there, since the sickness will leave through the patient's extremities and may endanger those in its path [CL].

M: If you please, sir, if you please. The day is good, the moment is right, the time has come.

T: I can't delay longer, taking part in this drama. I'd better go home for an audience with my ruler. Ah, saa . . .

[Transition music; the tok 'teri dances before Mat Din and his son who sits beside him. He reaches down, grabbing first their feet and then their heads with both his hands. He claps his hands together and thrusts them out in a casting-away motion. When the music stops, a friendlier persona has arrived. It is Pak Dogol, whose nickname is Pak Deh, one of the shaman's familiar spirits.]

M: Ah, a friend has arrived, but I don't know who he is. Who has come to visit me? What is your name, sir?

T: Me, sir? Why, I'm the inang's friend.

M: What is your name and what is your title?

T: Hey, I'm Pak Deh,[101] sir.

M: Be on the alert, Pak Deh, friend of the inang.

T: Yes, indeed.

M: Now I can speak to you politely, Pak Deh, since when I instruct the inang I also inform his penggawa . . .

T: Right, sir.

M: . . . in case there are misunderstandings and false steps.

T: Yes, indeed. Don't be suspicious, lay aside your cares, sir.

M: Ah, would that it were so, sir. You guard on the left, the right, behind, above, and below.

T: Right, sir.

M: If jin try to break in and rob, they can't; if mambang try to move in and seek shelter, they can't.

T: Yes, indeed.

M: Tonight I place my trust in you, foreign prince, and ask you to help and assist us by acting as physician and healer.

T: Cease your suspicions, lay aside your cares. I can help you to the best of my ability, in a rough-and-ready fashion.

M: True, sir.

T: Now, if you please, I'll return home to speak to my ruler.

M: If you please. The day is good, the moment is right, the time has come.

101. See n. 57.

T: Ah, saa . . .

[Transition music. The shaman takes on a new persona; now he speaks as Hitam Seri Penakluk, the Black Conqueror who rules the crossroads. He leans threateningly toward the minduk as the music stops.]

M: Hey, one person disappears and is exchanged for another. Who is it now that visits me in the palace courtyard?

T: Hey, I just wanted to come.

M: What is your name and what is your title? Who are you?

T: Ha! Black Seri Penakluk, who rules the four crossroads and the three branching paths; who levies taxes and demands tribute. I was busy hunting, involved in the chase, when I heard you call me. I came immediately.

M: Oh, is that so?

T: Yes, sir.

M: Black Seri Penakluk, brother of Seri Penaklik,[102] who rules the bays and villages, ridges and neighborhood in these parts.

T: Right, sir.

M: Now I can tell you politely why I summoned you.

T: Right.

M: Ah, if by chance you have brought any error at all into the discussion . . .

T: Right.

M: . . . from the halls of the earth's great gods to this lamb[103] here . . .

T: Right.

M: . . . tonight I ask a favor of you, I plead and coax you, sir.

T: You want to ask me?

M: Yes.

T: Does the physician mean to flatter me?

M: I want to petition you.

T: Oh, so you're asking me to remove my hot vapor which raises the temperature,[104] from the little lamb, from Adam, from Mat Din, sir.

102. Hitam Seri Penakluk means Illustrious Black Conqueror. Penaklik is just a sound-alike name used as a synonym.

103. The lamb is the patient.

104. See n. 84.

M: Yes, that's right.

T: Cease your suspicions, lay aside your cares. I can leave, remove my hot vapor, and lower the temperature. The atmosphere will not oppress, the vapor will not pile up upon Mat Din.

M: Oh, yes, if you please, sir, if you please. The day is good, the time has come.

T: I can't delay longer, taking part in this drama. Ah, saa . . .

[Transition music; the tok 'teri dances before Mat Din, changing persona to that of a spirit of the village, one of the Mighty Spirits (Hantu Raya).]

M: [*spoken*] Who is the friend who emerged with a rush, arms waving and body swaying, confused and heedless?

T: Hey, I'll give you my name. You can say I'm one of the troops of the Mighty Spirit, from the edge of the village, in the shadow of the groves.

M: Oh, my, the troops of the Seven Mighty Spirits from the edge of the village, from the sheltered groves.

T: Yes, sir.

M: Tonight I can tell you politely why I summoned you.

T: Right.

M: It's because I have carefully made ready the rice, sir, for the mother's feasts, the father's preparations, the grandsire's offerings.

T: Are they ready yet?

M: Yellow rice, pancakes, popped rice, a coconut, a betel quid, a drop of water, because I want to pamper you.

T: Yes, indeed.

M: Because I want to hold a discussion in the halls of the great gods of the earth, sir.

T: Ah, is that so, sir?

M: Yes.

T: If you want to have a discussion, ha! you'd better invoke the father of all polong, sir.

M: Oh, yes, that's true.

T: Yes, indeed. Our tribe is feeling uneasy.

M: Ah, right.

T: We've been keeping watch in the village and groves here. We want peace in the village and groves here.

M: Ah, that's true.

T: That's so.

M: Tonight, sir . . .

T: Yes, indeed.

M: If you have, even in the slightest way, brought error into the discussion . . .

T: Right.

M: . . . you should go home now and rest at the edge of the village, in the shelter of the groves.

T: Ah, right, sir.

M: Watch over the whole world: the four directions, five palaces, seven corners, eight counties.[105] May no errors enter into our discussion, sir.

T: Yes, indeed, sir.

M: Now, if you please.

T: If you please, sir. I can't stay any longer taking part in this drama.

[Transition music; as he dances, shaking his head, the tok 'teri changes his persona from that of a fierce hantu to that of a flirtatious young girl who wiggles her behind as she gracefully seats herself on the mat. It is Mek Bunga (Miss Flower), Pak Long's most cherished spirit familiar, who speaks in a high and gentle voice:]

M: Who is this who sifts the rice and winnows it up and down, to the left and to the right?[106]

T: [*laughs*] Do you mean me? My prince, don't you even know me a little? Have you forgotten?

M: I don't recall.

T: Ah, my name is Mek Bunga, the friend of the inang, his penggawa and jinjang, sir.

M: Oh, the beloved friend.

T: That's right.

M: Ah, your name is Miss Flower.

105. The four directions, five palaces, seven corners are the four elements, the five senses, the seven body parts. Adding one to the final group (eight counties) shows that it is not simply a symbolic reference to the human body but also refers to the world outside.

106. The tok 'teri in the persona of Mek Bunga, is making flirtatious girlish movements that Tok Daud compares to winnowing rice [CL].

T: Yes, indeed, sir.

M: A person to be reckoned with, a clever talker, good at discussions . . .

T: That's true, sir.

M: . . . who knows how to cajole, who knows how to love.

T: Yes, indeed.

M: Tonight you must be alert; when I instruct the inang I inform his jinjang. Let no one be forgetful, let no one make mistakes regarding the inang and his jinjang.

T: Ah, just so, sir. Cease your suspicions, lay aside your cares. I will take care of my inang. None shall attack him, none shall cause harm.

M: Ah, may the inang not suffer attack and destruction. Tonight I place my trust in you, foreign princess, and ask for your help and assistance.

[The tok 'teri rises and dances, using the graceful hand movements and small steps of the Mak Yong, while he sings this duet with the minduk:]

T: [*sung*] If you please, oh, if you please. A country has a ruler.

M: Ei, Mek. Guard the inang below . . .

T: [*spoken*] Yes, indeed.

M: [*sung*] . . . guard him above.

T: Ah.

M: Ah, run, run swiftly, glide, glide across the sky.

T: I will run swiftly. I will surely guard my king.

M: Eii, while you dwell with the Grandsire.

T: [*spoken*] Ah, that's right.

M: [*sung*] Yes, indeed, ah, look and gaze.

T: [*spoken*] Ah, yes, indeed.

M: May no errors enter into our discussion.

[The music ends and the tok 'teri assumes another persona, this time without the aid of transition music. The new persona, a spirit, never identifies himself. He intends to do a divination, but Mat Din has not provided the requisite beeswax candles. He asks Mat Din for the names of all of the spirits with whom he had made contracts, to make sure that none is left out.]

T: [*spoken*] Ha, ha! Here I am, my prince.

M: Yes?

T: I'm not the one who bothered him. I'm really angry at him.

M: At him? Well what do you know, now *he's* angry at him. He says he's going to make trouble.

T: Not yet I won't.

M: Oh.

T: Does he want to get rid of me, or does he want to give me offerings? What's up with Mat Din?

M: Ah, do you want to get rid of him or give him offerings?

MAT DIN: I want to get rid of him.

T: You want to get rid of me! Very well. Mat Din also harbored a large polong and some sea spirits. Try to remember, did you or didn't you?

MAT DIN: I did.

T: Ah, there we are.

MAT DIN: What do you want me to do now? Talk about what I learned first or what I studied recently? I don't really want to discuss the former.

T: Oh, right.

MAT DIN: The most important thing, I guess, is that I used magic here and there and didn't give the necessary offerings. In the second place, it was like this: I got a few bits of magic from these writings here . . .

T: Oh, right.

MAT DIN: . . . from these old spells and drawings written down here.[107]

T: I'd like some tapers, give me some candles, please. I'm going to hit Mat Din here a good one. What, there aren't any candles?[108]

MAT DIN: Well, I don't know. The magic I inherited, the first things I learned?

107. Mat Din had a paper upon which magical figures were inscribed, which he showed to Pak Long.

108. Pak Long just means that he wants to do a divination, using candles made from the wax of wild bees. The height, color, and shape of the flame are the criteria used in the divination. Only beeswax candles will do, since bees are considered the "hantu's friends" because they are beyond human control (at least on the east coast of Malaysia) and their sting is hot, like the breath of the spirits. Pak Long was unable to do this divination, since Mat Din had neglected to provide the beeswax.

T: Oh, well. Don't worry about that, it's the usual thing.[109]

Mat Din: You want to know about those first things?

T: It's because I can't do a divination.

Mat Din: Well, there are quite a lot of things I learned in the beginning. About the sea spirits, those of the land, and even from the hills. So, I called on the sea spirits in the manner of the sea, those of the land in the manner of the land, that's what I learned in the beginning.

T: In the beginning?

Mat Din: Yes, in the beginning.

T: And then, later, what are their names?[110]

Mat Din: Their names?

T: Their names.

Mat Din: There are all sorts. From the sea, the Black Commander and the Fierce Commander.

T: Oh, is that all? Very few. From the land?

Mat Din: From the land, the Earth Jin and the Earth Imp.

T: Ah, very few.

Mat Din: Ranks of dewa all the way to Nenek Betara Guru.

T: Ah, very few, ah.

Mat Din: The lineage of the Wayang Jawa.[111]

T: Ah, yes, indeed.

Mat Din: That's all. The whole lineage of the Wayang Jawa.

T: Is that all there is?

Mat Din: That's all there is.

T: Well then, I'll go after the troops of polong. I'll go inform those polong who were created by sorcery, who were created by magical pictures and spells. I'll go and bring back the polong now. Ah, saa . . .

[Transition music; another fierce persona arrives, one of the polong, a malevolent familiar spirit created for the purpose of serving its "master." He kneels before the minduk and leans forward, putting his face up near the minduk's face.]

T: Hey, physician!

109. He means that most Malays inherit some useful spells.

110. What follows is a list of all the spirits with whom Mat Din made compacts.

111. The *Wayang Jawa* is a form of the Malay shadow play that was close to extinction in 1970 (Sweeney 1972:3). The shadow play most often performed in Malaysia is the *Wayang Siam*.

M: Hey, sir, your vapor emerged with a rush, to meet the physician, changing the atmosphere, arms waving and body swaying, confused and heedless. What is your name, sir?

T: Ei, you mean me, sir?

M: Yes! What is your name and what is your title?

T: Hey, if I tell you, what then?

M: Ah, if you do, in that case . . . only then can we put an end to this story.

T: Cut off the discussion and end the account.

M: Cut off and end the account, sir.

T: Hey! I'm one of the Seven Polong, sir. We've been waiting for Mat Din.

M: Oh, my, one of the Seven Polong, one of the seven little mackerels.[112]

T: Ah, right, sir!

M: Hey, how can you have the heart to torment Mat Din from dawn until sunset, from sunset to dawn?

T: Hey! we've been with Mat Din for a long time. We haven't had the slightest taste or smell of the father's feasts, the mother's preparations. Hey! that's why we're after Mat Din now.

M: Well, in times past you used to eat the mother's feasts, the father's offerings, the grandsire's gifts.

T: That's true, sir.

M: Yellow rice, pancakes, popped rice, a coconut, a betel quid, a drop of water, and a stick of opium.[113]

T: Right, sir.

M: It's been a long time now.

T: It has.

M: Ha! Tonight, sir . . .

T: Right.

M: . . . he has called upon me to be the interpreter, the attorney in this affair, Dewa Mahalatah Raja.[114]

112. Tok Daud is making a play on words at the expense of the *polong* by pretending to have heard him give his name as *talang* (horse mackerel). Like most spirits, the polong is too stupid to perceive the insult.

113. The "stick of opium" is really a cigarette.

114. According to Tok Daud, Dewa Mahalatah Raja is judge over all the hantu.

T: Very true.

M: To be a judge and make a decision. Everything's ready and waiting for you: yellow rice, pancakes, popped rice, a coconut, a betel quid, a drop of water.

T: There is? Where is it?

M: Oh, it's over yonder, all prepared. Take a look over there.

T: Ah, I can see there's only a little.

M: Oh, over yonder.

T: OK. [*Walks over and looks at the offerings; then says, querulously*] Hey, there's nothing raw.[115]

M: There's nothing raw?

SOMEONE IN THE AUDIENCE [*in a reasoning tone of voice*]: People don't eat them raw. They aren't eaten raw. They're eaten cooked.

M: Well, now. I want to ask you a few questions.

T: All right.

M: Long ago, in the beginning, did you eat them raw? How did you eat them?

T: When I stayed with him, I ate them cooked. When I stayed with other people, I ate them either raw or cooked.

M: Ah, if you ate them cooked when you stayed with him, well then, eat them cooked!

T: I should eat them cooked?

M: Yes.

T: Did you invite me to go eat, huh?

M: I haven't invited you to eat yet.

T: Ah. Ah.

M: First you have to accept.[116]

T: I have to accept first?

M: When we reach that point, there's the place where you will eat; you can go over there and grab all you can. But now, if you haven't played false with Mat Din, I ask you to accept, to remove your vapor and let the atmosphere flow over to take its place.

T: All at the same time?

M: Yes.

115. The spirit is complaining that no raw eggs were included in the offerings.

116. First the spirit has to accept the offerings and their implications: that the compact between him and Mat Din has come to an end [CL].

T: Right away?

M: What do you mean, right away? You were asked to accept first, weren't you? You can go over there when it's time to grab the food.

T: Well, then, I'll accept right away and go wait over yonder, OK?

M: Oh, yes.

T: But before I leave, don't you want to trade with me?[117]

M: Ah, you want to trade? If you asked the price I wouldn't know what to say.

T: Even so, what's the price?

M: The price? It's pretty expensive.

T: True, true, true, true, true, true, true, true.

M: If I want to sell fairly cheaply, how would that be?

T: Yes, yes, yes, yes, yes.

M: I want to sell one kati three [*tahil*].

T: One kati three?

M: Yes.

T: Four, five?

M: I can't!

T: You can't do it? Would you have to take a loss?

M: I would!

T: Add three more.

M: How many would that make?

T: I don't know.

M: Ah, we'll do it this way. I'll take the price down.

T: Ha, right, right, right.

M: I'll take it down by three.

T: By three?

M: I'll sell one kati one [tahil], sir.

T: One kati one?

M: For one you can have it right away.

T: Well, that one consists of seven body parts, sir.[118]

M: How extraordinary!

117. This section follows the convention of inverted bargaining with spirits: the human seller, instead of lowering the price, actually increases it.

118. Here we finally have the meaning of the bargaining session. The spirit and the minduk are bargaining for the life and health of a human being (Mat Din)—one person formed from seven body parts.

T: That is the nature of Man, sir. Well, that's over. Now, if you please.

M: If there are seven, then there is one.

T: I agree. Ah, if you please. I can linger here no longer. If you please.

M: If you please. The day is good, the moment is right, the time has come.

T: Ah, saa . . .

[Transition music; the tok 'teri dances briefly, then his manner changes to that of an exaggeratedly flirtatious and forward woman. A female spirit, Mek Ketuk-ketak (Miss Click-clack), has arrived, looking for a man.]

M: Who is it?

T: Do you mean me?

M: Yes, I do.

T: Ha! You've summoned the troops of Miss Click-clack,[119] that's who I am.

M: Miss Click-clack?

T: Hmmm.

M: What does Miss Click-clack look like?

T: Miss Click-clack follows right after the polong.

M: Ah, is that so?

T: Yes, indeed, sir.

M: Ah, the troops of Miss Click-clack.

T: Right.

M: Ah, now, long ago, in the beginning, your friend followed after the Seven Polong.

T: Yes, indeed.

M: Tonight the polong has already accepted the offerings and has gone to wait for them.

T: Yes, indeed.

M: You should go follow after.

T: Follow after? First I want to look around a little.

M: You can.

T: Ah, it's a long time since I met a man; are there any men here?

119. Miss Click-clack (Mek Ketuk-ketak) is a sea spirit who sits upon the waves and guards Mat Din's fishing boat.

M: You certainly can. You can certainly get a man.

T: I'm going to look around. [*"Her" eyes scan the room and "she" smiles seductively at the men in the audience.*]

M: Oh, go get a man. Click-clack, click-clack.

T: Ah, there he is. There's Pak Samat.[120] [*drum beat emphasis*]

M: Yes, there's Pak Samat.

T: Ah, ha, ha! Oh, Gawd, that's done it.

[Laughter from the audience.]

M: You've only just now been able to get a man.

T: I always could get a man. Oh, now I'm leaving.

M: Right you are.

T: I'm going to get a man.

M: Ah, ah.

T: I'm going right away.

M: Ah, go. Now, if you please, ma'am, if you please.

T: Ah, saa . . .

[Transaction music during which the shaman says: "Watch over me, my many penggawa and crowds of friends." The persona that arrives is strong and swaggering and speaks in a loud voice, but does not act in a challenging or threatening manner as he kneels before the minduk, keeping a respectful distance. It is one of Pak Long's familiar spirits, Hanuman Ikan (Fish Hanuman), the son of Hanuman the White Monkey and the Fish Princess, a character from the shadow play with the body of a monkey and the tail of a fish.]

M: Hey, you emerged with a rush, arms waving and body swaying, confused and heedless . . .

T: Yes, indeed.

M: . . . looking up and down like a hungry tiger.

T: Hey!

M: Hey, you receive a new name and you change your character. What is your name and what is your title, sir?

T: Hey, I'm the grandson of Sang Sepit Bentala Naga, sir, Prince Hanuman Ikan is who I am, physician.

M: Oh my, Prince Hanuman Ikan, sir, the grandson of Nenek Sepit Bentala Naga, the king of all dragons . . .

120. Pak Samat was one of the onlookers at the seance.

T: Hey, oooh.

M: . . . from the center of the ocean where the magic mango grows, sir.[121]

T: True, sir.

M: Hey, you fine and mighty person.

T: That's true, sir.

M: Tonight, when I instruct the inang I inform his jinjang.

T: Hey, cease your worries, lay aside your cares, my prince.

M: Hey, your inang has kept watch on the left, the right, behind, before, above, and below. I want to ask for your aid and assistance in helping Mat Din on the palace verandah, in the village of the country, sir.

T: Help Mat Din, sir?

M: Yes.

T: Ah, when shall it be, sir?

M: Right now, if any errors have entered into the discussion, if one of his former friends has done something of the sort.

T: All right.

M: If any of the spirits he harbored in the past are here, let us confer together tonight and put an end to the discussion.

T: Ah, when shall it be? I can go after them right away.

M: You can go take a look around right now, sir.

T: I'll gird up my loins and roll up my sleeves. Ha! I'll swiftly enter a land. Ah, saa . . .

[Transition music; the tok 'teri dances close to Mat Din, shaking his head as he changes persona to that of a powerful sea spirit.]

M: Hey, your vapor emerged with a rush, changing the atmosphere, arms waving and body swaying, confused and heedless, to meet the illustrious healers here. What is your name, sir?

T: Hey, who are you talking about? Do you mean me?

M: I mean you, sir.

T: Well, if you want to know who I am, I'm from the troops of those they call Captain Fierce, Captain Foam, Captain Poison, Captain War, sir.

121. The *pauh janggi* is a legendary tree growing in the middle of the ocean. In traditional literature and the shadow play, as well as in incantations used by Pak Long to invoke Hanuman Ikan, he is always mentioned as dwelling in the *Pusat Tasik Pauh Janggi*—(the middle of the ocean where the magic [African] mango grows) [CL].

M: Oh my.

T: I'm a follower of Captain Pincers, sir.

M: Spirit troops from the ocean's depths, Captain Jebuh, Captain Jepun,[122] all the many warriors, the steadfast warriors, sir.

T: Yes, indeed.

M: The Black Captain from the ocean's depths, sir.

T: Hey!

M: Hey! Princess Coral Reef, sir.

T: Yes, sir.

M: Now I can tell you politely why I summoned you.

T: Right.

M: It's because Mat Din has asked me to act as his spokesman tonight.

T: Right, sir.

M: To have a discussion with you, sir.

T: Yes, indeed.

M: In the beginning, long ago, did Mat Din confer with you, sir?

T: Yes, he did, sir. And now, what's going on with him?

M: Now he says he wants to end the discussion and make a final reckoning, sir.

T: Mat Din loves me, doesn't he?

MAT DIN: No, I don't, not anymore.

[sung]

T: [*sobbing as he sings, and dancing with slow and stately steps before Mat Din*] My prince, you have the heart to . . . all his words strike me to the quick. He wants to get rid of me, he wants to get rid of me.

M: Oh, sir, black captains all, captain upon captain.

T: Oh, mother, now I must look for another friend. My feelings are hurt, he wants to leave me in the forest.

M: Hey, captain, little captain.

T: Yes.

M: Break the ties of affection, captain.

T: I'll tear the leaf, break the charcoal.[123]

122. *Jebuh* (*Dussumieria*) and *Jepun* (*Myripistis murjan*) are varieties of sea fish.

123. Break charcoal (*patah arang*) means to break completely, past mending.

M: Good.

T: My friends and I won't come visiting back and forth.

M: Oh, don't bother to come back and forth here . . .

T: All right.

M: . . . or peer in the windows in the middle of the night or stand here during the day.

T: Yes, my prince.

M: Yes.

T: Chase bad luck far away, kick it up to the skies. It's a pity I can't stay . . .

M: Ah.

T: . . . it's a pity I can't stay.

M: [*spoken; instrumental music continues*] Now, if you please, sir, the day is good, the moment is right, the time has come.

T: Guard me, my penggawa, my many friends, my crowds of penggawa. Be on the alert.

M: Ah, all the many jin, together with Hanuman Ikan. Hey, ogres, you must ask leave of Sang Gana Kaki Lima[124] to withdraw.

T: Ha, ha, ha . . .

[Transition music; the tok 'teri dances toward Mat Din, touching Mat Din's head and clapping his hands together in a casting-out gesture. When the music ends, the shaman has assumed the persona of Tok Jerambang, the Old Will-o-the-Wisp, another sea spirit.]

M: Who is this?

T: Huh?

M: Who is this?

T: You mean me?

M: What is your name?

T: What is my title?

M: Ah.

T: They call me Old Will-o-the-Wisp, sir.[125]

M: Ah, the Will-o-the-Wisp.

T: Ah, the rudder, the rudder, chug, chug, chug, chug, chug.

124. Tok Daud said that Sang Gana Kaki Lima was a character in the shadow play, but could not identify him further.

125. Tok Jerambang is a personification of St. Elmo's fire. He is a spirit harbored by fishermen to protect them and help them bring in a good catch [CL].

M: Ah, look here, Mr. Will-o-the-Wisp.

T: All right.

M: I can tell you politely why I called you here.

T: Good.

M: Tonight we want to make the final reckoning and end the discussion, sir.

T: What's this now? What's this now?

M: Long ago, in the beginning . . .

T: Hmm, hmm, hmm.

M: . . . well, they say that you and Mat Din used to speak to each other.

T: Ah, huh, huh?

M: Ah, tonight he said he wants to make the final reckoning and end the discussion, since he has made ready a feast with pancakes, popped rice, a coconut, a betel quid.

T: Well, he hasn't spoken to me lately. He didn't tell me to row off.

M: He already said row off.

T: He did? Then I should leave, shouldn't I?

M: Yes, you should.

T: I'm leaving.

M: That's good.

T: Ah, very well. Shall I remove my vapor and raise the atmosphere?

M: Yes, you should.

T: Well, I'm leaving and I won't come visit back and forth here again.

M: Flitting back and forth, laughing hilariously and telling stories, in the middle of the night and at dawn, you can't come and go here, don't even think of it, don't even think of it.

T: How about tomorrow or the next day?

M: Not the day after tomorrow nor any other day.

Mat Din: Leave right away.

T: Should I leave right away?

M: Leave, tear the leaf.

T: Ah.

M: If you break charcoal, it can never again be whole. If you break off a hair, it can grow back.

T: It can?

M: Yes.

T: If you divorce your wife, you can take her back again.[126]

M: You can take her back. Ah, we are tearing the leaf . . .

T: Ah?

M: . . . it can never grow back.

T: No, it never can grow back.

M: If you break charcoal, that's it, it can never grow together again.

T: If you break charcoal, it can never grow together again. Well, I'm going to break off with Mat Din once and for all.

M: Ah, once and for all.

MAT DIN: Well then, break off with me. As long as there is a sun and a moon in the sky we will never again be united.

T: Never again?

M: Ah, is he getting angry?

MAT DIN: Here is the sign. As long as there is a sun and a moon in the sky, you can never come back.

M: Ah, I agree, it would not be seemly. There's not just one beetle, there's not just one flowerbud.[127]

T: Yes, that's true.

M: There's not just one boat on the sea.

T: There's not just one boat on the sea.

M: Why should we mourn an old love? There's not just one sail to a ship.

T: There's not just one sail to a ship, there's not just one mast.

M: There's not just one mast.

T: Well, I'll return home right away.

M: If you please, sir, if you please. The day is good, the moment is right, the time has come.

T: Ah, saa . . .

[Transition music; the tok 'teri touches Mat Din's head and feet, removing evil influences. He changes persona to that of Pak Deh (Pak Dogol), a familiar spirit who has already appeared briefly earlier in the seance.]

M: Who's here now?

126. If a husband has spoken the formula of divorce fewer than three times, he can reconsider during the following three months and take his wife back.

127. The beetle is symbolic of young men, the flowerbud of young women.

T: Oh, me? I'm known as the inang's friend, his penggawa and jinjang.

M: If you eat your fill?

T: Not I. I ate hardly anything just now.

M: Oh, you ate very little. If you eat your fill you won't be able to prance around. You still have to prance around some more.[128]

T: If I can fill up by eating a little, more or less, that suits me.

M: What is your name and what is your title?

T: Well, it's like this. They call me Pak Deh, they do.

M: Pak Deh?

T: That's right.

M: The inang's friend?

T: Yes, yes, yes.

M: Ah, be on the alert Pak Deh, when I instruct the inang I inform his jinjang. Let no one be forgetful, let no one make mistakes regarding the inang and jinjang.

T: Ha! there's no flood here, the rains haven't come. Just now Pak Deh got his share, but there's no crust in it.[129]

[Break; tea is served. Then the seance resumes with a duet between Pak Deh and the minduk.]

T: [*sung*] Pak Deh travels alone, oh yes, he travels alone.

M: Ah, all alone, all by himself. He bends to the left and sways to the right in the palace hall.

T: [*spoken*] Ah, that's right, sir.

M: [*sung*] In the palace hall, in the courtyard of the palace, on the king's verandah.

T: [*sung*] Hey, I'm a penggawa, and old am I. Oh, ask my elder brother to come down here with me, to accept the offerings. It doesn't matter if the king is angry.

M: Hey, wake up Brother Persanta Gerga Jiwa and ask him.

T: [*spoken*] Very well.

128. "You eat your fill" is part of a phrase used in connection with Pak Dogol: "*Makan kenyang duduk diam*" (Eat your fill and then keep still). The "prancing" that Tok Daud is referring to is the dancing and shaking done by Pak Long during the course of the Main Peteri.

129. This entire conversation is about the tea being passed out to the assemblage. "The rains haven't come" means he hasn't got his cup of tea yet. "There's no crust" means no sugar has been added.

M: [*sung*] Let one be awake though the rest deeply sleep on the palace verandah.

T: Ah, I called and I beckoned. He hasn't emerged for a long long time.

M: Hey, stand guard, my friend, if you want to earn your pay.

T: [*spoken*] That's true.

M: The inang beckons, from the feet of Alif, in the shadow of Ba.

T: [*spoken*] Ah, saa!

[Transition music. The shaman assumes the persona of Persanta, a manifestation of Pak Dogol in the shadow play. He is one of the entities who entered into an agreement with Mat Din.]

M: [*spoken*] Hey, you emerged with a rush, arms waving and body swaying, to meet with the dalang.

T: Yes.

M: Hey, you receive a new name and you change your character. What is your name and what is your title? Who are you, sir?

T: Me, my prince?

M: What is your name and what is your title?

T: Ah, my title is Older Brother and my name is Roh Persanta. I flew down to the abode of mortals. I came to see the inang. I have come, my prince, to find out which of our holy company you still want to see.

M: Be on the alert, Brother Persanta.

T: All right, sir.

M: We will hold an audience in the palace courtyard. Tonight, while I instruct the inang, I inform his penggawa. Let no one be forgetful, let no one make mistakes.

T: He usually doesn't call me, my prince, but this time he bade me descend to him. Why is that?

M: Well, it's like this, sir.

T: Yes?

M: Sometimes he can't reach you.

T: True.

M: It's because you don't have a branch office.

T: That's true.

M: Tonight you will have a branch office.

T: A branch office for me, sir?

M: Yes.

T: Tonight?

M: Ah, tonight, sir, I want to ask you to speak to the Teacher.

T: To Nenek Betara Guru?

M: Ah, yes, indeed.

T: Hey, I'll step into my howdah and fly off to that person of refinement, Nenek Betara Guru.

M: Ah.

T: All right, sir.

M: Ah, I ask you, sir, to go to the feet of the Teacher and urge him; hey! to the airy heights of the Heavenly Abode.[130]

T: All right, sir.

M: Now, if you please, sir.

T: If you please, grandson, if you please.

M: The day is good, the moment is right, the time has come.

T: Ah, saa!

[Transition music. The shaman assumes the persona of Nenek Betara Guru, one of the chief deities of Kayangan, the Heavenly Abode of the dewa.]

M: Hey, you, whose vapor emerges with a rush, changing the atmosphere, arms waving and body swaying, confused and heedless, what is your name, sir?

T: Are you asking about me, sir?

M: Yes.

T: Hey! I am Nenek Betara Guru, sir. I have descended to the abode of mortals, I came to have an audience with the physician.

M: Oh, my.

T: I would like to ask you for some information. Due to what sickness, what calamity, what disloyalty, for what reason have you called me?

M: I can tell you, Teacher; I disturb you, at your feet, Teacher.

T: True, sir.

M: Lame and heedless, stiff, numb and itching, you flew down . . .

T: True.

M: . . . to the abode of mortals, to the level ground, to meet me, the dalang.

130. The Heavenly Abode of the dewa, called *kayangan, kekayangan, suralalaya, suralaya*, and *nagoro*, is distinct from *syurga*, the Islamic heaven.

T: Yes.

M: May I speak frankly? I disturb you, at your feet, Teacher, how did this scandal arise?

T: You may, sir.

M: Tonight, sir, I can tell you politely why I summoned you, Great Teacher.

T: Hey!

M: I want to confer with you, have a discussion. I don't mean to say that I wish to compete in wisdom or power with the Great Teacher's kinsmen. Oh, no.

T: Right, sir.

M: It's just that Mat Din has asked me to be his spokesman for awhile, sir.

T: Mat Din?

M: Yes.

T: Why did he want to involve you in this?

M: He asked me to speak to you, to confer with you, to have a discussion with you, sir.

T: Oh, is that so?

M: In times past . . .

T: Hey, he often used to speak to me himself and ask me to descend to earth.

M: Yes, that's been true up till now.

T: Yes, indeed.

M: Up till now, if he had any wishes, he had to speak to you.

T: True.

M: He wants to speak to you again tonight, and he has asked me to be his spokesman.

T: True.

M: He asked me to be his spokesman . . .

T: True.

M: . . . because he wants to make a final reckoning and end the discussion, because he feels it is no longer fitting, that it would be unseemly for him to confer with you now, Teacher.

T: With me?

M: Yes.

T: Oh, that's a pity. I would like to stay with Mat Din. I can't recall ever doing anything against Mat Din.

M: It's true that you are not to blame. He says he is not to blame, either.

T: True.

M: He doesn't blame you, Teacher; neither of you is to blame.

Mat Din: Neither is to blame.

T: I quite agree.

M: But he feels that it wouldn't be fitting or proper.

Mat Din: It wouldn't be fitting or proper.

T: To confer any longer with me?

M: To confer with you.

Mat Din: I have lots of children, lots of grandchildren, lots of them.

T: This house is dirty, filthy, stinking, rotten, putrid.

M: Extraordinary!

T: So I can't stay here any longer, sir.

M: No, you can't. You are a god; one of the myriads of gods.

T: True.

M: You can't bear to touch dirty things, sir.

T: I can't bear dirt and filth.

M: No, you can't.

T: [*sung; sobbing as he sings and dances in a slow and stately manner*] Oh me, oh Mat Din, Mat Din really wants to abandon me. Cease your worries, lay aside your cares, alas, alas.

M: Oh, Grandsire, please don't be offended and hold it against him.

T: [*spoken*] Very well, sir.

M: [*sung*] Grandsire, sever the relationship, soar back up to the Heavenly Abode.

T: [*sung*] Oh, I'll climb atop the Bird of Paradise and go to Heaven.

M: Grandsire of all the myriads of gods, I ask you to be at rest, go back to your holy meditation.

T: Mat Din must cease his worries and lay aside his cares. I will soar up to the Heavenly Abode. Mat Din can live alone.

M: Oh, if you please, sir, if you please, then.

T: [*spoken*] Very well.

M: [*sung*] Ah, Grandsire, forget all the ties of love and affection you had with him. Oh, Grandsire, don't return here again.

T: [*sung*] Ah, my prince, I won't stay here, I won't stay here with him.

M: Oh, you can't remain here or sleep along the way, Grandsire. If you please, Grandsire, return to your country, to the place of cool shadows.

T: [*spoken*] Ah, saa!

[Transition music. The shaman assumes the persona of Wak Long, Pak Dogol's comic sidekick in the shadow play, made from his own body dirt. He is one of the shaman's familiar spirits.]

M: [*spoken*] What friend has not appeared?

T: [*laughs, and speaks rapidly*] Are you finished now? Are you? Is there anything else?

M: What is your name and what is your title? Who are you?

T: They call me Mr. Long the Rich Man,[131] the inang's friend, his penggawa and jinjang, they do.

M: Mr. Long the Rich Man?

T: Yes, indeed.

M: Oh, that's a good one! He even has debts piling up at the store.

T: Not anymore I don't.

M: You don't?

T: But I haven't paid them yet, either.

M: Oh, yes, that's the kind of rich man he is.

T: That kind?

M: Yes, that kind.

T: Hmm, what's the reason for all this rushing about?

M: Ah, I can tell you politely why I summoned you, while your name is Mr. Long.[132]

T: Yes, indeed.

M: Friend of the inang, penggawa, jinjang, when I instruct the inang I inform his jinjang. Let no one be forgetful, let no one make mistakes. I ask you to guard the inner fortress, to strengthen the outer gates.

T: Don't be suspicious, lay aside your cares, my prince. I watch over

131. Mr. Long the Rich Man (Cik Long Kaya) is Wak Long. See n. 77.

132. ". . . while your name . . ." because his is a fleeting visitation; his personality is not the usual inhabitant of Pak Long Awang's body.

my inang to the seventh day, to the eighth night. My inang will suffer no harm at all.

M: Ah, may the inang not suffer attack or destruction.

T: Yes, indeed.

M: Now then, we still have some bones to pick here.

T: Is there something else?

M: Yes.

T: What do you suppose?

M: How should I know? You'd better ask the tree himself.[133] There's no way anyone else can know.

T: That's true.

M: How could his children know?

T: Where do we go from here?

M: Oh, come on and tell us.

T: What more is there?

M: What else shall we do, who else should be summoned, with whom should we confer?

MAT DIN: There's nothing else.

T: All finished?

MAT DIN: We finished with the sea spirits, the land spirits, Sultan Ahmad.[134]

M: We still have Sultan Ahmad?

MAT DIN: Mm, the land spirits, the spirits of the hills and valleys . . .

T: Hm, hm, hm.

MAT DIN: . . . have all been spoken to.

M: That's OK, that's OK.

MAT DIN: I've asked them all for peace, for rest, tonight.

T: Well, that's fine. Now we will travel to the dense forest, the spreading shade trees, for an audience with Budak Kecil,[135] the holy and powerful, ha! at this time, at this moment. Ah, saa!

[Transition music; another fierce and threatening persona arrives. It is Budak Kecil (Sonny Boy), a jungle spirit.]

T: Hey!

133. "The tree himself" is Mat Din.

134. Sultan Ahmad is an invisible being who guards the edges of the jungle. One must ask his permission to cut the trees down or risk having nightmares.

135. See n. 27.

M: Hey!

T: [*laughs menacingly*] Ha, ha, ha!

M: Your vapor emerged with a rush, changing the atmosphere, arms waving and body swaying, confused and heedless. What, then, is your name, sir?

T: Me, sir?

M: Yes.

T: Hey! they called me from the lonely jungle, the silent forest.

M: What is your name and what is your title?

T: I'm Budak Kecil the Learned and Clever, the holy and powerful, sir.

M: Oh my, Budak Kecil the Learned and Clever.

T: Yes, indeed.

M: The servant of that holy and powerful ruler, Grandsire White Syed.[136]

T: Right.

M: Grandsire Yellow Turban, Blue Turban, Green Turban, White Turban, sir.

T: Yes, indeed.

M: I can tell you politely now why I summoned you here to confer with me, to have a discussion . . .

T: What do you want to talk about?

M: . . . because tonight I've prepared a feast with Mat Din which is ready and waiting, sir, the mother's feast, the father's preparations, sir.

T: Is it tonight?

M: It is.

T: Why is Mat Din being so nice to me? [laughs]

M: Ah, we'll ask him that together.

Mat Din: I'd like to get this over in the best possible way. I want everyone to feel comfortable. I don't want to look for trouble. Let's not be friends anymore.

T: You don't want to be friends anymore?

Mat Din: No, I don't anymore.

T: Did you speak to Wak Peran Hutan[137] yet?

136. Syed is the title of male descendants of Mohammad.

137. Peran Hutan, like all the spirits mentioned in this section, dwells in the jungle. See n. 24, chap. 6.

Mat Din: I won't give any less, and I won't add any more.

T: You won't add any more?

Mat Din: No, that's as far as I go, that's all.

T: Well, all right then, I'm leaving. I'm going back to the lonely jungle, the silent forest. I'm removing my vapor and changing the temperature for Mat Din. Let there be no laughter or confrontations. Let there be no more discussion.

Mat Din: Let there be no more discussion.

M: Wait over there, sir, for the party and the feasting.

T: Very well, sir.

M: Now, if you please, sir, if you please.

T: Ah, saa!

[Transition music; the shaman assumes the persona of the Old Birdcatcher (Wak Tok Juara Mikat), who not only aids mortals in the hunt but also "catches" their semangat, the vital force conceptualized as a bird.]

M: Who is it?

T: [*slaps his thighs and crows like a cock*]

[The audience laughs. A man says: "I bet that's Tok Juara Mikat (the Old Birdcatcher)."]

M: Ah, who is it, is it the Old Birdcatcher?[138]

T: Yes it is, yes it is, you can say that again.

M: [*laughs*]

T: Right.

M: Tonight . . .

T: Right.

M: . . . I can tell you politely, oh man of the jungle clearing.

T: Right.

M: You who are called the Old Expert.

T: Right.

M: Oh, be on the alert, sir, with your snares and your nooses.

T: Right.

M: With a decoy, sir.

138. *Mikat* means to trap by means of a decoy. The Old Birdcatcher (Wak Tok Juara Mikat) is the guardian spirit of jungle fowl, who sees to it that they are protected from hunters. Each type of jungle animal has a guardian spirit. Hunters, like Mat Din, may enter into a compact with these spirits to achieve greater success in the hunt.

T: Right.

M: Now I want to confer with you, I want to have a discussion, sir. All the preparations have been made for the feast, all of the mother's offerings, the father's preparations, the grandsire's gifts: yellow rice, pancakes, popped rice, a coconut, a betel quid, a drop of water.

T: For me?

M: All the dishes are a gift from Mat Din.

T: He wants to give them to me?

M: Yes.

T: Is it because he wants to get rid of this old man?

M: He wants to make a final reckoning and end the discussion.

Mat Din: All of them are waiting over there.

T: Is that so, sir?

Mat Din: Don't keep coming back and forth here.

T: Well now, even though you want the troops to pull out, at least they need to know if you mean from these parts, from this room, from this *wakaf*,[139] from this land, from this whole place?

M: Oh, yes!

T: Even Tok Da'eh, Mak Da'eh, and the Mighty Spirit, too?[140]

M: Oh, yes!

T: Are you asking us to cease our relationship with Mat Din, at this time, at this moment, so all can be at rest, sir?

M: Oh, you who have supernatural power, the great and the mighty and those who are neither, tonight you will all receive coconuts.

T: Will Awang Longstride and the Armswinging Jin follow after the rest?

M: Yes.

T: Will Jungle Taproots be there, too?

M: Yes.

T: Well now, the small and the large, the old and the young, the whole lot of us will be there.

M: Yes.

T: Well, we will stop now, at this time, at this moment, and be at rest. The troops of Budak Kecil are leaving. Ah, saa!

139. A *wakaf* is a roadside stand. The spirit is asking how far they are being asked to withdraw.

140. Tok Da'eh and Mak Da'eh are the father and mother of the Hantu Raya.

[Transition music; the tok 'teri assumes the persona of Sultan Ahmad, a spirit that entered into a contract with Mat Din, promising to protect him from possible enemies.]

M: Who is this, eh?

T: Who, me, sir? I'm Sultan Ahmad, a friend of Mat Din's, that's who I am.

M: Ah, Sultan Ahmad.

T: That's right.

M: Ah, Mat Din's friend, with whom he used to confer, sir.

T: Right, sir.

M: Tonight, Sultan Ahmad . . .

T: Right.

M: . . . don't be offended and feel hurt, because Mat Din says . . .

T: Right.

M: . . . because Mat Din says he wants to make a final reckoning and end the discussion, he has had a feast all prepared and waiting, sir, with yellow rice, pancakes, popped rice, a coconut, a betel quid, and a drop of water, along with a coconut, sir.

T: Is he giving it to me?

M: Tonight he wants each one of you to remember the place, sir.

Mat Din: Ah.

T: Ah, each of us should know the place.

M: Ah.

T: He said before that he wanted to employ me; he asked me to guard every bay, every district.

M: Oh, yes.

T: Now he asks me to go back where I came from.

Mat Din: Yes, that's right.

M: Because he feels . . .

Mat Din: All tired out.

M: . . . all tired out.

T: Worn out already?

M: Worn out already.

T: Hmm, if he puts it that way, it's OK with me.

Mat Din: I'm worn out already.

T: Hmm, he's worn out, he's getting old.

MAT DIN: I don't want to continue the discussion. I have plenty of children, lots of grandchildren.

T: Hm, hm, hm.

M: Sir, remove your vapor and go wait for the party.

T: [*to Mat Din*] Don't do any other kind of work—go make yourself more grandchildren!

[General laughter.]

MAT DIN: Sultan Ahmad, don't be offended, Sultan Ahmad.

T: [*magnanimously*] Oh, very well, that's OK, Mat Din.

MAT DIN: Ah.

T: I'll leave now, all right?

MAT DIN: Ah, do.

T: Ah, saa!

[Transition music; an elderly doddering persona arrives. It is Wak Tok Nyadap (the Old Toddy Tapper), one of the shaman's familiar spirits.]

M: Who is this, eh?

T: Me? They call me the Old Toddy Tapper.[141]

M: The Old Toddy Tapper?

T: Mmm.

M: Where have you been keeping your toddy containers?

T: It's a long time since I had a container. My wife is old now.[142]

M: Be on the alert, Old Toddy Tapper, friend of the inang.

T: Very well.

M: In the past you were a man to be reckoned with.

T: Hey, that's right.

M: You used to climb the coconut trees and tap by candlelight.

T: [*laughs*] It's absolutely true, and I didn't use footholds to climb then, either. I used to sing, toten, toten, verses to make the sap run.[143] I wasn't just kidding around.

M: [*laughs*] In those times you certainly weren't kidding around.

141. Pak Long acquired this familiar spirit, The Old Toddy Tapper (Wak Tok Nyadap), when he was a young toddy tapper. The sugar palm's sap is collected to make cakes of palm sugar and is sometimes allowed to ferment and become an alcoholic drink.

142. A dirty joke.

143. *Toten, toten* = tralala. The poems (*pantun*) he recited were spells to increase the amount of sap running out.

T: No, I certainly wasn't.

M: They say you used to piss, chuu, chuu,[144] all day long, for months and years on end.

T: [*laughs*] That's right. That's what my youngest brother used to do.

[General laughter.]

T: Ah, that's right.

M: It came out in drops. [*laughs*] Ah, tonight I can tell you politely, friend of the inang, penggawa and jinjang, when I instruct the inang I inform his jinjang. Let no one be forgetful, let no one make mistakes regarding the inang and his jinjang.

T: Is that so, sir?

M: Yes.

T: Cease your suspicions, lay aside your cares. I will help my inang, my jinjang. To which bay shall I go now, to which island, sir?[145]

M: You'd better ask the one whose business this is.

T: Is there anything else?

M: What else is there?

Mat Din: I'd like to say that the discussion has come to an end.

[The tok 'teri has gone back to his own persona.]

T: All finished?

Mat Din: It's all finished. All the sea spirits, finished. The land spirits, finished. The gods, all finished. Nenek Betara Guru, finished. I don't have a single worry left. What remains is the magic I studied; I want to know if there's anything wrong with the things I learned, whether there's anything dangerous in the things I studied with my teacher. I want to recite them, I want to say them.

T: Hmm.

Mat Din: If I can use them, tell me I can. If I can't use them, tell me I can't.

T: Hmm.

Mat Din: Because they make things that you ask for come to pass.

144. Chuu is the sound of the stream of urine. As all the villagers know, Pak Long suffered from a urinary incontinence problem when he was a toddy tapper. The magic he employed to make the sap run also appears to have affected his bladder.

145. Familiar spirits are often used to search out and bring back other spirits to the seance [CL].

T: Hmm.

Mat Din: They're wondrous things, clever things.

T: Hmm.

M: Go on, recite them.

Mat Din: I'm going to recite some, and if I can keep on using them, I will.

T: Hmm.

Mat Din: If I can't use them anymore, I'll get rid of them.

T: Hmm.

Mat Din: Allah's Word is my shelter.
Allah's spittle is with me.
Allah's road is on my left,
He supports me from behind.
Believers in Islam, all over the world,
I have so much work.
Help me to do it.
Let none be ascetic for evil ends.
I turn my gaze to the earth.
Ah, blessed am I, making my little wish.

Ah, that's it. Can I use it or not?

T: There's nothing wrong with that one.

Mat Din: No problem?

T: No problem. What else?

Mat Din: Bismillah illaha illa'llah Muhammad'ur Rasulullah.
A, I, O, Um, blessed am I when I speak the name of the Call to Prayer
Which truly has no peer.
Bismillah illaha illa'llah Muhammad'ur Rasulullah.
A, I, O, Um, blessed am I when I speak the name of the Vizier's Weapon[146]
Which truly has no peer.
Bismillah illaha illa'llah Muhammad'ur Rasulullah.
Bismillah illaha illa'llah Muhammad'ur Rasulullah.

146. The Vizier is Mohammad, who stands in relation to God as a vizier to the sultan.

Blessed am I when I speak the name of Si Alam Tunggal[147]
Who truly has no peer.

Can I use it or not?

T: No problem.

MAT DIN: No problem?

T: No problem.

MAT DIN: Bismillah-hir rohman-nir rahim.

T: Recite the whole thing.

MAT DIN: Hey, fierce tiger!
Soar to the seventh heaven.
I climb aloft.
I tread upon the ground.
Ah, it's shut and it's locked.
Ah, it's shut and it's locked.
I ask that my enemies stay far away.

Ah, there it is. Can I use it or not?

T: Are you finished?

MAT DIN: I am.

T: It's all right.

M: Just a while ago you mentioned the "rogue elephant," if I'm not mistaken.

MAT DIN: The rogue elephant "locking charm," right?[148]
Oh, rogue elephant,
I climb aloft.
I balance the seven layers of heaven upon my head.
I tread upon the seven layers of earth.
Ah, it's shut and it's locked.
I ask that my enemies stay far away.

Ah, that's it, that's as far as it goes.

M: Ah, a little bit of everything.

MAT DIN: It's all right, isn't it? That's all there is.

T: Is that all? There isn't anything else?

147. The first two verses of this incantation are unimpeachably Muslim, while the third, particularly in this context, could be considered problematic by orthodox Muslims [CL].

148. A locking charm (*pengunci*) locks the gates of the body against alien invasion.

MAT DIN: No, no, there isn't.

T: Try hard to remember.

MAT DIN: There isn't any more. The sea spirits are all finished; the land spirits, all finished.

M: Pick up the offerings and set them out for the feast. Go at once.

MAN IN THE AUDIENCE: Go put them out.

MAT DIN: Ah, there's nothing else. The ones I just recited, can I use them all?

T: You can.

M: We haven't spoken to the Mighty Spirit yet, or the jungle spirits or the polong, and told them to go and make a farm there.

T: You people who want to go, take along an axe, some nails, and this piece of wood.

MAT DIN: Can I go, or not?

T: You can't.

MAT DIN: I can't. Since I can't go near there . . . there's a clump of coconut palms on the high ground there near the clearing, near the ditch. You'll need to light your way there.

M: Two or three of you others, go ahead.

MAT DIN: There's a trail there.

M: Two or three of you would be enough.

MAN IN THE AUDIENCE: Go look around for some nails.

MAT DIN: I've cut a path there, where the stream bed goes to the cape; take the right fork and turn toward the stream bed.

T: Well now, when you hammer the nails in firmly, you must say, "Should these nails fall out, only then can you return; should these nails not fall out, then you can never return."

MAT DIN: Ah, I cleared everything away to cut a path there.

T: Remember this well. You also have to say this, you must say this, "If my corn, millet, and beans don't grow, then you must wait here."[149]

MAN IN THE AUDIENCE: All right, I'll go.

T: Oh, good.

MAT DIN: Ah, in the underbrush. When you come close to the stream bed, near the main pipe back there, that's the place you turn off, the bend in the road. That's where you go, just up to there.

149. Using this grain, which had been fried and could therefore never grow, fools the spirits and prevents them from returning to Mat Din.

M: I want to tell you about that young coconut. When you get ready to go, lift the top off.

T: Put it in the crotch of a tree.

M: When you leave it there, make sure you don't leave it on the ground.

[As the men leave with the offerings, the players and audience discuss the events of the night. Then the minduk stops speaking in his everyday voice and continues in his "official" voice, marking the recommencement of the seance.]

M: [*spoken*] Let's "play" Mighty Spirit.[150] Ah, we can't linger here and drowse at every road, at every pier, sir.

T: Yes, indeed.

T: [*sung*] As I wend my way . . .

M: [*spoken, aside to man in audience*] They have to strew those fried seeds.

T: [*sung*] . . . as I go on patrol, ever watchful against pain and sickness. Let no one try to fight with me.

M: [*sung*] Ei, if you please, don't . . .

T: [*spoken*] Aha!

M: [*sung*] . . . don't linger on every road.

T: [*spoken*] Right!

M: [*sung*] Oh, yes, inang, we can't linger here on every road.

T: [*spoken*] Right.

M: [*sung*] We can't linger at every road and pier. While we journey we shall see that everything is in order.

T: [*sung*] And I travel alone, all by myself, counting on meeting the inang, flying along, searching for my brother.

M: Be sure to speak to our friends in the village, to all our many penggawa.

T: [*spoken*] Ah, right.

M: [*sung*] A long time ago a request was made, trust was placed.

T: [*spoken*] Ah, saa!

[Transition music; a strong and vigorous but unthreatening persona arrives. By his proud stance as he kneels before the minduk, it is obvious

150. He wants to send for the Hantu Raya in his most powerful manifestation, as the Mighty Gray Spirit (Sang Raya Uban).

to the minduk that this is Hanuman the White Monkey, one of Pak Long's penggawa.]

T: [*spoken*] Who am I, physician?

M: What is your name, sir?

T: I receive a new name and I change my character. I can tell you my name and my title, physician.

M: Oh, my, it's the fine and mighty, strong and brave person whose deeds are recounted in the old Panji tales. Hey, your name is Raja Hanuman the White Monkey, a great personage, Bersenu's lieutenant, the son of Raja Seri Rama, the grandson of Sirat Maharaja, sir.

T: That's right, sir. Ha, ha, ho, ho!

M: Tonight I can tell you politely that when I instruct the inang I inform his jinjang.

T: Cease your suspicions, lay aside your cares, sir.

M: Oh, may the inang not suffer attack or destruction. Tonight there is work which you well understand.

T: Well, what kind of work do you have for me?

M: Oh, I want to ask your noble self to soar above the borders of the village and its groves, and go fetch Grandsire Mighty Gray Spirit, sir.

T: When should I do it?

M: Right now.

T: Ah, I can't linger here any longer. I'll gird up my loins and roll up my sleeves. Ha! I'll go to the edge of the village, to the shady groves. Ah, saa!

[Transition music; the tok 'teri dances, vigorously shaking his head. The new persona is fierce and threatening. It is the Mighty Gray Spirit (Sang Raya Uban).]

M: Hey, who is it now, sir, who comes to meet me, emerging with a rush, arms waving and body swaying, confused and heedless?

T: Hey, sir, my name is Who's That.

M: Oh dear, that's a new one on me.

T: Hey, did he want to make the acquaintance of the Mighty Gray Spirit, physician?

M: Oh my, it's the Mighty Gray Spirit . . .

T: Hey, ha, ha!

M: . . . who comes from this village, from the orchards, bays, and ridges of this neighborhood.

T: That's right, sir.

M: In times past, in the beginning, Mat Din and you used to hold discussions.

T: That's right, sir.

M: Ah, tonight Mat Din has called upon me to confer with you, to discuss things with you, sir.

T: What do you want to discuss with me?

M: Well, sir, in times past, in the beginning, Mat Din made certain promises, came to certain agreements with you.

T: That's right.

M: Tonight he says that it wouldn't be fitting and proper, it wouldn't be seemly, for him to talk to you.

T: To me?

M: Because he has prepared yellow rice, pancakes, popped rice, a coconut, a betel quid, and a coconut, sir, because he wants to cut off the relationship, and a betal quid, and a stick of *ma'ajun*.[151]

T: He wants to give it to me?

M: He's giving it to you, sir, and he wants to ask you not to visit back and forth here, neither tomorrow nor any day to come.

T: Well, if he wants to give me offerings, will he take them to a farm?

M: [*to Mat Din*] Turn toward him. He wants to speak to you.

T: Well, what about it?

MAT DIN: So that you and your tribe won't come seeking satisfaction, I am giving you a farm with ducks and chickens, cows and buffalos.[152]

M: Ah.

MAT DIN: With as many goats and sheep as you'll need.

T: Right.

151. The "stick of ma'ajun" is actually an ordinary cigarette, but calling it *ma'ajun* gives it the connotation of something forbidden. The term *ma'ajun* can apply to various kinds of medicine, but in the past ma'ajun was often compounded with hemp or datura (Gimlette and Thomson 1971:153). See fn. 113.

152. Before the beginning of the Main Peteri, Pak Long modeled animals, people, and cooking utensils out of rice paste. The references to the ducks, pots, and so forth are to these figurines. For the spirits, a symbol is as good as the thing it stands for [CL].

MAT DIN: With all kinds of pots, pans, vats, and cauldrons, and I ask you to stay there.

T: We'll stay there and watch over it.

MAT DIN: Build a house there, make a farm.

MAN IN THE AUDIENCE: Everything is there—enough gold, enough silver.

T: Has anyone made a clearing for my farm?

MAT DIN: I did it just a while ago.

T: You cleared the area, hee, ha, ha! [*drumbeat emphasis*] Mat Din cleared the area and asks me to go wait.

MAT DIN: Yes, go wait there; until the corn and millet grow . . .

M: Don't come back until they do.

MAT DIN: . . . you can't come back to Mat Din.

T: Can't I come back?

MAT DIN: Wait there as long as possible.

T: As far as beasts with two legs go,[153] do you want me to bother them?

MAT DIN: No, you mustn't do that.

T: Beasts with four legs will be my prey. Ah, well, I'd better go off to the feast. Ah, saa!

[Transition music; the tok 'teri's dance is slow and stately, his arm gestures are graceful, his head-shaking movements are small. He has assumed the persona of Prince Potent Cure (Anak Raja Mahatawar), a manifestation of Wak Kedi Bomoh, the magical sage from the Siamese Monastery, an important character in the shadow play. He and his brother, Prince Mountain of Remedies (Anak Raja Segunung Tawar), who doesn't speak, preside over the final healing scene of the seance.]

[spoken]

M: Who is it now?

T: Me? They call me the old man from long ago, King Potent Cure.[154] I flew down here to the abode of mortals, sir.

M: Ah, Prince Mountain of Remedies, sir?

T: Yes indeed.

M: Now two brother gods have flown down.

T: Yes indeed.

153. Beasts with two legs—human beings.

154. See fn. 64, chap. 6.

M: I want to ask you to send down an antidote, sir, to neutralize all trace of jin vapor.

T: From the person of Mat Din?

M: Mambang vapor, bayu vapor, too. I want you to do this for all the people of this village.

T: All of them?

MAT DIN: Everyone in this house, everyone in this village.

M: Heal everyone, sir.

MAT DIN: I ask you to heal everyone.

M: Oh, godlike Flower of Healing . . .

T: Yes indeed.

M: . . . I ask you to heal this flower.

T: Ah, yes indeed, sir.

M: Make everyone strong and healthy according to ancient custom.

T: Sit over here, Mat Din, the children can sit there.

M: The whole family should spread out, with their legs extended like the father is doing. Spread out, spread out.

MAT DIN: Ah, that's fine.

[Mat Din's entire family sits down in the middle of the room, ready to undergo a ceremony of release, performed by Pak Long, the tok 'teri, and Tok Daud, the minduk. Pak Long places spots of neutralizing rice paste (tepung tawar) on the foreheads of all the players in the Main Peteri. Its earthy and watery qualities protect them against the airy and fiery nature of the spirits. Singing as they pass in front of the members of Mat Din's household, the tok 'teri and the minduk paint spots of rice paste on the head of each family member. Pak Long had previously prepared several "releasers" (pelepas—strips of coconut frond tied in double slipknots). During the song, he unties them to release the assemblage from spiritual dangers.]

[sung]

T: Truly blessed, I wend my way.

M: Yes, indeed, today it's true.

T: I finished the discussion and then I traveled on.

M: Yes indeed, we've had great success today. Yes indeed, those with white blood,[155] those with a single bracelet, command the inang.

155. White blood to a Malay is the same as blue blood to a European: a symbol of royalty.

T: Things that we ask for come to pass, alai, they do. Things that we want we can possess.

M: Things that we ask for we can have. Things that we want we can possess.

T: Things that we want we can possess.

M: I release you from all misfortune and evil influences whatsoever.

T: I release the lot of you, one and all.

M: Ah, let one and all be released. May two angels watch over each one.

T: Truly we will listen, truly we will walk. Release them all.

M: Let all be released. Let all harm retreat far away. I ask that they be released this month.

T: I ask that the two wise men, the physicians, also be released. May all be released.

M: Ah, Kumar Hakim, original physician, first healer.

T: Right.

M: Who has the power to release? Kumar Hakim has the power to release.

T: Ah, friend, I want to call upon my close friend, Kumar Hakim the healer.

M: Ah, yes indeed, it isn't I who has the power to release. The great holy ones of this place have the power to release.

T: The great holy ones of this place have the power to release.

M: Oh, yes, release the inang.

T: Oh, yes.

M: Ah, it isn't I who has the power to release. Ekoton Hujung[156] has the power to release. The Old Midwife, the Young Midwife,[157] they have the power to release.

T: Ah, I call upon my friend.

M: Ah, the Old Midwife, the Youngest Midwife have the power to release, they have the power to release.

T: The Old Midwife, the Youngest Midwife.

M: Ei, I ask for health for one and all. May we two travel in peace.

156. Ekoton Hujung is supposed to be Bomoh Kumar Hakim's name in Thai. (See fn. 5, chap. 6.)

157. A reference to the Heavenly Midwives. See fn. 73, chap. 6.

T: I ask for release for one and all. Who has the power to release? Release all who live in this vicinity.

M: I, too, ask that everyone, one and all be released, tonight. Hear me, one and all.

T: Listen, one and all, let there be no accusations. Who has the power to release? Kumar Hakim has the power to release.

M: Release one, release all. May all be strong and well.

T: Release one, release all. 1,2,3,4,5,6,7, you are released! Release one, release all.

M: I have no power to release, the great gods here have the power to release.

[Short break. The players wipe the sweat off their faces and drink some cool water. Tok Daud asks Pak Long:]

M: We've done a lot of work because of that business just now over yonder. Do you want to bathe them right away?

T: Yes, right away.

[Mat Din's family, having changed into old bathing sarongs, go into the kitchen, a room in the back of the house whose cement floor is lower than that of the large front room in which the Main Peteri has taken place. Two large pails of water had been drawn from the well. Pak Long cut up the limes, squeezed their juice into the water, and threw them in. He passed the dish of smoking benzoin three times around the pails. Then he ladled the water over Mat Din's family, making sure that they were thoroughly soaked. He picked up a handful of raw rice and threw it to the four cardinal directions, up to the ceiling, and down to the floor. Another handful of rice was thrown toward the newly released family. The cold and wet qualities of the water, limes, and rice would safeguard them against the hot and airy spirits at this moment of liminal vulnerability. Then they all returned to the front room, and the performers concluded the seance:]

[spoken]

M: Kings with kings, gods with gods.

T: Yes indeed, sir.

M: Courtiers with courtiers, nobles with nobles, warriors with warrios, penggawa with penggawa.

T: Ah, that's right, sir.

M: Let there be strength and health according to the ancient customs of times long past, sir.

T: If you please, sir. Ah, saa!

M: Penggawa with penggawa. Let no one be forgetful, let no one make mistakes.

T: Oh, penggawa, my friends. Ah, saa!

[The little band plays the music of transition for a final time, returning the participants to everyday time and space. When the music ends, the tok 'teri stretches and the players relax, drinking the coffee and eating the cakes served by Mat Din's wife.]

PART III

Afterword

9

Words and Meaning

The "meaning centered" approach to ritual has come under criticism by such figures as Foucault (1981), who has called for a "refusal of analyses couched in terms of the symbolic field or the domain of signifying structures, and a recourse to analyses in terms of the genealogy of relations of force, strategic developments, and tactics," and Bloch (1974), who believes that the efficacy of symbols in ritual must be located in their nonsemantic, rather than their semantic, content (see also Laderman 1987). But one must keep in mind that rituals span the gamut from those in which action dominates (such as mass participation in communal rites) to those performed with words alone, as is often the case in healing incantations (Tambiah 1968). In the Main Peteri, words, reinforced by music, gesture, and props, have the power to heal. Their content, while not the sole determiner of "meaning," is of prime importance.

Messages, both verbal and nonverbal, are conveyed by the ritual players to participants and audience, both spirit and mortal. They reach out to all senses—smell, sight, touch, and taste, as well as hearing. Sweet-smelling incense and jasmine water are essential to the seance, attracting spirits and contenting mortals with the beauty of their odors. Patients' bodies are touched by the shaman, sometimes gently, sometimes roughly, in his efforts to draw off evil influences. Foods of many kinds appear in the seance. Raw rice, with its earthy and watery qualities, acts as a barrier, repelling the airy, fiery spirits. Popped rice, which attracts the spirits because the dry heat of its preparation has neutralized

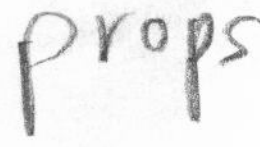

the repellent qualities, may be given to patients as medicine. The nasi guru (teacher's rice), hung from the rafters for familiar spirits to perch upon, provides them with "nourishment," as do the food offerings presented to the hantu. They "taste" the essence, leaving the material substance behind.

The onlookers' sight is soothed and gladdened by the beautiful mats that set the stage for the seance and the batik-covered pillows that hold the popped rice used in divination. The spirits (and many mortals) understand the messages encoded in the shaman's gestures as he signals his greetings and instructions. The ghostly visitors' characteristic stances and body movements provide clues to their identity, even before they speak. The Mute Spirit (Hantu Bisu) who cannot speak must convey his wishes entirely by gesture.

The Main Peteri, then, brings all of the senses into play, but the sense most intensely involved is hearing. Above all other talents and skills, a performer must possess a beautiful voice. Inability to produce a "delicious sound" (*bunyi sedap*) is fatal to a ritual healer's career. A healer with an unpleasing voice cannot help patients achieve trance; their Winds will not respond to vocal ugliness.

Music sets the stage for the seance. It is an essential part of the shaman's transition as he leaves one persona and attains another; it helps delineate the persona's character; and it aids in building and releasing tension in the drama. Instruments have roles to play beyond their functions in the ensemble: drum flourishes and serunai blasts also emphasize the meaning of words. Comments on Latip's unceremonious treatment of his puppets are accompanied by drum beats, as is the minduk's mocking of the Genie with the Look-alike Face; the players' insulting remarks about Latip's manner of sitting are underlined by both drum and serunai—the music makes sure that even the dullest listener is let in on the joke.

The spoken voice also sends out messages as it changes pitch, tone, and volume. Inarticulate cries accompany every change of persona, as the shaman momentarily sinks into chaos; the tok 'teri's exclamation, "Ah, saa!" cues the musicians to begin the music of transition; grunts and murmurs encourage a spirit to speak and a patient to trance; a Spirit Pig spices his speech with oinks, and fearsome genies threaten with shouts of "Hish!" Although all of these messages are pregnant with meaning, words are the real midwives of the seance.

An important aspect of the Main Peteri is the discovery, acquisition, and use of names. Spirits must be invoked and invited to the seance by name. Those ignored may strike out in resentment at having been forgotten,[1] so the shaman protects himself and his fellows by his plea to the spirits, "Hear me, big or small, old or young, even if I don't know the letters to call you by name." For each spirit visitation, the minduk's first question is, "What is your name and what is your title?" A recalcitrant spirit, like the Genie with the Look-alike Face, must be urged to reveal his name—knowing an entity's name gives power to the possessor of such knowledge. Similarly, knowing the etiology and nature of an illness—being able to name it—whether this knowledge is arrived at through popped rice divination or interpretation of biomedical tests, can be invaluable to healers and their patients, removing the feeling of powerlessness that accompanies dealings with the unknown.

The minduk's words, as he chants his invocation and sings his introductory song, are not sacred in the sense of Islamic prayer, but are, nevertheless, believed to carry power; a power that proceeds from the bomoh's breath, the outward manifestation of his Inner Wind. Ethnographers of magic in a number of cultures have remarked on the importance of the magician's breath as the medium of magical force (e.g., Malinowski 1965; Errington 1983). East coast Malays make the connection explicit. No one, they say, can successfully function in any calling without having inherited the appropriate Inner Wind. This is particularly vital in the case of bomoh (and midwives) whose Inner Wind emerges during treatment of their patients and allows them to transfer its efficacy, through the breath, to healing substances and directly to the patient's body, in the form of words and puffs of air. The power of the word emanates, moreover, from the quality of the bomoh's voice as well as from what he says. His voice rings out, his words are meant to be heard both by mortals and by spirits.

The seance is enhanced by the use of unusual language: Arabic prayer, Thai and Javanese words, and mysterious terms, such as "*bisik*," "*risik*," and "*hidu*," the meanings of which the shaman himself could

1. These resentful spirits are reminiscent of the Wicked Fairy in the Grimms' account of Sleeping Beauty: She cursed the baby because she was not invited to the christening.

not (or would not) explain. Such words are extremely rare, however, and, aside from these infrequent additions, the Main Peteri is conducted wholly in Kelantanese Malay (with occasional Trengganese expressions), a dialect understood and spoken by all those attending.

Malay shamans agree with their Sri Lankan counterparts (Kapferer 1983:57) that rites lose much of their effectiveness if a patient cannot understand their meaning. The importance of the meaning of words in a ritual setting was illuminated experientially for me when I was placed into trance by Pak Long. As the music played and the shaman rhythmically pounded on the floor, he recited portions of the legend of Dewa Muda, which he believed to be the archetype of my principal Inner Wind. My response convinced the audience that not only was his diagnosis of my personality correct but also that I now truly understood the content and meaning of his recitation. The same technique (including incense, darkness, and regular percussive noises, as well as speech), was unsuccessful when used on a visiting colleague whose Malay was not fluent and who had not internalized the symbolic content of the shaman's words.

The ritual relies upon tropes of all kinds to express the fullness of the seance's meaning. Some are common metaphors used in Malay poetry and flowery speech, such as "beetle and flowerbud" for "young man and young woman." Others, like "tear the leaf, break the charcoal" (end a relationship past mending), are everyday expressions. The use of Alif for Allah and Ba for Muhammad is understood by all. Hearing the minduk compare a patient to a trampled tree with drooping branches poses no problem for a Malay audience; nor do comical remarks, such as a shaman's complaint that "the rains have not yet come" when he has not been offered a drink, and "there's no crust here" because sugar was not added to his tea. It amuses the audience when a shaman compares his false teeth to scissors that don't cut properly (don't let him enunciate clearly), and when he compares his troupe to images or "pictures" (gambar) like the shadow puppets. Malays enjoy the players' puns: spirits are teased by twisting their names into new forms—*polong* (a type of spirit) becomes *talang* (mackerel) in the minduk's mouth; *serupa* ("looks like") becomes *sejubur* ("asshole"). They roar with laughter when a patient's immodest way of sitting is noted by the shaman as allowing people to see "the hole in his window" (implying that the patient's anus was visible). References to body parts and their functions can be used for their noble, as well as their comic, effect. Humanity, to the shaman, is "the fortress of excrement, the gateway to wisdom."

In the seance, emotions out of control are like a "great elephant whose driver is stupid, crazed elephant whose driver's a fool." During the divination, Islamic references combine with Hindu names from the Ramayana. The popped rice is a flowerbud which "falls to the palms of Fatimah (the daughter of the Prophet) [who] plants the flower . . . The name of the leaf is the Sword of Ali (Fatimah's husband). The name of the shoot is Arrow Gandewat (Rama's weapon)."

The tropes of conception used by the minduk are densely packed with meaning: "*Angin keluar di hujung yang kadim*," which I translated as "The Winds emerge from the tip of eternity," could also be rendered as "The child's personality (his angin) is inherited from the father, emerging, with semen, from the end of his penis"; or "The Inner Winds have existed from the beginning of Time and will exist forever more." All of these meanings, suggested to me by the minduk, are equally valid and simultaneously understood. Likewise, the fruit (*buah*) of the father, of which the minduk sings, is both his offspring (as the fruit is child to the tree) and his own testicles (*buah pelir*), the seat of his fruitfulness.

The performance of healing communicates an important message to its audience: interpret the words; they may contain meanings beyond those they carry under ordinary circumstances (Bauman 1984:9). As Turner (1967:45) points out, however, ritual speech encompasses levels of meaning and interpretation. Laymen will give simple and exoteric meanings, while specialists understand the deeper (and sometimes idiosyncratic) meanings of the text. The language of the Main Peteri makes extensive use of polysemy, the multivocality that Turner called a "fan" of meanings (a particularly apposite phrase, since, like a fan, it can conceal part of its contents within itself or spread out to display its fullness). Malays are accustomed to the interplay between macrocosm and microcosm in magic and philosophy: they know that when a bomoh speaks of the sea it is not merely the place to sail a boat but refers, as well, to the human bloodstream and to the stomach, the liquid center of the human body; a mountain is also the human head, the fields a human heart. Prior conception of a child within its father's brain is common, and not esoteric, knowledge. But not all of the metaphors are equally accessible. No layman I spoke to among Tok Mamat's audience knew that the "elephant with nine tusks" of which he sang was meant to symbolize the healthy sweat that pours from the body of a patient as evidence of a return to health, although some hazarded a guess that the number nine might refer to the nine orifices of the body (a much more common ritual allusion).

The language of the minduk's invocation and Bestirring Song, in its flowing poetic statement, is reminiscent of *hikayat*, Malay legends read aloud to audiences. Its use of metaphor, whether part of the shared vocabulary of the ritual practitioners and their audience or esoteric allusion, relates it to Malay poetry such as the *pantun*, a quatrain the first two lines of which suggest the last two lines, often quite obliquely. Malay poetry, particularly the love lyrics of the pantun, uses literary, historical, and mythic allusions to make subtle points and to convey emotions otherwise often unexpressed.

The ritual language of the seance is related, as well, to the everyday language of the villagers, which can be cryptic to a city dweller's ears in its use of elision and irony and its references to proverbs and tales. In any discourse between those who share experiences and beliefs, moreover, a good deal "goes without saying," making it difficult at times for outsiders to follow (Shweder 1984:38).

The legends of Dewa Muda and other archetypes occur in the context of the seance as bits and pieces of the whole, scarcely understandable to those previously unacquainted with them. The participants in the seance, however, have seen the story of Dewa Muda enacted by Mak Yong troupes and heard the tale of the Weretiger from their parents when they were young. A variation on a theme, such as the scene in which Little Prince Flower Play of Times Past appears (chapter 7), evokes the proper response from the audience, even though he is not the hero of a famous tale and only portions of his story are told. The audience may not have heard his particular tale before, but they are thoroughly familiar with the plot pattern, which echoes others better known to them (see also Sweeney 1987:207). The names themselves are evocative of the stories and their meanings.

The action of the Main Peteri is not confined solely to the ritual performers. The patient's participation is essential. He and his family provide refreshments for the players and audience, offerings for the spirits, and payments to the shaman and his troupe. Patients often go into trance and act out aspects of their personalities inexpressible in daily life. A patient may hold conversations with spirits that appear at the seance, bargaining with them about the extent of the promised offerings, asking them to leave, pleading with them for the return of health, and cajoling them with sweet words. The audience is not expected to sit in silence. Besides assisting with the preparation and disposal of the offerings, they often react aloud as the drama unfolds, laughing at the players' jokes and commenting to one another about the action. When a divination revealed that much of Latip's troubles were due to his Inner Winds, audible murmurs of agreement swept the audience.

Members of the audience know a good ideal about the behavior of individual spirits and can identify them from their actions in the seance even before they speak. For instance, when the shaman crowed like a cock after changing persona, a man in the audience cried, "I'll bet that's the Old Birdcatcher." When the Mute Spirit makes the universal gesture of sexual intercourse, jabbing a finger in and out of a circle made of two fingers of the opposite hand, the audience laughs, "He wants to get married." During the seance for the sick shaman, the entire small audience, consisting of the shaman's wife, my assistant, and me, joined the players in instructing the afflicting spirits to press their claims with the real culprits who neglected to give them their due and stop bothering the innocent shaman. Occasionally a member of the audience momentarily commands the stage, electrifying the proceedings by unexpectedly going into trance.

Listening to performances of Main Peteri, or reading the texts, one is struck by its great variety of speech forms. Ritual practitioners each have their own individual styles, and, beyond that, the language of each varies from one seance to another. Within each seance the minduk's language changes from the epic sweep of his prelude, through the lyric beauty of his Bestirring Song, to the slangy colloquialisms of his conversations with the spirits.

The prelude presents a vast panorama of the important divisions of the rural Malay world and the spirits that inhabit it: the earth, the waters, the jungle, the fields, and the village. The Bestirring Song is poignant in its invocation of the Inner Winds: "Wind as small as a sesame seed, Wind as small as a mustard seed . . . lit with five rays of light. It stands and recites six magical words. The Wind comes out with seven claps of thunder . . . Winds that interpret our very souls."

The minduk speaks to the noble forces of the body and the demigods of Kayangan with a formality that befits their status, calling them "foreign prince" and "fragrant person." Familiar spirits are treated like equals. They engage in good-humored bantering with the minduk, who calls them "big brother" and "beloved friend." Ordinary hantu are inferior to humans and can be teased: told to "row off," warned against premature "grabbing" of the offerings, and twitted about their ignorance of Islamic prayer.

A reading of the preceding translations shows that Firth's characterization of the language of the Main Peteri as stereotyped and formulaic (1967) is only partially borne out by the actuality. Set phrases recur in particular situations. For example, as a ghostly visitor arrives, the minduk exclaims, "*Ah, tuan hamba keluar dengan gaduh gupuh gawang goncang lorat langgar masa mengidap nama gelanggi bahsa tubuh bernama badan gelar. Siapa pula, hilang seorang menganti seorang*?" (Oh, sir, you emerged with a rush, arms waving and body swaying, receiving a new name and changing your character. One person has left and another has taken his place. Who is this, now?). But these formulae occur within a context of wide improvisation, as ritual speech and attempts at courtly usage alternate with broad colloquialisms.

The language of Main Peteri, as well as that of the Mak Yong and wayang kulit, includes both informal highly improvised speech and formal relatively fixed language. In general, most of the colloquial language occurs in comic scenes and in the dialogue of unrefined characters. Even then, the style takes on formality when the circumstances become more formal or the characters break into song (Ghulam-Sarwar 1976:95).

Even the sections that appear to be set pieces, like the minduk's prelude and the Bestirring Song, vary from performer to performer and from one seance to another. Although they answer to the same purpose, keep to a general form, and begin with similar words, Tok Daud's songs differed from one another in length, complexity, and language in the two seances included in this volume. The prelude he sang for the emergency seance held for Pak Long Awang is considerably shorter and less comprehensive than the one he used for Mat Din, reflecting the urgency of the treatment and the late hour of its beginning. The Bestirring Song for Pak Long's seance spoke at greater length than usual of the Winds, since the sick shaman's Winds had been dealt a nearly mortal blow by his negligent clients.

As Sweeney points out, the wisdom of an oral culture "is encapsulated in mnemonic patterns which must constantly be repeated if they are to survive. . . . It is for this reason that the discourse of an oral culture is heavily dependent upon the use of relatively fixed utterances in stylized form . . . their use of parallelism, assonance, alliteration, etc., ensures that the form produces its own, often distinctive rhythm" (Sweeney 1987:96). Although the patterns for much of Malay ritual speech are relatively fixed, they are by no means frozen. Like the European singer of tales studied by Lord (1976), the Malay minduk and shaman must develop the capacity to generate formulaic expressions on the model of fixed formulae whose ready-made character makes fluency possible. The elaboration of formulae, the systematic variation, and the use to which they put redundant and "flowery" speech allow the ritual pair time to collect their thoughts and avoid any hesitancy that might otherwise occur (cf. Bauman 1984:18; Zurbuchen 1987:152).

The Yugoslav bardic tradition was chosen by Lord as a living example of the circumstances under which the two greatest epic poems of Western culture, the Iliad and the Odyssey, must have been composed. The degree of freedom allowed within a formulaic structure, as realized by master poets, rather than total freedom and an emphasis on originality, produced an oral literature that still speaks to us across the centuries. It is to this tradition that the Main Peteri belongs. The Malay seance is far from a mere exotic curiosity. The best of its practitioners, such as Tok Daud, are poets of great worth, as well as healers of bodies and souls.

The Main Peteri is a dramatic totality, combining performers, audience, words, music, movement, setting, and props. It is a performance that relies upon an audience which does not merely observe, enjoy, and applaud. The audience, as well as the patient and healers, has a personal and immediate stake in the proceedings and their outcome, and its members do not hesitate to interject comments or even become spontaneous performers, rising in trance to sing or dance.

The words and the music, the movements and ritual objects of the Main Peteri, speak with a clear voice, conveying multiple meanings to the audience, both human and spirit. The seance takes place in ritual space, a small delimited area marked off from everyday concerns, but its meanings are embedded in a broad view of the universe, embracing all aspects of human existence. The Malay shaman, a person of dignity and power, convincingly changes into a flirtatious girl, a fearsome genie, a little monkey, a sluttish female spirit, a noble demigod, all for the purpose of healing his patients' afflictions. He exorcises the demons of disease and opens the floodgates of emotion; his vehicle encodes precepts of behavior and reveals truths about flesh and spirit, temperament and power, illness and health, death and birth.

APPENDIX A

A Shaman Speaks

The following is a verbatim transcription, which I translated, of a long interview I had with Mat Daud bin Panjak, a very successful Kelantanese tok 'teri now living in Trengganu. I was introduced to Mat Daud by the state representative of the Ministry of Youth, Sports, and Culture, who invited me to attend a seance. The cultural officer had recently moved to Trengganu from another state, where he had been in charge of sports. He clearly enjoyed the drama of the seance, but wondered at my eagerness to tape the proceedings, since, he said, the words were mostly gibberish that even Malays couldn't understand. His comment brings into sharp focus the fact that the language of the Main Peteri presents a formidable barrier to understanding for educated, urbanized Malays, especially those from states other than Kelantan and Trengganu.

Mat Daud proved to be not only a popular shaman but a very articulate speaker who was generous in sharing his knowledge, both musical and theoretical, with a foreign novice, when Pak Long Awang and I visited him the day after we had attended one of his seances.

Each of the anthropologist's brief questions elicited a waterfall of responses from the shaman. Readers who do not want to interrupt the flow of the shaman's speech can avoid the anthropologist's comments in italics, within brackets.

The interview began as I asked Mat Daud why he said, during the course of the seance, that if a spirit lands in one place he has one name, if he lands in another, he has another name.

CAROL: *Does that mean there are many hantu or just one with many names?*

MAT DAUD: One hantu and many names. That means, if we talk about those of the earth, the tribes of the earth, even the headman of the earth, until we have named all his subjects and people, then, finished with that, we land in the village and call on Tok Chor of the village, Hitam Seri Penaklak *[The Black Conqueror]*, Seri Pejajat *[The Wanderer]*, the likes of Hitam Batang Pengulit *[Black Crooner of Lullabies]*, Kuning Batang Pengedan *[Yellow Mad-for-Love]*, headmen all. These hantu, when it comes right down to it, are just one. They give birth to names, but when there are many names the bomoh has a lot to invoke. All of the *jembalang*, the *hantu*, the *jin*, *mambang*, all of them, they're all the same. *[Jembalang are the servants of the genies and hantu, something like imps. Mambang are powerful spirits, associated with the yellow glow of sunset.]*

The *dewa* are another story. There are also many dewa. The names of the dewa are *sekati sepekur*, two worlds, we call on them. *[The etymology of sekati is* keti, *a Sanskrit word meaning "a hundred thousand;" sepekur derives from* peku, *a Javanese word meaning "a thousand."]* What we mean by sepekur is "throughout the land." The world being finished *[i.e., the dewa having been invoked en masse]* then he *[the bomoh]* names dewa—Dewa Muda, Dewa Laleng, Dewa Penchil, names of dewa like those. If you count them, there are many names, but there's just one dewa, just one jin. Dewa started with one—who was that one? Dewa Si Alam Tunggal. He broke apart and separated, like Adam, he had offspring. We give birth to *sipat*, *tongkol*, *jiring*, *jising [aspects, a clot, the body, the spirit]*. You can't see the spirits, we call them *halus [impalpable]*, we bomoh, we call them. When we say hantu-hantu there are hantu, but if we people don't say hantu, then there aren't any. People talk about hantu, I talk about Hantu Pari *[female spirits of the fields]*, for instance, other people don't.

They say that Iblis looks just like us. In the past he was an angel most pure. Then a commandment came down but he didn't listen when God ordered him to prostrate himself before the Prophet Adam. He said he preceded Adam. He *[God]* said, "No, Adam came before you." He *[Iblis]* said, "I don't believe that he came first." Why was that? Because God commanded Gabriel, he ordered him to put something up the nose of the image of Adam. He *[Gabriel]* got halfway there when he wanted to see what it was, so he opened his hands, he opened them and there appeared a pure angel. *[This was Iblis before he Fell. Adam's body had already been created out of earth and water, although it was lacking the air and fire of nyawa. That is why God said that Adam came before Iblis.]* So Gabriel went back to God and he gave him something into his hands again, which he put up Adam's nose. He *[Adam]* sneezed and the substance went through his entire body. Right away he *[Gabriel]* went to bow down before God, but the image of Adam broke into a million pieces. He *[Gabriel]* went before God and God commanded him to weld it back together *['teri]*. He *[Gabriel]* picked up all the pieces it had broken into when the *nyawa [Breath of Life]* had entered and had torn apart the body of Adam completely. He *[Gabriel]* healed him with four kinds of water: (1) *air [water] hanyir [smells like fish]*; (2) *air pahit [bitter]*; (3) *air maung [stinking like blood]*; (4) *air busuk [rotten]*. Then he said *[to himself]* "You have to nail him together, but what can be used for nails?" There was nothing. Then there came down a Word, *patakuna rolati hewataku sujana waharah*. That means, go nail him up, go do 'teri. The way he welded him has now come to be called Main Teri. It's been known as Main Teri from the beginning. God is very powerful. He has a holy book.

Then, after welding the image of Adam together, one Being lived in Heaven. Then he *[Adam]* fell in love with Eve, he wanted a woman. I mean to say he wanted to find one. Then a Word descended again. He *[God]* ordered him *[Adam]* to pray a special prayer, doing two cycles of prayer movements, bow to the right, bow to the left—and there was Eve. Because of this there was a woman, Eve. Some people say Adam's rib, some people say God's power. Then Iblis, whom I mentioned before, he said, "I want to fool this Adam. How shall I do it?" He wants to fool us. Commanded to prostrate himself, he didn't want to do it. God cursed him, saying, "You will become a devil," said God, "because you have an unyielding gizzard *[stiff-necked, obstinate]*." Don't act like him; people are forbidden not to listen to God and to follow him *[Iblis]*. When God said, "Listen to me, you will become a devil," Iblis said, "I don't care." He fooled Adam. He even entered a snake's mouth. He went to Heaven and got the *buah khaldi [the forbidden fruit]*. Adam ate it and Eve ate it. Adam tried to chew it up, but he swallowed it down and it became the Adam's apple. Women don't have an Adam's apple. The woman ate it quickly and when she swallowed it it became menstrual blood. Then they had to pee, they had to shit, they had all kinds of desires. God commanded them to come forth, but Iblis fooled Grandsire Adam. Iblis made a lot of noise and confusion. Because of that, the tok 'teri recites, "*Hilang wap timbul kabut; hilang kabut timbul hawa; hilang asap timbul debu; hilang debu timbul kelang; hilang kelang timbul air [Vapor disappears and mist arises; mist disappears and air arises; smoke disappears and ashes arise; ashes disappear and confusion arises; confusion disappears and water arises.]*" Why does the red of the sunrise appear, the long clouds at the time when the thrush sings and the great king goes back to sleep, he who is called Dewa Si Alam Tunggal? Adam already had desires, we all had them. Then this is how it was—Dewa Si Alam Tunggal already existed. He met Jin Iblis, whom I already mentioned, and they made a pact. The desires, the feelings of mankind, that would be the affairs of the dewa. He would add to the desires that resulted from eating the fruit I mentioned before. Because of that, people have Angin Dewa Muda. They want to look handsome, they want things clean and neat, they want to wear fine clothes, smell sweet odors, they can't stand filth. Whether they are religious or ignorant of how to be a proper Muslim, they want only cleanliness. It started with the angel, the dewa. If one falls heir to Dewa Penchil, one's parents may chase one away; when such people eat, the food doesn't taste good, when they sleep they don't feel rested; that Wind is very *penchil [likes to be isolated; doesn't like to stay at home]*. Such a person's mother was like that, too. *[The implication is that the Wind is hereditary.]* If one falls heir to Dewa Laleng, he doesn't want to work, he gambles, he is *laleng*: he wants to play chess, he wants to play games, he wants to gamble, drink, steal other people's belongings. Think of a gambler, that's what I mean by laleng. If one falls heir to Dewa Samadaru, it's never peaceful in his home. If a husband is like that, a wife is like that, they're always fighting. That's their way. Dewa Muda, when he falls to humanity, he lies on our heartstrings.

When one goes into trance, he says *Yalah Awang wei*, he wants to speak like that, he doesn't want to say *bismillah*; even if he wants to say *Ya Allah, ya Tuhan*, he doesn't say it. He speaks in song and after a while his Wind comes. *[Mat Daud's statement should not be taken lit-*

erally, since Malay magic invariably employs Islamic prayer. He means to conceptually separate religious obligation from the healing that occurs when he "speaks in song." The tok 'teri I mentioned before, what does he do? He calls the rebab *akar kayu penawar [antidote made from herbs and roots]*. It becomes an antidote for sick people, people sick from Angin Dewa Muda. They are always losing their way, always worried. Song makes them feel well, refreshes their hearts.

Getting back to the Teri, Teri dates back to early times. Then there were many kinds of Main in those days. This means it was an invention; it had to be done well, it had to be attractive. That's why they say, "I am Radin Kecil Aulia Gunung Padang Terselor *[Little Prince Holy Mountain Interspersed by Fields]*." It brings peace. The tok 'teri calls on all the dewa, rather than just one, so it should feel good *[sedap]*.

He sets snares. That means he wants to make things attractive, use artistic words. Some people say, "*Tuan teri geliga jadi [the Princess becomes a bezoar/clever person]*." Some people say, "*Ismi dan ismawi dewa [names and 'attractive sounds' of dewa]*." Syed Saleh Mamat Dollah, a penggawa, comes—it's OK, none of it is a big deal. It's like what I just said—Jin Tanah *[Earth Genie]* from the depths of the earth, denizens of the earth, Black Conqueror, Yellow Wanderer, the whole lot of them. All the jin give birth to names. He says, "Hei Mek Batik Baju Hijau *[Miss Green Dress]*, your mother supports you, your father in the jungle supports you. Your mother tends the great jungle, the tongue of land where the water curls around the dragon."

There are all kinds, men, women, female, male, little, big, old, young. Loads of spirits in the town, if you could see them. Try to step, you can't; try to walk, you can't. Hordes of hantu *[he laughs]*. Sometimes they have enormous teeth like axes; eyes as big containers for lime *[an essential ingredient of betel quids]*, if you listen to what the bomoh recite. The physicians say their names; they are given titles by the bomoh. They order them to receive the services, the bomoh's offerings, such as they are. They say, "Drink this water; if there's not enough I won't add to it, I won't give more. Receive and taste, feel, sip, smell."

In the past, people used to hold *kenduri [feasts]* in the fields to *puja [a non-Islamic celebration to praise spirits and give them offerings]*. One after the other would bring things—one would bring rice, one would bring *pulut [sticky rice]* to make a kenduri and say special prayers like at the Main Pantai *[a yearly seaside celebration for the sea spirits]*; they would slaughter a water buffalo, make pulut, a plateful for each person; they ate it all up and couldn't bring any home. *[For more than a decade Malays have been forbidden to make offerings to the sea spirits, as they had done annually at the Main Pantai. Mat Daud is commenting on the greed that people had exhibited by eating everything at the feast and neglecting to bring some food home to their families, a serious lapse of behavior.]* When they came back home, the children screeched. As for us, we take stuff back home. The ones in the field then filled their bellies, and those at home went hungry. That means Iblis's titles, his names—like they say Sewah Raja Burung Teriak 'Stana Malam *[Swooping King of Birds Who Screams in the Palace by Night]*, like they say *puak angkatan* Anak Jin Putaran *[army of the Rotating or Twisting Genie]*—Winds that all dwell in mankind. If one is dealing with a person with a hot illness, we "play" *[take on the persona of]* Anak Borak Api Nenek Sebut Tari Sinar Tari *[Fiery Steed Grandsire Sun's Rays; "tari" = matahari]*, that's how we "play" hotness. "*Jaga 'balang asal kandang mula*" *[guard, oh warrior from the original byre]* for those who inherited Hala Rimau Besar Serjan Kilat *[the Wind of the Weretiger]*, people who are "hot." When you go to the doctor, he gives you a shot, he says it will make the hot sickness become cool. We village people recite spells to make it become cool. We say, "If there is hot vapor, I ask that it become cool; vapor of illness, I ask for healing; vapor of fever, I ask that it abate; if poison, I ask for an antidote; heavy, I ask for lightness." We ask it of those I mentioned before.

Well, about *Kayangan [the heavenly abode of the dewa-demigods]*, Nenek Betara Guru, his younger brother Betara Umar, they are a whole family—Betara Umar, Betara Semar, Nenek Antara Merada, Tok Mah Siku Mata Api, all the dewa. People say Dewa Sepatmi guards the Seven Golden Siamese Temples, he is the teacher of all the dewa. The true king is Dewa Si Alam Tunggal, king over all the jin and dewa. He becomes Sewah Budak Layangan Kuning in the speech of bomoh. They recite the names of the jin and the dwellers in Kayangan, but they can't soar up there. They can't abide dirt and filth *[a trait of the dewa who live in Kayangan]*, but they *[bomoh]* can't dwell in Kayangan. This means, the moral of it is, that we people on the outside can't become rajahs. It's forbidden *[entails a curse]*. He who is born a rajah is a rajah; he who is born to a noble family is a noble. *[Mat Daud's comments underline the Malay philosophy that health, whether in the human body, the body politic, or the universe, depends upon the harmony of the elements and upon everything being "in its place." Those who are born nobles must behave nobly, and commoners should not aspire to be kings. Inappropriate behavior throws the world out of kilter.]* This means that rajahs are people blessed with royal power just like the dewa. The dewa known as Bersenu *[Vishnu in the Hindu pantheon, but not so identified at the village level]* is filled with magical power; his blood is white, his throat is black, his spittle is salty, he fulfills requests, he can fly, he can perform sorcery. *[Malay royalty, and supernatural beings, are considered to have cool, white blood, rather than the hot, red blood of common humanity. "Salty spittle" signifies effective speech, in everyday life as well as in connection with magic.]* It's like you can see now in the movies about sorcery—anything one asks for can be had. People long ago, they could even fly, they could soar and do battle, they had knowledge. Then there was a bomoh, Guru Kumar Hakim, the original bomoh. Kumar Hakim had a wonderful antidote. God gave him this marvelous antidote. When someone died, he was able to restore them to life. After a while God called him to return it. "It's not true," he said, "what antidote are you talking about?" *[Kumar Hakim didn't get away with it, I was told later. God put him in a cave, and there he still dwells.]*

"I made all kinds of medicines descend," *[said God]*, "to fall upon the face of the earth." Everyone who is clever and skilled can seek them and heal people even now. Marvelous antidotes, great antidotes, powerful knowledge. Guru Mahatawar *[Teacher Great Antidote]* has medicines which he requested from the Prophet Elijah, who controls medicines, the Prophet Koibeh *[also known as the Prophet Khadzir, believed to have found and drunk the Water of Life, and so became immortal]*, he's the person who controls medicines. We get that medicine, we say we send greetings and ask the Prophet Elijah to heal the sick person, or ask Prophet Koibeh if you want to treat kids with worms. In the case of Prophet Koibeh one asks for medicine to give men who lust after women and women who lust after men. Prophet Elijah has the best medicine for sickness, the kinds that people who know want to get. My uncle got roots that were very effective; God was good to him.

We're talking from the standpoint of religion. We borrow the voice of Adam, our body hair rises; that doesn't mean that we are claiming to be jin. We are followers of the Prophet, servants of God, that's what we claim. If I say, "I am a jin," if I am Jin Putih 'balang Putih Afrit-afrit Jin, that means I have fallen into sin, if I am a jin. That's why I have to say I am adopting the attributes of jin, the behavior of devils who borrow the voice of Adam—Adam can talk, jin can't talk. If they bother you, you don't know it. People have attributes, too.

CAROL: *How do you know what to call them [spirits]?*

MAT DAUD: It's like this, it's a feeling. You test it on sick people. The sign is given to us who "play." At first you go into trance for the patient, you have to descend to the realms of the earth, the four earths, the seven countries. We call on the gates of the earth's realm. Why is that? The soles of humanity's feet—they are there. The jin there pierce the feet. They hurt the big toe. But if you want to see them you can't; you can't behold them. Women who have just delivered babies, they might be weakened. They *[the jin]* attempt to kick the mothers' big toe. They *[the mothers]* could be utterly destroyed *[punah]*. Even if he kicks lightly, blood flows heavily. Then we "play" until we finish the story of the earth. Then we go to the village. We go to the village to ask for more information. On behalf of the patient, to whom do we go? We say Mamat Jin Hitam Halalintar *[Genie Black Thunderbolt]*, Jin Kuning Panah Lat Juna Kilat Barat Sulung Tahun *[Genie Yellow Bow of Arjuna Western Lightning of the New Year]*, or Anak Jin Hitam Batu Laleng *[Genie Black Immovable Stone]* Batu Larut *[Dissolving Stone]*. That means Sang Babi Kepala Tujuh *[Seven-headed Pig]*, Hantu Raya *[Mighty Spirit]*, Si Tunjang Raya *[Mighty Kicker]*, Si Balik Raya *[Mighty Returner]*, all of them, the Raya, all. We incant about Hantu Raya, it's no joke. Awang Si Rambut Ekar Mata Merah Dada Bidang *[Awang of the Dishevelled Hair, Red Eyes, and Wide Chest]* if they are friends harbored by the bomoh. People long ago often harbored the Hantu Raya. When we go into trance we go there, too. The *tabib [physician]* calls them, too. The tabib asks them to leave and go home. After "playing" and eating cakes, they leave. But when it was devised, Main 'Teri, the songs were meant to move the *semangat*, to move our souls, to refresh our spirits after playing. To move the *jiwa*, *semangat*, *roh* means we ask for health. People with Wind sickness, if their jiwa and semangat are healthy, become strong. If they sweat, the sickness abates. The fever cools. If people with Wind sickness hear the instruments play, the rebab, gebana, gong, gendang, then they open their eyes wide. If they haven't been eating, they ask for their rice. When the instruments play, they regain their health, their Wind emerges. For fevers brought on by accosting spirits, there are also tunes. That means that the jiwa and semangat fly at the same time as the body moves.

Iblis lies in wait to strike us on the heel. Three kinds of sickness can result. Sometimes it's a sickness that old folks call *kelintasan [glossed by Mat Daud as falling down suddenly]*. That means, we are healthy and suddenly fall ill due to kelintasan. The second sickness people call *kena angin [due to Wind]*, that's its name. If it happens to a kid it's called *sawan [convulsions]*, if it happens to adults, they call it kelintasan. Their eyes go back and they froth at the mouth. Sometimes it's fatal. Sometimes when they recover, they aren't the way they used to be. Sometimes their legs and arms are limp or their mouth goes awry *[the description sounds like the symptoms of stroke]*, and there are many other after-effects. It's because they were startled, as I mentioned before.

Like when people have accidents and aren't aware of what they're doing and remember holding onto the steering wheel. There are lots of accidents where you want to move the wheel, not say *bismillah [pray]*. The car is like semangat: it goes far by itself. Semangat flies, one can't keep it in mind, then one is open to Iblis. Iblis wants to deceive us day and night. When he enters, he can destroy us. If we claim to be jin, this hantu or that, it's the destruction of Islam. That's why religious people are angry at people who perform Main Teri. Religious people call it sin, what we performers do. *[Mat Daud feels that religious people misunderstand the Main Peteri. They think that the shaman claims to* be *a jin, which would be a sin, rather than merely* acting *like a jin during the performance, for the benefit of a patient.]* They say that we actually claim that Dollah got sick at an anthill, at the head of a bridge. It's easy for them to think it's a sin. They don't know what they're talking about. It's like *they're* in a trance. Because we don't say that Iblis uses the voice of Adam when we "play." Plenty of people break God's laws in the coffee shops. They say we break God's laws because they don't know our intentions. Because we have true hearts and mean well by people, we do good, bring peace and tell stories that teach a moral lesson. God protects us. If we ask Him in that way, He covers our heads with safety.

He helps us find a way to aid people. They're glad to see Pak Daud *[himself]*; things are better when Pak Daud comes. According to them it's a sin. Well, we can help people anyhow. You have to say that what Pak Daud does is to help people along the way to health, that's all. If you follow what I'm saying, we don't claim to be jin. We take on their attributes because it's the way to help sick people. Many of those who fight with us about the Main Teri are just ignorant, stupid people.

Melenggang perut arose from people long ago. Melenggang perut goes to Iblis. *[The practice of melenggang perut, or rocking the abdomen, a ceremony performed for primagravidas during the seventh month of pregnancy, has been specifically condemned by the Trengganu Office of Religious Affairs as a disturbing vestige of Hindu customs; see Laderman 1981:146; Laderman 1983:87–90.]* Human mouths have speech, they talk about haunted trees *[pohon bunut]*. What are these hantu, we ask? The bunut is a tree that God made. *[In other words, it is an ordinary material part of God's creation, not a spirit.]* A tree has no *akal [power of reason]*. We can talk; a tree talks in its own fashion. If we take a knife we can't go cut it if we have no real reason. Perhaps we singlemindedly want to fulfill a vow to build a house, walls, and floor, that's all right. Maybe we want to build a house in which to place equipment. That's all right, too. *[Although they lack akal, trees possess semangat, which must be respected. Negligent or deliberate acts of violence toward any form of life constitutes disrespect for the universal life force. It is all right, however, to cut the tree for a valid purpose.]*

It's like what I just said about melenggang perut. I mean that wherever it falls, it's according to the view of the bomoh. According to the angry pious folk, it's not good. But if you examine it closely, if you really think about it, you can't stay angry. If they really thought hard, they wouldn't disagree. They'd find plenty of people in the marketplace making a racket. There are lots of sins worse than performing in Main Teri. If the Office of Religious Affairs wanted to prohibit it, that would be very tough. If they prohibited women from dressing smartly, oh my! There's plenty of adultery and fornication going on. We who "play," if we ask for mercy, ask for healing of the sick, people shouldn't slander us—we are good people—it isn't right. We ask Allah for help, Muhammad for aid, we point morals, we ask that disaster be removed far away. It's not as though we go asking for death to come quickly, oh no. That's why they want to forbid what we do. *[Mat Daud believes that the objections of religious authorities are based upon misunderstanding.]* If we roll an egg they say we shouldn't. To roll an egg and throw it away, that's forbidden, because edible things shouldn't be thrown away. Some do it anyhow. There are many subjects of Raja Suleiman *[King Solomon]*: dogs, cats even, come across it and eat it. *[Bomoh occasionally roll an egg over the body of a patient and then discard it as "infected." The Office of Religious Affairs has particularly condemned all magical practices that "waste food." Mat Daud comments that none of it is really wasted, since some of God's creatures, animals, will eat it.]* We bomoh make medicine to exchange the sickness in the body and soul, to give it another name. It's just like medicine in the hospital. We swallow it but aren't immediately well. If it's not in harmony with our blood nothing will happen, it won't be good. If it's in harmony and you take one pill when you have fever, you get well, if God does not intend for you to die. If someone hasn't eaten *[well]* for a year and a month and Pak Daud comes singing, he sits up and opens his eyes right away.

What's the use of the trance? We like to make a loud noise, shake our heads until we "forget." It's just like people with strong Winds *[berangin]*; if they go to the home of pious people they feel like muddying it. The vapor of Iblis comes upon them; it's a vapor you can't see; you can't see the wind. It's like wind, you can't see it as it blows among the trees. You feel it on your skin, you can't see it. When he *[the shaman]* trances, he says, "That person is harboring a *pelesit [a familiar spirit used by women to make them appear attractive to the opposite sex; the shaman in trance senses the presence of spirits]*." He *[the hantu]* says, "I can't go." He says, "I want to stay here. It's nice here with this sick man, I don't want to go anywhere else."

CAROL: *How does it feel to trance?*

MAT DAUD: When we go treat a patient it feels different. But, really, this work, this way, is inherited. If I want to tell you I can't. Before we speak of *berkat salam aleikum*. Now he sings *berkat tanggung sabillulah*; now he recites *sabillulah mendarah salam. [Mat Daud is once again separating the speech of prayer, berkat salam aleikum, from the speech of the Main Peteri, sabillulah, which, although it derives from "sabil Allah," or God's path, in context stands for "let the performance begin."]*

CAROL: *If you aren't descended from bomoh can you still study and become a bomoh?*

MAT DAUD: Yes, many do. Their Wind is harmonious with this kind of performance. They study and they are quickly able to do it. They quickly become performers. Someone in their family was skilled at it long ago. I used to listen to my father *[a bomoh]* when I was young. I didn't want to learn even though my father asked me to. Not until my sister fell ill. My father chose me to give his knowledge. I went before the minduk and was able to trance right off. When in trance I was able to say everything right away. My sister got well immediately. After that she was healthy and plump. My father became a religious man and didn't do Main Teri any more. He has Angin Dewa Muda. When he hears the music he starts to cry. I used to study Koran; I still do. Treating patients is breaking God's law *[maksiat]*, so is dikir barat, wayang kulit, fighting silat, learning to fly kites, all of it, to bring nasi semangat to your teacher. But they just worry about bomoh, everything else they forget about.

[Mat Daud has mentioned many of the pastimes that give east coast Malays particular pleasure: Dikir barat *is a type of antiphonal singing practiced by Kelantanese men. It can either be serious praise of God or funny, even scandalous, exchanges of sung quatrains. East coast men hugely enjoy competitive kite flying, using handmade, giant-sized, elaborately decorated kites. The* nasi semangat *Mat Daud refers to is a mound of glutinous rice cooked in coconut milk and colored yellow with turmeric; it forms part of the obligatory offerings that must be presented by a successful student to his teacher before he can be considered worthy of taking on the mantle of a fighter, healer, puppet master, and so forth. Islamic opposition to popular forms of entertainment has been noted elsewhere in Southeast Asia. Peacock (1968:19), writing about the proletarian theater in Java* (ludruk)*, notes that pious Muslims believe that it violates Islam by mixing male and female elements and "because ludruk laughs at everything and Islam is serious".]* One can support a wife and kids by being a bomoh. Now, while I'm strong, I can go here and there. In the future, when I'm old, who knows?

CAROL: *What are the signs of sakit berangin?*

MAT DAUD: Cold hands, hot body, a pulse that doesn't beat properly, a heart that thuds even when you're sitting still. It's as if the engine inside isn't working well. We're like a clock; if it's broken it can't run. If our blood is ruined, we can't walk. The blood and vigor can run up and down. It's like a punishment for things you shouldn't do. It means our *zat [true core, essence]* isn't good. When one is sick like this, the heart is troubled, oh Daddy, it's troubled. He doesn't want to go to the hospital; he doesn't want the village bomoh. That kind of sickness causes one to become thin and dried up. Then Pak Daud goes and recites jampi—hey! he *[the patient]* snarls or else he wants to punch someone; he cries a lot and acts like a hantu; he gets completely hysterical as if Iblis had entered him, like the kid I treated before who didn't laugh or cry, only her neck could turn. Before she just sat and laughed. It's the kind of Wind that kid had. Her semangat was weak, when she was accosted. First, when I came to *siup* her *[blow supernaturally cooled breath on her back while reciting jampi]*, it didn't work. The power of the jampi wasn't enough to make her well. When we Main Teri her Wind was released, her semangat could return.

There are many kinds of Wind: the Wind to "play" silat, to "play" Mak Yong. Because of this the bomoh calls on 199 Winds. Nine can make people sick, especially four of them: Angin Putih, Angin Merah, Angin Kuning, Angin Hitam [White Wind, Red Wind, Yellow Wind, Black Wind]. Angin Putih *[white]* is a rajah's title, white Wind, white blood. Angin Merah *[red]* is the title of Baginda Ali, hot-blooded when it's a matter of humanity. Angin Hitam *[black]* is Angin Raja Bali *[a violent character in the shadow play]* and why? Jin Hitam *[the Black Genie]*—a person with Jin Hitam has a nasty face, wants to hit people, doesn't care what he does, is quick to anger. For someone like that, if people give him advice he gets mad; it's because of his Wind, his black Wind. It's not that his Wind is a jin, oh no. Angin Kuning *[yellow]* is the Wind of dewa, you can reason with him, you can discuss things. He's good at discussions. Whatever people say, he can follow, and people follow him too. It's a fine Wind. Winds that aren't fine are hard to treat. Angin Merah, for instance. If you speak nicely to him, he still gets angry, he says it wasn't nice. It's not that hantu have entered him, it's the kind of Wind that makes him harbor angry desires. To treat short-tempered people you use *air tawar [magically treated water]* and ask God to take away his short temper, that's all. It doesn't help to Main Teri for this sickness. You put water into a jar, but don't let him know, and give it to him. It's like Angin Hitam, they become stupid and you can't talk to them. If you want to treat them you can't—they get angry.

CAROL: *How do you know which spirit accosted a person?*

MAT DAUD: Hantu are found here and there if the bomoh calls them by name. It comes back to desires *[nafsu]*. Their *[the patients]* desire, their fondness for whichever hantu. They say Awang Jambu Lebat because if you *[the bomoh]* don't say Awang Jambu Lebat *[Awang of the Abundant Guavas]*, they say you haven't finished. Their Wind isn't refreshed if you say all the things people say and leave out Awang Jambu Lebat. In the past they always praised Jambu Lebat, made him their friend. They said he didn't do [harm to] people, others did it. He just hitched on. Awang Jambu Lebat, Hantu Raya *[the Mighty Spirit]*, Awang Jangak *[Handsome Awang]*, *putarranggas [malevolent spirits who live in the brushwood* (ranggas)*]*, that's on the male side; on the female Mek Comel *[Miss Cutie]*, Mek Teri Masuk *[Miss Enter the "Play"]*, Mek Jin Kuning *[Miss Yellow Genie]*, Mek 'Stana Malam *[Miss Night Palace]*, Mak Baju Batik Cula Hijau *[Mother Green Jacket]*, Mek Telaga Rendam *[Miss Soaked in the Well]*. In the fields Mek Kopek Lanjut *[Miss Longbreasts]*, Belalang Kacung Si Dada Bidang *[Wide-chested Mantis]*. When you get to the fields they run quickly, long breasts swinging. They like you *[bomoh]* to call their names. If you don't mention them they *[patients]* say this tok 'teri is not adept. They say why didn't he call that one, he said he wouldn't change names, he spoke of origins *[usul]*, but he didn't speak about beginnnings *[asal]*. It's like that night when I "played," I didn't say Mak Beruk Besar *[Mother Large Macaque]*, Mak Pangan Langah *[Mother Gaping Jungle]*, Mak Pangan Putih *[Mother White Jungle]*. They said, "You haven't finished." When I "played" Anak Kera Beleh *[the name used by Hanuman the White Monkey as a child, in the shadow play]*, only then did he trance. His father, in the past, was used to that, too. After that he said, "For a sore throat do Beruk Besar." *[Mat Daud is making fun of patients who insist on having their "favorite hantu" mentioned even in the treatment of minor ailments]*.

Well, like drowsy people who feel indifferent, that's what it's like to be in trance—you don't know what's going on and you don't care. It's like when you sleep, according to some people. They jump on top of people's heads *[the behavior of some disturbed patients before treat-*

ment, figuratively speaking, of course]. When they are refreshed *[after coming out of trance]* they don't behave like that; they feel ashamed. When in trance, they aren't conscious. When they're released, they are conscious and embarrassed. They sit quietly. People say they aren't conscious yet, but they are, they sit still, they're just embarrassed.

CAROL: *How can you know the right name to call the hantu?*

MAT DAUD: We bomoh know plenty of names to call. It's an art, those words we use. It follows tradition. When you arrive there *[in the jampi]*, you mention the names of the hantu there. For example, if we go to a village, we look for the headman. *[He is not talking about the "shaman's spirit journey," or sending his soul to these places. "Going to the village" means reaching the place in the invocation where the bomoh speaks of the spirits of the village. It "follows tradition" since all bomoh learn the basic pattern of the invocation: the order in which spirits of various places must be invoked.]* Whoever he is, he can discuss things with people. The headman tells people this one made you sick, that one made you sick. I mean Awang Jangak is the headman. Awang Jambu Lebat is also a headman. They all have names, Cik Ali Lengah from the edge of the village in the shadow of the groves, the one who guards the village. The bomoh knows which place—he recites the place of the hantu and his feelings let him know which one did it. The bomoh says strong spells right away. He says spells and the patient feels it on his body hair. The bomoh have many names for hantu like *jin, syaitan, jembalang, jin empat bahsa, Iblis empat ragam [genies of four sorts, devils of four kinds]*, you can talk about all of them, but when you arrive at the place, your body hair rises. "Awang Jangak, you mustn't cause trouble here," the bomoh says. If the sick person feels it in his heart's desire, he gets well. If the bomoh trances he can make the sick well; if he has no *ilmu [specialized knowledge]*, he can't. We village people say the bomoh has a fence. If he has no fence he will fall. *[Mat Daud is referring to the "gate" surrounding healthy, whole, prudent people.]* He feels it in his hair, his cheeks feel like they're swelling, that's the sign that hantu are there. It's like at a kenduri. A kid goes to the store and gets five cents *[for running an errand].* You tell him *[the hantu]* to look after the farm *[actually rice-flour models of animals, people, and household utensils]* and give him a kenduri. Like a kid he cries, so you give him bananas. That's how it is with the spirits. *[He means that hantu are like children, continually whining for things but being satisfied with very little. He likens the offerings given to the spirits to induce them to return a patient to health, to a tip given to a child who runs errands. For a clearer understanding of his reference to a spirit "farm" and "kenduri," see Breaking Contracts with the Spirit World, chapter 8.]*

APPENDIX B

Music of the Main Peteri

The four transcriptions that follow (transcribed by Marina Roseman) are of music from the ceremony that I have called "Breaking Contracts with the Spirit World" (chapter 8). The first three are excerpts from the minduk's Introductory Song: The beginning, showing its basic structure; the elaborated middle section; and the ending, where the minduk's song leads into the first example of the music of transition, here merely a premonition of what will later be the trigger for and signal of the shaman's changes of persona. The fourth transcription is a duet sung by the minduk and the tok 'teri, in the persona of a Sea Spirit. We chose this excerpt above other possibilities because of its exceptional poignance, beauty, and intensity.

In the first excerpt, the minduk is accompanied by a rebab (spike fiddle) and a gebana (single-headed hand-held drum). In the second, a canang (floor gong), here substituted by an overturned pot, joins in. The same three instruments accompany the Sea Spirit duet.

Traditional Malay and Indonesian musical structure is usually defined by a repeating series of strokes on different-sized gongs. The larger the gong, the louder and lower-pitched the sound. Small gongs are struck to signal the end of a subdivision of the gongan; the large gong is struck to mark the end of a cycle. Gong cycles (*gongan*), once established, are unchanging and infinitely repeatable in any given piece of music.

Instruments used in Main Peteri may comprise a large group of elaborating instruments, such as the rebab, gebana, canang, and serunai (a type of oboe), plus a set of hanging gongs. Often, however, they are reduced to a minimum of rebab, gebana, and canang. The canang, although it is a type of gong, is used as an elaborating instrument and does not function as a division marker.

Since only elaborating instruments were used in this ceremony, and no hanging gongs were present to mark the musical divisions, it was decided to demonstrate the implied structure of the gong cycle by indicating where gong strokes would have occurred. For example, the minduk's Introductory Song is a 32-beat gongan with 8-beat subdivisions. The lower case letter g beneath the canang line indicates where the small hanging gong (*tawak anak*) would have sounded; the capital G beneath the canang line indicates the hypothetical striking of the large hanging gong (*tawak ibu*).

Unlike Western music, which often tends to have a four bar phrase structure with stress on the downbeats of the first and third bars, Southeast Asian gong cycles put stress on the second and fourth (6th and 8th) beats. In the transcriptions that follow, the weak beats are marked by ˘ and the strong beats by ‘. In the beginning of the first excerpt (Minduk's Introductory Song: Beginning), a few rebab notes were lost owing to problems in taping. This explains the rests that precede the minduk's vocal line, and accounts for the fact that the transcription starts with a strong beat. (For an extensive discussion of Malay gongan, see Matusky 1980).

The rebab line in the Sea Spirit duet was recorded very faintly. It was difficult to transcribe at best, and impossible to hear with any accuracy in some places. These have been indicated by question marks. An x in any staff indicates that the note is of indeterminant pitch. In the gebana and canang staves, x designates a regular drum stroke. In a vocal line, x indicates that the notes were produced in a manner intermediate between speech and song, as in contemporary German Sprechstimme. A diamond-shaped note in the gebana line represents a "ting" sound characterized by prominent high harmonics, as opposed to the duller sound represented by x.

Using Western notation to represent non-Western music is an attempt to portray this material in a form that is meaningful to a Western, nonspecialist audience. The attempt is inherently problematic: for example, the pitches produced do not correspond exactly to this notation. Interested readers are encouraged to obtain copies of the original tapes from the Columbia University Center for Ethnomusicology.

Minduk's Introductory Song: Beginning

♩ = 56

Minduk

Rebab

Gebana

Bis- mil- lah 'tu ham- ba deng- an sa- tu a- lif.

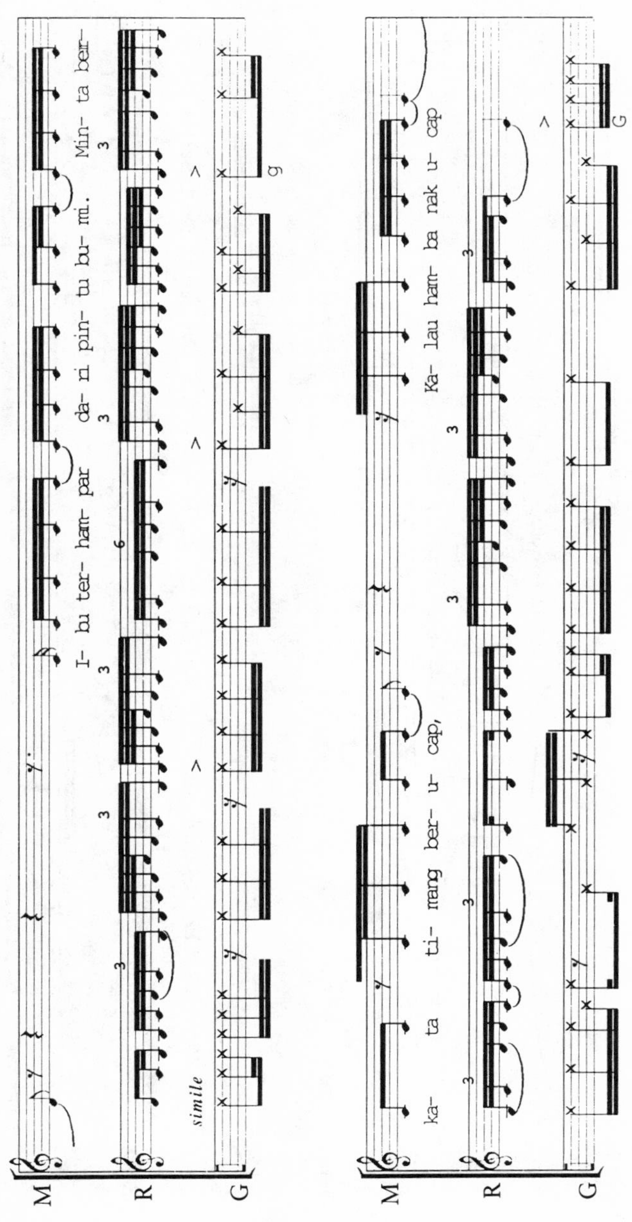
M
R
G
simile
I- bu ter- ham- par da- ri pin- tu bu- mi. Min- ta ber-
ka- ta ti- mang ber- u- cap, Ka- lau ham- ba nak u- cap

M
R
G
ti- mang ge- rak ja- ga.
Min- duk 'duk ti- dur gak,
nak gon- cang dan bang- un.

M

Ja- ga sung- guh min- duk tu- a, min- duk mu- da, Ja- ga se-

R

G

M

ka- li Tu- an 'te- ri mu- dah di la- man i- sta- na.

R

G

(continues)

Minduk's Introductory Song: Middle, Elaborated

M
R
G
C
Ser- ban Bi- ru, Se- er- ban dan Pu- tih o- rang k'ra-
mat ber- di- ri- ? ? di- si- ni gak Ma- sing ma- sing jang- an ba- wa hi- lap ki- ra be- lok deng-
an bi- ca- ra la- gi gak.
(continues)

Minduk's Introductory Song: End, to Transition Music

M
R
G
C
deng- ar dan bi- lang be- ri- ta dan ba- ri a- la-
g
-ai, tuan wei.
G

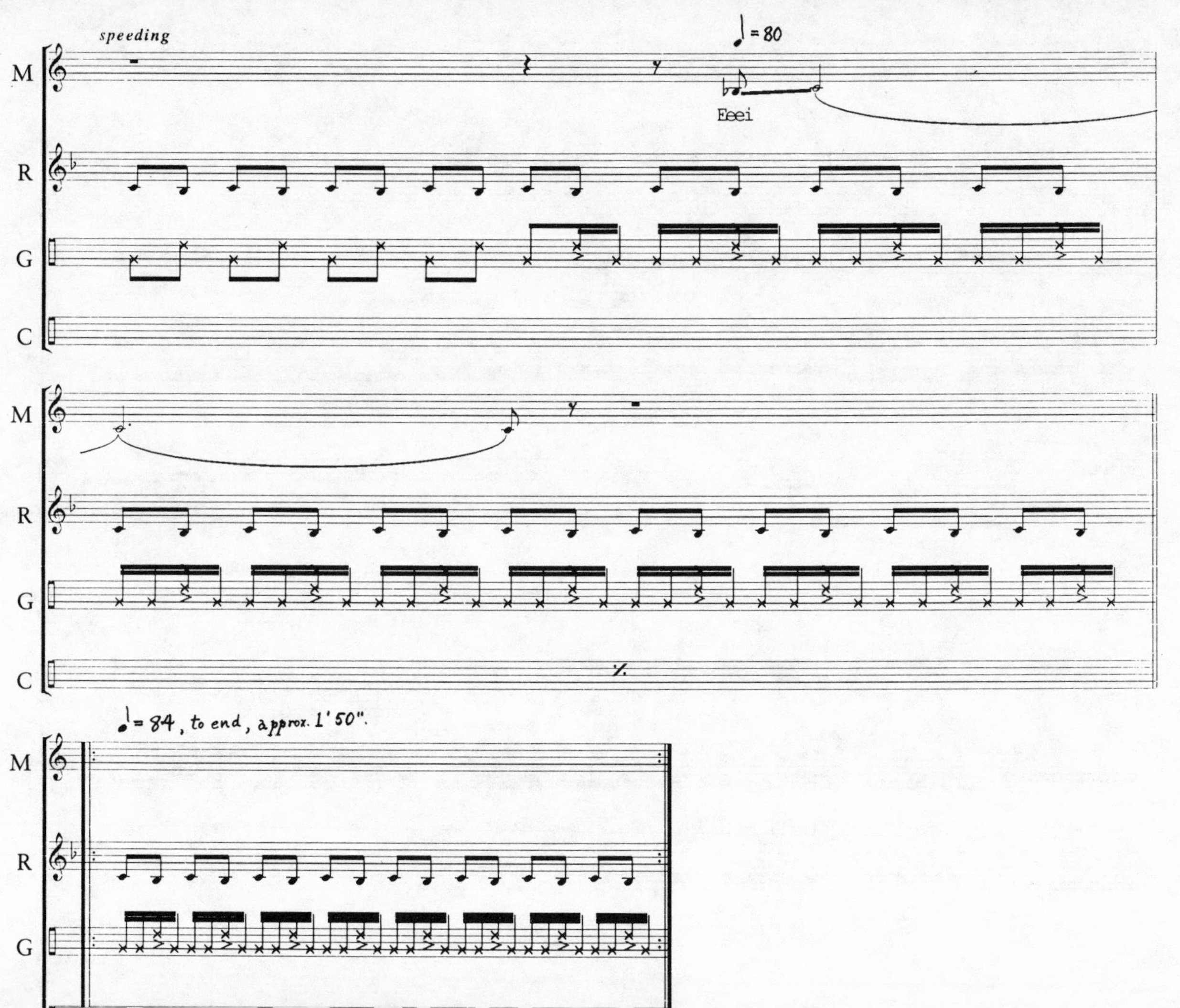
speeding
= 80
M
Eeei
R
G
C
M
R
G
C
= 84, to end, approx. 1'50".
M
R
G

Tok 'teri
Minduk
Rebab
Gebana
Canang
Ham- ba 'ni, mah- ko- ta, sam-
T
M
R
G
C
pai gak ha- ti, se- mua ka- ta sam- pai gak ra- sa ham- ba gak wei, ham-

T
M
R
G
C
ba, nak bu- ang ham- ba wei.
Ei, tu- an ham- ba,
ham- ba ham- ba gak, ham- ba, pang- li- ma

T
M
R
G
C
3
g
T
M
R
G
C
5
se- mu- a hi- tam gak, pang-
5
g

T
M
R
G
C
li- ma gan- da gak.
Ei, bon- da gak, bon-
G
g
da gak ham- ba, ham- ba, ham- ba nak ca- ri gak lain.
g

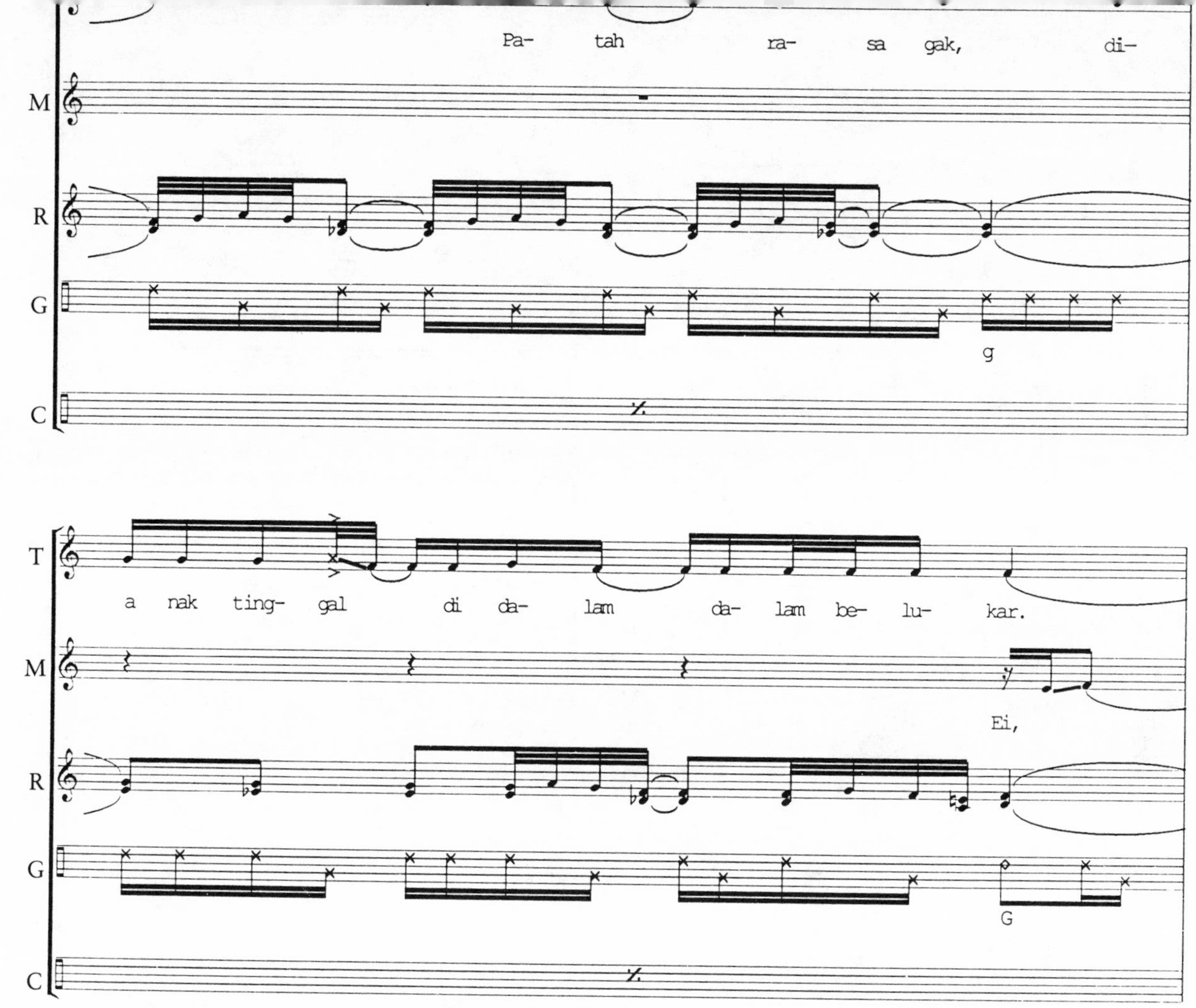
Pa- tah ra- sa gak, di-
M
R
G
g
C
T
a nak ting- gal di da- lam da- lam be- lu- kar.
M
Ei,
R
G
G
C

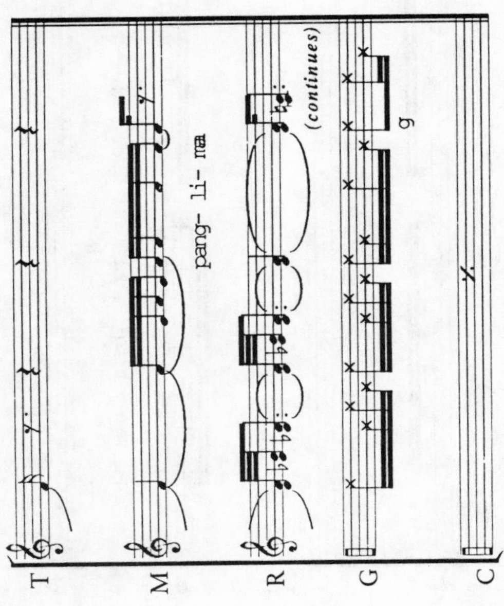

T
M
R
G
C
pang- li- ma
(continues)
g

GLOSSARY

Modern Malay orthography differs from that of English principally in that the sound "ch," as in the English "church," is represented in Malay by the letter "c;" and the sound "sh," as in the English "shut," is represented in Malay by the letters "sy." Pronunciation of standard Malay closely resembles pronunciation of standard Italian. Although I have retained the standard Malay orthography, readers should be aware of the fact that in the Kelantanese dialect of the performers of Main Peteri, pronunciation differs significantly from that of standard Malay. In Kelantanese dialect:

1. Final stops (k, p, b, t, and d) are all pronounced as glottal stops ('). Glottal stops substitute for other final consonants and are added to many words ending in vowels. For example, ambil, kecil, bawa, minta, juga, and pula are pronounded in dialect as ambi', keci', tahi', and so forth.
2. Final s is pronounced as h.
3. Final h is often pronounced as s.
4. Final l and r are indistinguishable from one another, and are often not sounded. Likewise, final au and ai, both generally pronounced in dialect as a, are indistinguishable from final al and ar.
5. Final m, n, and ng are indistinguishable from one another; they are all sounded as a nasalization of the preceding vowel. Nasals preceding voiced consonants are either not sounded or, more often, sounded softly.
6. Final a before k or h is pronounced ɔ.
7. Although the plural in standard Malay is usually formed by doubling a word (bomoh-bomoh), in Kelantanese dialect the same

word is often used to denote both singular and plural. Therefore, the word bomoh in Kelantanese dialect can refer either to one or several healers.

For further information, see Brown 1956 and Sweeney 1972.

akal - rationality, a quality of mind peculiar to humanity.

angin - wind. Refers to all kinds of wind, e.g., the wind blowing in the air, stomach wind (gas); however, in the context of the Main Peteri, angin refers to the Inner Winds: personality, talents, drives.

Angin Dewa Muda - the Wind of the Young Demigod, a personality type that craves admiration and material comforts.

Angin Hala - the Wind of the Weretiger, a personality type quick to anger.

Angin Dewa Penchil - the Wind of the Isolated Demigod, a personality type that likes to wander in foreign parts and behave in ways not befitting his station in life.

Awang - a common Malay male name, also used as the equivalent of "Sonny" when addressing or referring to male children.

berangin - (1) to be strongly inclined to or attracted to something, e.g., *berangin Mak Yong*; (2) to have Wind Sickness (penyakit, or sakit, angin), illness caused by a blockage of the Inner Winds.

berhantu - a variant of the shaman's seance as it was known in Perak and Selangor. See *hantu*.

berjin - *berhantu*, but, according to Gimlette, using no music. See *jin*.

bertih - raw rice that has been cooked by exposing it to dry heat, causing it to pop and puff up.

biasa - usual, ordinary.

bidan - midwife.

bidandari - the Celestial Midwives. The word has been formed by combining the Malay *bidan* (midwife) with the Sanskrit *bidadari* (the beautiful dancing-girls of Siva's heaven).

bomoh - Malay medicine-man; native healer.

bisa - (1) powerful; (2) exacerbating existing disharmonies; (3) toxic.
buka hutan - opening the jungle; a ritual in which offerings are presented to the jungle spirits before the land is cleared for agriculture.
buka mulut - opening the mouth; before a newborn baby is fed, its mouth is touched with silver, gold, sugar, and salt.
canang - small floor gongs.
Cik - Mr. or Ms.
dadar kuah - *dadar* are pancakes made from wheat flour, coconut milk, sugar, and eggs; the *kuah* (sauce) served with them is a kind of custard.
daeng - a Bugis title of nobility.
dalang - the puppet master of the shadow play.
dewa - a demigod.
dikir barat - exchanging of quatrains in song by a male group with a leader, done as entertainment in Kelantan; there are serious ones in praise of Allah, and funny ones, some obscene and others critical of political leaders.
doa - prayer (other than the five daily prayers of Islamic obligation).
gebana - hand drum (sometimes called *rebana*).
Gerak Angin - literally, to move the Wind (referring to the Inner Winds); the song sung by the minduk to assist the shaman in achieving trance.
gila - crazy
haji - a Muslim who has made the pilgrimage to Mecca.
hala - weretiger.
hantu - a disembodied spirit.
ilmu - knowledge; in the context of the Main Peteri, magical knowledge.
jampi - spell, incantation.
jembalang - imp, the servant of jin and powerful hantu.
jin - genie.
jinjang - see *penggawa*.
jiwa - human spirit, soul; also used to refer to life, feelings, thoughts, hopes.

joget - a dance done by men and women, facing but not touching one another.

kampung - village, hamlet.

kemenyan - benzoin, the aromatic resin of a tree used as incense.

kenduri - feast, especially on religious or ceremonial occasions.

keramat - wonderworking, holy, endowed with supernatural power.

kuwung - powerful evil influences.

lagu - tune.

limau nipis - thin-skinned lime, used widely in traditional Malay medicine and magic.

luar biasa - unusual, out of the ordinary.

lupa - to forget; said of shaman when in trance.

main - play, in every sense of the word.

Main Bagih - similar to Main Peteri, but performed without instrumentalists.

Main Pantai - festivities at the seashore, held annually, and featuring performances of wayang kulit, Mak Yong, joget, and, occasionally, the showing of a film. In the past, offerings (often large ones, such as a goat or water buffalo) were put out to sea for the Sea Spirits; however, this has been forbidden by religious and civil law.

Mak Yong - a traditional Malay dramatic performance employing instrumental music, song, and dance.

Mek - a term of address, on the east coast, for a female younger than the speaker.

melenggang perut - "rocking the abdomen," a protective ritual performed during the seventh month of a woman's first pregnancy.

menerima (*terima*) - to receive a teacher's blessings; acceptance by the teacher of a student's final payment, signifying his satisfaction with the student's accomplishments and giving the student a professional imprimatur.

minduk - the shaman's partner, who does not go into trance. Often called "master of the spirits," he converses with each spirit-visitation, frequently accompanies his and the shaman's songs on the rebab, and acts as leader of the instrumentalists.

nasi guru - the "teacher's rice"; the offering made to the "original bomoh" or "first teacher," and to the familiar spirits that assist in the seance.

nasi semangat - "life-force rice"; glutinous rice cooked in coconut milk and colored yellow (the royal color), an integral part of many ritual occasions such as *melenggang perut* and *menerima*, q. v.

nyawa - life, soul; associated with the breath.

orang ghaib - invisible people.

Pak - father; used as a term of respect to adult men.

pawang - used interchangeably in the literature with *bomoh*, q.v., but on the east coast only refers to experts on the jungle and its inhabitants, animal, vegetable, mineral, and spirit.

pelepas - "releaser," made of two long strips of palm frond tied in double slipknots. At the close of an incantation, the bomoh recites, "1,2,3,4,5,6,7, I release you," and pulls the ends of the pelepas, untying the slipknots, and thereby releasing the patient from a state of vulnerability.

pelesit - a spirit harbored by women who wish to appear attractive to the opposite sex.

penggawa - a helpful familiar spirit.

pengasuh - in literary convention, refers to attendants of royal children; in the Mak Yong, the comic companion of the prince.

penghulu - headman.

polong - a familiar spirit used for selfish or harmful purposes, usually by men.

puja pantai - "invocations at the seaside"; now known as Main Pantai, q.v.

pulut kuning - yellow sticky rice, cooked with tumeric and coconut milk. Yellow is the color of royalty in Malaysia; it is often used in Malay magic as a symbol of the Sultan's protection of his subjects. Spirits fear the Sultan's power, since all Malay sultans are considered to be descendants of King Solomon who subjugated the genies.

rebab - spike-fiddle; a two- or three-stringed instrument played with a bow, whose player sits on a floor mat.

serunai - a reed instrument similar to the oboe.
sesuai - harmonious, suitable, matching, complementary.
silat - the Malay martial art.
sirih - the leaf of a climbing plant (Piper betel) chewed with areca nut, lime, and sometimes tobacco, to make up the quid of betel.
tepung tawar - neutralizing rice paste, a frequent constituent of Malay materia magica.
tok - an honorific, used for males and females of age and/or distinction; from *datok* (*datuk* in the new orthography).
Toki - Grandpa, in Trengganu dialect.
tok 'teri - the shaman in the Main Peteri.
Wayang Jawa - a form of the Malay shadow play (wayang kulit) primarily used as entertainment for aristocrats, now largely fallen into disuse.
Wayang Siam - the popular form of the Kelantanese shadow play.
wayang kulit - the generic name for the Malay shadow play.

BIBLIOGRAPHY

Andaya, B. W., and L. Andaya
1982 *A History of Malaysia.* London: The MacMillan Press Ltd.

Annandale, Nelson
1903*a* "Primitive Beliefs and Customs of the Patani Fisherman." In *Fasciculi Malayenses I*, ed. N. Annandale and H. C. Robinson. Liverpool: Liverpool University Press, pp. 73–88.
1903*b* "Religion and Magic among the Malays of the Patani States." In *Fasciculi Malayenses I*, ed. N. Annandale and H. C. Robinson. Liverpool: Liverpool University Press, pp. 89–104.
1904*a* "Religion and Magic among the Malays of the Patani States," pt. 2. In *Fasciculi Malayenses IIa*, ed. N. Annandale and H. C. Robinson. Liverpool: Liverpool University Press, pp. 21–57.
1904*b* "Customs of the Malayo-Siamese." In *Fasciculi Malayenses IIa*, ed. N. Annandale and H. C. Robinson. Liverpool: Liverpool University Press, pp. 61–89.

Annandale, Nelson, and Herbert C. Robinson
1903–1904 *Fasciculi Malayenses: Anthropological and Zoological Results of an Expedition to Perak and the Siamese Malay States 1901–1902.* Liverpool: University Press of Liverpool.

Asad, Talal
1986 "The Concept of Cultural Translation in British Social Anthropology." In *Writing Culture: The Poetics and Politics of Ethnography*, ed. James Clifford and George E. Marcus. Berkeley, Los Angeles, London: University of California Press.

Atkinson, Jane M.
1989 *The Art and Politics of Wana Shamanship.* Berkeley, Los Angeles, London: University of California Press.

Awang Sudjai Hairul, and Yusoff Khan
1977 *Kamus Lengkap.* Petaling Jaya: Pustaka Zaman.

Banks, David J.
1976 *Trance and Dance in Malaya: The Hindu-Buddhist Complex in Northwest Malay Folk Religion.* Buffalo: Council on International Studies, SUNY at Buffalo, Special Studies #74.

Bibliography

Basso, Ellen
1984 *A Musical View of the Universe: Kalapalo Myth and Ritual Performances*. Philadelphia: University of Pennsylvania Press.

Bauman, Richard
1984 *Verbal Art as Performance*. Prospect Heights, Ill.: Waveland Press. (First published 1977.)

Benjamin, Geoffrey
1979 "Indigenous Religious Systems of the Malay Peninsula." In *The Imagination of Reality: Essays in Southeast Asian Coherence Systems*, ed. A. L. Becker and Aram A. Yengoyan. Norwoods, N.J.: Ablex Publishing Corp.

Blacking, J.
1985 "The Context of Venda Possession Music: Reflection on the Effectiveness of Symbols." *Yearbook of Traditional Music* 17:64–87.

Blagden, C. Otto
1896 "Notes on the Folklore and Popular Religion of the Malays." *Journal of the Royal Asiatic Society*, Straits Branch 29:1–12.

Bloch, M.
1974 "Symbols, Song, Dance and Features of Articulation." *Eur. J. of Sociology* 15:55–81.

Blumberg, H.
1961 *Averroe's Epitome of Parva Naturalis*. Cambridge, Mass.: The Mediaeval Academy of America.

Brandon, James
1972 *Traditional Asian Plays*. New York: Hill & Wang.

Brown, C. C.
1956 *Studies in Country Malay*. London: Luzac & Co., Ltd.
1970 *Sejarah Melayu* (Malay Annals). Kuala Lumpur: Oxford University Press.

Burkill, I. H.
1966 *A Dictionary of the Economic Products of the Malay Peninsula*. Kuala Lumpur: Ministry of Agriculture and Cooperatives.

Chen, P. C. Y.
1979 "Main Puteri: An Indigenous Kelantanese Form of Psychotherapy." *Int. J. Soc. Psychiat.* 25:167–175.

Coèdes, George
1968 *The Indianized States of Southeast Asia*. Honolulu: East-West Center.

Cogliati, Arano L.
1976 *The Medieval Health Handbook (Taciunum Sanitatis)*. New York: George Braziller.

Colson, Anthony C.
1971 *The Prevention of Illness in a Malay Village: An Analysis of Con-*

cepts and Behavior. Monograph Series Two. Winston Salem: Wake Forest University.

Connor, Linda

1984 "The Unbounded Self: Balinese Therapy in Theory and Practice." In *Cultural Conceptions of Mental Health and Therapy*, ed. Anthony J. Marsella and Geoffrey M. White. Dordrecht: D. Reidel Publishing Company.

Connor, Linda, Patsy Asch, and Timothy Asch

1986 *Jero Tapakan: A Balinese Healer*. New York: Cambridge University Press.

Crapanzano, Vincent

1973 *The Hamadsha: A Study in Moroccan Ethnopsychiatry*. Berkeley, Los Angeles, London: University of California Press.

1977 "Introduction." In *Case Studies in Spirit Possession*, V. Crapanzano and V. Garrison. New York: John Wiley & Sons, pp. 1–40.

Cuisinier, Jeanne

1936 *Danses Magiques de Kelantan*. Travaux et Memoires de l'Institut d'Ethnologie de l'Universite de Paris, 22.

1951 *Sumangat: l'Ame et son Culte en Indochine et en Indonesie*. Paris: Gallimard.

De Danaan, Llyn

1984 "Performance and Transformation: Mystery and Myth in Malay Healing Arts." Ph. D. dissertation, The Union for Experimenting Colleges and Universities.

Dentan, Robert K.

1964 Senoi. In *Ethnic Groups of Mainland Southeast Asia*, ed. F. K. Lebar, G. C. Hickey, and J. K. Musgrove. New Haven: HRAF Press.

1965 "Some Senoi Semai Dietary Restrictions: A Study of Food Behavior in a Malayan Hill Tribe." Ph. D. dissertation, Department of Anthropology, Yale University.

Devereux, George

1956 "Normal and Abnormal: The Key Problem of Psychiatric Anthropology." *In Some Uses of Anthropology: Theoretical and Applied*, ed. J. B. Casagrande and T. Gladwin. Washington: Anthropological Society of Washington.

Dols, Michael W.

1984 *Medieval Islamic Medicine*. Berkeley, Los Angeles, London: University of California Press.

Doust, John W. L., and Denis Leigh

1953 "Studies on the Physiology of Awareness: The Interrelations of Emotions, Life Situations, and Anoxemia in Patients with Bronchial Asthma." *Psychosomatic Medicine* 15:292–311.

Eissler, K.
1967 "Genius, Psychopathology, and Creativity." *American Imago* 24:35–81.

Elgood, C.
1970 *Safavid Medical Practice*. London: Luzac & Co., Ltd.

Endicott, K. M.
1970 *An Analysis of Malay Magic*. London: Oxford University Press.
1979 *Batek Negrito Religion*. Oxford: Clarendon Press.

Epton, Nina
1966 "Sumarah and the Ghostly Sultan." In *Trances*, ed. Stuart Wavell, Audrey Butt, and Nina Epton. London: George Allen & Unwin Ltd.

Errington, Shelly
1975 "A Study of Genre: Meaning and Form in the Malay Hikayat Hang Tuah." Ph. D. dissertation, Dept. of Anthropology, Cornell University.
1983 "Embodied Sumange' in Luwu." *J. Asian Studies* XLII: 545–570.

Fabrega, Horacio Jr.
1974 *Disease and Social Behavior: An Interdisciplinary Perspective*. Cambridge: MIT Press.

Ferrand, G.
1919 "Le K'Ouen-Louen et les Anciennes Navigations Interoceaniques dans les Mers du Sud." *Journal Asiatique*, 11th series, July-August.

Filliozat, J.
1964 *The Classical Doctrine of Indian Medicine: Its Origins and Its Greek Parallels*. Delhi: Munshiram Manoharlal.

Finkler, Kaja
1985 *Spiritualist Healers in Mexico: Successes and Failures of Alternative Therapeutics*. New York: Bergin & Garvey.

Firth, Raymond
1967 "Ritual and Drama in Malay Spirit Mediumship." *Comparative Studies in Society and History* 9:190–201.
1974 "Faith and Skepticism in Kelantanese Village Magic." In *Kelantan: Religion, Society and Politics in a Malay State*, ed. William R. Roff. Kuala Lumpur: Oxford University Press.

Foster, George W., and Barbara G. Anderson
1978 *Medical Anthropology*. New York: John Wiley & Sons.

Foucault, Michel
1981 *Power/Knowledge*. New York: Pantheon Books.

Frank, Jerome D.
1974 *Persuasion and Healing: A Comparative Study of Psychotherapy*. New York: Schocken Books.

Freeman, Derek
1970 *Report on the Iban*. New York: Athlone Press.

Fried, E., A. Bloomgarden, W. Lewis, I. Mermelstein, R. Spiegel, V. Watts.
1964 *Artistic Productivity and Mental Health*. Springfield, Ill.: Charles C. Thomas.

French, Thomas M.
1939 "Psychogenic Factors in Asthma." *Amer. J. of Psychiatry* 96:89.

Freud, Sigmund
1924 *Collected Papers*, vol. 1. New York: International Psychoanalytic Press.
1949 *Three Essays on the Theory of Sexuality*, trans. J. Strachey. London: Imago. (1st ed. 1905.)

Freud, Sigmund, and Joseph Breuer
1895 *Studies on Hysteria*. New York: Avon Books. (Reprinted 1966.)

Frith, Simon
1981 *Sound Effects*. New York: Pantheon Books.

Garrison, Vivian
1977 "The 'Puerto Rican Syndrome' in Psychiatry and *Espiritismo*." In *Case Studies in Spirit Possession*, ed. V. Crapanzano and V. Garrison. New York: John Wiley & Sons, pp. 383–449.

Gerber, Eleanor Ruth
1985 "Rage and Obligation: Samoan Emotion in Conflict." In *Person, Self and Experience: Exploring Pacific Ethnopsychologies*, ed. Geoffrey M. White and John Kirkpatrick. Berkeley, Los Angeles, London: University of California Press.

Ghulam-Sarwar Yousof
1976 "The Kelantan 'Mak Yong' Dance Theatre: A Study of Performance Structure." Ph.D. dissertation, Dept. of Drama and Theatre, University of Hawaii.

Gimlette, John D.
1913 "Some Superstitious Beliefs Occurring in the Theory and Practice of Malay Medicine." *Journal of the Royal Asiatic Society*, Straits Branch 65:29–35.
1971 *Malay Poisons and Charm Cures*. Kuala Lumpur: Oxford University Press. (First printed 1915.)

Gimlette, John D., and H. W. Thomson
1971 *A Dictionary of Malayan Medicine*. Kuala Lumpur: Oxford University Press. (First edition, 1915.)

Golomb, Louis
1985 *An Anthropology of Curing in Multiethnic Thailand*. Illinois Studies in Anthropology No. 15. Urbana and Chicago: University of Illinois Press.

Gorlin, E.
1961 *Maimonides "On Sexual Intercourse."* Brooklyn: Rambash Publishing Co.

Hamid, Wan
1964 "Religion and Culture of the Modern Malay." In *Malaysia*, ed. Wang Gungwu. Singapore: Donald Moore Books.
Harington, Sir John
1920 *The School of Salernum: Regimen Sanitatis Salernitanum*. New York: P. B. Hoeber.
Hart, Donn V., P. A. Rajadhon, and R. Coughlin
1965 *Southeast Asian Birth Customs: Three Studies in Human Reproduction*. New Haven: HRAF Press.
Hartog, Joseph, and Gerald Resner
1972 "Malay Folk Treatment Concepts and Practices with Special Reference to Mental Disorders." *Ethnomedizin* I, 3/4:353–372.
Horne, Elinor C.
1974 *Javanese-English Dictionary*. New Haven: Yale University Press.
Horney, Karen
1945 *Our Inner Conflicts*. New York: W. W. Norton.
1950 *Neurosis and Human Growth: The Struggle Toward Self-Realization*. New York: W. W. Norton.
Horowitz, Allan V.
1982 *The Social Control of Mental Illness*. New York: Academic Press.
Howell, Signe
1981 *Society and Cosmos: Chewong of Peninsular Malaysia*. Singapore: Oxford University Press.
Hsu, Francis L. K.
1985 "The Self in Cross-cultural Perspective." In *Culture and Self: Asian and Western Perspectives*, ed. Anthony J. Marsella, George DeVos, and Francis L. K. Hsu. New York: Tavistock Publications.
Huard, Pierre, and M. Wong
1968 *Chinese Medicine*. London: World University Library.
Hussein Alatas, Syed
1968 "Occupational Prestige Amongst the Malays in Malaysia." *J. of the Royal Asiatic Society,* Malaysian Branch 41(1):146–156.
Hymes, Dell
1981 "*In Vain I Tried to Tell You.*" Philadelphia: University of Pennsylvania Press.
Iskandar, T.
1970 *Kamus Dewan*. Kuala Lumpur: Dewan Pustaka dan Bahasa.
Ismail Hussein
1974 *The Study of Malay Traditional Literature with a Selected Bibliography*. Kuala Lumpur: Dewan Bahasa dan Pustaka.
Jacobi, Jolande
1973 *Psychology of C. G. Jung*. New Haven: Yale University Press.

Jung, Carl G.
1958 *Psychology and Religion: West and East*. Collected Works, vol. 11. Princeton: Princeton University Press.
1969 *The Archetype and the Collective Unconscious*. Collected Works, vol. 9, pt. 1. Princeton: Princeton University Press.
1976 "Introduction." In M. Esther Harding, *Woman's Mysteries*, 2d ed. New York: Harper & Row, pp. ix–xii.

Kapferer, Bruce
1983 *A Celebration of Demons: Exorcism and the Aesthetics of Healing in Sri Lanka*. Bloomington: Indiana University Press.

Katz, Richard
1982 *Boiling Energy: Community Healing among the Kalahari Kung*. Cambridge: Harvard University Press.

Kendall, Laurel
1985 *Shamans, Housewives, and Other Restless Spirits: Women in Korean Ritual Life*. Honolulu: University of Hawaii Press.

Kessler, Clive S.
1977 "Conflict and Sovereignty in Spirit Seances." In *Case Studies in Spirit Possession*, ed. V. Crapanzano and V. Garrison. New York: John Wiley & Sons.

Kiersey, David, and Marilyn Bates
1978 *Please Understand Me: Character and Temperament Types*. Del Mar, Calif.: Prometheus Nemesis.

Kiev, Ari
1964 *Magic, Faith and Healing*. New York: The Free Press.
1972 *Transcultural Psychiatry*. New York: The Free Press.

Kleinman, Arthur
1980 *Patients and Healers in the Context of Culture*. Berkeley, Los Angeles, London: University of California Press.

Kloss, C. Boden
1908 "Some Ethnological Notes." *Journal of the Royal Asiatic Society*, Straits Branch 50:73–77.

Knappert, Jan
1980 *Malay Myths and Legends*. Petaling Jaya: Heinemann Educational Books (Asia) Ltd.

Koran
1955 Trans. A. J. Arberry. 2 vols. New York: Macmillan Co.

Koss, Joan D.
1975 "Therapeutic Aspects of Puerto Rican Cult Practices." *Psychiatry* 38:160–171.

Kramer, Brett Hart
1970 "Psychotherapeutic Implications of a Traditional Healing Cere-

mony: The Malaysian Main Puteri." *Transcultural Research Review* 7:149–51.

nd "The Malaysian Main Puteri: A Traditional Healing Ceremony." Unpublished manuscript.

nd "A Tentative Framework for the Comparative Analysis of Ethnopsychiatric Systems." Unpublished manuscript.

Krueger, H. C.

1963 *Avicenna's Poem on Medicine*. Springfield, Ill.: Charles C. Thomas.

Kubie, Lawrence S.

1958 *Neurotic Distortion of the Creative Process*. Lawrence: University of Kansas Press.

Lad, Vasant

1984 *Ayurveda: The Science of Self-Healing*. Santa Fe, N.M.: Lotus Press.

Laderman, Carol

1979 "Conceptions and Preconceptions: Childbirth and Nutrition in Rural Malaysia." Ph.D. dissertation, Department of Anthropology, Columbia University.

1980 "Taming the Wind of Desire: Malay Shamanism." *Asia* 2(5):34–39.

1981 "Symbolic and Empirical Reality: A New Approach to the Analysis of Food Avoidances." *American Ethnologist* 9(3):468–493. Special issue on Symbolism and Cognition.

1983 *Wives and Midwives: Childbirth and Nutrition in Rural Malaysia*. Berkeley, Los Angeles, London: University of California Press.

1987 "The Ambiguity of Symbols in the Structure of Healing." *Social Science & Medicine* 24(4):293–301.

1988 "Wayward Winds: Malay Shamanism and Theory of Personality." In *Techniques of Healing in Southeast Asia*, a special issue of *Social Science and Medicine* (vol. 27, no. 8), ed. Carol Laderman and P. Van Esterik.

Forthcoming *Main Peteri: Malay Shamanism*. Federation Museums Journal, Kuala Lumpur.

Laird, Peter

1985 Personal communication concerning Temoq.

Leslie, Charles

1976 *Asian Medical Systems: A Comparative Study*. Berkeley, Los Angeles, London: University of California Press.

Lévi-Strauss, Claude

1963 *Structural Anthropology*. New York: Basic Books, Inc.

Levy, Robert I.

1984 "Emotion, Knowing, and Culture." In *Culture Theory: Essays on*

Mind, Self, and Emotion, ed. Richard A. Schweder and Robert A. LeVine. New York: Cambridge University Press.

Lewis, I. M.
1971 *Ecstatic Religion: An Anthropological Study of Spirit Possession and Shamanism*. Baltimore: Penguin Books.

Lex, Barbara
1979 "The Neurobiology of Ritual Trance." In *The Spectrum of Ritual: A Biogenetic Structural Analysis*, ed. Eugene G. d'Aquili, C. D. Laughlin, Jr., and John McManus. New York: Columbia University Press, pp. 117–151.

Lord, Albert
1976 *The Singer of Tales*. New York: Atheneum. (First published 1960.)

Lutz, Catherine
1985 "Ethnopsychology Compared to What? Explaining Behavior and Consciousness Among the Ifaluk." In *Person, Self, and Experience: Exploring Pacific Ethnopsychologies*, ed. Geoffrey M. White and John Kirkpatrick. Berkeley, Los Angeles, London: University of California Press.

Maclean, I.
1980 *The Renaissance Notion of Woman*. London: Cambridge University Press.

Mahmud Salim bin Haji Mhd. (Haji)
1976 *Al Iman* (The Faithful). Trengganu Office of Religious Affairs.

Maimonides
1970 *Medical Aphorisms*, ed. and trans. F. Rosner and S. Munter. New York: Yeshiva University Press.
1981 *The Book of Knowledge*, trans. H. M. Russell and Rabbi J. Weinberg. Edinburgh: Royal College of Physicians.

Malinowski, Bronislav
1965 *Coral Gardens and Their Magic*. In Bloomington: University of Indiana Press.

Malm, William P.
1969 "Music of the Ma'yong." *Tenggara* 5:114–120.
1974 "Music in Kelantan, Malaysia and Some of its Cultural Implications." In *Studies in Malaysian Oral and Musical Tradition*. Michigan Papers on South and Southeast Asia, no. 8. Ann Arbor: University of Michigan Center for South and Southeast Asia Studies.

Marsden, William
1784 *The History of Sumatra*, 2d ed. London: Privately printed.

Marsella, Anthony
1977 "Depressive Experience and Disorder Across Cultures." In *Handbook of Cross-Cultural Psychology*, vol. 5: *Culture and Psycho-*

pathology, ed. H. Triandis and J. Draguns. Boston: Allyn and Bacon.

1984 "Culture and Mental Health: An Overview." In *Cultural Conceptions of Mental Health and Therapy*, ed. Anthony J. Marsella and Geoffrey M. White. Dordrecht: D. Reidel Publishing Company.

1985 "Culture, Self, and Mental Disorder." In *Culture and Self: Asian and Western Perspectives*, ed. Anthony Marsella, George DeVos, and Francis L. K. Hsu. New York: Tavistock Publications.

Marsella, Anthony J., George De Vos, Frances L. K. Hsu

1985 *Culture and Self: Asian and Western Perspectives* Tanistock Publications.

Marsella, Anthony J., and Geoffrey M. White, eds.

1984 *Cultural Conceptions of Mental Health and Therapy.* Dordrecht: D. Reidel Publishing Company.

Massard, Josiane

1988 "Doctoring by Go-between: Aspects of Health Care for Malay Children." *Social Science and Medicine* 27(8):789–798.

Matusky, Patricia Ann

1980 "Music in the Malay Shadow Puppet Theater." Ph.D. dissertation, Department of Music, University of Michigan.

Maxwell, Sir George

1907 *In Malay Forests*. Edinburgh: Wm. Blackwood & Sons.

Maxwell, W. E.

1881 "Folklore of Malays." *J. of the Royal Asiatic Soc.*, Straits Branch 7:11–29.

1883 "Shamanism in Perak." *J. of the Royal Asiatic Soc.*, Straits Branch 12:222–232.

May, Rollo

1975 *The Courage to Create*. New York: W. W. Norton.

McHugh, J. N.

1959 *Hantu-hantu: An Account of Ghost Belief in Modern Malaya*. Singapore: Eastern Universities, Ltd.

McVaugh, M.

1975 "Discussion of Medicinal Degrees at Montpellier by Henry of Winchester." *Bull Hist. Med.* 9:57–69.

Mishkat Al-Masabih

1965 Trans. James Robson. Lahore: Sh. Muhammad Ashraf.

Mohd. Hood Salleh

1978 "Semelai Rituals of Curing." Ph.D. dissertation, St. Catherine's College, Oxford University.

Mohd. Taib Osman

1972 "Patterns of Supernatural Premises Underlying the Institution of

the Bomoh in Malay Culture." *Bijdragen Tot de Taal-, Land- en Volkenkunde* 128 (2/3):219–234.
1976 "The Bomoh and the Practice of Malay Medicine." *The South East Asian Review* I(1):16–26.

Nagata, Suichi
1985 Personal communication concerning Kintaq.

Naguib al-Attas, Syed
1963 *Some Aspects of Sufism as Understood and Practised among the Malays*, ed. by Shirle Gordon. Singapore: Malaysian Sociological Research Institute Ltd.

Needham, Rodney
1967 "Percussion and Transition." *Man* II:606–614.

Neher, A.
1962 "A Physiological Explanation of Unusual Behavior in Ceremonies Involving Drums." *Human Biology* 34:151–161.

Newbold, T. J.
1839 *Political and Statistical Account of the British Settlements in the Straits of Malacca, viz. Pinang, Malacca and Singapore; With a History of the Malayan States on the Peninsula of Malacca*. London: J. Murray.

Nida, Eugene
1964 *Toward a Science of Translating*. Leiden: E. J. Brill.

Obeyesekere, Gannanath
1969 "The Ritual Drama of the *Sanni* Demons: Collective Representations of Disease in Ceylon." *Comparative Studies in Society and History* 11(2):174–216.
1981 *Medusa's Hair*. Chicago: University of Chicago Press.

Ornstein, R.
1972 *The Psychology of Consciousness*. San Francisco: Freeman.

Peacock, James
1968 *Rites of Modernization: Symbols and Social Aspects of Indonesian Proletarian Drama*. Chicago: University of Chicago Press.

Pillsbury, Barbara L. K.
1982 "Doing the Month: Confinement and Convalesence of Chinese Women After Childbirth." In *Anthropology of Human Birth*, ed. M. A. Kay. Philadelphia: F. A. Davis Co.

Prince, Raymond
1977 "Foreword." In *Case Studies in Spirit Possession*, ed. V. Crapanzano and V. Garrison. New York: John Wiley & Sons, pp. xi–xvi.
1980 "Variations in Psychotherapeutic Procedures." In *Handbook of Cross-Cultural Psychology*, vol. 6, ed. H. C. Triandis and J. G. Draguns. Boston: Allyn & Bacon, pp. 291–349.

Provencher, Ronald
1979 "Orality as a Pattern of Symbolism in Malay Psychiatry." *The Imagination of Reality: Essays in Southeast Asian Coherence Systems*, ed. A. L. Becker and A. A. Yengoyan. Norwood, N.J.: Ablex, pp. 43–53.

Raybeck, Douglas
1974 "Social Stress and Social Structure in Kelantan Village Life." In *Kelantan: Religion, Society and Politics in a Malay State*, ed. William R. Roff. Kuala Lumpur: Oxford University Press.

Rentse, Anker
1934 "A History of Kelantan." *J. of the Royal Asiatic Soc.*, Malayan Branch 12(2):44–62.

Rogler, Lloyd, and A. Hollingshead
1961 "The Puerto Rican Spiritualist as a Psychiatrist." *The American Journal of Sociology* VXVII(1):17–21.

Roseman, Marina
1984 "The Social Structuring of Sound: The Temiar Example." *Ethnomusicology* 28:411–445.
1985 Personal communication regarding Temiar.
1986 "Sound in Ceremony: Power and Performance in Temiar Curing Ritual." Ph.D. dissertation, Department of Anthropology, Cornell University.
1988 "The Pragmatics of Aesthetics: The Performance of Healing among Senoi Temiar." *Social Science & Medicine* 27(8):811–818.

Rosenblatt, Paul C., R. Patricia Walsh, and Douglas A. Jackson
1976 *Grief and Mourning in Cross-Cultural Perspective*. New Haven: HRAF Press.

Rouget, Gilbert
1985 *Music and Trance: A Theory of the Relations between Music and Possession*. Chicago: University of Chicago Press.

Rowland, Beryl
1981 *The Medieval Woman's Guide to Health*. Kent: Kent State University Press.

Ryan, N. J.
1965 *The Making of Modern Malaya: A History From Earliest Times to Independence*, 2d ed. Kuala Lumpur: Oxford University Press.

Ryle, Gilbert
1949 *The Concept of Mind*. New York: Barnes & Noble.

Schebesta, Paul
1957 "Die Negrito Asiens." *Studia Instituti Anthropos* 13, II.

Scheff, T. J.
1979 *Catharsis in Healing, Ritual, and Drama*. Berkeley, Los Angeles, London: University of California Press.

Shah, M. H.
1966 *The General Principles of Avicenna's Canon of Medicine.* Karachi: Naveed Clinic.

Shaw, William
1973 "Miscellaneous Notes on Malaysian Magic and Aspects of Spirit-Mediumship in Peninsular Malaysia." *Federation Museums Journal* XVII, new series.

Shellabear, Rev. W. G.
1916 *An English-Malay Dictionary.* Singapore: Methodist Publishing House.

Sheppard, Mubin
1961 "Puteri Sadong of Kelantan." *Straits Times Annual*:78–80 (writing under the name of Kijang Putih).
1972 *Taman Indera: Malay Decorative Arts and Pastimes.* Kuala Lumpur: Oxford University Press.
1974 *Cerita-cerita Makyung* (Stories from the Makyung), bk. 1. Kuala Lumpur: Federal.

Shweder, Richard
1984 "Anthropology's Romantic Rebellion." In *Culture Theory: Essays on Mind, Self, and Emotion*, ed. Richard A. Shweder and Robert A. LeVine. New York: Cambridge University Press.

Shweder, Richard A., and Robert A. LeVine, eds.
1984 *Culture Theory: Essays on Mind, Self, and Emotion.* New York: Cambridge University Press.

Siegel, James
1979 *Shadow and Sound: The Historical Thought of a Sumatran People.* Chicago: University of Chicago Press.

Siti Hasmah
1975 "The Role of Traditional Birth Attendants in Family Health." Paper presented at Workshop for the Instruction and Practice of Midwifery, Kuala Lumpur.

Skeat, W. W.
1898 "Some Records of Malay Magic by an Eye-Witness." *J. the Royal Asiatic Soc., Straits Branch* 31:1–61.
1972 *Malay Magic: Being an Introduction to the Folklore and Popular Religion of the Malay Peninsula.* New York: Benjamin Blom, Inc. (First published 1900.)

Skeat, W. W., and C. O. Blagden
1906 *Pagan Races of the Malay Peninsula.* 2 vols. London: MacMillan & Co., Ltd.

Slaff, Bertram
1981 "Creativity: Blessing or Burden?" *Adolescent Psychiatry* 9:78–87.

Soyer, Raphaël
1986 Statement. *Artists Observed*, ed. E. King. New York: Abrams, p. 16.

Sweeney, P. L. Amin
1971 "Peran Hutan, A Malay Wayang Drama." *J. of the Royal Asiatic Soc.*, Malayan Branch 44(2):79–107.
1972 *The Ramayana and the Malay Shadow-Play*. Kuala Lumpur: The National University of Malaysia Press.
1987 *A Full Hearing: Orality and Literacy in the Malay World*. Berkeley, Los Angeles, London: University of California Press.

Swettenham, Sir Frank
1895 *Malay Sketches*. London: John Lane.

Tambiah, Stanley J.
1968 "The Magical Power of Words." *Man* 3:175–208.

Tedlock, Dennis
1983 *The Spoken Word and the Word of Interpretation*. Philadelphia; Univeristy of Pennsylvania Press.

Thakkur, C. G.
1965 *Introduction to Ayurveda*. Bombay: The Times of India Press.

Torrey, E. Fuller
1972 *The Mind Game*. New York: Emerson Hall.

Trilling, Lionel
1963 "Art and Neurosis." In *Art and Psychoanalysis*, ed. William Phillips. New York: World, pp. 502–520.

Turner, Victor
1967 *The Forest of Symbols: Aspects of Ndembu Ritual*. Ithaca: Cornell University Press.
1981 *The Drums of Affliction: A Study of Religious Processes Among the Ndembu of Zambia*. Ithaca: Cornell University Press. (First published 1968.)

Von Franz, Marie-Louise
1964 "The Process of Individuation." In *Man and His Symbols*, ed. C. Jung. New York: Doubleday, pp. 158–229.
1970 *An Introduction to the Psychology of Fairy Tales*. New York: Spring.

Wazir-Jahan Karim
1981 *Ma' Betisek Concepts of Living Things*. London: The Athlone Press, Ltd.

Weiner, Herbert
1977 *Psychobiology and Human Disease*. New York: Elsevier.

White, Geoffrey M.
1985 "Premises and Purposes in a Solomon Islands Ethnopsychology." In *Person, Self, and Experience: Exploring Pacific Ethnopsychologies*. Berkeley, Los Angeles, London: University of California Press.

White, Geoffrey M., and John Kirkpatrick, eds.
1985 *Person, Self, and Experience: Exploring Pacific Ethnopsychologies.* Berkeley, Los Angeles, London: University of California Press.
Whitmont, Edward C.
1969 *The Symbolic Quest: Basic Concepts of Analytical Psychology.* London: Barrie & Rackliff.
Wilkinson, R. J.
1908 *The Incidents of Malay Life.* Pt. I of Life and Customs, Papers on Malay Subjects, 1st series. Kuala Lumpur, Government Printer.
1959 *A Malay-English Dictionary.* London: Macmillan.
Winstedt, Richard O.
1920 "Propiating the Spirits of a District (*menjamu negeri*)" *Journal of the F.M.S. Museums* 9:93–95.
1922 "A Malay Pantheist Charm." *J. of the Royal Asiatic Soc.*, Straits Branch 86:261–267.
1935 *A History of Malaya.* Published as v. 13, pt. 1, *J. of the Royal Asiatic Soc.*, Malay Branch.
1951 *The Malay Magician.* London: Routledge & Kegan Paul. (First published in 1925.)
1961 *The Malays: A Cultural History.* London: Routledge & Kegan Paul. (First ed. 1947.)
1966 *An Unabridged English-Malay Dictionary*, 4th ed. enlarged. Kuala Lumpur: Marican & Sons Sdn. Berhad.
Wittkower, Rudolph, and Margot Wittkower
1963 *Born Under Saturn.* New York: Norton.
Wright, Barbara A. S.
1980 "Wayang Siam: An Ethnographic Study of the Malay Shadow Play of Kelantan." Ph.D. dissertation, Department of Anthropology, Yale University.
Zainal-Abidin bin Ahmad
1922 "The Tiger-breed families." *J. of the Royal Asiatic Soc.*, Straits Branch 85:36–39.
1947 "The Various Significations of the Malay Word *Sejok.*" *J. of the Royal Asiatic Soc.*, Malay Branch 20(2):41–44.
Zurbuchen, Mary S.
1987 *The Language of Balinese Shadow Theater.* Princeton: Princeton University Press.

INDEX

Index

Index

Index

Designer: Sandy Drooker
Compositor: Auto-Graphics
Text: 10/13 Sabon
Display: Sabon
Printer: Thomson Shore
Binder: Thomson Shore

Fri-
6:30-8pm

Sun
10am